(ISC)²

Certified Cloud Security Professional

Official Practice Tests

Second Edition

(ISC)² CCSP

Certified Cloud Security Professional

Official Practice Tests

Second Edition

Ben Malisow

SYBEX®
A Wiley Brand

For Robin, again, for another one

Acknowledgments

The author would like to thank the tawdry circus of characters who nursed this project to completion. First, Jim Minatel, who is unlike any other editor in this realm, in that he is actually helpful, kind, somewhat intelligent, and a pleasure to work with. Kelly Talbot is the real reason this book got done at all. His patience and professionalism are unmatched by any mortal being, and there is not enough praise that can be directed his way. Kelly— thank you. That's all I can say. Katie Wisor is constantly charming and always seems happy, which is maddening and bizarre when most of the people involved in the publishing world are in no way like that whatsoever. She's also incredibly capable and thorough in every way, and she was instrumental in making this book useful and correct. The technical reviewer, Jerry Rayome, fixed so many, many problems, improving amazingly on my feeble efforts, offering great suggestions, and nailing down pieces I'd completely missed. Finally, the author's partner, Robin, who exhibited a virtuoso patience of her own, while constantly offering support, and the dog Jake, who didn't live to see the end of the writing of the book but was a constant joy throughout the parts he was around for.

About the Author

Ben Malisow, CISSP, CISM, CCSP, SSCP, Security+, has been involved in INFOSEC and education for more than 20 years. At Carnegie Mellon University, he crafted and delivered the CISSP prep course for CMU's CERT/SEU. Malisow was the ISSM for the FBI's most highly classified counterterror intelligence-sharing network, served as a U.S. Air Force officer, and taught grades 6–12 at a reform school in the Las Vegas public school district (probably his most dangerous employment to date). His latest work has included the *CCSP (ISC)² Certified Cloud Security Professional Official Study Guide*, Second Edition, also from Sybex/Wiley 2017, and *How to Pass Your INFOSEC Certification Test: A Guide to Passing the CISSP, CISA, CISM, Network+, Security+, and CCSP*, available from Amazon Direct 2017. In addition to other consulting and teaching, Ben is a certified instructor for (ISC)², delivering CISSP and CCSP courses. You can find more information about the CCSP and other INFOSEC-related topics at his blog, www.securityzed.com.

About the Technical Editor

Jerry K. Rayome, BS/MS Computer Science, worked as a member of the Cyber Security Program at Lawrence Livermore National Laboratory for over 20 years providing cybersecurity services, including software development, penetrative testing, incident response, firewall implementation, firewall auditing, cyber forensic investigations, NIST 900-53 control implementation/assessment, cloud risk assessment, and cloud security auditing.

Contents

Introduction

There is no magic formula for passing the Certified Cloud Security Professional (CCSP) certification exam, just as there is no single source that will prepare you sufficiently to pass the actual test. You can, however, prepare yourself for the challenge. This book is all about preparation.

We've included more than 1,000 questions related to the CCSP material in this book, which also includes access to the online databank (the same questions but in a point-and-click format). They were created in accordance with the (ISC)² CCSP Common Body of Knowledge (CBK), the CCSP Training Guide, the *Official CCSP Study Guide*, Second Edition, and the CCSP Exam Outline, which is also referred to as the CCSP Exam Outline (www.isc2.org/-/media/ISC2/Certifications/Exam-Outlines/CCSP-Exam-Outline.ashx), which lists all the elements of practice that the candidate is expected to know for the certification.

The questions in this book are not necessarily indicative of what you'll see on the actual CCSP exam. Instead, these questions are intended for study purposes, to help you review and understand the concepts that you may be tested on when you take the certification exam. Be aware that some of these questions may be easier, and some may be harder, than what you'll be faced with if you try to become a CCSP.

How This Book Is Organized

The questions have been arranged in the order of the CBK, with varying amounts in proportion to the (ISC)² published matrix describing how the exam is constructed, as shown in Table I.1.

TABLE I.1   How the exam is constructed

Domains	Weight
1. Cloud Concepts, Architecture, and Design	17%
2. Cloud Data Security	19%
3. Cloud Platform and Infrastructure Security	17%
4. Cloud Application Security	17%
5. Cloud Security Operations	17%
6. Legal, Risk, and Compliance	13%

There are six chapters, one for each of the CBK domains; each chapter contains a fraction of the hundreds of practice questions, reflecting the questions from the respective domain on the exam (for example, Chapter 1 reflects Domain 1 of the CBK and has over 100 questions). There are also two full-length practice exams, 125 questions each, at the end of the book (Chapters 7 and 8).

Who Should Read This Book

This book is intended for CCSP candidates. To earn the CCSP, you are expected to have professional experience in the field of information security/IT security, particularly experience related to cloud computing. Candidates will also need to provide evidence of their professional experience to (ISC)^2 in the event of passing the exam.

The author has drawn on his own experience studying for and passing the exam as well as years of teaching the Certified Information Systems Security Professional (CISSP) and CCSP preparation courses for (ISC)^2. He also solicited feedback from colleagues and former students who have taken the prep course and the exam. The book should reflect the breadth and depth of question content you are likely to see on the exam. Some of the questions in this book are easier than what you will see on the exam; some of them may be harder. Hopefully, the book will prepare you for what you might encounter when you take the test.

The one thing I chose not to simulate in the book is the "interactive" questions; (ISC)^2 has stated that the current tests may go beyond the regular multiple-choice format and could include "matching" questions (a list of multiple answers and multiple terms, where the candidate has to arrange them all in order), drag-and-drop questions (where the candidate uses the mouse to arrange items on the screen), and "hot spot" questions (where the candidate uses the mouse to point at specific areas of the screen to indicate an answer). There will probably not be many of these on the exam you take, but they are weighted more in your score than the multiple-choice questions, so pay attention and be extra careful answering those.

Tools You Will Need

In addition to this book, I recommend the *CCSP (ISC)^2 Certified Cloud Security Professional Official Study Guide, Second Edition*, also from Wiley (2019). There is, as stated in this introduction, no magic formula for passing the exam. No single particular book or source with all the answers to the exam exists. If someone claims to be able to provide you with such a product, realize that they are mistaken or, worse, misleading you.

However, you can augment your studying by reviewing a significant portion of the likely sources used by the professionals who created the test. The following is a just a *sampling* of the possible professional resources the cloud practitioner should be familiar with:

- The Cloud Security Alliance's *Notorious Nine*

    https://downloads.cloudsecurityalliance.org/initiatives/top_threats/
    The_Notorious_Nine_Cloud_Computing_Top_Threats_in_2013.pdf

- The OWASP's *Top 10*

  www.owasp.org/index.php/Top_10_2013-Top_10

- The OWASP's *XSS (Cross-Site Scripting) Prevention Cheat Sheet*

  www.owasp.org/index.php/XSS_(Cross_Site_Scripting)_Prevention_Cheat_Sheet

- The OWASP's *Testing Guide (v4)*

  www.owasp.org/images/1/19/OTGv4.pdf

- NIST SP 500-292, *NIST Cloud Computing Reference Architecture*

  http://ws680.nist.gov/publication/get_pdf.cfm?pub_id=909505

- The CSA's *Security Guidance v4.0*:

  https://cloudsecurityalliance.org/research/guidance

- ENISA's *Cloud Computing Risk Assessment*:

  www.enisa.europa.eu/publications/cloud-computing-risk-assessment

- The Uptime Institute's *Tier Standard: Topology* and *Tier Standard: Operational Sustainability* (the linked page includes download options for the documents)

  https://uptimeinstitute.com/publications

CCSP Certified Cloud Security Professional Objective Map

Domain 1 Cloud Concepts, Architecture, and Design

- 1.1. Understand cloud computing concepts
  - 1.1.1 Cloud computing definitions
  - 1.1.2 Cloud computing roles (e.g., cloud service customer, cloud service provider, cloud service partner, cloud service broker)
  - 1.1.3 Key cloud computing characteristics (e.g., on-demand self-service, broad network access, multitenancy, rapid elasticity and scalability, resource pooling, measured service)
  - 1.1.4 Building block technologies (e.g., virtualization, storage, networking, databases, orchestration)
- 1.2 Describe cloud reference architecture
  - 1.2.1 Cloud computing activities
  - 1.2.2 Cloud service capabilities (e.g., application capability types, platform capability types, infrastructure capability types)

- 1.2.3 Cloud service categories (e.g., Software as a Service (SaaS), Infrastructure as a Service (IaaS), Platform as a Service (PaaS))

- 1.2.4 Cloud deployment models (e.g., public, private, hybrid, community)

- 1.2.5 Cloud shared considerations (e.g., interoperability, portability, reversibility, availability, security, privacy, resiliency, performance, governance, maintenance and versioning, service levels and Service Level Agreements (SLA), auditability, regulatory)

- 1.2.6 Impact of related technologies (e.g., machine learning, artificial intelligence, blockchain, Internet of Things (IoT), containers, quantum computing)

- 1.3 Understand security concepts relevant to cloud computing

  - 1.3.1 Cryptography and key management

  - 1.3.2 Access control

  - 1.3.3 Data and media sanitization (e.g., overwriting, cryptographic erase)

  - 1.3.4 Network security (e.g., network security groups)

  - 1.3.5 Virtualization security (e.g., hypervisor security, container security)

  - 1.3.6 Common threats

- 1.4 Understand design principles of secure cloud computing

  - 1.4.1 Cloud secure data lifecycle

  - 1.4.2 Cloud-based Disaster Recovery (DR) and Business Continuity (BC) planning

  - 1.4.3 Cost benefit analysis

  - 1.4.4 Functional security requirements (e.g., portability, interoperability, vendor lock-in)

  - 1.4.5 Security considerations for different cloud categories (e.g., Software as a Service (SaaS), Infrastructure as a Service (IaaS), Platform as a Service (PaaS))

- 1.5 Evaluate cloud service providers

  - 1.5.1 Verification against criteria (e.g., International Organization for Standardization/International Electrotechnical Commission (ISO/IEC) 27017, Payment Card Industry Data Security Standard (PCI DSS))

  - 1.5.2 System/subsystem product certifications (e.g., Common Criteria (CC), Federal Information Processing Standard (FIPS) 140-2)

Domain 2 Cloud Data Security

- 2.1 Describe cloud data concepts

  - 2.1.1 Cloud data lifecycle phases

  - 2.1.2 Data dispersion

- 2.2 Design and implement cloud data storage architectures
    - 2.2.1 Storage types (e.g. long term, ephemeral, raw-disk)
    - 2.2.2 Threats to storage types
- 2.3 Design and apply data security technologies and strategies
    - 2.3.1 Encryption and key management
    - 2.3.2 Hashing
    - 2.3.3 Masking
    - 2.3.4 Tokenization
    - 2.3.5 Data Loss Prevention (DLP)
    - 2.3.6 Data obfuscation
    - 2.3.7 Data de-identification (e.g., anonymization)
- 2.4 Implement data discovery
    - 2.4.1 Structured data
    - 2.4.2 Unstructured data
- 2.5 Implement data classification
    - 2.5.1 Mapping
    - 2.5.2 Labeling
    - 2.5.3 Sensitive data (e.g., Protected Health Information (PHI), Personally Identifiable Information (PII), card holder data)
- 2.6 Design and implement Information Rights Management (IRM)
    - 2.6.1 Objectives (e.g., data rights, provisioning, access models)
    - 2.6.2 Appropriate tools (e.g., issuing and revocation of certificates)
- 2.7 Plan and implement data retention, deletion, and archiving policies
    - 2.7.1 Data retention policies
    - 2.7.2 Data deletion procedures and mechanisms
    - 2.7.3 Data archiving procedures and mechanisms
    - 2.7.4 Legal hold
- 2.8 Design and implement auditability, traceability, and accountability of data events
    - 2.8.1 Definition of event sources and requirement of identity attribution
    - 2.8.2 Logging, storage, and analysis of data events
    - 2.8.3 Chain of custody and non-repudiation

Domain 3 Cloud Platform and Infrastructure Security

- 3.1 Comprehend cloud infrastructure components
  - 3.1.1 Physical environment
  - 3.1.2 Network and communications
  - 3.1.3 Compute
  - 3.1.4 Virtualization
  - 3.1.5 Storage
  - 3.1.6 Management plane
- 3.2 Design a secure data center
  - 3.2.1 Logical design (e.g., tenant partitioning, access control)
  - 3.2.2 Physical design (e.g., location, buy or build)
  - 3.2.3 Environmental design (e.g., Heating, Ventilation, and Air Conditioning (HVAC), multi-vendor pathway connectivity)
- 3.3 Analyze risks associated with cloud infrastructure
  - 3.3.1 Risk assessment and analysis
  - 3.3.2 Cloud vulnerabilities, threats, and attacks
  - 3.3.3 Virtualization risks
  - 3.3.4 Counter-measure strategies
- 3.4 Design and plan security controls
  - 3.4.1 Physical and environmental protection (e.g., on-premise)
  - 3.4.2 System and communication protection
  - 3.4.3 Virtualization systems protection
  - 3.4.4 Identification, authentication, and authorization in cloud infrastructure
  - 3.4.5 Audit mechanisms (e.g., log collection, packet capture)
- 3.5 Plan Disaster Recovery (DR) and Business Continuity (BC)
  - 3.5.1 Risks related to the cloud environment
  - 3.5.2 Business requirements (e.g., Recovery Time Objective (RTO), Recovery Point Objective (RPO), Recovery Service Level (RSL))
  - 3.5.3 Business Continuity/Disaster Recovery strategy
  - 3.5.4 Creation, implementation, and testing of plan

Domain 4 Cloud Application Security

Domain 5 Cloud Security Operations

- 5.1 Implement and build physical and logical infrastructure for cloud environment
  - 5.1.1 Hardware-specific security configuration requirements (e.g., Basic Input Output System (BIOS) settings for virtualization and Trusted Platform Module (TPM), storage controllers, network controllers)
  - 5.1.2 Installation and configuration of virtualization management tools
  - 5.1.3 Virtual hardware-specific security configuration requirements (e.g., network, storage, memory, Central Processing Unit (CPU))
  - 5.1.4 Installation of guest Operating System (OS) virtualization toolsets
- 5.2 Operate physical and logical infrastructure for cloud environment
  - 5.2.1 Configure access control for local and remote access (e.g., Secure Keyboard Video Mouse (KVM), Console-based access mechanisms, Remote Desktop Protocol (RDP))
  - 5.2.2 Secure network configuration (e.g., Virtual Local Area Networks (VLAN), Transport Layer Security (TLS), Dynamic Host Configuration Protocol (DHCP), Domain Name System (DNS), Virtual Private Network (VPN))
  - 5.2.3 Operating System (OS) hardening through the application of baselines (e.g., Windows, Linux, VMware)
  - 5.2.4 Availability of stand-alone hosts
  - 5.2.5 Availability of clustered hosts (e.g., Distributed Resource Scheduling (DRS), Dynamic Optimization (DO), storage clusters, maintenance mode, high availability)
  - 5.2.6 Availability of guest Operating System (OS)
- 5.3 Manage physical and logical infrastructure for cloud environment
  - 5.3.1 Access controls for remote access (e.g., Remote Desktop Protocol (RDP), Secure Terminal Access, Secure Shell (SSH))
  - 5.3.2 Operating System (OS) baseline compliance monitoring and remediation
  - 5.3.3 Patch management
  - 5.3.4 Performance and capacity monitoring (e.g., network, compute, storage, response time)
  - 5.3.5 Hardware monitoring (e.g., disk, Central Processing Unit (CPU), fan speed, temperature)
  - 5.3.6 Configuration of host and guest Operating System (OS) backup and restore functions
  - 5.3.7 Network security controls (e.g., firewalls, Intrusion Detection Systems (IDS), Intrusion Prevention Systems (IPS), honeypots, vulnerability assessments, network security groups)
  - 5.3.8 Management plane (e.g., scheduling, orchestration, maintenance)

- 5.4 Implement operational controls and standards (e.g., Information Technology Infrastructure Library (ITIL), International Organization for Standardization/International Electrotechnical Commission (ISO/IEC) 20000-1)
  - 5.4.1 Change management
  - 5.4.2 Continuity management
  - 5.4.3 Information security management
  - 5.4.4 Continual service improvement management
  - 5.4.5 Incident management
  - 5.4.6 Problem management
  - 5.4.7 Release management
  - 5.4.8 Deployment management
  - 5.4.9 Configuration management
  - 5.4.10 Service level management
  - 5.4.11 Availability management
  - 5.4.12 Capacity management
- 5.5 Support digital forensics
  - 5.5.1 Forensic data collection methodologies
  - 5.5.2 Evidence management
  - 5.5.3 Collect, acquire, and preserve digital evidence
- 5.6 Manage communication with relevant parties
  - 5.6.1 Vendors
  - 5.6.2 Customers
  - 5.6.3 Partners
  - 5.6.4 Regulators
  - 5.6.5 Other stakeholders
- 5.7 Manage security operations
  - 5.7.1 Security Operations Center (SOC)
  - 5.7.2 Monitoring of security controls (e.g., firewalls, Intrusion Detection Systems (IDS), Intrusion Prevention Systems (IPS), honeypots, vulnerability assessments, network security groups)
  - 5.7.3 Log capture and analysis (e.g., Security Information and Event Management (SIEM), log management)
  - 5.7.4 Incident management

Domain 6 Legal, Risk, and Compliance

- 6.1 Articulate legal requirements and unique risks within the cloud environment
    - 6.1.1 Conflicting international legislation
    - 6.1.2 Evaluation of legal risks specific to cloud computing
    - 6.1.3 Legal frameworks and guidelines
    - 6.1.4 eDiscovery (e.g., International Organization for Standardization/International Electrotechnical Commission (ISO/IEC) 27050, Cloud Security Alliance (CSA) Guidance)
    - 6.1.5 Forensics requirements
- 6.2 Understand privacy issues
    - 6.2.1 Difference between contractual and regulated private data (e.g., Protected Health Information (PHI), Personally Identifiable Information (PII))
    - 6.2.2 Country-specific legislation related to private data (e.g., Protected Health Information (PHI), Personally Identifiable Information (PII))
    - 6.2.3 Jurisdictional differences in data privacy
    - 6.2.4 Standard privacy requirements (e.g., International Organization for Standardization/International Electrotechnical Commission (ISO/IEC) 27018, Generally Accepted Privacy Principles (GAPP), General Data Protection Regulation (GDPR))
- 6.3 Understand audit process, methodologies, and required adaptations for a cloud environment
    - 6.3.1 Internal and external audit controls
    - 6.3.2 Impact of audit requirements
    - 6.3.3 Identify assurance challenges of virtualization and cloud
    - 6.3.4 Types of audit reports (e.g., Statement on Standards for Attestation Engagements (SSAE), Security Operations Center (SOC), International Standard on Assurance Engagements (ISAE))
    - 6.3.5 Restrictions of audit scope statements (e.g., Statement on Standards for Attestation Engagements (SSAE), International Standard on Assurance Engagements (ISAE))
    - 6.3.6 Gap analysis
    - 6.3.7 Audit planning
    - 6.3.8 Internal Information Security Management System (ISMS)
    - 6.3.9 Internal information security controls system
    - 6.3.10 Policies (e.g., organizational, functional, cloud computing)
    - 6.3.11 Identification and involvement of relevant stakeholders

- 6.3.12 Specialized compliance requirements for highly-regulated industries (e.g., North American Electric Reliability Corporation/Critical Infrastructure Protection (NERC/CIP), Health Insurance Portability and Accountability Act (HIPAA), Payment Card Industry (PCI))
    - 6.3.13 Impact of distributed Information Technology (IT) model (e.g., diverse geographical locations and crossing over legal jurisdictions)
- 6.4 Understand implications of cloud to enterprise risk management
    - 6.4.1 Assess providers risk management programs (e.g., controls, methodologies, policies)
    - 6.4.2 Difference between data owner/controller vs. data custodian/processor (e.g., risk profile, risk appetite, responsibility)
    - 6.4.3 Regulatory transparency requirements (e.g., breach notification, Sarbanes-Oxley SOX, General Data Protection Regulation (GDPR))
    - 6.4.4 Risk treatment (i.e., avoid, modify, share, retain)
    - 6.4.5 Different risk frameworks
    - 6.4.6 Metrics for risk management
    - 6.4.7 Assessment of risk environment (e.g., service, vendor, infrastructure)
- 6.5 Understand outsourcing and cloud contract design
    - 6.5.1 Business requirements (e.g., Service Level Agreement (SLA), Master Service Agreement (MSA), Statement of Work (SOW))
    - 6.5.2 Vendor management
    - 6.5.3 Contract management (e.g., right to audit, metrics, definitions, termination, litigation, assurance, compliance, access to cloud/data, cyber risk insurance)
    - 6.5.4 Supply-chain management (e.g., International Organization for Standardization/International Electrotechnical Commission (ISO/IEC) 27036)

Online Test Bank

To practice in an online testing setting of the same questions, visit www.wiley.com/go/sybextestprep and register your book to get access to the Sybex Test Platform. Online, you can mix questions from the domain chapters and practice exams, take timed tests, and have your answers scored.

As you go through the questions in this book, please remember the abbreviation RTFQ, which is short for "read the *full* question." There is no better advice you can possibly receive than this. Read every word of every question. Read every possible answer before selecting the one you like. The exam is 125 questions over three hours. You have more than enough time to consider each question thoroughly. There is no cause for hurry. Make sure you understand what the question is asking before responding.

Good luck on the exam. I'm hoping this book helps you pass.

Chapter

1

Domain 1: Cloud Concepts, Architecture, and Design

Domain 1 of the Certified Cloud Security Professional (CCSP) Exam Outline is an introductory section that touches on almost every other element of the exam outline so you'll find a wide breadth of content and subject matter ranging over many topics. The questions in this chapter will reflect that broad scope but will also get into some level of detail on certain aspects you'll find pertinent to the exam.

1. Alice is the CEO for a software company; she is considering migrating the operation from the current traditional on-premises environment into the cloud. Which cloud service model should she most likely consider for her company's purposes?

   A. Platform as a service (PaaS)

   B. Software as a service (SaaS)

   C. Backup as a service (Baas)

   D. Infrastructure as a service (IaaS)

2. Alice is the CEO for a software company; she is considering migrating the operation from the current traditional on-premises environment into the cloud. Which aspect of cloud computing should she be *most* concerned about, in terms of security issues?

   A. Multitenancy

   B. Metered service

   C. Service-level agreement (SLA)

   D. Remote access

3. Alice is the CEO for a software company; she is considering migrating the operation from the current traditional on-premises environment into the cloud. In order to protect her company's intellectual property, Alice might want to consider implementing all these techniques/solutions *except* _____.

   A. Egress monitoring

   B. Encryption

   C. Turnstiles

   D. Digital watermarking

4. Alice is the CEO for a software company; she is considering migrating the operation from the current traditional on-premises environment into the cloud. What is probably the biggest factor in her decision?

   A. Network scalability

   B. Off-site backup capability

   C. Global accessibility

   D. Reduced overall cost due to outsourcing administration

5. In which of the following situations does the data owner have to administer the OS?

   A. IaaS

   B. PaaS

   C. Off-site archive

   D. SaaS

6. You are setting up a cloud implementation for an online retailer who will accept credit card payments. According to the Payment Card Industry Data Security Standard (PCI DSS), what can you never store for any length of time?

   A. Personal data of consumers

   B. The credit card verification (CCV) number

    C. The credit card number

    D. Home address of the customer

7. The Payment Card Industry Data Security Standard (PCI DSS) distinguishes merchants by different tiers, based on _____.

    A. Number of transactions per year

    B. Dollar value of transactions per year

    C. Geographic location

    D. Jurisdiction

8. What is usually considered the difference between business continuity (BC) efforts and disaster recovery (DR) efforts?

    A. BC involves a recovery time objective (RTO), and DR involves a recovery point objective (RPO).

    B. BC is for events caused by humans (like arson or theft), whereas DR is for natural disasters.

    C. BC is about maintaining critical functions during a disruption of normal operations, and DR is about recovering to normal operations after a disruption.

    D. BC involves protecting human assets (personnel, staff, users), whereas DR is about protecting property (assets, data).

9. For business continuity and disaster recovery (BC/DR) purposes, the contract between the primary cloud provider and customer should include all of the following *except* _____.

    A. Which party will be responsible for initiating a BC/DR response activity

    B. How a BC/DR response will be initiated

    C. How soon the customer's data can be ported to a new cloud provider in the event a disruptive event makes the current provider unable to continue service

    D. How much a new cloud provider will charge the customer if data has to be ported from the current cloud provider because of a disruptive event

10. When the cloud customer requests modifications to the current contract or service-level agreement (SLA) for business continuity/disaster recovery (BD/DR) purposes, who should absorb the cost of modification?

    A. The customer absorbs the cost.

    B. The provider absorbs the cost.

    C. The cost should be split equally.

    D. Modifications don't cost anything.

11. Which of the following is *not* a factor an organization might use in the cost–benefit analysis when deciding whether to migrate to a cloud environment?

    A. Pooled resources in the cloud

    B. Shifting from IT investment as capital expenditures to operational expenditures

    C. The time savings and efficiencies offered by the cloud service

    D. Branding associated with which cloud provider might be selected

12. Which of the following is the *least* important factor an organization might use in the cost–benefit analysis when deciding whether to migrate to a cloud environment?

    A. Depreciation of IT assets

    B. Shift in focus from IT dependencies to business process opportunities

    C. Whether the provider bills on a monthly or weekly basis

    D. Costs associated with utility consumption

13. Which of the following is an aspect of IT costs that will likely be reduced by moving from a traditional, on-premises IT environment into the cloud?

    A. Number of users

    B. Cost of software licensing

    C. Number of applications

    D. Number of clientele

14. Which of the following is an aspect of IT costs that will likely be reduced by moving from a traditional, on-premises IT environment to the cloud?

    A. Utilities costs

    B. Security costs

    C. Landscaping costs

    D. Travel costs

15. Which of the following is an aspect of IT costs that will likely be reduced by moving from a traditional, on-premises IT environment to the cloud?

    A. Personnel training

    B. Personnel turnover

    C. Capital expenses for IT assets

    D. Loss due to an internal data breach

16. Although cloud migration might offer significant cost savings for an organization, which of the following factors might reduce the actual financial benefit the organization realizes in a cloud environment?

    A. Altitude of the cloud data center

    B. Security controls and countermeasures

    C. Loss of ownership of IT assets

    D. Costs of Internet connectivity for remote users

17. What is the international standard that dictates creation of an organizational information security management system (ISMS)?

    A. NIST SP 800-53

    B. PCI DSS

    C. ISO 27001

    D. NIST SP 800-37

18. ISO 27001 favors which type of technology?

    A. Open source

    B. PC

    C. Cloud-based

    D. None

19. Why might an organization choose to comply with the ISO 27001 standard?

    A. Price

    B. Ease of implementation

    C. International acceptance

    D. Speed

20. Why might an organization choose to comply with NIST SP 800-series standards?

    A. Price

    B. Ease of implementation

    C. International acceptance

    D. Speed

21. Which standard contains guidance for selecting, implementing, and managing information security controls mapped to an information security management system (ISMS) framework?

    A. ISO 27002

    B. Payment Card Industry Data Security Standard (PCI DSS)

    C. NIST SP 800-37

    D. Health Insurance Portability and Accountability Act (HIPAA)

22. The current American Institute of Certified Public Accountants (AICPA) publishes the _____ standard, from which the Service Organization Control (SOC) reports are derived.

    A. Sherwood Applied Business Security Architecture (SABSA)

    B. Statement on Standards for Attestation Engagements (SSAE) 18

    C. Biba

    D. NIST SP 800-53

23. Which U.S. federal law affects banking and insurance companies?

    A. NIST 800-53

    B. HIPAA

    C. Sarbanes-Oxley Act (SOX)

    D. Gramm-Leach-Bliley Act (GLBA)

24. The Statement on Standards for Attestation Engagements 18 (SSAE 18) Service Organization Control (SOC) reports are audit tools promulgated by the American Institute of Certified Public Accountants (AICPA). What kind of entities were SOC reports designed to audit?

A. U.S. federal government

B. Privately held companies

C. Companies that provide services

D. Nonprofit organizations

25. The Statement on Standards for Attestation Engagements (SSAE) 18 Service Organization Control (SOC) reports are audit tools promulgated by the American Institute of Certified Public Accountants (AICPA). As an IT security professional, when reviewing SOC reports for a cloud provider, which report would you *most* like to see?

A. SOC 1

B. SOC 2, Type 1

C. SOC 2, Type 2

D. SOC 3

26. The Statement on Standards for Attestation Engagements (SSAE) 18 Service Organization Control (SOC) reports are audit tools promulgated by the American Institute of Certified Public Accountants (AICPA). As an investor, when reviewing SOC reports for a cloud provider, which report would you *most* like to see?

A. SOC 1

B. SOC 2, Type 1

C. SOC 2, Type 2

D. SOC 3

27. The Statement on Standards for Attestation Engagements (SSAE) 18 Service Organization Control (SOC) reports are audit tools promulgated by the American Institute of Certified Public Accountants (AICPA). You are an IT security professional working for an organization that is considering migrating from your on-premises environment into the cloud. Assuming some have passed SSAE 18 audits and some haven't, which SOC report might be best to use for your initial review of several different cloud providers in order to narrow down the field of potential services in a fast, easy way?

A. SOC 1

B. SOC 2, Type 1

C. SOC 2, Type 2

D. SOC 3

28. Which of the following entities would *not* be covered by the Payment Card Industry Data Security Standard (PCI DSS)?

A. A bank issuing credit cards

B. A retailer accepting credit cards as payment

    C. A business that processes credit card payments on behalf of a retailer

    D. A company that offers credit card debt repayment counseling

29. What sort of legal enforcement may the Payment Card Industry (PCI) Security Standards Council *not* bring to bear against organizations that fail to comply with the Payment Card Industry Data Security Standard (PCI DSS)?

    A. Fines

    B. Jail time

    C. Suspension of credit card processing privileges

    D. Subject to increased audit frequency and scope

30. The Payment Card Industry Data Security Standard (PCI DSS) merchant levels are based on _____.

    A. Dollar value of transactions over the course of a year

    B. Number of transactions over the course of a year

    C. Location of the merchant or processor

    D. Dollar value and number of transactions over the course of a year

31. In terms of greatest stringency and requirements for security validation, which is the highest merchant level in the Payment Card Industry (PCI) standard?

    A. 1

    B. 2

    C. 3

    D. 4

32. The Payment Card Industry Data Security Standard (PCI DSS) requires _____ security requirements for entities involved in credit card payments and processing.

    A. Technical

    B. Nontechnical

    C. Technical and nontechnical

    D. Neither technical nor nontechnical

33. According to the Payment Card Industry Data Security Standard (PCI DSS), if a merchant is going to store credit cardholder information for any length of time, what type of security protection *must* be used?

    A. Tokenization or masking

    B. Obfuscation or tokenization

    C. Masking or obfuscation

    D. Tokenization or encryption

34. What element of credit cardholder information may *never* be stored for any length of time, according to the Payment Card Industry Data Security Standard (PCI DSS)?

A. The full credit card number

B. The card verification value (CVV)

C. The cardholder's mailing address

D. The cardholder's full name

35. When reviewing IT security products that have been subjected to Common Criteria certification, what does the Evaluation Assurance Level (EAL) tell you?

A. How secure the product is from an external attack

B. How thoroughly the product has been tested

C. The level of security the product delivers to an environment

D. The level of trustworthiness you can have if you deploy the product

36. Which Common Criteria Evaluation Assurance Level (EAL) is granted to those products that are functionally tested by their manufacturer/vendor?

A. 1

B. 3

C. 5

D. 7

37. Which Common Criteria Evaluation Assurance Level (EAL) is granted to those products that are formally verified in terms of design and tested by an independent third party?

A. 1

B. 3

C. 5

D. 7

38. Who pays for the Common Criteria certification of an IT product?

A. National Institute of Standards and Technology (NIST)

B. The vendor/manufacturer

C. The cloud customer

D. The end user

39. Who publishes the list of cryptographic modules validated according to the Federal Information Processing Standard (FIPS) 140-2?

A. The U.S. Office of Management and Budget (OMB)

B. The International Standards Organization (ISO)

C. International Information System Security Certification Consortium, or (ISC)[2]

D. The National Institute of Standards and Technology (NIST)

40. Who performs the review process for hardware security modules (HSMs) in accordance with the Federal Information Processing Standard (FIPS) 140-2?

   A. The National Institute of Standards and Technology (NIST)

   B. The National Security Agency (NSA)

   C. Independent (private) laboratories

   D. The European Union Agency for Network and Information Security (ENISA)

41. In terms of the number of security functions offered, which is the highest Federal Information Processing Standard (FIPS) 140-2 security level a cryptographic module can achieve in certification?

   A. 1

   B. 2

   C. 3

   D. 4

42. What distinguishes the Federal Information Processing Standard (FIPS) 140-2 security levels for cryptographic modules?

   A. The level of sensitivity of data they can be used to protect

   B. The amount of physical protection provided by the product, in terms of tamper resistance

   C. The size of the IT environment the product can be used to protect

   D. The geographic locations in which the product is allowed

43. For U.S. government agencies, what level of data sensitivity/classification may be processed by cryptographic modules certified according to the Federal Information Processing Standard (FIPS) 140-2 criteria?

   A. Sensitive but unclassified (SBU)

   B. Secret

   C. Top Secret

   D. Sensitive Compartmentalized Information (SCI)

44. Who pays for cryptographic modules to be certified in accordance with Federal Information Processing Standard (FIPS) 140-2 criteria?

   A. The U.S. government

   B. Module vendors

   C. Certification laboratories

   D. Module users

45. The Open Web Application Security Project (OWASP) Top Ten is a list of web application security threats that is created by a member-driven OWASP committee of application development experts and published approximately every 24 months. What is probably the single *most* important way of countering the highest number of items on the OWASP Top Ten (regardless of year)?

   A. Social engineering training

   B. Disciplined coding practices and processes

   C. White-box source code testing

   D. Physical controls at all locations at which the application is eventually used

46. The Open Web Application Security Project (OWASP) Top Ten is a list of web application security threats that is created by a member-driven OWASP committee of application development experts and published approximately every 24 months. The OWASP Top Ten list usually includes "injection." In most cases, what is the attacker trying to do with an injection attack?

   A. Get the user to allow access for the attacker.

   B. Insert malware onto the system.

   C. Trick the application into running commands.

   D. Penetrate the facility hosting the software.

47. The Open Web Application Security Project (OWASP) Top Ten is a list of web application security threats that is created by a member-driven OWASP committee of application development experts and published approximately every 24 months. The OWASP Top Ten list usually includes "injection." In most cases, what is the method for reducing the risk of an injection attack?

   A. User training

   B. Hardening the OS

   C. Input validation/bounds checking

   D. Physical locks

48. The Open Web Application Security Project (OWASP) Top Ten is a list of web application security threats that is created by a member-driven OWASP committee of application development experts and published approximately every 24 months. The OWASP Top Ten list often includes "broken authentication and session management." Which of the following is a good method for reducing the risk of broken authentication and session management?

   A. Do not use custom authentication schemes.

   B. Implement widespread training programs.

   C. Ensure that strong input validation is in place.

   D. Use X.400 protocol standards.

49. The Open Web Application Security Project (OWASP) Top Ten is a list of web application security threats that is created by a member-driven OWASP committee of application development experts and published approximately every 24 months. The OWASP Top Ten list often includes "broken authentication and session management." Which of the following is *not* a practice/vulnerability that can lead to broken authentication and infringe on session management?

   A. Session identification exposed in URLs

   B. Unprotected stored credentials

   C. Lack of session timeout

   D. Failure to follow Health Insurance Portability and Accountability Act (HIPAA) guidance

50. The Open Web Application Security Project (OWASP) Top Ten is a list of web application security threats that is created by a member-driven OWASP committee of application development experts and published approximately every 24 months. The OWASP Top Ten list often includes "broken authentication and session management." Which of the following is *not* a practice/vulnerability that can lead to broken authentication and infringe on session management?

   A. Failure to rotate session IDs after a successful login

   B. Easily guessed authentication credentials

   C. Weak physical entry points in the data center

   D. Credentials sent over unencrypted lines

51. The Open Web Application Security Project (OWASP) Top Ten is a list of web application security threats that is created by a member-driven OWASP committee of application development experts and published approximately every 24 months. The OWASP Top Ten list usually includes "cross-site scripting (XSS)." Which of the following is *not* a method for reducing the risk of XSS attacks?

   A. Put untrusted data in only allowed slots of HTML documents.

   B. HTML escape when including untrusted data in any HTML elements.

   C. Use the attribute `escape` when including untrusted data in attribute elements.

   D. Encrypt all HTML documents.

52. The Open Web Application Security Project (OWASP) Top Ten is a list of web application security threats that is created by a member-driven OWASP committee of application development experts and published approximately every 24 months. The OWASP Top Ten list usually includes "cross-site scripting (XSS)." Which of the following is *not* a method for reducing the risk of XSS attacks?

   A. Use an auto-escaping template system.

   B. Use XML escape for all identity assertions.

   C. Sanitize HTML markup with a library designed for the purpose.

   D. HTML escape JSON values in an HTML context and read the data with `JSON.parse`.

53. The Open Web Application Security Project (OWASP) Top Ten is a list of web application security threats that is created by a member-driven OWASP committee of application development experts and published approximately every 24 months. The OWASP Top Ten list often includes "insecure direct object references." Which of these is an example of an insecure direct object reference?

   A. `www.sybex.com/authoraccounts/benmalisow`

   B. `10 ? "sybex accounts"; 20 goto 10`

   C. `mysql -u [bmalisow] -p [database1];`

   D. `bmalisow@sybex.com`

54. The Open Web Application Security Project (OWASP) Top Ten is a list of web application security threats that is created by a member-driven OWASP committee of application development experts and published approximately every 24 months. The OWASP Top Ten list often includes "insecure direct object references." Which of these is a method to counter the risks of insecure direct object references?

   A. Perform user security training.

   B. Check access each time a direct object reference is called by an untrusted source.

   C. Install high-luminosity interior lighting throughout the facility.

   D. Append each object with sufficient metadata to properly categorize and classify based on asset value and sensitivity.

55. The Open Web Application Security Project (OWASP) Top Ten is a list of web application security threats that is created by a member-driven OWASP committee of application development experts and published approximately every 24 months. The OWASP Top Ten list often includes "security misconfiguration." Which of these is an example of a security misconfiguration?

   A. Not providing encryption keys to untrusted users

   B. Having a public-facing website

   C. Leaving default accounts unchanged

   D. Using turnstiles instead of mantraps

56. The Open Web Application Security Project (OWASP) Top Ten is a list of web application security threats that is created by a member-driven OWASP committee of application development experts and published approximately every 24 months. The OWASP Top Ten list often includes "security misconfiguration." Which of these is an example of a security misconfiguration?

   A. Having unpatched software in the production environment

   B. Leaving unprotected portable media in the workplace

   C. Letting data owners determine the classifications/categorizations of their data

   D. Preventing users from accessing untrusted networks

57. The Open Web Application Security Project (OWASP) Top Ten is a list of web application security threats that is created by a member-driven OWASP committee of application development experts and published approximately every 24 months. The OWASP Top Ten list often includes "security misconfiguration." Which of these is a technique to reduce the potential for a security misconfiguration?

   A. Enforce strong user access control processes.

   B. Have a repeatable hardening process for all systems/software.

   C. Use encryption for all remote access.

   D. Use encryption for all stored data.

58. The Open Web Application Security Project (OWASP) Top Ten is a list of web application security threats that is created by a member-driven OWASP committee of application development experts and published approximately every 24 months. The OWASP Top Ten list usually includes "security misconfiguration." Which of these is a technique to reduce the potential for a security misconfiguration?

   A. Broad user training that includes initial, recurring, and refresher sessions

   B. Deeper personnel screening procedures for privileged users than is used for regular users

   C. A repeatable patching process that includes updating libraries as well as software

   D. Randomly auditing all user activity, with additional focus on privileged users

59. The Open Web Application Security Project (OWASP) Top Ten is a list of web application security threats that is created by a member-driven OWASP committee of application development experts and published approximately every 24 months. The OWASP Top Ten list usually includes "security misconfiguration." Which of these is a technique to reduce the potential for a security misconfiguration?

   A. Purchase only trusted devices/components.

   B. Follow a published, known industry standard for baseline configurations.

   C. Hire only screened, vetted candidates for all positions.

   D. Update policy on a regular basis, according to a proven process.

60. The Open Web Application Security Project (OWASP) Top Ten is a list of web application security threats that is created by a member-driven OWASP committee of application development experts and published approximately every 24 months. The OWASP Top Ten list usually includes "security misconfiguration." Which of these is a technique to reduce the potential for a security misconfiguration?

   A. Get regulatory approval for major configuration modifications.

   B. Update the business continuity and disaster recovery (BC/DR) plan on a timely basis.

   C. Train all users on proper security procedures.

   D. Perform periodic scans and audits of the environment.

61. The Open Web Application Security Project (OWASP) Top Ten is a list of web application security threats that is created by a member-driven OWASP committee of application development experts and published approximately every 24 months. The OWASP Top Ten list often includes "sensitive data exposure." Which of these is a technique to reduce the potential for a sensitive data exposure?

- **A.** Extensive user training on proper data handling techniques
- **B.** Advanced firewalls inspecting all inbound traffic, to include content-based screening
- **C.** Ensuring the use of utility backup power supplies
- **D.** Roving security guards

62. The Open Web Application Security Project (OWASP) Top Ten is a list of web application security threats that is created by a member-driven OWASP committee of application development experts and published approximately every 24 months. The OWASP Top Ten list often includes "sensitive data exposure." All of the following are techniques for reducing the possibility of exposing sensitive data, *except* _____.

- **A.** Destroying sensitive data as soon as possible
- **B.** Avoiding categorizing data as sensitive
- **C.** Using proper key management when encrypting sensitive data
- **D.** Disabling autocomplete on forms that collect sensitive data

63. The Open Web Application Security Project (OWASP) Top Ten is a list of web application security threats that is created by a member-driven OWASP committee of application development experts and published approximately every 24 months. The OWASP Top Ten list sometimes includes "missing function level access control." Which of these is a technique to reduce the potential for a missing function-level access control?

- **A.** Set the default to deny all access to functions, and require authentication/authorization for each access request.
- **B.** HTML escape all HTML attributes.
- **C.** Restrict permissions based on an access control list (ACL).
- **D.** Refrain from including direct access information in URLs.

64. The Open Web Application Security Project (OWASP) Top Ten is a list of web application security threats that is created by a member-driven OWASP committee of application development experts and published approximately every 24 months. The OWASP Top Ten list sometimes includes "missing function level access control." Which of these is a technique to reduce the potential for a missing function-level access control?

- **A.** Run a process as both user and privileged user, compare results, and determine similarity.
- **B.** Run automated monitoring and audit scripts.
- **C.** Include browser buttons/navigation elements to secure functions.
- **D.** Enhance user training to include management personnel.

65. The Open Web Application Security Project (OWASP) Top Ten is a list of web application security threats that is created by a member-driven OWASP committee of application development experts and published approximately every 24 months. The OWASP Top Ten list often includes "cross-site request forgery" (CSRF). Which of these is a technique to reduce the potential for a CSRF?

A. Train users to detect forged HTTP requests.

B. Have users remove all browsers from their devices.

C. Don't allow links to or from other websites.

D. Include a CAPTCHA code as part of the user resource request process.

66. The Open Web Application Security Project (OWASP) Top Ten is a list of web application security threats that is created by a member-driven OWASP committee of application development experts and published approximately every 24 months. The OWASP Top Ten list often includes "cross-site request forgery" (CSRF). A CSRF attack might be used for all the following malicious actions *except* _____.

A. The attacker could have the user log into one of the user's online accounts.

B. The attacker could collect the user's online account login credentials, to be used by the attacker later.

C. The attacker could have the user perform an action in one of the user's online accounts.

D. The attacker could trick the user into calling a fraudulent customer service number hosted by the attacker and talk the user into disclosing personal information.

67. The Open Web Application Security Project (OWASP) Top Ten is a list of web application security threats that is created by a member-driven OWASP committee of application development experts and published approximately every 24 months. The OWASP Top Ten list often includes "cross-site request forgery" (CSRF). Which of the following is a good way to deter CSRF attacks?

A. Have your website refuse all HTTP resource requests.

B. Ensure that all HTTP resource requests include a unique, unpredictable token.

C. Don't allow e-commerce on your website.

D. Process all user requests with only one brand of browser, and refuse all resource requests from other browsers.

68. The Open Web Application Security Project (OWASP) Top Ten is a list of web application security threats that is created by a member-driven OWASP committee of application development experts and published approximately every 24 months. The OWASP Top Ten list often includes "using components with known vulnerabilities." Which of the following is a good way to protect against this problem?

A. Use only components your organization has written.

B. Update to current versions of component libraries as soon as possible.

C. Never use anyone else's component library.

D. Apply patches to old component libraries.

69. The Open Web Application Security Project (OWASP) Top Ten is a list of web application security threats that is created by a member-driven OWASP committee of application development experts and published approximately every 24 months. The OWASP Top Ten list often includes "using components with known vulnerabilities." Why would an organization ever use components with known vulnerabilities to create software?

    A. The organization is insured.

    B. The particular vulnerabilities exist only in a context not being used by developers.

    C. Some vulnerabilities exist only in foreign countries.

    D. A component might have a hidden vulnerability.

70. The Open Web Application Security Project (OWASP) Top Ten is a list of web application security threats that is created by a member-driven OWASP committee of application development experts and published approximately every 24 months. The OWASP Top Ten list often includes "using components with known vulnerabilities." Which of the following is a good way to protect against this problem?

    A. Use only standard libraries.

    B. Review all updates/lists/notifications for components your organization uses.

    C. Be sure to HTML escape all attribute elements.

    D. Increase the user training budget.

71. The Open Web Application Security Project (OWASP) Top Ten is a list of web application security threats created by a member-driven OWASP committee of application development experts and published approximately every 24 months. The OWASP Top Ten list sometimes includes "unvalidated redirects and forwards." Which of the following is a good way to protect against this problem?

    A. HTML escape all HTML attributes.

    B. Train users to recognize invalidated links.

    C. Block all inbound resource requests.

    D. Implement audit logging.

72. The Open Web Application Security Project (OWASP) Top Ten is a list of web application security threats that is created by a member-driven OWASP committee of application development experts and published approximately every 24 months. The OWASP Top Ten list often includes "unvalidated redirects and forwards." Which of the following is a good way to protect against this problem?

    A. Don't use redirects/forwards in your applications.

    B. Refrain from storing credentials long term.

    C. Implement security incident/event monitoring (security information and event management [SIEM]/security information management [SIM]/security event management [SEM]) solutions.

    D. Implement digital rights management (DRM) solutions.

73. You are the security subject matter expert (SME) for an organization considering a transition from a traditional IT enterprise environment into a hosted cloud provider's data center. One of the challenges you're facing is whether your current applications in the on-premises environment will function properly with the provider's hosted systems and tools. This is a(n) _____ issue.

   A. Interoperability

   B. Portability

   C. Stability

   D. Security

74. You are the security subject matter expert (SME) for an organization considering a transition from a traditional IT enterprise environment into a hosted cloud provider's data center. One of the challenges you're facing is whether the provider will have undue control over your data once it is within the provider's data center; will the provider be able to hold your organization hostage because they have your data? This is a(n) _____ issue.

   A. Interoperability

   B. Portability

   C. Stability

   D. Security

75. You are the security subject matter expert (SME) for an organization considering a transition from a traditional IT enterprise environment into a hosted cloud provider's data center. One of the challenges you're facing is whether the cloud provider will be able to comply with the existing legislative and contractual frameworks your organization is required to follow. This is a _____ issue.

   A. Resiliency

   B. Privacy

   C. Performance

   D. Regulatory

76. You are the security subject matter expert (SME) for an organization considering a transition from a traditional IT enterprise environment into a hosted cloud provider's data center. One of the challenges you're facing is whether the cloud provider will be able to allow your organization to substantiate and determine with some assurance that all of the contract terms are being met. This is a(n) _____ issue.

   A. Regulatory

   B. Privacy

   C. Resiliency

   D. Auditability

77. Encryption is an essential tool for affording security to cloud-based operations. While it is possible to encrypt every system, piece of data, and transaction that takes place on the cloud, why might that not be the optimum choice for an organization?

    A. Key length variances don't provide any actual additional security.

    B. It would cause additional processing overhead and time delay.

    C. It might result in vendor lockout.

    D. The data subjects might be upset by this.

78. Encryption is an essential tool for affording security to cloud-based operations. While it is possible to encrypt every system, piece of data, and transaction that takes place on the cloud, why might that not be the optimum choice for an organization?

    A. It could increase the possibility of physical theft.

    B. Encryption won't work throughout the environment.

    C. The protection might be disproportionate to the value of the asset(s).

    D. Users will be able to see everything within the organization.

79. Which of the following is *not* an element of the identification component of identity and access management (IAM)?

    A. Provisioning

    B. Management

    C. Discretion

    D. Deprovisioning

80. Which of the following entities is *most* likely to play a vital role in the identity provisioning aspect of a user's experience in an organization?

    A. The accounting department

    B. The human resources (HR) office

    C. The maintenance team

    D. The purchasing office

81. Why is the deprovisioning element of the identification component of identity and access management (IAM) so important?

    A. Extra accounts cost so much extra money.

    B. Open but unassigned accounts are vulnerabilities.

    C. User tracking is essential to performance.

    D. Encryption has to be maintained.

82. All of the following are reasons to perform review and maintenance actions on user accounts *except* _____.

    A. To determine whether the user still needs the same access

    B. To determine whether the user is still with the organization

    C. To determine whether the data set is still applicable to the user's role

    D. To determine whether the user is still performing well

83. Who should be involved in review and maintenance of user accounts/access?

    A. The user's manager

    B. The security manager

    C. The accounting department

    D. The incident response team

84. Which of the following protocols is *most* applicable to the identification process aspect of identity and access management (IAM)?

    A. Secure Sockets Layer (SSL)

    B. Internet Protocol Security (IPSec)

    C. Lightweight Directory Access Protocol (LDAP)

    D. Amorphous ancillary data transmission (AADT)

85. Privileged user (administrators, managers, and so forth) accounts need to be reviewed more closely than basic user accounts. Why is this?

    A. Privileged users have more encryption keys.

    B. Regular users are more trustworthy.

    C. There are extra controls on privileged user accounts.

    D. Privileged users can cause more damage to the organization.

86. The additional review activities that might be performed for privileged user accounts could include all of the following *except* _____.

    A. Deeper personnel background checks

    B. Review of personal financial accounts for privileged users

    C. More frequent reviews of the necessity for access

    D. Pat-down checks of privileged users to deter against physical theft

87. If personal financial account reviews are performed as an additional review control for privileged users, which of the following characteristics is *least* likely to be a useful indicator for review purposes?

    A. Too much money in the account

    B. Too little money in the account

    C. The bank branch being used by the privileged user

    D. Specific senders/recipients

88. How often should the accounts of privileged users be reviewed?

    A. Annually

    B. Twice a year

    C. Monthly

    D. More often than regular user account reviews

89. Privileged user account access should be _____.

   A. Temporary

   B. Pervasive

   C. Thorough

   D. Granular

90. The Cloud Security Alliance (CSA) publishes the Notorious Nine, a list of common threats to organizations participating in cloud computing. According to the CSA's Notorious Nine list, data breaches can be _____.

   A. Overt or covert

   B. International or subterranean

   C. From internal or external sources

   D. Voluminous or specific

91. The Cloud Security Alliance (CSA) publishes the Notorious Nine, a list of common threats to organizations participating in cloud computing. According to the CSA, an organization that operates in the cloud environment and suffers a data breach may be required to _____.

   A. Notify affected users

   B. Reapply for cloud service

   C. Scrub all affected physical memory

   D. Change regulatory frameworks

92. The Cloud Security Alliance (CSA) publishes the Notorious Nine, a list of common threats to organizations participating in cloud computing. According to the CSA, an organization that suffers a data breach might suffer all of the following negative effects *except* _____.

   A. Cost of compliance with notification laws

   B. Loss of public perception/goodwill

   C. Loss of market share

   D. Cost of detection

93. The Cloud Security Alliance (CSA) publishes the Notorious Nine, a list of common threats to organizations participating in cloud computing. According to the CSA, in the event of a data breach, a cloud customer will likely need to comply with all the following data breach notification requirements *except* _____.

   A. Multiple state laws

   B. Contractual notification requirements

   C. All standards-based notification schemes

   D. Any applicable federal regulations

94. The Cloud Security Alliance (CSA) publishes the Notorious Nine, a list of common threats to organizations participating in cloud computing. According to the CSA, data loss can be suffered as a result of _____ activity.

   A. Malicious or inadvertent

   B. Casual or explicit

   C. Web-based or stand-alone

   D. Managed or independent

95. The Cloud Security Alliance (CSA) publishes the Notorious Nine, a list of common threats to organizations participating in cloud computing. According to the CSA, all of the following activity can result in data loss *except* _____.

   A. Misplaced crypto keys

   B. Improper policy

   C. Ineffectual backup procedures

   D. Accidental overwrite

96. The Cloud Security Alliance (CSA) publishes the Notorious Nine, a list of common threats to organizations participating in cloud computing. According to the CSA, service traffic hijacking can affect which portion of the CIA triad?

   A. Confidentiality

   B. Integrity

   C. Availability

   D. All of the triad

97. The Cloud Security Alliance (CSA) publishes the Notorious Nine, a list of common threats to organizations participating in cloud computing. The CSA recommends the prohibition of _____ in order to diminish the likelihood of account/service traffic hijacking.

   A. All user activity

   B. Sharing account credentials between users and services

   C. Multifactor authentication

   D. Interstate commerce

98. The Cloud Security Alliance (CSA) publishes the Notorious Nine, a list of common threats to organizations participating in cloud computing. According to the CSA, which aspect of cloud computing makes it particularly susceptible to account/service traffic hijacking?

   A. Scalability

   B. Metered service

   C. Remote access

   D. Pooled resources

99. The Cloud Security Alliance (CSA) publishes the Notorious Nine, a list of common threats to organizations participating in cloud computing. According to the CSA, what is one reason the threat of insecure interfaces and APIs is so prevalent in cloud computing?

    A. Most of the cloud customer's interaction with resources will be performed through APIs.

    B. APIs are inherently insecure.

    C. Attackers have already published vulnerabilities for all known APIs.

    D. APIs are known carcinogens.

100. The Cloud Security Alliance (CSA) publishes the Notorious Nine, a list of common threats to organizations participating in cloud computing. According to the CSA, what is one reason the threat of insecure interfaces and APIs is so prevalent in cloud computing?

    A. Cloud customers and third parties are continually enhancing and modifying APIs.

    B. APIs can have automated settings.

    C. It is impossible to uninstall APIs.

    D. APIs are a form of malware.

101. The Cloud Security Alliance (CSA) publishes the Notorious Nine, a list of common threats to organizations participating in cloud computing. According to the CSA, what is one reason the threat of insecure interfaces and APIs is so prevalent in cloud computing?

    A. APIs are always used for administrative access.

    B. Customers perform many high-value tasks via APIs.

    C. APIs are cursed.

    D. It is impossible to securely code APIs.

102. The Cloud Security Alliance (CSA) publishes the Notorious Nine, a list of common threats to organizations participating in cloud computing. According to the CSA, why are denial of service (DoS) attacks such a significant threat to cloud operations?

    A. DoS attackers operate internationally.

    B. There are no laws against DoS attacks, so they are impossible to prosecute.

    C. Availability issues prevent productivity in the cloud.

    D. DoS attacks that can affect cloud providers are easy to launch.

103. The Cloud Security Alliance (CSA) publishes the Notorious Nine, a list of common threats to organizations participating in cloud computing. According to the CSA, what do we call denial of service (DoS) attacks staged from multiple machines against a specific target?

    A. Invasive denial of service (IDoS)

    B. Pervasive denial of service (PDoS)

    C. Massive denial of service (MDoS)

    D. Distributed denial of service (DDoS)

104. The Cloud Security Alliance (CSA) publishes the Notorious Nine, a list of common threats to organizations participating in cloud computing. According to the CSA, what aspect of managed cloud services makes the threat of malicious insiders so alarming?

   A. Scalability

   B. Multitenancy

   C. Metered service

   D. Flexibility

105. The Cloud Security Alliance (CSA) publishes the Notorious Nine, a list of common threats to organizations participating in cloud computing. According to the CSA, what aspect of managed cloud services makes the threat of abuse of cloud services so alarming from a management perspective?

   A. Scalability

   B. Multitenancy

   C. Resiliency

   D. Broadband connections

106. The Cloud Security Alliance (CSA) publishes the Notorious Nine, a list of common threats to organizations participating in cloud computing. According to the CSA, which of the following is *not* an aspect of due diligence that the cloud customer should be concerned with when considering a migration to a cloud provider?

   A. Ensuring that any legacy applications are not dependent on internal security controls before moving them to the cloud environment

   B. Reviewing all contractual elements to appropriately define each party's roles, responsibilities, and requirements

   C. Assessing the provider's financial standing and soundness

   D. Vetting the cloud provider's administrators and personnel to ensure the same level of trust as the legacy environment

107. The Cloud Security Alliance (CSA) publishes the Notorious Nine, a list of common threats to organizations participating in cloud computing. A cloud customer that does not perform sufficient due diligence can suffer harm if the cloud provider they've selected goes out of business. What do we call this problem?

   A. Vendor lock-in

   B. Vendor lockout

   C. Vendor incapacity

   D. Unscaled

108. Which of the following is *not* a method for creating logical segmentation in a cloud data center?

   A. Virtual local area networks (VLANs)

   B. Network address translation (NAT)

   C. Bridging

   D. Hubs

109. According to (ISC)², the lack/ambiguity of physical endpoints as individual network components in the cloud environment creates what kind of threat/concern?

A. The lack of defined endpoints makes it difficult to uniformly define, manage, and protect IT assets.

B. Without physical endpoints, it is impossible to apply security controls to an environment.

C. Without physical endpoints, it is impossible to track user activity.

D. The lack of physical endpoints increases the opportunity for physical theft/damage.

110. When should cloud providers allow platform as a service (PaaS) customers shell access to the servers running their instances?

A. Never

B. Weekly

C. Only when the contract stipulates that requirement

D. Always

111. In a PaaS implementation, each instance should have its own user-level permissions; when instances share common policies/controls, the cloud security professional should be careful to reduce the possibility of _____ and _____ over time.

A. Denial of service (DoS)/physical theft

B. Authorization creep/inheritance

C. Sprawl/hashing

D. Intercession/side-channel attacks

112. In a platform as a service (PaaS) environment, user access management often requires that data about user activity be collected, analyzed, audited, and reported against rule-based criteria. These criteria are usually based on _____.

A. International standards

B. Federal regulations

C. Organizational policies

D. Federation directives

113. An essential element of access management, _____ is the practice of confirming that an individual is who they claim to be.

A. Authentication

B. Authorization

C. Nonrepudiation

D. Regression

114. An essential element of access management, _____ is the practice of granting permissions based on validated identification.

   A. Authentication

   B. Authorization

   C. Nonrepudiation

   D. Regression

115. What is the usual order of an access management process?

   A. Access-authorization-authentication

   B. Authentication-authorization-access

   C. Authorization-authentication-access

   D. Authentication-access-authorization

116. Why are platform as a service (PaaS) environments at a higher likelihood of suffering backdoor vulnerabilities?

   A. They rely on virtualization.

   B. They are often used for software development.

   C. They have multitenancy.

   D. They are scalable.

117. Backdoors are sometimes left in software by developers _____.

   A. In lieu of other security controls

   B. As a means to counter denial of service (DoS) attacks

   C. Inadvertently or on purpose

   D. As a way to distract attackers

118. Alice is staging an attack against Bob's website. She is able to introduce a string of command code into a database Bob is running, simply by entering the command string into a data field. This is an example of which type of attack?

   A. Insecure direct object reference

   B. Buffer overflow

   C. SQL injection

   D. Denial of service

119. Bob is staging an attack against Alice's website. He is able to embed a link on her site that will execute malicious code on a visitor's machine if the visitor clicks on the link. This is an example of which type of attack?

   A. Cross-site scripting

   B. Broken authentication/session management

   C. Security misconfiguration

   D. Insecure cryptographic storage

120. Alice is staging an attack against Bob's website. She has discovered that Bob has been storing cryptographic keys on a server with a default admin password and is able to get access to those keys and violate confidentiality and access controls. This is an example of which type of attack?

   A. SQL injection

   B. Buffer overflow

   C. Using components with known vulnerabilities

   D. Security misconfiguration

121. Which of the following is a management risk that organizations migrating to the cloud will have to address?

   A. Insider threat

   B. Virtual sprawl

   C. Distributed denial of service (DDoS) attacks

   D. Natural disasters

122. Which kind of hypervisor is the preferred target of attackers, and why?

   A. Type 1, because it is more straightforward

   B. Type 1, because it has a greater attack surface

   C. Type 2, because it is less protected

   D. Type 2, because it has a greater attack surface

123. Which of the following would make a good provision to include in the service-level agreement (SLA) between cloud customer and provider?

   A. Location of the data center

   B. Amount of data uploaded/downloaded during a pay period

   C. Type of personnel security controls for network administrators

   D. Physical security barriers on the perimeter of the data center campus

124. What is the *most* significant aspect of the service-level agreement (SLA) that incentivizes the cloud provider to perform?

   A. The thoroughness with which it details all aspects of cloud processing

   B. The financial penalty for not meeting service levels

   C. The legal liability for violating data breach notification requirements

   D. The risk exposure to the cloud provider

125. From a customer perspective, all of the following are benefits of infrastructure as a service (IaaS) cloud services *except* _____.

   A. Reduced cost of ownership

   B. Reduced energy costs

   C. Metered usage

   D. Reduced cost of administering the operating system (OS) in the cloud environment

126. From an academic perspective, what is the main distinction between an event and an incident?

   A. Incidents can last for extended periods (days or weeks), whereas an event is momentary.

   B. Incidents can happen at the network level, whereas events are restricted to the system level.

   C. Events are anything that can occur in the IT environment, whereas incidents are unscheduled events.

   D. Events occur only during processing, whereas incidents can occur at any time.

127. The cloud computing characteristic of elasticity promotes which aspect of the CIA triad?

   A. Confidentiality

   B. Integrity

   C. Availability

   D. None

128. A hosted cloud environment is great for an organization to use as _____.

   A. Storage of physical assets

   B. A testbed/sandbox

   C. A platform for managing unsecured production data

   D. A cost-free service for meeting all user needs

129. What is the entity that created the Statement on Standards for Attestation Engagements (SSAE) auditing standard and certifies auditors for that standard?

   A. National Institute of Standards and Technology (NIST)

   B. European Network and Information Security Agency (ENISA)

   C. General Data Protection Regulation (GDPR)

   D. American Institute of Certified Public Accountants (AICPA)

130. The current American Institute of Certified Public Accountants (AICPA) standard codifies certain audit reporting mechanisms. What are these called?

   A. Sarbanes-Oxley Act (SOX) reports

   B. Secure Sockets Layer (SSL) audits

   C. Sherwood Applied Business Structure Architecture (SABSA)

   D. System and Organization Controls (SOC) reports

131. Which of the following is *not* a report used to assess the design and selection of security controls within an organization?

   A. Consensus Assessments Initiative Questionnaire (CAIQ)

   B. Cloud Security Alliance Cloud Controls Matrix (CSA CCM)

   C. SOC 1

   D. SOC 2 Type 1

132. Which of the following is a report used to assess the implementation and effectiveness of security controls within an organization?

    A. SOC 1

    B. SOC 2 Type 1

    C. SOC 2 Type 2

    D. SOC 3

133. _____ is an example of due care, and _____ is an example of due diligence.

    A. Privacy data security policy; auditing the controls dictated by the privacy data security policy

    B. The European Union General Data Protection Regulation (GDPR); the Gramm-Leach-Bliley Act (GLBA)

    C. Locks on doors; turnstiles

    D. Perimeter defenses; internal defenses

134. In a Lightweight Directory Access Protocol (LDAP) environment, each entry in a directory server is identified by a _____.

    A. Domain name (DN)

    B. Distinguished name (DN)

    C. Directory name (DN)

    D. Default name (DN)

135. Each of the following is an element of the Identification phase of the identity and access management (IAM) process _except_ _____.

    A. Provisioning

    B. Inversion

    C. Management

    D. Deprovisioning

136. Which of the following is true about two-person integrity?

    A. It forces all employees to distrust one another.

    B. It requires two different identity and access management matrices (IAM).

    C. It forces collusion for unauthorized access.

    D. It enables more thieves to gain access to the facility.

137. All of the following are statutory regulations _except_ the _____.

    A. Gramm-Leach-Bliley Act (GLBA)

    B. Health Information Portability and Accountability Act (HIPAA)

    C. Federal Information Systems Management Act (FISMA)

    D. Payment Card Industry Data Security Standard (PCI DSS)

138. A cloud data encryption situation where the cloud customer retains control of the encryption keys and the cloud provider only processes and stores the data could be considered a _____.

    A. Threat

    B. Risk

    C. Hybrid cloud deployment model

    D. Case of infringing on the rights of the provider

139. Which of the following is one of the benefits of a private cloud deployment?

    A. Less cost

    B. Higher performance

    C. Retaining control of governance

    D. Reduction in need for maintenance capability on the customer side

140. What are the two general delivery modes for the software as a service (SaaS) model?

    A. Ranked and free

    B. Hosted application management and software on demand

    C. Intrinsic motivation complex and undulating perspective details

    D. Framed and modular

141. Your organization has migrated into a platform as a service (PaaS) configuration. A network administrator within the cloud provider has accessed your data and sold a list of your users to a competitor. Who is required to make data breach notifications in accordance with all applicable laws?

    A. The network admin responsible

    B. The cloud provider

    C. The regulators overseeing your deployment

    D. Your organization

142. If an organization wants to retain the *most* control of their assets in the cloud, which service and deployment model combination should they choose?

    A. Platform as a service (PaaS), community

    B. Infrastructure as a service (IaaS), hybrid

    C. Software as a service (SaaS), public

    D. Infrastructure as a service (IaaS), private

143. If an organization wants to realize the *most* cost savings by reducing administrative overhead, which service and deployment model combination should they choose?

    A. Platform as a service (PaaS), community

    B. Infrastructure as a service (IaaS), hybrid

    C. Software as a service (SaaS), public

    D. Infrastructure as a service (IaaS), private

Chapter

2

Domain 2: Cloud Data Security

In Domain 2, the exam outline focuses on the data owned by the cloud customer, hosted in the cloud. The domain discusses methods for securing the data, including specific tools and techniques.

1. In which of these options does the encryption engine reside within the application accessing the database?

   A. Transparent encryption

   B. Symmetric-key encryption

   C. Application-level encryption

   D. Homomorphic encryption

2. You are the security team leader for an organization that has an infrastructure as a service (IaaS) production environment hosted by a cloud provider. You want to implement an event monitoring (security information and event management [SIEM]/security information management [SIM]/security event management [SEM]) solution in your production environment in order to acquire better data for security defenses and decisions. Which of the following is probably your *most* significant concern about implementing this solution in the cloud?

   A. The solution should give you better analysis capability by automating a great deal of the associated tasks.

   B. Dashboards produced by the tool are a flawless management benefit.

   C. You will have to coordinate with the cloud provider to ensure that the tool is acceptable and functioning properly.

   D. Senior management will be required to approve the acquisition and implementation of the tool.

3. Which of the following is *not* a step in the crypto-shredding process?

   A. Encrypt data with a particular encryption engine.

   B. Encrypt first resulting keys with another encryption engine.

   C. Save backup of second resulting keys.

   D. Destroy original second resulting keys.

4. Which of the following sanitization methods is feasible for use in the cloud?

   A. Crypto-shredding

   B. Degaussing

   C. Physical destruction

   D. Overwriting

5. Which of the following is *not* a method for enhancing data portability?

   A. Crypto-shredding

   B. Using standard data formats

   C. Avoiding proprietary services

   D. Favorable contract terms

6. When implementing a digital rights management (DRM) solution in a cloud environment, which of the following does *not* pose an additional challenge for the cloud customer?

   A. Users might be required to install a DRM agent on their local devices.

   B. DRM solutions might have difficulty interfacing with multiple different operating systems and services.

   C. DRM solutions might have difficulty interacting with virtualized instances.

   D. Ownership of intellectual property might be difficult to ascertain.

7. When implementing cryptography in a cloud environment, where is the worst place to store the keys?

   A. With the cloud provider

   B. Off the cloud, with the data owner

   C. With a third-party provider, in key escrow

   D. Anywhere but with the cloud provider

8. Which of the following is *not* a security concern related to archiving data for long-term storage?

   A. Long-term storage of the related cryptographic keys

   B. Format of the data

   C. Media the data resides on

   D. Underground depth of the storage facility

9. Data dispersion is a cloud data security technique that is most similar to which legacy implementation?

   A. Business continuity and disaster recovery (BC/DR)

   B. Redundant Array of Inexpensive Disks (RAID)

   C. Software-defined networking (SDN)

   D. Content delivery network (CDN)

10. Data dispersion uses _____, where the traditional implementation is called "striping."

    A. Chunking

    B. Vaulting

    C. Lumping

    D. Grouping

11. Data dispersion uses _____, where the traditional implementation is called "parity bits."

    A. Smurfing

    B. Snarfing

    C. Erasure coding

    D. Real-time bitlinking

12. Data dispersion provides protection for all the following security aspects *except* _____.

    A. Protecting confidentiality against external attack on the storage area

    B. Loss of availability due to single-storage-device failure

    C. Loss due to seizure by law enforcement in a multitenant environment

    D. Protecting against loss due to user error

13. Your organization is migrating the production environment to an infrastructure as a service (IaaS) cloud implementation. Your users will need to be able to get access to their data, install programs, and partition memory space for their own purposes. You should configure the cloud memory as _____.

    A. Object

    B. Volume

    C. Synthetic

    D. Database

14. Your organization is migrating the production environment to an infrastructure as a service (IaaS) cloud implementation. Your users will need to be able to get access to their data and share data with other users in a defined way, according to a hierarchy. You should configure the cloud memory as _____.

    A. Object storage

    B. Volume storage

    C. Synthetic storage

    D. Databases

15. What is one of the benefits of implementing an egress monitoring solution?

    A. Preventing distributed denial of service (DDoS) attacks

    B. Inventorying data assets

    C. Interviewing data owners

    D. Protecting against natural disasters

16. Egress monitoring solutions usually include a function that _____.

    A. Arbitrates contract breaches

    B. Performs personnel evaluation reviews

    C. Discovers data assets according to classification/categorization

    D. Applies another level of access control

17. Egress monitoring solutions usually include a function that _____.

    A. Uses biometrics to scan users

    B. Inspects incoming packets

    C. Resides on client machines

    D. Uses stateful inspection

18. Digital rights management (DRM) solutions (sometimes referred to as information rights management, or IRM) can be used to protect all sorts of sensitive data but are usually particularly designed to secure _____.

    A. Personally identifiable information (PII)

    B. Intellectual property

    C. Plans and policies

    D. Marketing material

19. Digital rights management (DRM) solutions (sometimes referred to as information rights management, or IRM) often protect unauthorized distribution of what type of intellectual property?

    A. Patents

    B. Trademarks

    C. Personally identifiable information (PII)

    D. Copyright

20. Which of the following characteristics is associated with digital rights management (DRM) solutions (sometimes referred to as information rights management, or IRM)?

    A. Persistence

    B. Influence

    C. Resistance

    D. Trepidation

21. Which of the following characteristics is associated with digital rights management (DRM) solutions (sometimes referred to as information rights management, or IRM)?

    A. Automatic expiration

    B. Multilevel aggregation

    C. Enhanced detail

    D. Broad spectrum

22. Which of the following characteristics is associated with digital rights management (DRM) solutions (sometimes referred to as information rights management, or IRM)?

    A. Transparent encryption modification

    B. Bilateral enhancement

    C. Continuous audit trail

    D. Encompassing flow

23. Which of the following characteristics is associated with digital rights management (DRM) solutions (sometimes referred to as information rights management, or IRM)?

    A. Mapping to existing access control lists (ACLs)

    B. Delineating biometric catalogs

    C. Preventing multifactor authentication

    D. Prohibiting unauthorized transposition

24. According to the (ISC)² Cloud Secure Data Lifecycle, which phase comes soon after (or at the same time as) the Create phase?

    A. Store

    B. Use

    C. Deploy

    D. Archive

25. According to the (ISC)² Cloud Secure Data Lifecycle, which phase comes immediately before the Share phase?

    A. Create

    B. Destroy

    C. Use

    D. Encrypt

26. Why is the term (ISC)² Cloud Secure Data Lifecycle actually somewhat inaccurate?

    A. The term is not used only by (ISC)².

    B. Not all phases are secure.

    C. Not all phases take place in the cloud.

    D. It's not actually a cycle.

27. According to the (ISC)² Cloud Secure Data Lifecycle, in which phase should the process of categorization/classification of data occur?

    A. Create

    B. Store

    C. Define

    D. Use

28. Which of the following should occur during the final phase of the Cloud Secure Data Lifecycle?

    A. Data dispersion

    B. Crypto-shredding

    C. Cryptoparsing

    D. Cryptosporidium

29. At what phase of the Cloud Secure Data Lifecycle does data enter long-term storage?

    A. The first

    B. The second

    C. The fourth

    D. The fifth

30. What is a form of cloud storage where data is stored as objects, arranged in a hierarchal structure, like a file tree?

    A. Volume storage

    B. Databases

    C. Content delivery network (CDN)

    D. Object storage

31. What is a form of cloud storage where data is stored in a logical storage area assigned to the user but not necessarily physically attached or even geographically proximate to the compute node the user is utilizing?

    A. Volume storage

    B. Databases

    C. Content delivery network (CDN)

    D. Object storage

32. What is a form of cloud storage often used for streaming multimedia data to users?

    A. Volume storage

    B. Databases

    C. Content delivery network (CDN)

    D. Neutral storage

33. What type of data storage is often used in platform as a service (PaaS) arrangements?

    A. Ephemeral

    B. Database

    C. Long-term

    D. Nefarious

34. What is a form of cloud data protection where data is spread across multiple storage devices/locations, similar to RAID in the legacy environment?

    A. Infringing

    B. Data dispersion

    C. Voiding

    D. Crypto-shredding

35. Erasure coding, in the cloud, is similar to what element of RAID implementations in a traditional IT environment?

    A. Deltas

    B. Inversion

    C. Parity bits

    D. Transposition

36. DLP (data loss prevention or data leak protection) solutions are implemented in the hopes of securing _____.

    A. Sensitive data that may leave the organization's control

    B. All data within the organization's control

    C. Data being processed by the organization's users

    D. Data that could be intercepted while out of the organization's control

37. Which of the following will DLP (data loss prevention or data leak protection) solutions most likely *not* inspect?

    A. Email content

    B. FTP traffic

    C. Material saved to portable media

    D. Voice over Internet Protocol (VoIP) conversations

38. DLP (data loss prevention or data leak protection) solutions may use all of the following techniques to identify sensitive data *except* _____.

    A. Pattern matching

    B. Inference

    C. Keyword identification

    D. Metadata tags

39. You are the security manager of a small firm that has just purchased an egress monitoring solution to implement in your cloud-based production environment. In which of the following cases would you *not* have to get permission from the cloud provider to install and implement the tool?

    A. If it's hardware-based and your production environment is in an infrastructure as a service (IaaS) model

    B. If you purchased it from a vendor other than the cloud provider

    C. If it's software-based and your production environment is in a platform as a service (PaaS) model

    D. If it affects all guest instances on any given host device

40. You are the security manager of a small firm that has just purchased an egress monitoring solution to implement in your cloud-based production environment. Before implementing the solution, what should you explain to senior management?

    A. The additional risks of external attack associated with using the tool

    B. The production impact it will have on the environment

    C. What the price of the tool was

    D. How the solution works

41. You are the security manager of a small firm that has just purchased an egress monitoring solution to implement in your cloud-based production environment. Which of these activities should you perform before deploying the tool?

    A. Survey your company's departments about the data under their control.

    B. Reconstruct your firewalls.

    C. Harden all your routers.

    D. Adjust the hypervisors.

42. You are the security manager of a small firm that has just purchased an egress monitoring solution to implement in your cloud-based production environment. What should you expect immediately following the implementation of the tool?

    A. Immediate decrease in lost data

    B. A series of false-positive indications

    C. Increase in morale across the organization

    D. Increase in gross revenue

43. You are the security manager of a small firm that has just purchased an egress monitoring solution to implement in your cloud-based production environment. What should you *not* expect the tool to address?

    A. Sensitive data sent inadvertently in user emails

    B. Sensitive data captured by screenshots

    C. Sensitive data moved to external devices

    D. Sensitive data in the contents of files sent via File Transfer Protocol (FTP)

44. You are the security manager of a small firm that has just purchased an egress monitoring solution to implement in your cloud-based production environment. In order to get truly holistic coverage of your environment, you should be sure to include _____ as a step in the deployment process.

    A. Getting signed user agreements from all users

    B. Installation of the solution on all assets in the cloud data center

    C. Adoption of the tool in all routers between your users and the cloud provider

    D. Ensuring that all your customers install the tool

45. You are the security manager of a small firm that has just purchased an egress monitoring solution to implement in your cloud-based production environment. In order to increase the security value of the tool, you should consider combining it with _____.

    A. Digital rights management (DRM) and security event and incident management (SIEM) tools

    B. An investment in upgraded project management software

    C. Digital insurance policies

    D. The Uptime Institute's Tier certification

46. You are the security manager of a small firm that has just purchased an egress monitoring solution to implement in your cloud-based production environment. You are interested in fielding the solution as an awareness tool to optimize security for your organization through conditioning user behavior. You decide to set the solution to _____.

    A. Suspend user accounts and notify the security office when it detects possible sensitive data egress attempted by a user

    B. Halt the transaction and notify the user's supervisor when the user attempts to transfer sensitive data

    C. Query the user as to whether they intend to send sensitive data upon detection of an attempted transfer

    D. Sever remote connections upon detection of a possible sensitive data transfer

47. You are the security manager of a small firm that has just purchased an egress monitoring solution to implement in your cloud-based production environment. You understand that all of the following aspects of cloud computing may make proper deployment of the tool difficult or costly *except* _____.

    A. Data will not remain in one place or form in the cloud

    B. The cloud environment will include redundant and resilient architecture

    C. There will be a deleterious impact on production upon installing the tool

    D. You might not have sufficient proper administrative rights in the cloud infrastructure

48. Egress monitoring solutions can aid all of the following security-related efforts *except* _____.

    A. Access control

    B. Data exfiltration

    C. E-discovery/forensics

    D. Data categorization/classification

49. The cloud security professional should be aware that encryption would most likely be necessary in all the following aspects of a cloud deployment *except* _____.

    A. Data at rest

    B. Data in motion

    C. Data in use

    D. Data of relief

50. As with the traditional IT environment, cloud data encryption includes all the following elements *except* _____.

    A. The user

    B. The data itself

    C. The encryption engine

    D. The encryption keys

51. Volume storage encryption in an infrastructure as a service (IaaS) arrangement will protect against data loss due to all of the following activities *except* _____.

  A. Physical loss or theft of a device

  B. Disgruntled users

  C. Malicious cloud administrators accessing the data

  D. Virtual machine snapshots stolen from storage

52. In an infrastructure as a service (IaaS) arrangement, all of the following are examples of object storage encryption *except* _____.

  A. File-level encryption

  B. Digital rights management (DRM)

  C. Application-level encryption

  D. Transport Layer Security (TLS)

53. All of the following are database encryption options that could be used in a platform as a service (PaaS) implementation *except* _____.

  A. File-level encryption

  B. Secure Sockets Layer (SSL)

  C. Transparent encryption

  D. Application-level encryption

54. In application-level encryption, where does the encryption engine reside?

  A. In the application accessing the database

  B. In the operating system on which the application is run

  C. Within the database accessed by the application

  D. In the volume where the database resides

55. Which of the following database encryption techniques can be used to encrypt specific tables within the database?

  A. File-level encryption

  B. Transparent encryption

  C. Application-level encryption

  D. Object-level encryption

56. Which of the following database encryption techniques makes it difficult to perform database functions (searches, indexing, etc.)?

  A. File-level encryption

  B. Transparent encryption

  C. Application-level encryption

  D. Volume encryption

57. According to (ISC)², where should the cloud customer's encryption keys be stored?

    A. With the cloud customer

    B. With a third-party provider

    C. At the cloud provider data center

    D. Anywhere but with the cloud provider

58. Which of the following is *not* used to determine data retention requirements?

    A. Legislation

    B. Business needs

    C. Average media longevity

    D. Contracts

59. Event monitoring tools (security information and event management [SIEM]/security information management [SIM]/security event management [SEM]) can aid in which of the following efforts?

    A. External hacking detection

    B. Prediction of physical device theft

    C. Data classification/categorization issues

    D. Social engineering attacks

60. Event monitoring tools (security information and event management [SIEM]/security information management [SIM]/security event management [SEM]) can aid in which of the following efforts?

    A. Detecting untrained personnel

    B. Predicting system outages

    C. Sending alerts for conflicts of interest

    D. Enforcing mandatory vacation

61. Event monitoring tools (security information and event management [SIEM]/security information management [SIM]/security event management [SEM]) can aid in which of the following efforts?

    A. Reducing workload for production personnel

    B. Decreasing size of log files

    C. Optimizing performance

    D. Ensuring adequate lighting of workspaces

62. Event monitoring tools (security information and event management [SIEM]/security information management [SIM]/security event management [SEM]) can aid in which of the following efforts?

    A. Detecting ambient heating, ventilation, and air-conditioning (HVAC) problems

    B. Ensuring proper cloud migration

    C. Deciding risk parameters

    D. Protecting all physical entry points against the threat of fire

63. In addition to predictive capabilities, event monitoring tools (security information and event management [SIEM]/security information management [SIM]/security event management [SEM]) are instrumental in what other security function?

   A. Personnel safety

   B. Vehicle tracking

   C. Incident evidence

   D. Acoustic dampening

64. Which of the following is one of the benefits of event monitoring tools (security information and event management [SIEM]/security information management [SIM]/security event management [SEM])?

   A. Greater physical security

   B. Psychological deterrence

   C. Cost savings

   D. More logs can be reviewed, at faster speeds

65. As in a traditional IT environment, proper key management is crucial in the cloud. Which of the following principles is *not* true regarding key management?

   A. It is good practice to introduce pseudorandom numbers when generating keys.

   B. Public keys should never be shared with anyone.

   C. Losing the keys is equivalent to losing the data.

   D. Symmetric keys should be passed out of band.

66. Which of the following is a good business case for the use of data masking?

   A. The shipping department should get only a masked version of the customer's address.

   B. The customer service department should get only a masked version of the customer's Social Security (SS) number.

   C. The billing department should get only a masked version of the customer's credit card number.

   D. The Human Resources (HR) department should get only a masked version of the employee's driver's license number.

67. All of the following are methods of data masking suggested by (ISC)² *except*

_____.

   A. Random substitution

   B. Algorithmic substitution

   C. Deletion

   D. Conflation

68. If data masking is being performed for software testing purposes, which of the following is *not* a good masking technique to use?

   A. Random substitution

   B. Shuffling

   C. Deletion

   D. Algorithmic substitution

69. For which use case would it probably be best to use static masking?

   A. Creating a test environment for a new application

   B. Allowing a customer service representative limited access to account data

   C. Providing detailed reports to regulators

   D. Notifying shareholders

70. For which use case would it probably be best to use dynamic masking?

   A. Creating a test environment for a new application

   B. Allowing a customer service representative limited access to account data

   C. Sending incident response notifications

   D. Implementing business continuity and disaster recovery (BC/DR)

71. What is one possible risk associated with the use of algorithmic masking for obscuring a data set?

   A. You could corrupt the production data.

   B. The data could be subject to easy inadvertent disclosure.

   C. Algorithms are two-way operations.

   D. A null set has no test value.

72. _____ is a direct identifier, and _____ is an indirect identifier.

   A. Username; password

   B. User's name; user's age

   C. User's IP address; user's media access control (MAC) address

   D. Location; income level

73. Anonymization is the process of removing _____ from data sets.

   A. Access

   B. Cryptographic keys

   C. Numeric values

   D. Identifying information

74. Tokenization is a method of obscuring data that, other than encryption, can be used to comply with _____ standards.

   A. Gramm-Leach-Bliley Act (GLBA)

   B. Payment Card Industry (PCI)

   C. Child Online Protection Act (COPA)

   D. Sarbanes-Oxley Act (SOX)

75. Tokenization requires at least __ database(s).

   A. One

   B. Two

   C. Three

   D. Four

76. Data owners might consider using tokenization for all of the following reasons *except* _____.

   A. Regulatory or contractual compliance

   B. Inference

   C. Reduced cost of compliance

   D. Mitigating risk from data lost to intrusion

77. Bit-splitting, also known as data dispersion, might be thought of as _____ in the cloud.

   A. RAID

   B. BIOS

   C. DDoS

   D. SYN-ACK

78. Bit-splitting also provides security against data breaches by _____.

   A. Removing all access to unauthorized parties

   B. Ensuring that an unauthorized user only gets a useless fragment of data

   C. Moving data across jurisdictional boundaries

   D. Tracking all incoming access requests

79. If bit-splitting is used to store data sets across multiple jurisdictions, how may this enhance security?

   A. By making seizure of data by law enforcement more difficult

   B. By hiding it from attackers in a specific jurisdiction

   C. By ensuring that users can only accidentally disclose data to one geographic area

   D. By restricting privilege user access

80. Which of the following is a possible negative aspect of bit-splitting?

   A. Less security

   B. Greatest risk of unauthorized access

   C. Significantly greater processing overhead

   D. Violating regulatory compliance

81. Which of the following is a possible negative aspect of bit-splitting?

   A. It may require trust in additional third parties beyond the primary cloud service provider.

   B. There may be cause for management concern that the technology will violate internal policy.

   C. Users will have far greater difficulty understanding the implementation.

   D. Limited vendors make acquisition and support challenging.

82. Which of the following is a possible negative aspect of bit-splitting?

   A. Greater chance of physical theft of assets

   B. Loss of public image

   C. Some risk to availability, depending on the implementation

   D. A small fire hazard

83. Which of the following is a theoretical technology that is intended to allow encrypted material to be processed and manipulated without decrypting it first?

   A. Inverse postulation

   B. Homomorphic encryption

   C. Didactic alignment

   D. Obverse reinstantiation

84. Which of the following is a data discovery approach used by e-commerce retailers to discern and predict shoppers' needs?

   A. Big data

   B. Real-time analytics

   C. Agile analytics

   D. Agile business intelligence

85. Which of the following is a data discovery approach that offers insight to trends of trends, using both historical and predictive approaches?

   A. Obverse polyglotism

   B. Big data

   C. Real-time analytics

   D. Agile analytics/business intelligence

86. Which of the following is *not* a data discovery technique?

    A. Metadata

    B. Labels

    C. Content analysis

    D. Data hover

87. Which of the following data discovery techniques involves using extra information automatically appended/included with the intended data when the data is created?

    A. Metadata

    B. Labels

    C. Content analysis

    D. Data hover

88. When labeling is used as a data discovery technique, who should be applying the labels?

    A. The security office

    B. Users

    C. Data owners

    D. Regulators

89. When data labels are being used in an environment (for discovery and other purposes), when should the labels be applied?

    A. During the risk assessment

    B. As part of the business impact analysis (BIA)

    C. At collection/creation

    D. When the discovery tools are implemented

90. Which of the following tools might be useful in data discovery efforts that are based on content analysis?

    A. Egress monitoring solutions

    B. Digital rights management (DRM)

    C. iSCSI

    D. Fibre Channel over Ethernet (FCoE)

91. All of the following might be used as data discovery characteristics in a content-analysis-based data discovery effort *except* _____.

    A. Keywords

    B. Pattern matching

    C. Frequency

    D. Inheritance

92. What is the risk to the organization posed by dashboards that display data discovery results?

    A. Increased chance of external penetration

    B. Flawed management decisions based on edited displays

    C. Higher likelihood of inadvertent disclosure

    D. Raised incidence of physical theft

93. Which of these is *most* likely to have the greatest negative impact on data discovery effort?

    A. Bandwidth latency issues

    B. Poor physical security of the data center

    C. Severe statutory regulation

    D. Inaccurate or incomplete data

94. Cloud customers performing data discovery efforts will have to ensure that the cloud provider attends to all of the following requirements *except* _____.

    A. Allowing sufficient access to large volumes of data

    B. Preserving metadata tags

    C. Assigning labels

    D. Preserving and maintaining the data

95. Where should the cloud provider's data discovery requirements be listed?

    A. National Institute of Standards and Technology (NIST) Special Publication (SP) 800-53

    B. Applicable laws and regulations

    C. Payment Card Industry Data Security Standard (PCI DSS)

    D. The managed services contract and SLA

96. Who will determine data classifications for the cloud customer?

    A. The cloud provider

    B. National Institute of Standards and Technology (NIST)

    C. Regulators

    D. The cloud customer

97. An organization's data classification scheme *must* include which of the following categories?

    A. File size

    B. Origin of the data

    C. Sensitivity of the data

    D. Whatever the data owner decides

98. Classification is usually considered a facet of data _____.

   A. Security

   B. Labeling

   C. Control

   D. Markup

99. Data classification can be _____ or _____.

   A. Inverse or obverse

   B. Automatic or manual

   C. Correct or incorrect

   D. Diurnal or nocturnal

100. Data may need to be reclassified for all the following reasons *except* _____.

   A. Color change

   B. Time

   C. Repurposing

   D. Transfer of ownership

101. Proper _____ need(s) to be assigned to each data classification/category.

   A. Dollar values

   B. Metadata

   C. Security controls

   D. Policies

102. Data transformation in a cloud environment should be of great concern to organizations considering cloud migration because _____ could affect data classification processes and implementations.

   A. Multitenancy

   B. Virtualization

   C. Remote access

   D. Physical distance

103. Who is ultimately responsible for a data breach that includes personally identifiable information (PII), in the event of negligence on the part of the cloud provider?

   A. The user

   B. The subject

   C. The cloud provider

   D. The cloud customer

104. In a personally identifiable information (PII) context, who is the subject?

    A. The cloud customer

    B. The cloud provider

    C. The regulator

    D. The individual

105. In a personally identifiable information (PII) context, who is the processor?

    A. The cloud customer

    B. The cloud provider

    C. The regulator

    D. The individual

106. In a personally identifiable information (PII) context, who is the controller?

    A. The cloud customer

    B. The cloud provider

    C. The regulator

    D. The individual

107. In a personally identifiable information (PII) context, which of the following is *not* normally considered "processing"?

    A. Storing

    B. Viewing

    C. Destroying

    D. Printing

108. Which of the following countries does *not* have a national privacy law that concerns personally identifiable information (PII) and applies to all entities?

    A. Argentina

    B. The United States

    C. Italy

    D. Australia

109. In protections afforded to personally identifiable information (PII) under the U.S. Health Information Portability and Accountability Act (HIPAA), the subject must _____ in order to allow the vendor to share their personal data.

    A. Opt in

    B. Opt out

    C. Undergo screening

    D. Provide a biometric template

110. In protections afforded to personally identifiable information (PII) under the U.S. Gramm-Leach-Bliley Act (GLBA), the subject must _____ in order to prevent the vendor from sharing their personal data.

    A. Opt in

    B. Opt out

    C. Undergo screening

    D. Provide a biometric template

111. The European Union (EU), with its implementation of privacy directives and regulations, treats individual privacy as _____.

    A. A passing fad

    B. A human right

    C. A legal obligation

    D. A business expense

112. If your organization collects/creates privacy data associated with European Union (EU) citizens and you operate in the cloud, you must *prevent* your provider from storing/moving/processing that data where?

    A. Argentina

    B. The United States

    C. Japan

    D. Israel

113. European Union (EU) personal privacy protections include the right to be _____.

    A. Secure

    B. Delivered

    C. Forgotten

    D. Protected

114. The Cloud Security Alliance (CSA) has developed a model for cloud privacy frameworks called the Privacy Level Agreement (PLA). Why might a cloud service provider be reluctant to issue or adhere to a PLA?

    A. A PLA might limit the provider's liability.

    B. A PLA would force the provider to accept more liability.

    C. A PLA is nonbinding.

    D. A PLA is not enforceable.

115. The Cloud Security Alliance Cloud Controls Matrix (CSA CCM) lists security controls from all the following frameworks *except* _____.

    A. ISACA's Control Objectives for Information and Related Technology (COBIT)

    B. Payment Card Industry Data Security Standard (PCI DSS)

    C. The Capability Maturity Model (CMM)

    D. International Organization for Standardization (ISO) 27001

116. The Cloud Security Alliance Cloud Controls Matrix (CSA CCM) lists security controls from all the following laws *except* _____.

    A. Health Information Portability and Accountability Act (HIPAA)

    B. Family Education Rights and Privacy Act (FERPA)

    C. Personal Information Protection and Electronic Documents Act (PIPEDA)

    D. Digital Millennium Copyright Act (DMCA)

117. Digital rights management (DRM) tools might be used to protect all the following assets *except* _____.

    A. A trusted device

    B. Proprietary software

    C. Medical records

    D. Financial data

118. Deploying digital rights management (DRM) tools in a bring-your-own-device (BYOD) environment will require _____.

    A. User consent and action

    B. Enhanced security protocols

    C. Use of the cloud

    D. Newer, upgraded devices

119. Deploying digital rights management (DRM) tools in a bring-your-own-device (BYOD) environment will require _____.

    A. A uniform browser installation

    B. Platform-agnostic solutions

    C. Turnstiles

    D. A secondary business continuity and disaster recovery (BC/DR) vendor

120. The Cloud Security Alliance Cloud Controls Matrix (CSA CCM) addresses all the following security architecture elements *except* _____.

    A. Physical security

    B. Infrastructure as a service (IaaS)

    C. Application security

    D. Business drivers

121. DRM requires that every data resource be provisioned with _____.

    A. A tracking device

    B. An access policy

    C. A hardware security module (HSM)

    D. A biometric system

122. Digital rights management (DRM) tools can be combined with _____ to enhance security capabilities.

    A. Roaming identity services (RIS)

    B. Egress monitoring solutions (DLP)

    C. Internal hardware settings (BIOS)

    D. The TEMPEST program

123. Digital rights management (DRM) tools should enforce _____, which is the characteristic of access rights following the object, in whatever form or location it might be or move to.

    A. Continuous audit trail

    B. Limiting printing output

    C. Persistence

    D. Automatic expiration

124. Digital rights management (DRM) tools should enforce _____, which is the practice of capturing all relevant system events.

    A. Continuous audit trail

    B. Limiting printing output

    C. Persistence

    D. Automatic expiration

125. Digital rights management (DRM) tools should enforce _____, which is the capability to revoke access based on the decision of the object owner or an administrator action.

    A. Integration with email filtering engines

    B. Disabling screencap capabilities

    C. Continuous audit trail

    D. Dynamic policy control

126. Digital rights management (DRM) tools should enforce _____, which is the revocation of access based on time.

    A. Persistence

    B. Disabling screencap capabilities

    C. Automatic expiration

    D. Dynamic policy control

127. Digital rights management (DRM) tools should enforce _____, which is interoperability with the organization's other access control activities.

  A. Persistence

  B. Support for existing authentication security infrastructure

  C. Continuous audit trail

  D. Dynamic policy control

128. In a data retention policy, what is perhaps the *most* crucial element?

  A. Location of the data archive

  B. Frequency of backups

  C. Security controls in long-term storage

  D. Data recovery procedures

129. _____ is the practice of taking data out of the production environment and putting it into long-term storage.

  A. Deletion

  B. Archiving

  C. Crypto-shredding

  D. Storing

130. In general, all policies within an organization should include each of the following elements *except* _____.

  A. The date on which the policy will expire

  B. The assignment of an entity to review the applicability of the possibility occasionally

  C. The assignment of an entity to monitor and maintain the process described in the policy

  D. A list of the laws, regulations, practices, and/or standards that drove the creation of the policy

131. The goals of secure sanitization (or "data destruction") include all of the following *except* _____.

  A. Removing data objects or files

  B. Minimizing or eliminating data remanence

  C. Removing pointers and metadata about specific files or objects

  D. Creating a secure, archived copy for business continuity and disaster recovery (BC/DR) purposes

132. Why is deleting a file or object insufficient for secure sanitization purposes?

  A. Drives and disks must be demagnetized for true secure destruction.

  B. Physical destruction is the only acceptable method of secure sanitization.

  C. Deletion usually only removes pointers or indicators of file location.

  D. Only administrators should be allowed to delete files or objects.

133. Data destruction in the cloud is difficult because _____.

    A. Cloud data doesn't have substance

    B. Regulations prevent it

    C. The hardware belongs to the provider

    D. Most of the data is subterranean

134. Data destruction in the cloud is difficult because _____.

    A. Data in the cloud is constantly being replicated and backed up

    B. Delete commands are prohibited in the cloud

    C. Internet service providers (ISPs) will not allow destruction of data stored in the cloud

    D. The end clients may prevent it

135. Data destruction in the cloud is difficult because _____.

    A. Only law enforcement is permitted to destroy cloud data

    B. The largest cloud vendors have prevented customers from destroying data

    C. Cloud data renews itself automatically

    D. The cloud is often a multitenant environment

136. Which of the following is the best and only completely secure method of data destruction?

    A. Degaussing

    B. Crypto-shredding

    C. Physical destruction of resources that store the data

    D. Legal order issued by the prevailing jurisdiction where the data is geographically situated

137. Aside from the fact that the cloud customer probably cannot reach the physical storage assets of the cloud provider and that wiping an entire storage space would impact other customers, why would degaussing probably not be an effective means of secure sanitization in the cloud?

    A. All the data storage space in the cloud is already gaussed.

    B. Cloud data storage may not be affected by degaussing.

    C. Federal law prohibits it in the United States.

    D. The blast radius is too wide.

138. Is overwriting a feasible secure sanitization method in the cloud?

    A. Yes, but only if you use multiple passes.

    B. No, because you can't get physical access to cloud storage resources.

    C. Yes, but it requires a final pass with all zeros or ones.

    D. No, because the logical location of the stored data is almost impossible to determine.

139. All of the following are reasons overwriting is not a viable secure sanitization method for data stored in the cloud *except* _____.

   A. Overwriting an entire storage resource would affect other tenants' data

   B. Regulators usually frown on the practice

   C. Locating the specific storage locations of cloud data is almost impossible

   D. Data is being backed constantly in the cloud; before you finished overwriting an entire data set, it would have been replicated elsewhere

140. Which of the following might make crypto-shredding difficult or useless?

   A. The cloud provider also managing the organization's keys

   B. Lack of physical access to the environment

   C. External attackers

   D. Lack of user training and awareness

141. Crypto-shredding requires at least ___ cryptosystem(s).

   A. One

   B. Two

   C. Three

   D. Four

142. In addition to having it for business continuity and disaster recovery (BC/DR) purposes, data archiving might also be useful for _____.

   A. Ensuring profitability

   B. Increasing performance

   C. Motivating users

   D. Correcting accidental errors

143. In addition to having it for business continuity and disaster recovery (BC/DR) purposes, data archiving might also be useful for _____.

   A. Team building and morale

   B. Forensic investigation

   C. Choosing security controls

   D. Enhancing quality

144. In addition to having it for business continuity and disaster recovery (BC/DR) purposes, data archiving might also be useful for _____.

   A. Compliance/audit

   B. Monitoring performance

   C. Gathering investment

   D. Enforcing policy

145. Who is responsible for performing archiving activities in a managed cloud environment?

    A. The cloud customer

    B. The cloud provider

    C. The customer's regulator

    D. Depends on the contract

146. Data archiving and retention policies should include _____.

    A. How long the data must be kept before destruction

    B. The depth of underground storage bunkers used for archiving

    C. The names of specific personnel tasked with restoring data in the event of data loss in the operational environment

    D. The name(s) of regulators approving the policy

147. What should data archiving and retention policies include?

    A. Names of personnel allowed to receive backup media, if third-party off-site archiving services are used

    B. Explicit statement of data formats and types of storage media

    C. A list of personnel whose data will be archived on a regular basis

    D. Which Internet service provider (ISP) should be used for backup procedures

148. If the organization operates in a cloud environment, security operations procedures should include specific contact information for all of the following *except* _____.

    A. Applicable regulatory entities

    B. Federal and local law enforcement

    C. The originator or publisher of the governing policy

    D. The cloud provider's security response office

149. If the organization operates in a cloud environment, security operations procedures should include guidance for all of the following audit or logging processes *except* _____.

    A. Definition of security events and incidents

    B. The brand or vendor of the cloud provider's audit or logging tool

    C. Process for adding new audit or logging rules

    D. Process for filtering out false positives by amending the rule set

150. What does *nonrepudiation* mean?

    A. Prohibiting certain parties from a private conversation

    B. Ensuring that a transaction is completed before saving the results

    C. Ensuring that someone cannot turn off auditing capabilities while performing a function

    D. Preventing any party that participates in a transaction from claiming that it did not

Chapter

3

Domain 3: Cloud Platform and Infrastructure Security

The third domain of the Certified Cloud Security Professional (CCSP) Exam Outline concerns the underlying infrastructure of the cloud, including both hardware and software, the concept of pooled resources, and a detailed discussion of identity and access management (IAM).

1. You are in charge of creating the business continuity and disaster recovery (BC/DR) plan and procedures for your organization. Your organization has its production environment hosted in a cloud environment. You are considering using cloud backup services for your BC/DR purposes as well. What would probably be the best strategy for this approach, in terms of redundancy and resiliency?

   A. Have your cloud provider also provide BC/DR backup.

   B. Keep a BC/DR backup on the premises of your corporate headquarters.

   C. Use another cloud provider for the BC/DR backup.

   D. Move your production environment back into your corporate premises, and use your cloud provider to host your BC/DR backup.

2. You are in charge of creating the business continuity and disaster recovery (BC/DR) plan and procedures for your organization. You decide to have a tabletop test of the BC/DR activity. Which of the following will offer the best value during the test?

   A. Have all participants conduct their individual activities via remote meeting technology.

   B. Task a moderator well versed in BC/DR actions to supervise and present scenarios to the participants, including randomized special events.

   C. Provide copies of the BC/DR policy to all participants.

   D. Allow all users in your organization to participate.

3. You are in charge of creating the business continuity and disaster recovery (BC/DR) plan and procedures for your organization. Your organization has its production environment hosted by a cloud provider, and you have appropriate protections in place. Which of the following is a significant consideration for your BC/DR backup?

   A. Enough personnel at the BC/DR recovery site to ensure proper operations

   B. Good cryptographic key management

   C. Access to the servers where the BC/DR backup is stored

   D. Forensic analysis capabilities

4. You are in charge of creating the business continuity and disaster recovery (BC/DR) plan and procedures for your organization. You are going to conduct a full test of the BC/DR plan. Which of the following strategies is an optimum technique to avoid major issues?

   A. Have another full backup of the production environment stored prior to the test.

   B. Assign all personnel tasks to perform during the test.

   C. Have the cloud provider implement a simulated disaster at a random moment in order to maximize realistic testing.

   D. Have your regulators present at the test so they can monitor performance.

5. A Security Assertion Markup Language (SAML) identity assertion token uses the _____ protocol.

   A. Extensible Markup Language (XML)

   B. Hypertext Transfer Protocol (HTTP)

   C. Hypertext Markup Language (HTML)

   D. American Standard Code for Information Interchange (ASCII)

6. The minimum essential characteristics of a cloud data center are often referred to as "ping, power, pipe." What does this term mean?

   A. Remote access for customer to racked devices in the data center; electrical utilities; connectivity to an Internet service provider (ISP)/the Internet

   B. Application suitability; availability; connectivity

   C. Infrastructure as a service (IaaS); software as a service (SaaS); platform as a service (PaaS)

   D. Anti-malware tools; controls against distributed denial of service (DDoS) attacks; physical/environmental security controls, including fire suppression

7. To support all aspects of the CIA triad (confidentiality, integrity, availability), all of the following aspects of a cloud data center need to be engineered with redundancies *except* _____.

   A. Power supply

   B. HVAC

   C. Administrative offices

   D. Internet service provider (ISP)/connectivity lines

8. Who is the cloud carrier?

   A. The cloud customer

   B. The cloud provider

   C. The regulator overseeing the cloud customer's industry

   D. The ISP between the cloud customer and provider

9. Which of the following terms describes a means to centralize logical control of all networked nodes in the environment, abstracted from the physical connections to each?

   A. Virtual private network (VPN)

   B. Software-defined network (SDN)

   C. Access control lists (ACLs)

   D. Role-based access control (RBAC)

10. In software-defined networking (SDN), the northbound interface (NBI) usually handles traffic between the _____ and the _____.

    A. Cloud customer; ISP

    B. SDN controllers; SDN applications

    C. Cloud provider; ISP

    D. Router; host

11. Software-defined networking (SDN) allows network administrators and architects to perform all the following functions *except* _____.

    A. Reroute traffic based on current customer demand

    B. Create logical subnets without having to change any actual physical connections

    C. Filter access to resources based on specific rules or settings

    D. Deliver streaming media content in an efficient manner by placing it closer to the end user

12. Which of the following is a device specially purposed to handle the issuance, distribution, and storage of cryptographic keys?

    A. Key management box (KMB)

    B. Hardware security module (HSM)

    C. Ticket-granting ticket (TGT)

    D. Trusted computing base (TCB)

13. When discussing the cloud, we often segregate the data center into the terms *compute*, *storage*, and *networking*. *Compute* is made up of _____ and _____.

    A. Routers; hosts

    B. Application programming interface (APIs); northbound interface (NBIs)

    C. Central processing unit (CPU); random-access memory (RAM)

    D. Virtualized; actual hardware devices

14. All of the following can be used to properly apportion cloud resources *except* _____.

    A. Reservations

    B. Shares

    C. Cancellations

    D. Limits

15. Which of the following is a method for apportioning resources that involves setting guaranteed minimums for all tenants/customers within the environment?

    A. Reservations

    B. Shares

    C. Cancellations

    D. Limits

16. Which of the following is a method for apportioning resources that involves setting maximum usage amounts for all tenants/customers within the environment?

  A. Reservations

  B. Shares

  C. Cancellations

  D. Limits

17. Which of the following is a method for apportioning resources that involves prioritizing resource requests to resolve contention situations?

  A. Reservations

  B. Shares

  C. Cancellations

  D. Limits

18. A bare-metal hypervisor is Type _____.

  A. 1

  B. 2

  C. 3

  D. 4

19. A hypervisor that runs inside another operating system (OS) is a Type _____ hypervisor.

  A. 1

  B. 2

  C. 3

  D. 4

20. A Type _____ hypervisor is probably more difficult to defend than other hypervisors.

  A. 1

  B. 2

  C. 3

  D. 4

21. One of the security challenges of operating in the cloud is that additional controls must be placed on file storage systems because _____.

  A. File stores are always kept in plain text in the cloud

  B. There is no way to sanitize file storage space in the cloud

  C. Virtualization necessarily prevents the use of application-based security controls

  D. Virtual machines are stored as snapshotted files when not in use

22. What is the main reason virtualization is used in the cloud?

    A. Virtual machines (VMs) are easier to administer.

    B. If a VM is infected with malware, it can be easily replaced.

    C. With VMs, the cloud provider does not have to deploy an entire hardware device for every new user.

    D. VMs are easier to operate than actual devices.

23. Orchestrating resource calls is the job of the _____.

    A. Administrator

    B. Router

    C. VM

    D. Hypervisor

24. Which of the following terms describes a cloud storage area that uses a filesystem/hierarchy?

    A. Volume storage

    B. Object storage

    C. Logical unit number (LUN)

    D. Block storage

25. Typically, which form of cloud storage is used in the near term for snapshotted virtual machine (VM) images?

    A. Volume storage

    B. Object storage

    C. Logical unit number (LUN)

    D. Block storage

26. Who operates the management plane?

    A. Regulators

    B. End consumers

    C. Privileged users

    D. Privacy data subjects

27. What is probably the *optimum* way to avoid vendor lock-in?

    A. Use nonproprietary data formats.

    B. Use industry-standard media.

    C. Use strong cryptography.

    D. Use favorable contract language.

28. Who will determine whether your organization's cloud migration is satisfactory from a compliance perspective?

A. The cloud provider

B. The cloud customer

C. The regulator(s)

D. The Internet service provider (ISP)

29. What is probably the best way to avoid problems associated with vendor lock-out?

A. Use strong contract language.

B. Use nonproprietary data and media formats.

C. Use strong cryptography.

D. Use another provider for backup purposes.

30. In a public cloud services arrangement, who creates governance that will determine which controls are selected for the data center and how they are deployed?

A. The cloud provider

B. The cloud customer

C. The regulator(s)

D. The end user

31. What is the term that describes the situation when a malicious user or attacker can exit the restrictions of a virtual machine (VM) and access another VM residing on the same host?

A. Host escape

B. Guest escape

C. Provider exit

D. Escalation of privileges

32. What is the term that describes the situation when a malicious user or attacker can exit the restrictions of a single host and access other nodes on the network?

A. Host escape

B. Guest escape

C. Provider exit

D. Escalation of privileges

33. _____ is/are probably the main cause of virtualization sprawl.

A. Malicious attackers

B. Lack of provider controls

C. Lack of customer controls

D. Ease of use

34. Sprawl is mainly a(n) _____ problem.
    A. Technical
    B. External
    C. Management
    D. Logical

35. Which of the following risks exists in the traditional environment but is dramatically increased by moving into the cloud?
    A. Physical security breaches
    B. Loss of utility power
    C. Financial upheaval
    D. Man-in-the-middle attacks

36. A fundamental aspect of security principles, _____ should be implemented in the cloud as well as in traditional environments.
    A. Continual uptime
    B. Defense in depth
    C. Multifactor authentication
    D. Separation of duties

37. From a security perspective, automation of configuration aids in _____.
    A. Enhancing performance
    B. Reducing potential attack vectors
    C. Increasing ease of use of the systems
    D. Reducing need for administrative personnel

38. _____ is the *most* prevalent protocol used in identity federation.
    A. Hypertext Transfer Protocol (HTTP)
    B. Security Assertion Markup Language (SAML)
    C. File Transfer Protocol (FTP)
    D. WS-Federation

39. A user signs on to a cloud-based social media platform. In another browser tab, the user finds an article worth posting to the social media platform. The user clicks on the platform's icon listed on the article's website, and the article is automatically posted to the user's account on the social media platform. This is an example of what?
    A. Single sign-on
    B. Insecure direct identifiers
    C. Identity federation
    D. Cross-site scripting

40. A group of clinics decides to create an identification federation for their users (medical providers and clinicians). If they opt to review each other, for compliance with security governance and standards they all find acceptable, what is this federation model called?

   A. Cross-certification

   B. Proxy

   C. Single sign-on

   D. Regulated

41. A group of clinics decides to create an identification federation for their users (medical providers and clinicians). If they opt to hire a third party to review each organization, for compliance with security governance and standards they all find acceptable, what is this federation model called?

   A. Cross-certification

   B. Proxy

   C. Single sign-on

   D. Regulated

42. A group of clinics decides to create an identification federation for their users (medical providers and clinicians). If they opt to use the web of trust model for federation, who is/are the identity provider(s)?

   A. Each organization

   B. A trusted third party

   C. The regulator overseeing their industry

   D. All of their patients

43. A group of clinics decides to create an identification federation for their users (medical providers and clinicians). If they opt to use the web of trust model for federation, who is/are the service providers?

   A. Each organization

   B. A trusted third party

   C. The regulator overseeing their industry

   D. All of their patients

44. A group of clinics decides to create an identification federation for their users (medical providers and clinicians). In this federation, all of the participating organizations would need to be in compliance with what U.S. federal regulation?

   A. Gramm-Leach-Bliley Act (GLBA)

   B. Family and Medical Leave Act (FMLA)

   C. Payment Card Industry Data Security Standard (PCI DSS)

   D. Health Information Portability and Accountability Act (HIPAA)

45. What is the process of granting access to resources?

    A. Identification

    B. Authentication

    C. Authorization

    D. Federation

46. The process of identity management includes all the following elements *except* _____.

    A. Provisioning

    B. Maintenance

    C. Deprovisioning

    D. Redaction

47. Which organizational entity usually performs the verification part of the provisioning element of the identification process?

    A. Information technology (IT)

    B. Security

    C. Human resources (HR)

    D. Sales

48. Of the following options, which is a reason cloud data center audits are often less easy to verify than traditional audits?

    A. Data in the cloud can't be audited.

    B. Controls in the cloud can't be audited.

    C. Getting physical access can be difficult.

    D. There are no regulators for cloud operations.

49. Of the following options, which is a reason cloud data center audits are often less easy to verify than traditional audits?

    A. Cryptography is present.

    B. Auditors don't like the cloud.

    C. Cloud equipment is resistant to audit.

    D. They often rely on data the provider chooses to disclose.

50. Of the following options, which is a reason cloud data center audits are often less easy to verify than audits in standard data centers?

    A. They frequently rely on third parties.

    B. The standards are too difficult to follow.

    C. The paperwork is cumbersome.

    D. There aren't enough auditors.

51. The cloud customer will usually not have physical access to the cloud data center. This enhances security by _____.

   A. Reducing the need for qualified personnel

   B. Limiting access to sensitive information

   C. Reducing jurisdictional exposure

   D. Ensuring statutory compliance

52. Which of the following controls would be useful to build into a virtual machine baseline image for a cloud environment?

   A. GPS tracking/locator

   B. Automated vulnerability scan on system startup

   C. Access control list (ACL) of authorized personnel

   D. Write protection

53. Which of the following controls would be useful to build into a virtual machine baseline image for a cloud environment?

   A. Automatic registration with the configuration management system

   B. Enhanced user training and awareness media

   C. Mechanisms that prevent the file from being copied

   D. Keystroke loggers

54. Virtual machine (VM) configuration management (CM) tools should probably include _____.

   A. Biometric recognition

   B. Anti-tampering mechanisms

   C. Log file generation

   D. Hackback capabilities

55. Using a virtual machine baseline image could be very useful for which of the following options?

   A. Physical security

   B. Auditing

   C. Training

   D. Customization

56. What can be revealed by an audit of a baseline virtual image, used in a cloud environment?

   A. Adequate physical protections in the data center

   B. Potential criminal activity before it occurs

   C. Whether necessary security controls are in place and functioning properly

   D. Lack of user training and awareness

57. Using one cloud provider for your operational environment and another for your BC/DR backup will also give you the additional benefit of _____.

    A. Allowing any custom VM builds you use to be instantly ported to another environment

    B. Avoiding vendor lock-in/lock-out

    C. Increased performance

    D. Lower cost

58. Having your BC/DR backup stored with the same cloud provider as your production environment can help you _____.

    A. Maintain regulatory compliance

    B. Spend less of your budget on traveling

    C. Train your users about security awareness

    D. Recover quickly from minor incidents

59. If you use the cloud for BC/DR purposes, even if you don't operate your production environment in the cloud, you can cut costs by eliminating your _____.

    A. Security personnel

    B. BC/DR policy

    C. Old access credentials

    D. Need for a physical hot site/warm site

60. If the cloud is used for BC/DR purposes, the loss of _____ could gravely affect your organization's RTO.

    A. Any cloud administrator

    B. A specific VM

    C. Your policy and contract documentation

    D. ISP connectivity

61. What is the *most* important asset to protect in cloud BC/DR activities?

    A. Intellectual property

    B. Hardware at the cloud data center

    C. Personnel

    D. Data on portable media

62. When considering cloud data replication strategies (i.e., whether you are making backups at the block, file, or database level), which element of your organization's BC/DR plan will be *most* affected by your choice?

    A. Recovery time objective

    B. Recovery point objective

    C. Maximum allowable downtime

    D. Mean time to failure

63. In addition to BC/DR, what other benefit can your data archive/backup provide?

   A. Physical security enforcement

   B. Access control methodology

   C. Security control against data breach

   D. Availability for data lost accidentally

64. Which of the following risks is probably *most* significant when choosing to use one cloud provider for your operational environment and another for BC/DR backup/archive?

   A. Physical intrusion

   B. Proprietary formats/lack of interoperability

   C. Vendor lock-in/lock-out

   D. Natural disasters

65. Return to normal operations is a phase in BC/DR activity when the emergency is over and regular production can resume. Which of the following can sometimes be the result when the organization uses two different cloud providers for the production and BC/DR environments?

   A. Both providers are affected by the emergency, extending the time before return to normal can occur.

   B. The BC/DR provider becomes the new normal production environment.

   C. Regulators will find the organization in violation of compliance guidance.

   D. All data is lost irretrievably.

66. Which of these determines the critical assets, recovery time objective (RTO), and recover point objective (RPO) for BC/DR purposes?

   A. Business drivers

   B. User input

   C. Regulator mandate

   D. Industry standards

67. What artifact—which should already exist within the organization—can be used to determine the critical assets necessary to protect in the BC/DR activity?

   A. Quantitative risk analysis

   B. Qualitative risk analysis

   C. Business impact analysis

   D. Risk appetite

68. Which of the following is probably the *most* important element to address if your organization is using two different cloud providers for the production and BC/DR environments?

   A. Do they cost the same?

   B. Do they have similar facility protections in place?

   C. What level of end-user support do they each offer?

   D. Can the backup provider meet the same SLA requirements as the primary?

69. In a managed cloud services arrangement, who invokes a BC/DR action?

    A. The cloud provider

    B. The cloud customer

    C. Depends on the contract

    D. Any user

70. What do you need to do in order to fully ensure that a BC/DR action will function during a contingency?

    A. Audit all performance functions.

    B. Audit all security functions.

    C. Perform a full-scale test.

    D. Mandate this capability in the contract.

71. Which of the following is probably the *most* important activity, of those listed?

    A. Regularly update the BC/DR plan/process.

    B. Have contact information for all personnel in the organization.

    C. Have contact information for essential BC/DR personnel.

    D. Have contact information for local law enforcement.

72. The BC/DR plan/policy should include all of the following *except* _____.

    A. Tasking for the office responsible for maintaining/enforcing the plan

    B. Contact information for essential entities, including BC/DR personnel and emergency services agencies

    C. Copies of the laws/regulations/standards governing specific elements of the plan

    D. Checklists for BC/DR personnel to follow

73. The BC/DR plan/process should be written and documented in such a way that it can be used by _____.

    A. Users

    B. Essential BC/DR team members

    C. Regulators

    D. Someone with the requisite skills

74. Which of the following probably poses the *most* significant risk to the organization?

    A. Not having essential BC/DR personnel available during a contingency

    B. Not including all BC/DR elements in the cloud contract

    C. Returning to normal operations too soon

    D. Telecommunications outages

75. Which of the following probably poses the *most* significant risk to the organization?

    A. Lack of data confidentiality during a contingency

    B. Lack of regulatory compliance during a contingency

    C. Returning to normal operations too late

    D. Lack of encrypted communications during a contingency

76. Why does the physical location of your data backup and/or BC/DR failover environment matter?

    A. It may affect regulatory compliance.

    B. Lack of physical security

    C. Environmental factors such as humidity

    D. It doesn't matter. Data can be saved anywhere without consequence.

77. According to the European Union Agency for Network and Information Security (ENISA), a cloud risk assessment should provide a means for customers to accomplish all these assurance tasks *except* _____.

    A. Assess risks associated with cloud migration

    B. Compare offerings from different cloud providers

    C. Reduce the risk of regulatory noncompliance

    D. Reduce the assurance burden on cloud providers

78. The European Union Agency for Network and Information Security's (ENISA's) definition of cloud computing differs slightly from the definition offered by (ISC)² (and, for instance, NIST). What is one of the characteristics listed by ENISA but *not* included in the (ISC)² definition?

    A. Metered service

    B. Shared resources

    C. Scalability

    D. Programmatic management

79. Risk should always be considered from a business perspective. Risk is often balanced by corresponding _____.

    A. Profit

    B. Performance

    C. Cost

    D. Opportunity

80. When considering the option to migrate from an on-premise environment to a hosted cloud service, an organization should weigh the risks of allowing external entities to access the cloud data for collaborative purposes against _____.

    A. Not securing the data in the traditional environment

    B. Disclosing the data publicly

    C. Inviting external personnel into the traditional workspace in order to enhance collaboration

    D. Sending the data outside the traditional environment for collaborative purposes

81. There are many ways to handle risk. However, the usual methods for addressing risk are not all possible in the cloud because _____.

    A. Cloud data risks cannot be mitigated

    B. Migrating into a cloud environment necessarily means you are accepting all risks

    C. Some risks cannot be transferred to a cloud provider

    D. Cloud providers cannot avoid risk

82. In which cloud service model does the customer lose the *most* control over governance?

    A. Infrastructure as a service (IaaS)

    B. Platform as a service (PaaS)

    C. Software as a service (SaaS)

    D. Private cloud

83. Which of the following poses a *new* risk in the cloud, not affecting the traditional, on-premise IT environment?

    A. Internal threats

    B. Multitenancy

    C. Natural disasters

    D. Distributed denial of service (DDoS) attacks

84. In addition to the security offered by the cloud provider, a cloud customer must consider the security offered by _____.

    A. The respective regulator

    B. The end user(s)

    C. Any vendor the cloud customer previously used in the on-premise environment

    D. Any third parties the provider depends on

85. Which of the following poses a *new* risk in the cloud, not affecting the traditional, on-premise IT environment?

    A. User carelessness

    B. Inadvertent breach

    C. Device failure

    D. Resource exhaustion

86. Where is isolation failure probably *least* likely to pose a significant risk?

   A. Public cloud

   B. Private cloud

   C. PaaS environment

   D. SaaS environment

87. Which of the following poses a *new* risk in the cloud, not affecting the traditional, on-premise environment?

   A. Fire

   B. Legal seizure of another firm's assets

   C. Mandatory privacy data breach notifications

   D. Flooding

88. Which of these does the cloud customer need to ensure protection of intellectual property created in the cloud?

   A. Digital rights management (DRM) solutions

   B. Identity and access management (IAM) solutions

   C. Strong contractual clauses

   D. Crypto-shredding

89. What could be the result of failure of the cloud provider to secure the hypervisor in such a way that one user on a virtual machine can see the resource calls of another user's virtual machine?

   A. Unauthorized data disclosure

   B. Inference attacks

   C. Social engineering

   D. Physical intrusion

90. Key generation in a cloud environment might have less entropy than the traditional environment for all the following reasons *except* _____.

   A. Lack of direct input devices

   B. No social factors

   C. Uniform build

   D. Virtualization

91. Lack of industry-wide standards for cloud computing creates a potential for _____.

   A. Privacy data breach

   B. Privacy data disclosure

   C. vendor lock-in

   D. vendor lock-out

92. What can hamper the ability of a cloud customer to protect their assets in a managed services arrangement?

    A. Prohibitions on port scanning and penetration testing

    B. Geographical dispersion

    C. Rules against training users

    D. Laws that prevent them from doing so

93. Cloud administration almost necessarily violates the principles of the _____ security model.

    A. Brewer-Nash (Chinese Wall)

    B. Graham-Denning

    C. Bell-LaPadula

    D. Biba

94. The physical layout of a cloud data center campus should include redundancies of all the following *except* _____.

    A. Physical perimeter security controls (fences, lights, walls, etc.)

    B. The administration/support staff building

    C. Electrical utility lines

    D. Communications connectivity lines

95. Best practice for planning the physical resiliency for a cloud data center facility includes _____.

    A. Having one point of egress for personnel

    B. Ensuring that any cabling/connectivity enters the facility from different sides of the building/property

    C. Ensuring that all parking areas are near generators so that personnel in high-traffic areas are always illuminated by emergency lighting, even when utility power is not available

    D. Ensuring that the foundation of the facility is rated to withstand earthquake tremors

96. The physical layout of a cloud data center campus should include redundancies of all the following *except* _____.

    A. Generators

    B. HVAC units

    C. Generator fuel storage

    D. Points of personnel ingress

97. There are two reasons to conduct a test of the organization's recovery from backup in an environment other than the primary production environment. Which of the following is one of them?

   A. It costs more to conduct a test at the same location as the primary workplace.

   B. You don't want to waste travel budget on what is only a test.

   C. The risk of negative impact to both production and backup is too high.

   D. There won't be enough room for everyone to sit in the primary facility.

98. There are two reasons to conduct a test of the organization's recovery from backup in an environment other than the primary production environment. Which of the following is one of them?

   A. It is good to invest in more than one community.

   B. You want to approximate contingency conditions, which includes not operating in the primary location.

   C. It is good for your personnel to see other places occasionally.

   D. Your regulators won't follow you off-site, so you'll be unobserved during your test.

99. In an IaaS arrangement, who accepts responsibility for securing cloud-based applications?

   A. The cloud provider

   B. The cloud customer

   C. The regulator

   D. The end user/client

100. Industry best practices dictate that cloud customers do not _____.

   A. Create their own identity and access management (IAM) solutions

   B. Create contract language that favors them over the provider

   C. Retrain personnel for cloud operations

   D. Encrypt data before it reaches the cloud

101. It is possible for the cloud customer to transfer _____ risk to the provider, but the cloud customer always retains ultimate legal risk.

   A. Market

   B. Perception

   C. Data

   D. Financial

102. A process for _____ can aid in protecting against data disclosure due to lost devices.

   A. User punishment

   B. Credential revocation

   C. Law enforcement notification

   D. Device tracking

103. All of the following can be used in the process of anomaly detection *except*
_____.

   A. The ratio of failed to successful logins

   B. Transactions completed successfully

   C. Event time of day

   D. Multiple concurrent logins

104. Critical components should be protected with _____.

   A. Strong passwords

   B. Chain-link fences

   C. Homomorphic encryption

   D. Multifactor authentication

105. It's important to maintain a current asset inventory list, including surveying your environment on a regular basis, in order to _____.

   A. Prevent unknown, unpatched assets from being used as back doors to the environment

   B. Ensure that any lost devices are automatically entered into the acquisition system for repurchasing and replacement

   C. Maintain user morale by having their devices properly catalogued and annotated

   D. Ensure that billing for all devices is handled by the appropriate departments

106. Which of the following can enhance data portability?

   A. Interoperable export formats

   B. Egress monitoring solutions

   C. Strong physical protections

   D. Agile business intelligence

107. Which of the following can enhance application portability?

   A. Using the same cloud provider for the production environment and archiving

   B. Conducting service trials in an alternate cloud provider environment

   C. Providing cloud-usage training for all users

   D. Tuning web application firewalls (WAFs) to detect anomalous activity in inbound communications

108. What should the cloud customer do to ensure that disaster recovery activities don't exceed the maximum allowable downtime (MAD)?

   A. Make sure any alternate provider can support the application needs of the organization.

   B. Ensure that contact information for all first responder agencies are correct and up-to-date at all times.

   C. Select an appropriate recovery time objective (RTO).

   D. Regularly review all regulatory directives for disaster response.

109. Which of the following would probably best aid an organization in deciding whether to migrate from a traditional environment to a particular cloud provider?

 A. Rate sheets comparing a cloud provider to other cloud providers

 B. Cloud provider offers to provide engineering assistance during the migration

 C. The cost/benefit measure of closing the organization's relocation site (hot site/warm site) and using the cloud for disaster recovery instead

 D. SLA satisfaction surveys from other (current and past) cloud customers

110. A cloud provider will probably require all of the following *except* _____ before a customer conducts a penetration test.

 A. Notice

 B. Description of scope of the test

 C. Physical location of the launch point

 D. Knowledge of time frame/duration

111. Cloud providers will probably not allow _____ as part of a customer's penetration test.

 A. Network mapping

 B. Vulnerability scanning

 C. Reconnaissance

 D. Social engineering

112. A cloud customer performing a penetration test without the provider's permission is risking _____.

 A. Malware contamination

 B. Excessive fees for SLA violations

 C. Loss of market share

 D. Prosecution

113. When a customer performs a penetration test in the cloud, why isn't the test an optimum simulation of attack conditions?

 A. Attackers don't use remote access for cloud activity.

 B. Advanced notice removes the element of surprise.

 C. When cloud customers use malware, it's not the same as when attackers use malware.

 D. Regulator involvement changes the attack surface.

114. Managed cloud services exist because the service is less expensive for each customer than creating the same services for themselves in a traditional environment. What is the technology that creates most of the cost savings in the cloud environment?

 A. Emulation

 B. Secure remote access

 C. Crypto-shredding

 D. Virtualization

115. Managed cloud services exist because the service is less expensive for each customer than creating the same services for themselves in a traditional environment. From the customer perspective, most of the cost differential created between the traditional environment and the cloud through virtualization is achieved by removing _____.

    A. External risks

    B. Internal risks

    C. Regulatory compliance

    D. Sunk capital investment

116. Managed cloud services exist because the service is less expensive for each customer than creating the same services for themselves in a traditional environment. Using a managed service allows the customer to realize significant cost savings through the reduction of _____.

    A. Risk

    B. Security controls

    C. Personnel

    D. Data

117. Which of the following is a risk posed by the use of virtualization?

    A. Internal threats interrupting service through physical accidents (spilling drinks, tripping over cables, etc.)

    B. The ease of transporting stolen virtual machine images

    C. Increased susceptibility of virtual systems to malware

    D. Electromagnetic pulse

118. The tasks performed by the hypervisor in the virtual environment can be most likened to the tasks of the _____ in the traditional environment.

    A. Central processing unit (CPU)

    B. Security team

    C. Operating system (OS)

    D. Pretty Good Privacy (PGP)

119. Mass storage in the cloud will most likely currently involve _____.

    A. Spinning platters

    B. Tape drives

    C. Magnetic disks

    D. Solid-state drives (SSDs)

120. What is the type of cloud storage arrangement that involves the use of associating metadata with the saved data?

    A. Volume

    B. Block

    C. Object

    D. Redundant

121. According to the *NIST Cloud Computing Reference Architecture*, which of the following is most likely a cloud carrier?

    A. Amazon Web Services

    B. Netflix

    C. Verizon

    D. Nessus

122. Resolving resource contentions in the cloud will most likely be the job of the _____.

    A. Router

    B. Emulator

    C. Regulator

    D. Hypervisor

123. Security controls installed on a guest virtual machine operating system (VM OS) will *not* function when _____.

    A. The user is accessing the VM remotely

    B. The OS is not scanned for vulnerabilities

    C. The OS is not subject to version control

    D. The VM is not active while in storage

124. Typically, SSDs are _____.

    A. More expensive than spinning platters

    B. Larger than tape backup

    C. Heavier than tape libraries

    D. More subject to malware than legacy drives

125. Typically, SSDs are _____.

    A. Harder to install than magnetic memory

    B. Faster than magnetic drives

    C. Harder to administer than tape libraries

    D. More likely to fail than spinning platters

126. Typically, SSDs are _____.

    A. Impossible to destroy physically

    B. Not vulnerable to degaussing

    C. Subject to a longer warranty

    D. Protected by international trade laws

127. Of the following control techniques/solutions, which can be combined to enhance the protections offered by each?

  A. Fences/firewalls

  B. Asset inventories/personnel training

  C. Data dispersion/encryption

  D. Intrusion prevention solutions/intrusion detection solutions

128. Of the following control techniques/solutions, which can be combined to enhance the protections offered by each?

  A. Razor tape/background checks

  B. Least privilege/generators

  C. DLP/DRM

  D. Personnel badging/secure baselines

129. Risk assessment is the responsibility of _____.

  A. Companies offering managed cloud services

  B. Regulatory bodies

  C. Every organization

  D. Legislative entities

130. Which entity can *best* aid the organization in avoiding vendor lock-in?

  A. Senior management

  B. The IT security office

  C. General counsel

  D. The cloud security representative

131. Perhaps the best method for avoiding vendor lock-out is also a means for enhancing BC/DR capabilities. This is _____.

  A. Having a warm site within 250 miles of the primary production environment

  B. Using one cloud provider for primary production and another for backup purposes

  C. Building a data center above the flood plain

  D. Cross-training all personnel

132. _____ can often be the result of inadvertent activity.

  A. DDoS

  B. Phishing

  C. Sprawl

  D. Disasters

133. Of the following, which is probably the *most* significant risk in a managed cloud environment?

   A. DDoS

   B. Management plane breach

   C. Guest escape

   D. Physical attack on the utility service lines

134. What is the optimal number of entrances to the cloud data center campus?

   A. One

   B. Two

   C. Three

   D. Four

135. The cloud data center campus physical access point should include all of the following *except* _____.

   A. Reception area

   B. Video surveillance

   C. Badging procedure

   D. Mantrap structures

136. Where should multiple egress points be included?

   A. At the power distribution substation

   B. Within the data center

   C. In every building on the campus

   D. In the security operations center

137. Which of the following is a risk in the cloud environment that does not exist or is not as prevalent in the traditional environment?

   A. DDoS

   B. Isolation failure

   C. External attack

   D. Internal attack

138. All security controls necessarily _____.

   A. Are expensive

   B. Degrade performance

   C. Require senior management approval

   D. Will work in the cloud environment as well as they worked in the traditional environment

139. Which of the following is a risk in the cloud environment that does not exist or is not as prevalent in the traditional environment?

    A. Legal liability in multiple jurisdictions

    B. Loss of productivity due to DDoS

    C. Ability of users to gain access to their physical workplace

    D. Fire

140. Which of the following is a risk in the cloud environment that does not exist or is not as prevalent in the traditional environment?

    A. Loss of availability due to DDoS

    B. Loss of value due to DDoS

    C. Loss of confidentiality due to DDoS

    D. Loss of liability due to DDoS

141. DDoS attacks do not affect _____ for cloud customers.

    A. Productivity

    B. Availability

    C. Connectivity

    D. Integrity

142. Sprawl in the cloud can lead to significant additional costs to the organization because of _____.

    A. Larger necessary physical footprint

    B. Much larger utility consumption

    C. Software licensing

    D. Requisite additional training

143. It is best to use variables in _____.

    A. Baseline configurations

    B. Security control implementations

    C. Contract language

    D. BC/DR tests

Chapter 4

Domain 4: Cloud Application Security

The fourth domain of the Certified Cloud Security Professional (CCSP) Exam Outline covers applications in the cloud, from software development to challenges involved in migrating apps from the traditional IT environment. It also addresses software security and performance testing methods as well as proper identity and access management (IAM) principles. Because it is weighted less than the previous domains (according to this table published by (ISC)[2], https://cccure.training/m/articles/view/CISSP-domains-weight-percentage-on-the-real-exam), there are considerably fewer questions in this chapter.

1. ISO 27034 mandates a framework for application security within an organization. According to the standard, each organization should have a(n) _____, and each application within the organization should have its own _____.

    A. Organizational Normative Framework (ONF), Application Normative Framework (ANF)

    B. Application Normative Framework (ANF), Organizational Normative Framework (ONF)

    C. Standard Application Security (SAS), Application Normative Framework (ANF)

    D. Organizational Normative Framework (ONF), Standard Application Security (SAS)

2. According to ISO 27034, there is one Organizational Normative Framework (ONF) in the organization, and _____ Application Normative Framework (ANF[s]) for each application within that organization.

    A. Many

    B. Three

    C. No

    D. One

3. What language is used in the Simple Object Access Protocol (SOAP) application design protocol?

    A. Hypertext Markup Language (HTML)

    B. X.509

    C. Extensible Markup Language (XML)

    D. Hypertext Transfer Protocol (HTTP)

4. Typically, representational state transfer (REST) interactions do *not* require _____.

    A. Credentials

    B. Sessions

    C. Servers

    D. Clients

5. Representational state transfer (REST) application programming interfaces (APIs) use _____ protocol verbs.

    A. Hypertext Markup Language (HTML)

    B. Hypertext Transfer Protocol (HTTP)

    C. Extensible Markup Language (XML)

    D. American Standard Code for Information Interchange (ASCII)

6. The architecture of the World Wide Web, as it works today, is _____.

    A. JavaScript Open Notation (JSON)

    B. Denial of service (DoS)

   C. Representational state transfer (REST)

   D. Extensible Markup Language (XML)

7. RESTful responses can come from the server in _____ or _____ formats.

   A. Extensible Markup Language (XML), JavaScript Open Notation (JSON)

   B. Hypertext Transfer Protocol (HTTP), X.509

   C. American Standard Code for Information Interchange (ASCII), text

   D. Hypertext Markup Language (HTML), Extensible Markup Language (XML)

8. Which of the following is an informal industry term for moving applications from a traditional environment into the cloud?

   A. Instantiation

   B. Porting

   C. Grandslamming

   D. Forklifting

9. Developers creating software for the cloud environment should bear in mind cloud-specific risks such as _____ and _____.

   A. DoS and DDoS (denial of service and distributed denial of service)

   B. Multitenancy and third-party administrators

   C. Unprotected servers and unprotected clients

   D. Default configurations and user error

10. When an organization considers cloud migrations, the organization's software developers will need to know which _____ and which _____ the organization will be using, in order to properly and securely create suitable applications.

   A. Geographic location, native language

   B. Legal restrictions, specific ISP

   C. Service model, deployment model

   D. Available bandwidth, telecommunications country code

11. Which of the following is perhaps the best method for reducing the risk of a specific application *not* delivering the proper level of functionality and performance when it is moved from the traditional environment into the cloud?

   A. Remove the application from the organization's production environment and replace it with something else.

   B. Negotiate and conduct a trial run in the cloud environment for that application before permanently migrating.

   C. Make sure the application is fully updated and patched according to all vendor specifications.

   D. Run the application in an emulator.

12. Software developers designing applications for the cloud should expect to include options to ensure all of the following capabilities *except* _____.

    A. Encryption of data at rest

    B. Encryption of data in transit

    C. Data masking

    D. Hashing database fields

13. In a platform as a service (PaaS) model, who should *most* likely be responsible for the security of the applications in the production environment?

    A. Cloud customer

    B. Cloud provider

    C. Regulator

    D. Programmers

14. In the testing phase of the software development lifecycle (SDLC), software performance and _____ should both be reviewed.

    A. Quality

    B. Brevity

    C. Requirements

    D. Security

15. Regardless of which model the organization uses for system development, in which phase of the software development lifecycle (SDLC) will user input be requested and considered?

    A. Define

    B. Design

    C. Develop

    D. Detect

16. Which phase of the software development lifecycle (SDLC) is most likely to involve crypto-shredding?

    A. Define

    B. Design

    C. Test

    D. Disposal

17. Where are business requirements most likely to be mapped to software construction?

    A. Define

    B. Design

    C. Test

    D. Secure Operations

18. All of the following are usually nonfunctional requirements *except*
_____.

    A. Color

    B. Sound

    C. Security

    D. Function

19. Designers making applications for the cloud have to take into consideration risks and operational constraints that did not exist or were not as pronounced in the traditional environment. Which of the following is an element cloud app designers may have to consider incorporating in software for the cloud that may not have been as important in the traditional environment?

    A. Identity and access management (IAM) capability

    B. Distributed denial of service (DDoS) resistance

    C. Encryption for data at rest and in motion

    D. Field validation

20. Designers making applications for the cloud have to take into consideration risks and operational constraints that did not exist or were not as pronounced in the traditional environment. Which of the following is an element cloud app designers may have to consider incorporating in software for the cloud that might not have been as important in the traditional environment?

    A. Application isolation

    B. Inference framing

    C. Known secure library components

    D. Testing that uses known bad data

21. Designers making applications for the cloud have to take into consideration risks and operational constraints that did not exist or were not as pronounced in the traditional environment. Which of the following is an element cloud app designers may not be able to use as readily in the cloud environment as it was deployed in the traditional environment?

    A. Cryptography

    B. STRIDE testing

    C. Field validation

    D. Logging

22. All of these can affect the quality of service expected from an application *except*
_____.

    A. Encryption

    B. Egress monitoring

    C. Anti-malware tools

    D. Use of known secure libraries/components

23. The possibility that a user could gain access or control of an application so as to take on administrator or management capabilities is called _____.

    A. Inversion

    B. Spoofing

    C. Repudiation

    D. Escalation of privilege

24. Which of the following is *not* checked when using the STRIDE threat model?

    A. The ability of users to gain administrative access rights without proper permission

    B. The ability of internal personnel to trigger business continuity/disaster recovery activities

    C. The ability of a participant in a transaction to refute that they've taken part in the transaction

    D. The ability of an unauthorized user to pretend to be an authorized user

25. It is very likely that your organization's users will use unapproved application programming interfaces (APIs), especially in a bring your own device (BYOD) environment, because _____.

    A. Users are constantly trying to break the security of your environment

    B. APIs can't ever be secure

    C. Hackers are constantly infiltrating all APIs

    D. Users enhance their productivity however they can

26. Some current software developers are not aware of security problems within the programs they're creating because _____.

    A. Young programmers are not nearly as disciplined in their coding practices as older programmers

    B. Some current programmers don't write code line by line and instead use code component libraries

    C. Coding languages have not been secure for 20 years

    D. Users are not clear in defining their requirements at the outset of the software development lifecycle (SDLC)

27. What is the *most* secure form of code testing and review?

    A. Open source

    B. Proprietary/internal

    C. Neither open source nor proprietary

    D. Combination of open source and proprietary

28. What is the major difference between authentication and authorization?

    A. Code verification/code implementation

    B. Identity validation/access permission

    C. Inverse incantation/obverse instantiation

    D. User access/privileged access

29. Access should be based on _____.

    A. Regulatory mandates

    B. Business needs and acceptable risk

    C. User requirements and management requests

    D. Optimum performance and security provision

30. Who should determine which users have access to which specific objects?

    A. The cloud provider

    B. Senior management

    C. Data owners

    D. System administrators

31. All of the following are identity federation standards commonly found in use today *except* _____.

    A. WS-Federation

    B. OpenID

    C. OAuth (Open Authorization)

    D. Pretty Good Privacy (PGP)

32. Which of the following is a federation standard/protocol that does *not* rely on Simple Object Access Protocol (SOAP), Security Assertion Markup Language (SAML), or Extensible Markup Language (XML)?

    A. WS-Federation

    B. OpenID Connect

    C. Service Organization Control (SOC) 2

    D. Open Web Application Security Project (OWASP)

33. Authentication mechanisms typically include any or all of the following *except* _____.

    A. Something you know

    B. Someone you know

    C. Something you have

    D. Something you are

34. Which of the following constitutes a multifactor authentication process or procedure?

    A. Using an automated teller machine (ATM) to get cash with your credit or debit card

    B. Using a password and personal identification number (PIN) to log into a website

    C. Presenting a voice sample and fingerprint to access a secure facility

    D. Displaying a birth certificate and a credit card

35. Typically, multifactor authentication should be used _____.

    A. In every IT transaction

    B. For high-risk operations and data that is particularly sensitive

    C. When remote users are logging into the cloud environment

    D. Only in the traditional environment

36. A web application firewall (WAF) usually operates at Layer _____ of the Open Systems Interconnection (OSI) model.

    A. 2

    B. 3

    C. 7

    D. Q

37. A web application firewall (WAF) can understand and act on _____ traffic.

    A. Malicious

    B. Simple Mail Transfer Protocol (SMTP)

    C. Internet Control Message Protocol (ICMP)

    D. Hypertext Transfer Protocol (HTTP)

38. WAFs can be used to reduce the likelihood that _____ attacks will be successful.

    A. Social engineering

    B. Physical theft

    C. Obverse inflection

    D. Cross-site scripting

39. A database activity monitor (DAM) tool usually operates at Layer _____ of the Open Systems Interconnection (OSI) model.

    A. 2

    B. 3

    C. 7

    D. Q

40. Database activity monitors (DAMs) can be used to reduce the potential success of _____ attacks.

    A. SQL injection

    B. Cross-site scripting

    C. Insecure direct-object reference

    D. Social engineering

41. Which security tool can perform content inspection of Secure File Transfer Protocol (SFTP) communications?

    A. Web application firewall (WAF)

    B. Database activity monitor (DAM)

    C. Extensible Markup Language (XML) gateway

    D. Single sign-on (SSO)

42. To deploy a set of microservices to clients instead of building one monolithic application, it is best to use a(n) _____ to coordinate client requests.

    A. Extensible Markup Language (XML) gateway

    B. Application programming interface (API) gateway

    C. Web application firewall (WAF)

    D. Database activity monitor (DAM)

43. Firewalls can detect attack traffic by using all these methods *except* _____.

    A. Known past behavior in the environment

    B. Identity of the malicious user

    C. Point of origination

    D. Signature matching

44. Transport Layer Security (TLS) provides _____ and _____ for communications.

    A. Privacy, security

    B. Security, optimization

    C. Privacy, integrity

    D. Enhancement, privacy

45. Transport Layer Security (TLS) uses a new _____ for each secure connection.

    A. Symmetric key

    B. Asymmetric key

    C. Public-private key pair

    D. Inverse comparison

46. A virtual private network (VPN) is used to protect data in transit by _____.

    A. Securing each end of a client-server connection

    B. Creating an encrypted tunnel between two endpoints

    C. Encrypting databases

    D. Restricting key access to only eight parties

47. The employment of users in dynamic software testing should best be augmented by
_____.

    A. Having the developers review the code

    B. Having the developers perform dynamic testing

    C. Using automated agents to perform dynamic testing

    D. Social engineering

48. Why do developers have an inherent conflict of interest in testing software they've created?

    A. They are notoriously bad, as a group, at testing.

    B. They work for the same department as the testing personnel.

    C. They have a vested interest in having the software perform well.

    D. They are never trained on testing procedures.

49. Sandboxing can often be used for _____.

    A. Optimizing the production environment by moving processes that are not frequently used into the sandbox

    B. Allowing secure remote access for users who need resources in the cloud environment

    C. Running malware for analysis purposes

    D. Creating secure subnets of the production environment

50. Sandboxing can often be used for _____.

    A. Testing user awareness and training

    B. Testing security response capabilities

    C. Testing software before putting it into production

    D. Testing regulatory response to new configurations and modifications

51. Application virtualization can typically be used for _____.

    A. Running an application in a non-native environment

    B. Installing updates to a system's operating system (OS)

    C. Preventing escalation of privilege by untrusted users

    D. Enhancing performance of systems

52. Application virtualization can typically be used for _____.

    A. Denying access to untrusted users

    B. Detecting and mitigating distributed denial of service (DDoS) attacks

    C. Replacing encryption as a necessary control

    D. Running an application on an endpoint without installing it

53. Any organization that complies with ISO 27034 will have a maximum of
_____ Organizational Normative Framework(s) (ONF)(s).

   A. 0

   B. 1

   C. 5

   D. 25

54. Under ISO 27034, every application within a given organization will have an attendant
set of controls assigned to it; the controls for a given application are listed in the
_____.

   A. ONF

   B. ANF

   C. TTF

   D. FTP

55. Static application security testing (SAST) is usually considered a _____
form of testing.

   A. White-box

   B. Black-box

   C. Gray-box

   D. Parched field

56. Static application security testing (SAST) examines _____.

   A. Software outcomes

   B. User performance

   C. System durability

   D. Source code

57. Dynamic application security testing (DAST) is usually considered a
_____ form of testing.

   A. White-box

   B. Black-box

   C. Gray-box

   D. Parched field

58. Dynamic application security testing (DAST) checks software functionality in
_____.

   A. The production environment

   B. A runtime state

   C. The cloud

   D. An IaaS configuration

59. Vulnerability scans are dependent on _____ in order to function.

    A. Privileged access

    B. Vulnerability signatures

    C. Malware libraries

    D. Forensic analysis

60. Due to their reliance on vulnerability signatures, vulnerability scanners will not detect _____.

    A. User error

    B. Improper control selection

    C. Cloud vulnerabilities

    D. Unknown vulnerabilities

61. Penetration testing is a(n) _____ form of security assessment.

    A. Active

    B. Comprehensive

    C. Total

    D. Inexpensive

62. Dynamic software security testing should include _____.

    A. Source code review

    B. User training

    C. Penetration testing

    D. Known bad data

63. According to Open Web Application Security Project (OWASP) recommendations, active software security testing should include all of the following *except* _____.

    A. Information gathering

    B. User surveys

    C. Configuration and deployment management testing

    D. Identity management testing

64. According to Open Web Application Security Project (OWASP) recommendations, active software security testing should include all of the following *except* _____.

    A. Authentication testing

    B. Authorization testing

    C. Session management testing

    D. Privacy review testing

65. According to Open Web Application Security Project (OWASP) recommendations, active software security testing should include all of the following *except* _____.

   A. Session initiation testing

   B. Input validation testing

   C. Testing for error handling

   D. Testing for weak cryptography

66. According to Open Web Application Security Project (OWASP) recommendations, active software security testing should include all of the following *except* _____.

   A. Business logic testing

   B. Client-side testing

   C. Intuition testing

   D. Information gathering

67. Static software security testing typically uses _____ as a measure of how thorough the testing was.

   A. Number of testers

   B. Flaws detected

   C. Code coverage

   D. Malware hits

68. Dynamic software security testing typically uses _____ as a measure of how thorough the testing was.

   A. User coverage

   B. Code coverage

   C. Path coverage

   D. Total coverage

69. Software security testing should involve both known good and known bad data in order to simulate both _____ and _____.

   A. Managers, users

   B. Regulators, users

   C. Vendors, users

   D. Users, attackers

70. Training programs should be tracked and monitored in order to fulfill both
_____ and _____ requirements. Choose the best response.

  A. Business, security

  B. Regulatory, legal

  C. User, managerial

  D. Vendor, supplier

71. Task-centric training is typically for _____.

  A. All personnel

  B. Specific personnel

  C. Management personnel

  D. HR personnel

72. Awareness training is typically for _____.

  A. All personnel

  B. Specific personnel

  C. Management personnel

  D. HR personnel

73. Why is cloud security training particularly important for software developers?

  A. Software developers are the mainstay of every cloud environment.

  B. You can't have a cloud environment without software developers.

  C. Security controls cannot be added to software after the fact and must be included from the very first steps of software development.

  D. Many modern software developers don't understand how the code underlying the libraries they use actually works.

74. Software developers should receive cloud-specific training that highlights the challenges involved with having a production environment that operates in the cloud. One of these challenges is _____.

  A. The massive additional hacking threat, especially from foreign sources

  B. The prevalent use of encryption in all data life-cycle phases

  C. Drastic increase of risk due to distributed denial of service (DDoS) attacks

  D. Additional regulatory mandates

75. Software developers should receive cloud-specific training that highlights the challenges involved with having a production environment that operates in the cloud. One of these challenges is _____.

  A. Lack of management oversight

  B. Additional workload in creating governance for two environments (the cloud data center and client devices)

    C. Increased threat of malware

    D. The need for process isolation

76. Which security technique is *most* preferable when creating a limited functionality for customer service personnel to review account data related to sales made to your clientele?

    A. Anonymization

    B. Masking

    C. Encryption

    D. Training

77. At which phase of the software development lifecycle (SDLC) is user involvement *most* crucial?

    A. Define

    B. Design

    C. Develop

    D. Test

78. At which phase of the software development lifecycle (SDLC) should security personnel first be involved?

    A. Define

    B. Design

    C. Develop

    D. Test

79. At which phase of the software development lifecycle (SDLC) is it probably *most* useful to involve third-party personnel?

    A. Define

    B. Design

    C. Develop

    D. Test

80. In software development lifecycle (SDLC) implementations that include a Secure Operations phase, which of the following security techniques or tools are implemented during that phase?

    A. Vulnerability assessments and penetration testing

    B. Performance testing and security control validation

    C. Requirements fulfillment testing

    D. Threat modeling and secure design review

81. A cloud environment that lacks security controls is vulnerable to exploitation, data loss, and interruptions. Conversely, excessive use of security controls _____.

    A. Can lead to data breaches

    B. Causes electromagnetic interference

    C. Will affect quality of service

    D. Can cause regulatory noncompliance

82. A cloud environment that lacks security controls is vulnerable to exploitation, data loss, and interruptions. Conversely, excessive use of security controls _____.

    A. Can lead to distributed denial of service (DDoS)

    B. Allows malware infections

    C. Increases the risk of adverse environmental effects

    D. Is an unnecessary expense

83. A cloud environment that lacks security controls is vulnerable to exploitation, data loss, and interruptions. Conversely, excessive use of security controls _____.

    A. Can lead to customer dissatisfaction

    B. Is a risk to health and human safety

    C. Brings down the organization's stock price

    D. Negates the need for insurance

84. You are the security manager for an online retail sales company with 100 employees and a production environment hosted in a platform as a service (PaaS) model with a major cloud provider. According to your company policies, personnel are allowed to work equally from the company offices and their own homes or other locations, using their personal IT devices. The policies also dictate which application programming interfaces (APIs) can be used to access and manipulate company data and the process for getting an API added to the list of approved programs. You conduct an approved scan of the company data set in the cloud, with the provider's permission. This allows you to catalog all APIs that have accessed and manipulated company data through authorized user accounts in the last month. The scan reveals that 300 different APIs were used by authorized personnel. Of these, 30 had been approved by the company and were on the list. Of the following, what is the *most* reasonable immediate action?

    A. Delete accounts of all users who had utilized unapproved APIs to access company data.

    B. Suspend access for all users who had utilized unapproved APIs to access company data.

    C. Block all unapproved APIs from accessing company data.

    D. Notify whomever you report to in the company hierarchy, and suggest bringing the matter to the attention of senior management immediately.

85. You are the security manager for an online retail sales company with 100 employees and a production environment hosted in a platform as a service (PaaS) model with a major cloud provider. According to your company policies, personnel are allowed to work equally from the company offices and their own homes or other locations, using their personal IT devices. The policies also dictate which application programming interfaces (APIs) can be used to access and manipulate company data and the process for getting an API added to the list of approved programs. You conduct an approved scan of the company data set in the cloud, with the provider's permission. This allows you to catalog all APIs that have accessed and manipulated company data through authorized user accounts in the last month. The scan reveals that 300 different APIs were used by authorized personnel. Of these, 30 had been approved by the company and were on the list. You've brought the matter to the attention of the chief executive officer (CEO), who understands the issue and asks for your recommendation. What is probably the best suggestion?

A. Gather more data about how users are utilizing the APIs and for what purposes.

B. Delete accounts of all users who had utilized unapproved APIs to access company data.

C. Suspend access for all users who had utilized unapproved APIs to access company data.

D. Block all unapproved APIs from accessing company data.

86. You are the security manager for an online retail sales company with 100 employees and a production environment hosted in a platform as a service (PaaS) model with a major cloud provider. According to your company policies, personnel are allowed to work equally from the company offices and their own homes or other locations, using their personal IT devices. The policies also dictate which application programming interfaces (APIs) can be utilized to access and manipulate company data and the process for getting an API added to the list of approved programs. You conduct an approved scan of the company data set in the cloud, with the provider's permission. This allows you to catalog all APIs that have accessed and manipulated company data through authorized user accounts in the last month. The scan reveals that 300 different APIs were used by authorized personnel. Of these, 30 had been approved by the company and were on the list. Upon performing an information-gathering investigation at the behest of the chief executive officer (CEO), you determine that these APIs increased productivity 387 percent over the period since they were adopted, at a cost that is negligible compared to getting even one API through the company's current approval process. What is your suggestion on how to handle the situation?

A. Retroactively put all the APIs currently in use through the formal approval process, and require that all future APIs users want to install also get approved.

B. Have the CEO waive formal approval processing for all APIs currently in use, granting them approval, but require all future APIs be approved through that process.

C. Punish all employees who have installed or used any of the rogue APIs for violating company policy.

D. Change the policy.

87. You are the security manager for an online retail sales company with 100 employees and a production environment hosted in a platform as a service (PaaS) model with a major cloud provider. According to your company policies, personnel are allowed to work equally from the company offices and their own homes or other locations, using their personal IT devices. The policies also dictate which application programming interfaces (APIs) can be utilized to access and manipulate company data and the process for getting an API added to the list of approved programs. You conduct an approved scan of the company data set in the cloud, with the provider's permission. This allows you to catalog all APIs that have accessed and manipulated company data through authorized user accounts in the last month. The scan reveals that 300 different APIs were used by authorized personnel. Of these, 30 had been approved by the company and were on the list. As a subject matter expert, what should you also recommend to the chief executive officer (CEO)?

A. Reward the users who committed the infractions, for aiding the company even when they were violating the policy.

B. Replace all the personnel that violated the policy, and have the new personnel use the new policy from their start of hire.

C. Restrict user access to possible APIs.

D. Augment the current set of security controls used by the company in order to offset risks posed by the anticipated use of even more APIs from unknown sources.

88. You are the security manager for an online retail sales company with 100 employees and a production environment hosted in a platform as a service (PaaS) model with a major cloud provider. According to your company policies, personnel are allowed to work equally from the company offices and their own homes or other locations, using their personal IT devices. The policies also allow users to select which application programming interfaces (APIs) they install and use on their own devices in order to access and manipulate company data. Of the following, what is a security control you'd like to implement to offset the risk(s) incurred by this practice?

A. Encrypt all routers between mobile users and the cloud.

B. Use additional anti-malware detection capabilities on both user devices and the environment to which they connect.

C. Implement strong multifactor authentication on all user-owned devices.

D. Employ regular performance monitoring in the cloud environment to ensure that the cloud provider is meeting the service level agreement (SLA) targets.

89. You are the security manager for an online retail sales company with 100 employees and a production environment hosted in a platform as a service (PaaS) model with a major cloud provider. According to your company policies, personnel are allowed to work equally from the company offices and their own homes or other locations, using their personal IT devices. The policies also allow users to select which application programming interfaces (APIs) they install and use on their own devices in order to access and manipulate company data. Of the following, what is a security control you'd like to implement to offset the risk(s) incurred by this practice?

A. Regular and widespread integrity checks on sampled data throughout the managed environment

B. More extensive and granular background checks on all employees, particularly new hires

C. Inclusion of references to all applicable regulations in the policy documents

D. Increased enforcement of separation of duties for all workflows

90. You are the security manager for an online retail sales company with 100 employees and a production environment hosted in a platform as a service (PaaS) model with a major cloud provider. According to your company policies, personnel are allowed to work equally from the company offices and their own homes or other locations, using their personal IT devices. The policies also allow users to select which application programming interfaces (APIs) they install and use on their own devices in order to access and manipulate company data. Of the following, what is a security control you'd like to implement to offset the risk(s) incurred by this practice?

A. Enact secure connections between the user devices and the cloud environment using end-to-end encryption.

B. Enact secure connections between the user devices and the cloud environment using link encryption.

C. Employ additional user training.

D. Tunnel all connections with a virtual private network (VPN).

91. Users in your organization have been leveraging application programming interfaces (APIs) for enhancing their productivity in the cloud environment. To ensure that you are securing API access to the production environment, you should deploy _____ and _____.

A. Secure Sockets Layer (SSL) and message-level cryptography

B. Transport Layer Security (TLS) and message-level cryptography

C. SSL and whole drive encryption

D. TLS and whole drive encryption

92. You implement identity and access management (IAM) in order to control access between subjects and objects. What is the ultimate purpose of this effort?

A. Identification. Determine who the specific, individual subjects are.

B. Authentication. Verify and validate any identification assertions.

C. Authorization. Grant subjects permissions to objects once they've been authenticated.

D. Accountability. Be able to reconstruct a narrative of who accessed what.

93. _____ is perhaps the main external factor driving identity and access management (IAM) efforts.

A. Regulation

B. Business need

C. The evolving threat landscape

D. Monetary value

94. Whether in a cloud or traditional environment, it is important to implement both _____ and _____ access controls.

    A. Internal and managed

    B. Provider and customer

    C. Physical and logical

    D. Administrative and technical

95. Access to specific data sets should be granted by _____.

    A. The data subjects

    B. The data owners

    C. The data processors

    D. The data regulators

96. Access should be granted based on all of the following *except* _____.

    A. Policy

    B. Business needs

    C. Performance

    D. Acceptable risk

97. Federation allows _____ across organizations.

    A. Role replication

    B. Encryption

    C. Policy

    D. Access

98. Federation should be _____ to the users.

    A. Hostile

    B. Proportional

    C. Transparent

    D. Expensive

99. A web application firewall (WAF) understands which protocol(s)?

    A. All protocols that use the Internet as a medium

    B. Transport Layer Security (TLS)

    C. Hypertext Transfer Protocol (HTTP)

    D. File Transfer Protocol (FTP)

100. Web application firewalls and database activity monitors function at levels
_____ and _____ of the Open Systems Interconnection
(OSI) model, respectively.

A. 1 and 7

B. 7 and 1

C. 7 and 7

D. 3 and 4

101. What can tokenization be used for?

A. Encryption

B. Compliance with the Payment Card Industry Data Security Standard (PCI DSS)

C. Enhancing the user experience

D. Giving management oversight to e-commerce functions

102. Merchants who accept credit card payments can avoid some of the compliance burden
for the Payment Card Industry Data Security Standard (PCI DSS) by outsourcing the
tokenization function to _____.

A. A third party

B. The data owner

C. The data subject

D. The PCI Security Standards Council

103. Which of the following is an example of useful and sufficient data masking of the string
"CCSP"?

A. XCSP

B. PSCC

C. TtLp

D. 3X91

104. A cloud-based sandbox should *not* be used for _____.

A. Application interoperability testing

B. Processing sensitive data

C. Application security testing

D. Malware analysis

105. Which of the following should occur at each stage of the software development lifecycle
(SDLC)?

A. Added functionality

B. Management review

C. Verification and validation

D. Repurposing of any newly developed components

106. Software that includes security elements from the outset of the software development lifecycle (SDLC) process will be _____.

    A. More secure in deployment

    B. Less secure in deployment

    C. More likely to malfunction

    D. Less likely to malfunction

107. Software that includes security elements from the outset of the software development lifecycle (SDLC) process will _____.

    A. Be less expensive to operate securely in the production environment

    B. Be more expensive to operate securely in the production environment

    C. Not be interoperable with other software and systems in the production environment

    D. Have a greater likelihood of interoperability with other software and systems in the production environment

108. The inclusion of security controls in the software design process is dictated by _____.

    A. The National Institute of Standards and Technology (NIST) 800-37

    B. The American Institute of Certified Public Accountants (AICPA)

    C. ISO 27034

    D. The Health Insurance Portability and Accountability Act (HIPAA)

109. Software development should be perceived as _____.

    A. Including all members of the organization

    B. The paramount goal of the organization

    C. The greatest risk to the organization

    D. A lifecycle

110. Dynamic testing of software is perhaps most useful for _____.

    A. Simulating negative test cases

    B. Finding errors in the source code

    C. Determining the effect of social engineering

    D. Penetration tests

Chapter 5

Domain 5: Cloud Security Operations

Domain 5 in the Certified Cloud Security Professional (CCSP) Exam Outline both introduces some significant new concepts, such as the physical design of a data center and the attendant standards and guidelines, and restates some material covered in earlier domains, such as multitenancy, resource pooling, and the like.

1. What is the *primary* incident response goal?

    A. Remediating the incident

    B. Reverting to the last known good state

    C. Determining the scope of the possible loss

    D. Outcomes dictated by business requirements

2. You are in charge of building a cloud data center. Which raised floor level is sufficient to meet standard requirements?

    A. 10 inches

    B. 8 inches

    C. 18 inches

    D. 2 feet

3. You are in charge of building a cloud data center. What purposes does the raised floor serve?

    A. Allows airflow and increases structural soundness for holding large components

    B. Cold air feed and a place to run wires for the machines

    C. Additional storage for critical components and a dedicated access to a landline

    D. Fire suppression systems and personnel safety

4. You are in charge of building a cloud data center. Which of the following is a useful rack configuration for regulating airflow?

    A. Exhaust fans on racks facing the inlet vents of other racks

    B. Inlet fans on racks facing exhaust fans of other racks

    C. All racks perpendicular to each other

    D. Exhaust fans on racks facing exhaust fans on other racks

5. An event is something that can be measured within the environment. An incident is a(n) _____ event.

    A. Deleterious

    B. Negative

    C. Unscheduled

    D. Major

6. Which of the following factors would probably *most* affect the design of a cloud data center?

    A. Geographic location

    B. Functional purpose

    C. Cost

    D. Aesthetic intent

7. All of the following elements must be considered in the design of a cloud data center *except* _____.

   A. External standards, such as ITIL or ISO 27001

   B. Physical environment

   C. Types of services offered

   D. Native language of the majority of customers

8. In designing a data center to meet their own needs and provide optimum revenue/profit, the cloud provider will most likely aim to enhance _____.

   A. Functionality

   B. Automation of services

   C. Aesthetic value

   D. Inherent value

9. You are the security officer for a small cloud provider offering public cloud infrastructure as a service (IaaS); your clients are predominantly from the education sector, located in North America. Of the following technology architecture traits, which is probably the one your organization would most likely want to focus on?

   A. Reducing mean time to repair (MTTR)

   B. Reducing mean time between failure (MTBF)

   C. Reducing the recovery time objective (RTO)

   D. Automating service enablement

10. What is perhaps the *main* way in which software-defined networking (SDN) solutions facilitate security in the cloud environment?

   A. Monitoring outbound traffic

   B. Monitoring inbound traffic

   C. Segmenting networks

   D. Preventing distributed denial of service (DDoS) attacks

11. The logical design of a cloud environment can enhance the security offered in that environment. For instance, in a software as a service (SaaS) cloud, the provider can incorporate _____ capabilities into the application itself.

   A. High-speed processing

   B. Logging

   C. Performance-enhancing

   D. Cross-platform functionality

12. You are tasked with managing a cloud data center in Los Angeles; your customers are mostly from the entertainment industry, and you are offering both platform as a service (PaaS) and software as a service (SaaS) capabilities. From a physical design standpoint, you are probably going to be most concerned with _____.

   A. Offering digital rights management (DRM) capabilities

   B. Insuring against seasonal floods

   C. Preventing all malware infection potential

   D. Ensuring that the racks and utilities can endure an earthquake

13. You are the security manager for a small retail business involved mainly in direct e-commerce transactions with individual customers (members of the public). The bulk of your market is in Asia, but you do fulfill orders globally. Your company has its own data center located within its headquarters building in Hong Kong, but it also uses a public cloud environment for contingency backup and archiving purposes. Your cloud provider is changing its business model at the end of your contract term, and you have to find a new provider. In choosing providers, which tier of the Uptime Institute rating system should you be looking for, if minimizing cost is your ultimate goal?

   A. 1

   B. 3

   C. 4

   D. 8

14. You are the security manager for a small retail business involved mainly in direct e-commerce transactions with individual customers (members of the public). The bulk of your market is in Asia, but you do fulfill orders globally. Your company has its own data center located within its headquarters building in Hong Kong, but it also uses a public cloud environment for contingency backup and archiving purposes. Your cloud provider is changing its business model at the end of your contract term, and you have to find a new provider. In choosing providers, which of the following functionalities will you consider absolutely essential?

   A. Distributed denial of service (DDoS) protections

   B. Constant data mirroring

   C. Encryption

   D. Hashing

15. You are the security manager for a small retail business involved mainly in direct e-commerce transactions with individual customers (members of the public). The bulk of your market is in Asia, but you do fulfill orders globally. Your company has its own data center located within its headquarters building in Hong Kong, but it also uses a public cloud environment for contingency backup and archiving purposes. Which of the following standards are you most likely to adopt?

   A. National Institute of Standards and Technology (NIST) 800-37

   B. General Data Protection Regulation (GDPR)

   C. ISO 27001

   D. Sarbanes–Oxley Act (SOX)

16. You are the security manager for a small retail business involved mainly in direct e-commerce transactions with individual customers (members of the public). The bulk of your market is in Asia, but you do fulfill orders globally. Your company has its own data center located within its headquarters building in Hong Kong, but it also uses a public cloud environment for contingency backup and archiving purposes. Your company has decided to expand its business to include selling and monitoring life-support equipment for medical providers. What characteristic do you need to ensure is offered by your cloud provider?

    A. Full automation of security controls within the cloud data center

    B. Tier 4 of the Uptime Institute certifications

    C. Global remote access

    D. Prevention of ransomware infections

17. When designing a cloud data center, which of the following aspects is *not* necessary to ensure continuity of operations during contingency operations?

    A. Access to clean water

    B. Broadband data connection

    C. Extended battery backup

    D. Physical access to the data center

18. You are the security manager for a small surgical center. Your organization is reviewing upgrade options for its current, on-premises data center. In order to best meet your needs, which one of the following options would you recommend to senior management?

    A. Building a completely new data center

    B. Leasing a data center that is currently owned by another firm

    C. Renting private cloud space in a Tier 2 data center

    D. Staying with the current data center

19. When building a new data center within an urban environment, which of the following is probably the *most* restrictive aspect?

    A. The size of the plot

    B. Utility availability

    C. Staffing

    D. Municipal codes

20. When you are building a new data center in a rural setting, which of the following is probably the *most* restrictive aspect?

    A. Natural disasters

    B. Staffing

    C. Availability of emergency services

    D. Municipal codes

21. All tiers of the Uptime Institute standards for data centers require _____ hours of on-site generator fuel.

   A. 6

   B. 10

   C. 12

   D. 15

22. The American Society of Heating, Refrigeration, and Air Conditioning Engineers (ASHRAE) guidelines for internal environmental conditions within a data center suggest that a temperature setting of _____ degrees (F) would be too high.

   A. 93

   B. 80

   C. 72

   D. 32

23. Internal data center conditions that exceed the American Society of Heating, Refrigeration, and Air Conditioning Engineers (ASHRAE) guidelines for humidity could lead to an increase of the potential for all of the following *except* _____.

   A. Biological intrusion

   B. Electrical shorting

   C. Corrosion/oxidation

   D. Social engineering

24. Setting thermostat controls by measuring the _____ temperature will result in the highest energy costs.

   A. Server inlet

   B. Return air

   C. Under-floor

   D. External ambient

25. Heating, ventilation, and air conditioning (HVAC) systems cool the data center by pushing warm air into _____.

   A. The server inlets

   B. Underfloor plenums

   C. HVAC intakes

   D. The outside world

26. It is important to include _____ in the design of underfloor plenums if they are also used for wiring.

   A. Mantraps

   B. Sequestered channels

   C. Heat sinks

   D. Tight gaskets

27. Cable management includes all of the following *except* _____.

   A. Tagging cables

   B. Removing unused/obsolete cables

   C. Banding and bundling cables

   D. Removing unused machines

28. How often should cable management efforts take place?

   A. Annually

   B. Continually

   C. Quarterly

   D. Weekly

29. You are designing a private cloud data center for an insurance underwriter, to be located in a major metropolitan area. Which of the following airflow management schemes is preferable?

   A. Hot aisle

   B. Cold aisle

   C. Either hot aisle or cold aisle

   D. Free flow

30. Which of the following factors will probably have the *most* impact on the cost of running your heating, ventilation, and air conditioning (HVAC) systems?

   A. Whether you choose hot or cold aisle containment

   B. The external ambient environment

   C. The initial cost of the HVAC systems

   D. Proper cable maintenance

31. You are designing a Tier 4 data center for a large hospital. In order to plan for the possibility of losing utility power, in addition to having sufficient generators, you should plan to locate the data center _____.

   A. In an urban setting

   B. In a rural environment

   C. Near a coast

   D. At the border of different counties, regions, or states

32. Because most cloud environments rely heavily on virtualization, it is important to lock down or harden the virtualization software, or any software involved in virtualization. Which of the following is *not* an element of hardening software?

   A. Removing unused services and libraries

   B. Maintaining a strict license catalog

   C. Patching and updating as necessary

   D. Removing default accounts

33. Which of the following is *not* an aspect of host hardening?

    A. Removing all unnecessary software and services

    B. Patching and updating as needed

    C. Performing more frequent and thorough audits on the host

    D. Installing a host-based firewall and an intrusion detection system (IDS)

34. Which of the following is *not* an element of ongoing configuration maintenance?

    A. Penetration tests of guest OSs and hosts

    B. Social engineering tests of all users

    C. Patch management of guest OSs, hosts, and applications

    D. Vulnerability scans of guest OSs and hosts

35. Storage controllers will be used in conjunction with all the following protocols *except* _____.

    A. HTTPS

    B. Internet Small Computer Systems Interface (iSCSI)

    C. Fibre Channel

    D. Fibre Channel over Ethernet

36. Which of these characteristics of a virtualized network adds risks to the cloud environment?

    A. Redundancy

    B. Scalability

    C. Pay-per-use

    D. Self-service

37. Security best practices in a virtualized network environment would include which of the following?

    A. Using distinct ports and port groups for various virtual local area networks (VLANs) on a virtual switch rather than running them through the same port

    B. Running Internet Small Computer Systems Interface (iSCSI) traffic unencrypted in order to have it observed and monitored by a network intrusion detection system (NIDS)

    C. Adding a host-based intrusion detection system (HIDS) to all virtual guests

    D. Hardening all outward-facing firewalls in order to make them resistant to attack

38. In order to enhance virtual environment isolation and security, a best practice is to _____.

    A. Ensure that all virtual switches are not connected to the physical network

    B. Ensure that management systems are connected to a different physical network than the production systems

    C. Never connect a virtual switch to a physical host

    D. Connect physical devices only with virtual switches

39. Which of the following is a risk that stems from a virtualized environment?

    A. Live virtual machines in the production environment are moved from one host to another in the clear.

    B. Cloud data centers can become a single point of failure.

    C. It is difficult to find and contract with multiple utility providers of the same type (electric, water, etc.).

    D. Modern service level-agreement (SLA) demands are stringent and very hard to meet.

40. Which of the following is a risk that stems from a pooled-resources environment?

    A. Loss of data to widespread phishing attacks

    B. Loss of availability due to widespread distributed denial of service (DDoS) attacks

    C. Loss of data to widespread insider threat

    D. Loss of data to law enforcement seizure of neighboring assets

41. Modern managed cloud service providers will often use secure keyboard/video/mouse (KVM) devices within their data centers. These devices are extremely expensive compared to their non-secured counterparts. Which of the following is one of the reasons cloud service providers do this?

    A. They have plenty of revenue and can afford it.

    B. They have invested heavily in the secure KVM market.

    C. Cloud data centers need very few of these devices.

    D. Managed cloud providers often manufacture their own devices as well.

42. The American Society of Heating, Refrigeration, and Air Conditioning Engineers (ASHRAE) guidelines for internal environmental conditions within a data center suggest that a temperature setting of _____ degrees (F) would be too low.

    A. 93

    B. 80

    C. 72

    D. 32

43. Modern managed cloud service providers will often use secure keyboard/video/mouse (KVM) devices within their data centers. These devices are extremely expensive compared to their non-secured counterparts. Which of the following is one of the reasons cloud service providers do this?

    A. The risk of transferring data from one customer to another is significant.

    B. The risk of devices leaving the cloud data center is significant.

    C. It makes physical inventories much easier to maintain.

    D. Audit purposes

44. A truly air-gapped machine selector will _____.

    A. Terminate a connection before creating a new connection

    B. Be made of composites and not metal

    C. Have total Faraday properties

    D. Not be portable

45. Which of the following cloud data center functions do *not* have to be performed on isolated networks?

    A. Customer access provision

    B. Management system control interface

    C. Storage controller access

    D. Customer production activities

46. Which of the following is *not* a characteristic of a virtual local area network (VLAN)?

    A. Broadcast packets sent by a machine inside the VLAN will reach all other machines in that VLAN.

    B. Broadcast packets sent from outside the VLAN will not reach other machines outside the VLAN.

    C. Broadcast packets sent from a machine outside the VLAN will not reach machines inside the VLAN.

    D. Broadcast packets sent by a machine inside the VLAN will not reach machines outside the VLAN.

47. In order for communications from inside a virtual local area network (VLAN) to reach endpoints outside the VLAN, _____.

    A. The communications must go through a gateway

    B. The traffic must be encrypted

    C. A repeater must be used

    D. The external endpoint must be in receive mode

48. Transport Layer Security (TLS) uses _____ to authenticate a connection and create a shared secret for the duration of the session.

    A. Security Assertion Markup Language (SAML) 2.0

    B. X.509 certificates

    C. 802.11X

    D. The Diffie-Hellman process

49. Halon is now illegal to use for data center fire suppression. What is the reason it was outlawed?

    A. It poses a threat to health and human safety when deployed.

    B. It can harm the environment.

    C. It does not adequately suppress fires.

    D. It causes undue damage to electronic systems.

50. When cloud computing professionals use the term *ping, power, pipe*, which of the following characteristics is *not* being described?

    A. Logical connectivity

    B. Human interaction

    C. Electricity

    D. Heating, ventilation, and air conditioning (HVAC)

51. Which of the following is *not* a goal of a site survey?

    A. Threat definition

    B. Target identification

    C. Penetration testing

    D. Facility characteristics

52. Designing system redundancy into a cloud data center allows all the following capabilities *except* _____.

    A. Incorporating additional hardware into the production environment

    B. Preventing any chance of service interruption

    C. Load-sharing/balancing

    D. Planned, controlled failover during contingency operations

53. Gaseous fire suppression systems that function by displacing oxygen need to be installed in conjunction with _____.

    A. Water cooling

    B. Filters

    C. Occupant training

    D. Failsafe or "last person out" switches

54. What aspect of data center planning occurs first?

    A. Logical design

    B. Physical design

    C. Audit

    D. Policy revision

55. Which of the following are *not* examples of personnel controls?

    A. Background checks

    B. Reference checks

    C. Strict access control mechanisms

    D. Continuous security training

56. Updating virtual machine management tools will require _____.

   A. An infusion of capital

   B. An alternate data center

   C. Sufficient redundancy

   D. Peer review

57. Access control to virtualization management tools should be _____.

   A. Rule-based

   B. Role-based

   C. User-based

   D. Discretionary

58. Before deploying a specific brand of virtualization toolset, it is important to configure it according to _____.

   A. Industry standards

   B. Prevailing law of that jurisdiction

   C. Vendor guidance

   D. Expert opinion

59. Which of the following is essential for getting full security value from your system baseline?

   A. Personnel training

   B. Documentation

   C. Host-based intrusion detection system (HIDS)

   D. Encryption

60. Which of the following is essential for getting full security value from your system baseline?

   A. Capturing and storing an image of the baseline

   B. Keeping a copy of upcoming suggested modifications to the baseline

   C. Having the baseline vetted by an objective third party

   D. Using a baseline from another industry member so as not to engage in repetitious efforts

61. Patching can be viewed as a configuration modification and therefore subject to the organization's configuration management program and methods. What may also be an aspect of patching in terms of configuration management?

   A. Patching doesn't need to be performed as a distinct effort; patching can go through the normal change request process like all other modifications.

   B. Any patches suggested or required by vendors to maintain compliance with service contracts must be made immediately, regardless of internal process restrictions.

C. Any patches suggested by third parties should not be considered as they may invalidate service contracts or warranties and negatively affect the organization's security posture.

D. The configuration or change management committee or board may grant blanket approval for patches (at a certain impact level) without the need to go through the formal change process.

62. Clustering hosts allows you to do all the following *except* _____.

    A. Meet high-availability demands

    B. Optimize performance with load balancing

    C. Enhance scalability

    D. Apply updates, patches, or configuration modifications instantly

63. Which of the following is *not* a way to apportion resources in a pooled environment?

    A. Reservations

    B. Limits

    C. Tokens

    D. Shares

64. A loosely coupled storage cluster will have performance and capacity limitations based on the _____.

    A. Physical backplane connecting it

    B. Total number of nodes in the cluster

    C. Amount of usage demanded

    D. The performance and capacity in each node

65. When putting a system into maintenance mode, it's important to do all of the following *except* _____.

    A. Transfer any live virtual guests off the host

    B. Turn off logging

    C. Lock out the system from accepting any new guests

    D. Notify customers if there are any interruptions

66. Typically, a cloud customer seeking stand-alone hosting will expect all of the following *except* _____.

    A. More control over governance of the environment

    B. Greater administrative control of the environment

    C. Higher overall security of the environment

    D. Lower costs for the environment

67. Methods for achieving "high availability" cloud environments include all of the following except _____.

   A. Extreme redundancy

   B. Multiple system vendors for the same services

   C. Explicitly documented business continuity and disaster recovery (BC/DR) functions in the service-level agreement (SLA) or contract

   D. Failover capability back to the customer's on-premises environment

68. You are in charge of a cloud migration for your organization. You anticipate attack traffic from various sources, each using a variety of both automated and manual intrusion techniques. In order to deter novel attacks used only against your organization, you would be wise to employ firewalls that use _____ to detect threats.

   A. Attack signatures

   B. Behavioral outliers

   C. Content filters

   D. Biometric templates

69. Firewalls can be included in all the following aspects of a cloud environment except _____.

   A. The guest OS

   B. The cloud data center IT architecture

   C. Bandwidth providers used to connect to the cloud

   D. Applications used to manipulate data in the cloud

70. A honeypot can be used for all the following purposes except _____.

   A. Gathering threat intelligence

   B. Luring attackers

   C. Distracting attackers

   D. Delaying attackers

71. Which of the following should honeypots contain?

   A. Inward-facing connections

   B. Network schematics

   C. Production data

   D. Detection systems

72. Because all cloud access is remote access, contact between users and the environment should include all of the following except _____.

   A. Encryption

   B. Secure login with complex passwords

   C. Once in-all in

   D. Logging and audits

73. Most attacks that overcome encryption protections exploit _____.

    A. Mathematical principles

    B. Misconfigurations

    C. Supercomputers

    D. Statistical probabilities

74. Administrators and engineers who work for cloud service providers will have a significant amount of control over multiple customer environments and therefore pose a severe risk. Which of the following is *not* a technique used to mitigate this level of increased risk from privileged users in the cloud data center?

    A. Two-person control

    B. Enhanced logging of administrative activity

    C. Granting privileged access only on a temporary basis

    D. Assigning permanent administrators to select customer accounts

75. Which of these is a vital action to determine whether the business continuity and disaster recovery (BC/DR) effort has a chance of being successful?

    A. Perform an integrity check on archived data to ensure that the backup process is not corrupting the data.

    B. Encrypt all archived data to ensure that it can't be exposed while at rest in the long term.

    C. Periodically restore from backups.

    D. Train all personnel on BC/DR actions they should take to preserve health and human safety.

76. Patches do all the following *except* _____.

    A. Address newly discovered vulnerabilities

    B. Solve cloud interoperability problems

    C. Add new features and capabilities to existing systems

    D. Address performance issues

77. When applying patches, it is necessary to do all of the following *except* _____.

    A. Test the patch in a sandbox that simulates the production environment

    B. Put the patch through the formal change management process

    C. Be prepared to roll back to the last known good build

    D. Inform users of any impact or interruptions

78. Which of the following is a risk associated with automated patching?

    A. Users can be leveraged by intruders.

    B. A patch may not be applicable to a given environment.

    C. Patches can come loaded with malware, in a Trojan horse attack.

    D. Automated patching is slow and inefficient.

79. Which of the following is a risk associated with automated patching, especially in the cloud?

    A. Snapshot/saved virtual machine (VM) images won't take a patch.

    B. Remote access disallows patching.

    C. Cloud service providers aren't responsible for patching.

    D. Patches aren't applied among all cloud data centers.

80. Which of the following is a risk associated with automated patching, especially in the cloud?

    A. Patches may interfere with some tenants' production environments.

    B. Patches don't work with software as a service (SaaS) service models.

    C. Patches don't work with private cloud builds.

    D. Vendors don't issue patches to cloud providers.

81. Which of the following is a risk associated with manual patching, especially in the cloud?

    A. It can happen too quickly.

    B. Vendors release patches that work only with their proprietary automated tools.

    C. It's not scalable.

    D. Users can be tricked into installing malware that looks like a patch.

82. Which of the following is a risk associated with manual patching especially in the cloud?

    A. No notice before the impact is realized

    B. There is a lack of applicability to the environment.

    C. Patches may or may not address the vulnerability they were designed to fix.

    D. The possibility for human error exists.

83. You are the security manager for an organization that uses the cloud for its production environment. According to your contract with the cloud provider, your organization is responsible for patching. A new patch is issued by one of your vendors. You decide not to apply it immediately for fear of interoperability problems. What additional risk are you accepting?

    A. The cloud provider will suspend your access for violating its terms of service.

    B. The cloud provider may sue your organization for breach of contract.

    C. Your organization is subject to the vulnerability the patch addresses.

    D. Your end clients will no longer trust your organization, and this will hurt your revenue flow.

84. You are the security manager for an organization that uses the cloud for its production environment. According to your contract with the cloud provider, your organization is responsible for patching. A new patch is issued by one of your vendors. You decide not to apply it immediately for fear of interoperability problems. Who may impose penalties on your organization for this decision if the vulnerability is exploited?

    A. The cloud provider

    B. Regulators

    C. Your end clients

    D. Your Internet service provider (ISP)

85. Which of the following aspects of a cloud environment is *most* likely to add risk to the patch management process?

    A. Variations in user training and familiarity with the cloud

    B. A cloud services contract that specifies which parties are responsible for which aspects of patching

    C. VMs located physically in one location but operating in different time zones

    D. The prevalence of attacker activity at the time the patch is applied

86. Which type of web application monitoring most closely measures actual activity?

    A. Synthetic performance monitoring

    B. Real-user monitoring (RUM)

    C. Security information and event management (SIEM)

    D. Database application monitor (DAM)

87. When using real-user monitoring (RUM) for web application activity analysis, which of the following do you need to take into account?

    A. False positives

    B. Attacker baseline actions

    C. Privacy concerns

    D. Sandboxed environments

88. Synthetic performance monitoring may be preferable to real-user monitoring (RUM) because _____.

    A. It costs less

    B. It is a more accurate depiction of user behavior

    C. It is more comprehensive

    D. It can take place in the cloud

89. You are the security manager for an organization with a cloud-based production environment. You are tasked with setting up the event monitoring and logging systems. In your jurisdiction, private entities are allowed to monitor all activity involving their systems, without exception. Which of the following best describes a logging scheme you would recommend?

    A. Logging every event, at all levels of granularity, including continual screen shots, keystroke logging, and browser history

    B. Sufficient logging to reconstruct a narrative of events at some later date

    C. Logging only data related to incidents after they have occurred

    D. Logging specific data sets recommended by industry standards and guidelines

90. Who should be performing log review?

    A. Only certified, trained log review professionals with a great deal of experience with the logging tool

    B. The internal audit body

    C. External audit providers

    D. Someone with knowledge of the operation and a security background

91. Which of these subsystems is probably *most* important for acquiring useful log information?

    A. Fan

    B. RAM

    C. Clock

    D. Uninterruptible power supply (UPS)

92. A SIEM (security information and event management) system does *not* eliminate the need for human participation in _____.

    A. Log collection

    B. Responding to alerts

    C. Mathematical normalization of different logs

    D. Detecting and alerts

93. Log data should be protected _____.

    A. One level below the sensitivity level of the systems from which it was collected

    B. At least at the same sensitivity level as the systems from which it was collected

    C. With encryption in transit, at rest, and in use

    D. According to National Institute of Standards and Technology (NIST) guidelines

94. Risk is usually viewed with consideration for all the following elements *except* _____.

    A. Impact that could occur if a given circumstance is realized

    B. The likelihood or probability a circumstance will occur

   C. In the context of specific threats to an organization

   D. According to risks recently realized by other organizations in the same industry

95. Risk management entails evaluating all of the following *except* _____.

   A. Threats

   B. Vulnerabilities

   C. Countermeasures

   D. Customers

96. Impact resulting from risk being realized is often measured in terms of _____.

   A. Amount of data lost

   B. Money

   C. Amount of property lost

   D. Number of people affected

97. You are the security officer for a small nonprofit organization. You are tasked with performing a risk assessment for your organization; you have one month to complete it. The IT personnel you work with have been with the organization for many years and have built the systems and infrastructure from the ground up. They have little training and experience in the field of risk. Which type of risk assessment would you choose to conduct?

   A. Quantitative

   B. Qualitative

   C. Pro forma

   D. Informal

98. Which of the following is *most* useful in determining the single loss expectancy (SLE) of an asset?

   A. The frequency with which you expect that type of loss to occur

   B. The dollar value of the asset

   C. The sensitivity of the asset

   D. The size and scope of the asset

99. Which of the following will likely *best* help you predict the annualized rate of occurrence (ARO) of a specific loss?

   A. Threat intelligence data

   B. Historical data

   C. Vulnerability scans

   D. Aggregation analysis

100. Which of the following has the *most* effect on exposure factor (EF)?

   A. The type of threat vector

   B. The source location of the attack

   C. The target of the attack

   D. The jurisdiction where the attack takes place

101. You are a consultant, performing an external security review on a large manufacturing firm. You determine that its newest assembly plant, which cost $24 million, could be completely destroyed by a fire but that a fire suppression system could effectively protect the plant. The fire suppression system costs $15 million. An insurance policy that would cover the full replacement cost of the plant costs $1 million per month. What is the annual rate of occurrence (ARO) in this scenario?

   A. 12

   B. $24 million

   C. 1

   D. $10 million

102. You are a consultant performing an external security review on a large manufacturing firm. You determine that its newest assembly plant, which cost $24 million, could be completely destroyed by a fire but that a fire suppression system could effectively protect the plant. The fire suppression system costs $15 million. An insurance policy that would cover the full replacement cost of the plant costs $1 million per month. What would you recommend?

   A. Accept the risk of fire, and save money by not spending anything on controls/countermeasures.

   B. Get the fire suppression system.

   C. Get the insurance policy.

   D. It is impossible to decide from this information.

103. You are a consultant performing an external security review on a large manufacturing firm. You determine that its newest assembly plant, which cost $24 million, could be completely destroyed by a fire but that a fire suppression system could effectively protect the plant. The fire suppression system costs $15 million. An insurance policy that would cover the full replacement cost of the plant costs $1 million per month. In order to establish the true annualized loss expectancy (ALE), you would need all of the following information *except* _____.

   A. The amount of revenue generated by the plant

   B. The rate at which the plant generates revenue

   C. The length of time it would take to rebuild the plant

   D. The amount of product the plant creates

104. You are a consultant performing an external security review on a large manufacturing firm. You determine that its newest assembly plant, which cost $24 million, could be completely destroyed by a fire but that a fire suppression system could effectively protect the plant. The fire suppression system costs $15 million. An insurance policy that would cover the full replacement cost of the plant costs $1 million per month. The plant generates $2 million of revenue each month. The time to rebuild the plant at the current location is six months. What should you recommend?

    A. Accept the risk of fire, and save money by not spending anything on controls and countermeasures.

    B. Get the fire suppression system.

    C. Get the insurance policy.

    D. It is impossible to decide from this information.

105. Risk mitigation must *always* also entail which other method of addressing risk?

    A. Risk acceptance

    B. Risk avoidance

    C. Risk transfer

    D. Risk attenuation

106. Which of the following poses a secondary risk?

    A. Fire exit signs

    B. Oxygen-displacing fire suppression

    C. Automated fire detection systems

    D. Fail-safe fire egress paths

107. Which of the following is *not* true about risk mitigation?

    A. A given control/countermeasure should never cost more than the impact of the risk it mitigates.

    B. Risk cannot be reduced to zero.

    C. The end state of risk mitigation is risk at a tolerable level.

    D. Risk mitigation is always the best means to address risk.

108. Which of the following is *not* true about risk mitigation?

    A. The cost of the control/countermeasure per year is simple: the overall cost (of acquisition, implementation, and maintenance) divided by life span, in years.

    B. Ignoring risk is not risk mitigation; ignoring risk is risk acceptance.

    C. The cost of mitigation can be compared against the cost of a control/countermeasure to determine the optimum course of action.

    D. Risk is fluid, so all risk assessments are pointless.

109. Which comes first?

   A. Accreditation

   B. Operation

   C. Maintenance

   D. Certification

110. The National Institute of Standards and Technology (NIST) Risk Management Framework (RMF) is required for federal agencies in the United States. Which of the following is *not* a characteristic of the RMF?

   A. Automation of controls wherever possible

   B. Focuses on continual improvement and near real-time risk management

   C. Is based on cost metrics and perceived threats

   D. Links risk management at the process level to risk management at the managerial level

111. Symmetric encryption involves _____.

   A. Two key pairs, mathematically related

   B. Unknown parties, sharing information

   C. Signed certificates

   D. A shared secret

112. Symmetric encryption involves _____.

   A. The Diffie-Hellman key exchange

   B. Passing keys out of band

   C. Mathematically related key pairs

   D. A one-way mathematical algorithm for validating messages

Chapter

6

Domain 6: Legal, Risk, and Compliance

Domain 6 contains material that some candidates find the most awkward and confusing: the legal and policy elements. It also delves into compliance and how cloud customers ensure that their organization is fulfilling regulatory requirements. It is weighted much less than the previous domains on the exam, though, so this chapter is much shorter than the ones you've seen so far.

1. Which of the following is a U.S. audit standard often used to evaluate cloud providers?

   A. ISO 27001

   B. SOX

   C. SSAE 18

   D. IEC 43770

2. The Cloud Security Alliance (CSA) Security, Trust, and Assurance Registry (STAR) program has _____ tiers.

   A. Two

   B. Three

   C. Four

   D. Eight

3. The Cloud Security Alliance (CSA) Security, Trust, and Assurance Registry (STAR) program's tier of self-assessment is which of the following?

   A. Tier 1

   B. Tier 2

   C. Tier 5

   D. Tier 8

4. Alice and Bob want to use the Internet to communicate privately. They each have their own asymmetric key pairs and want to use them to create temporary symmetric keys for each connection or session. Which of the following will enable them to do this?

   A. Remote Authentication Dial-In User Service (RADIUS)

   B. Rivest-Shamir-Adelman (RSA) encryption

   C. Diffie-Hellman exchange

   D. Terminal Access Controller Access-Control System (TACACS)

5. Under European Union (EU) law, a cloud customer who gives sensitive data to a cloud provider is still legally responsible for the damages resulting from a data breach caused by the provider; the EU would say that it is the cloud customer's fault for choosing the wrong provider. This is an example of insufficient _____.

   A. Proof

   B. Evidence

   C. Due diligence

   D. Application of reasonableness

6. Which of the following is *not* an enforceable governmental request?

   A. Warrant

   B. Subpoena

   C. Court order

   D. Affidavit

7. Which of the following is *not* a way of managing risk?

    A. Mitigation

    B. Acceptance

    C. Avoidance

    D. Streamlining

8. The Organisation for Economic Cooperation and Development (OECD) is a multinational entity that creates nonbinding policy suggestions for its member countries. The OECD has published recommendations for privacy laws. One of the characteristics the OECD suggests that privacy laws include is the _____.

    A. Amorphous curtailment principle

    B. Collection limitation principle

    C. State-based incorporation principle

    D. Hard-copy instantiation principle

9. The Organisation for Economic Cooperation and Development (OECD) is a multinational entity that creates nonbinding policy suggestions for its member countries. The OECD has published recommendations for privacy laws. One of the characteristics the OECD suggests that privacy laws include is the _____.

    A. Data quality principle

    B. Transformative neologism principle

    C. Encryption matrices principle

    D. Restful state principle

10. The Organisation for Economic Cooperation and Development (OECD) is a multinational entity that creates nonbinding policy suggestions for its member countries. The OECD has published recommendations for privacy laws. One of the characteristics the OECD suggests that privacy laws include is the _____.

    A. Archipelago enhancement principle

    B. Solidity restoration principle

    C. Netherworking substrate principle

    D. Purpose specification principle

11. The Organisation for Economic Cooperation and Development (OECD) is a multinational entity that creates nonbinding policy suggestions for its member countries. The OECD has published recommendations for privacy laws. One of the characteristics the OECD suggests that privacy laws include is the _____.

    A. Use limitation principle

    B. Erstwhile substitution principle

    C. Flatline cohesion principle

    D. Airstream fluidity principle

12. The Organisation for Economic Cooperation and Development (OECD) is a multinational entity that creates nonbinding policy suggestions for its member countries. The OECD has published recommendations for privacy laws. One of the characteristics the OECD suggests that privacy laws include is the _____.

    A. Transient data principle

    B. Security safeguards principle

    C. Longtrack resiliency principle

    D. Arbitrary insulation principle

13. The Organisation for Economic Cooperation and Development (OECD) is a multinational entity that creates nonbinding policy suggestions for its member countries. The OECD has published recommendations for privacy laws. One of the characteristics the OECD suggests that privacy laws include is the _____.

    A. Volcanic principle

    B. Inherency principle

    C. Repository principle

    D. Openness principle

14. The Organisation for Economic Cooperation and Development (OECD) is a multinational entity that creates nonbinding policy suggestions for its member countries. The OECD has published recommendations for privacy laws. The OECD privacy principles influenced which lawmaking body and are readily apparent in the law(s) it created?

    A. U.S. Congress

    B. European Union (EU)

    C. Politburo

    D. International Standards Organization (ISO)

15. Which of the following is *not* a way in which an entity located outside the European Union (EU) can be allowed to gather and process privacy data belonging to EU citizens?

    A. Be located in a country with a nationwide law that complies with the EU laws.

    B. Appeal to the EU High Court for permission.

    C. Create binding contractual language that complies with the EU laws.

    D. Join the Privacy Shield program in its own country.

16. The Privacy Shield program is _____.

    A. Voluntary for non–European Union (EU) entities

    B. Mandatory for all EU entities

    C. Mandatory for all non-EU entities

    D. Voluntary for all EU entities

17. Which of the following countries does *not* have a federal privacy law that complies with the European Union (EU) General Data Protection Regulation?

   A. Canada

   B. United States

   C. Switzerland

   D. Japan

18. Which of the following countries does *not* have a federal privacy law that complies with the European Union (EU) General Data Protection Regulation?

   A. Argentina

   B. Israel

   C. Australia

   D. Brazil

19. In the United States, who manages the Privacy Shield program for voluntary compliance with European Union (EU) data privacy laws?

   A. Department of State

   B. Department of Interior

   C. Department of Trade

   D. Department of Commerce

20. You're a sophomore at a small, private medical teaching college in the midwestern United States; you make your tuition payments directly from your bank account via a debit card. Which of the following laws and standards will *not* be applicable to you, your personal data, or the data you work with as a student?

   A. Sarbanes-Oxley Act (SOX)

   B. Health Information Portability and Accountability Act (HIPAA)

   C. Payment Card Industry Data Security Standards (PCI DSS)

   D. Family Educational Rights and Privacy Act (FERPA)

21. U.S. federal entities are required to use cloud data centers within the borders of the United States only. Which law, standard, or requirement mandates this?

   A. Federal Information Security Management Act (FISMA)

   B. Federal Risk and Authorization Management Program (FedRAMP)

   C. Organisation for Economic Cooperation and Development (OECD)

   D. General Data Protection Regulation (GDPR)

22. The Cloud Security Alliance (CSA) Security, Trust, and Assurance Registry (STAR) program includes a level of certification for cloud providers that acquire third-party assessments of their environment and controls. Which STAR level is this?

    A. 1

    B. 2

    C. 3

    D. 4

23. _____ is the legal concept whereby a cloud customer is held to a reasonable expectation for providing security of its users' and clients' privacy data.

    A. Due care

    B. Due diligence

    C. Liability

    D. Reciprocity

24. Under European Union law, what is the difference between a directive and a regulation?

    A. A directive is enforced by the member states; a regulation is enforced by an international body.

    B. A directive is put in place by statute; a regulation is put in place by precedent.

    C. A directive is for local laws; a regulation is for laws dealing with matters outside the EU.

    D. A directive allows member states to create their own laws; a regulation is applied to all member states.

25. You work for a European government agency providing tax counseling services to taxpayers. On your website home page, you include a banner with the following text: "As a visitor to this website, I agree that any information I disclose to the Tax Counseling Agency can be used for any and all purposes under the General Data Protection Regulation (GDPR)." This is followed by a button that says, "I Agree": users have to click the button, or they are taken to a page that says, "Goodbye. Thank you for visiting the Tax Counseling Agency, and have a nice day."

    This method of collecting personal information is _____.

    A. Illegal under the GDPR because it is electronic and needs to be in hard copy

    B. Legal under the GDPR

    C. Illegal under the GDPR because it doesn't allow service if the visitor refuses

    D. Illegal under the GDPR because it doesn't ask the nationality of the visitor

26. Administrative penalties for violating the General Data Protection Regulation (GDPR) can range up to _____.

    A. US$100,000

    B. 500,000 euros

    C. 20,000,000 euros

    D. 1,000,000 euros

27. The European Union (EU) General Data Protection Regulation (GDPR) addresses performance by _____.

    A. Data subjects

    B. Data controllers

    C. Data processors

    D. Data controllers and processors

28. You are the security manager for a mid-sized nonprofit organization. Your organization has decided to use a software as a service (SaaS) public cloud provider for its production environment. A service contract audit reveals that while your organization has budgeted for 76 user accounts, there are currently 89 active user accounts. Your organization is paying the contract price, plus a per-account fee for every account over the contracted number.

    This is an example of costs incurred by _____.

    A. Data breach

    B. Shadow IT

    C. Intrusions

    D. Insider threat

29. An audit against the _____ will demonstrate that an organization has a holistic, comprehensive security program.

    A. Statement on Auditing Standards (SAS) 70 standard

    B. Statement on Standards for Attestation Engagements (SSAE) 18 standard

    C. Service Organization Control (SOC) 2, Type 2 report matrix

    D. ISO 27001 certification requirements

30. An audit against the _____ reporting mechanism will demonstrate that an organization has an adequate security control design.

    A. Service Organization Control (SOC) 1

    B. SOC 2, Type 1

    C. SOC 2, Type 2

    D. SOC 3

31. A(n) _____ includes reviewing the organization's current position/ performance as revealed by an audit against a given standard.

    A. Service Organization Control (SOC) report

    B. Gap analysis

    C. Audit scoping statement

    D. Federal guideline

32. An audit against the _____ will demonstrate that an organization has adequate security controls to meet its ISO 27001 requirements.

   A. Statement on Auditing Standards (SAS) 70 standard

   B. Statement on Standards for Attestation Engagements (SSAE) 18 standard

   C. ISO 27002 certification criteria

   D. National Institute of Standards and Technology (NIST) Special Publication (SP) 800-53

33. An audit scoping statement might include constraints on all of the following aspects of an environment *except* _____.

   A. Time spent in the production space

   B. Business areas and topics to be reviewed

   C. Automated audit tools allowed in the environment

   D. Not reviewing illicit activities that may be discovered

34. An audit scoping statement might include all of the following constraints *except* _____.

   A. Limitation on destructive techniques

   B. Prohibition of all personnel interviews

   C. Prohibition on access to the production environment

   D. Mandate of particular time zone review

35. You are the IT director for a European cloud service provider. In reviewing possible certifications your company may want to acquire for its data centers, you consider the possibilities of the Cloud Security Alliance (CSA) Security, Trust, and Assurance Registry (STAR) program, the Uptime Institute's tier certification motif, and _____.

   A. The National Institute of Standards and Technology (NIST) Risk Management Framework (Special Publication [SP] 800-37)

   B. The Federal Risk and Authorization Management Program (FedRAMP)

   C. ISO 27034

   D. The EuroCloud Star Audit (ECSA) program

36. Who should perform the gap analysis following an audit?

   A. The security office

   B. The auditor

   C. A department other than the audit target

   D. An external audit body other than the original auditor

37. An IT security audit is designed to reveal all of the following *except* _____.

    A. Financial fraud

    B. Malfunctioning controls

    C. Inadequate controls

    D. Failure to meet target standards and guidelines

38. What was the first international privacy standard specifically for cloud providers?

    A. National Institute of Standards and Technology (NIST) Special Publication (SP) 800-37

    B. Personal Information Protection and Electronic Documents Act

    C. Payment Card Industry

    D. ISO 27018

39. Choose the entity that has *not* published a privacy principle document that includes recognizing a subject's right to access any of their own privacy data; limitations on the use of privacy data collected from subjects; and security measures for privacy data.

    A. Organisation for Economic Cooperation and Development (OECD)

    B. American Institute of Certified Public Accountants (AICPA)

    C. The European Union (EU) parliament

    D. U.S. Congress

40. The field of digital forensics does *not* include the practice of securely _____ data.

    A. Collecting

    B. Creating

    C. Analyzing

    D. Presenting

41. Which of the following is a legal practice of removing a suspect from one jurisdiction to another in order for the suspect to face prosecution for violating laws in the latter?

    A. Applicable law

    B. Judgments

    C. Criminal law

    D. Extradition

42. In which court must the defendant be determined to have acted in a certain fashion according to the preponderance of the evidence?

    A. Civil court

    B. Criminal court

    C. Religious court

    D. Tribal court

43. You are the security manager for a retail sales company that uses a software as a service (SaaS) public cloud service. One of your employees uploads sensitive information they were *not* authorized to put in the cloud. An administrator working for the cloud provider accesses that information and uses it for an illegal purpose, benefiting the administrator and causing harm to your organization.

After you perform all the incident-response activity related to the situation, your organization determines that the price of the damage was US$125,000. Your organization sues the cloud provider, and the jury determines that your organization shares in the blame (liability) for the loss because it was your employee performing an unauthorized action that created the situation.

If the jury determines that 25 percent of the evidence shows that the situation was your organization's fault and 75 percent of the evidence shows that the situation was the cloud provider's fault, what is the likely outcome?

A. Your organization owes the cloud provider $31,250.

B. The cloud provider owes your organization $93,750.

C. Neither side owes the other party anything.

D. The cloud provider owes your organization $125,000.

44. You are the security manager for a small American tech firm and investigate an incident. Upon analysis, you determine that one of your employees was stealing proprietary material and selling it to a competitor. You inform law enforcement and turn over the forensic data with which you determined the source and nature of the theft. The prosecutor can use the material you delivered because of _____.

A. The doctrine of plain view

B. The silver platter doctrine

C. The General Data Protection Regulation (GDPR)

D. The Federal Information System Management Act (FISMA)

45. You are the security director for an online retailer in Belgium. In February 2019, an audit reveals that your company may have been responsible for exposing personal data belonging to some of your customers over the previous month. Which law is applicable in this instance?

A. Belgian law

B. The General Data Protection Regulation (GDPR)

C. National Institute of Standards and Technology (NIST) Special Publication (SP) 800-53

D. The Federal Information Systems Management Act (FISMA)

46. You are the security manager for a software company that uses platform as a service (PaaS) in a public cloud service. Your company's general counsel informs you that they have received a letter from a former employee who is filing a lawsuit against your company. You should immediately issue a(n) _____ to all personnel and offices within your company.

    A. Litigation hold notice

    B. Audit scoping letter

    C. Stop loss memo

    D. Memorandum of agreement

47. You are the security manager for a software company that uses platform as a service (PaaS) in a public cloud service. Your company's general counsel informs you that they have received a letter from a former employee who is filing a lawsuit against your company. If you do not take proper steps to retain, capture, and deliver pertinent data to the person making the request (or their attorney), the company could be facing legal problems with _____ as well as the lawsuit.

    A. Spoliation

    B. Fraud

    C. Jurisdiction

    D. Recompositing

48. You are the chief information officer (CIO) for an IT hardware manufacturer. Your company uses cloud-based software as a service (SaaS) services, including email. You receive a legal request for data pertinent to a case. Your e-discovery efforts will largely be dependent on _____.

    A. The cloud provider

    B. Regulators

    C. The cloud customer

    D. Internal IT personnel

49. You work for a company that operates a production environment in the cloud. Another company using the same cloud provider is under investigation by law enforcement for racketeering. Your company should be concerned about this because of the cloud characteristic of _____.

    A. Virtualization

    B. Pooled resources

    C. Elasticity

    D. Automated self-service

50. You are the security manager for a software company that uses platform as a service (PaaS) in a public cloud service. Your company's general counsel informs you that they have received a letter from a former employee who is filing a lawsuit against your company. What is one of the common practices used in your industry that will have to be halted until the resolution of the case?

    A. Versioning

    B. Patching

    C. Threat modeling

    D. Secure destruction

51. Your company receives a litigation hold notice from a customer that is suing you for harm caused by one of your products. You are using a managed cloud service for your production environment. You determine that the data requested by the litigant is vast and is going be very difficult to review for pertinence to the case.

    The senior executive at your firm who is making decisions about this case suggests handing over all data the company has archived for the time frame related to the case, whether or not it may be pertinent, in order to both allow the litigant to find the pertinent data and reduce the costs your company would incur if it performed the reform.

    What should be your response to the executive?

    A. This is an excellent idea; it fulfills the company's legal requirements and reduces the overall costs of the litigation.

    B. This is a good idea; it may alleviate some of the costs associated with the court case.

    C. This is a bad idea; the company might not realize the full cost savings that it expects.

    D. This is a horrible idea; it could lead to extensive unauthorized disclosure and additional lawsuits.

52. Your company receives a litigation hold notice from a customer that is suing you for harm caused by one of your products. You are using a managed cloud service for your production environment. You determine that the data requested by the litigant is vast and is going be very difficult to review for pertinence to the case.

    Which security control mechanism may also be useful in the e-discovery effort?

    A. Trained and aware personnel

    B. An egress monitoring solution (data loss prevention or data leak protection [DLP])

    C. A digital rights management (DRM) solution

    D. A multifactor authentication implementation

53. When targeting a cloud customer, a court grants an order allowing a law enforcement entity to seize _____.

    A. Electronic data

    B. Hardware

    C. Electronic data and the hardware on which it resides

    D. Only data extracted from hardware

54. Your company is defending itself during a civil trial for a breach of contract case. Personnel from your IT department have performed forensic analysis on event logs that reflect the circumstances related to the case.

    In order for your personnel to present the evidence they collected during forensic analysis as expert witnesses, you should ensure that _____.

    A. Their testimony is scripted, and they do not deviate from the script

    B. They present only evidence that is favorable to your side of the case

    C. They are trained and certified in the tools they used

    D. They are paid for their time while they are appearing in the courtroom

55. In some jurisdictions, it is mandatory that personnel conducting forensic analysis collection or analysis have a proper _____.

    A. Training credential

    B. License

    C. Background check

    D. Approved toolset

56. You run an IT security incident response team. When seizing and analyzing data for forensic purposes, your investigative personnel modify the data from its original content. For courtroom evidentiary purposes, this makes the data _____.

    A. Inadmissible

    B. Less believable, if the changes aren't documented

    C. Harder to control

    D. Easily refutable

57. You are the security manager for a small investing firm. After a heated debate regarding security control implementation, one of your employees strikes another employee with a keyboard. The local media hear about the incident and broadcast/publish stories about it under the title "Computer-related attack."

    What may be the result of this situation?

    A. A criminal trial

    B. A civil case

    C. Both criminal and civil proceedings

    D. Federal racketeering charges

58. You are the security manager for a small investing firm. After a heated debate regarding security control implementation, one of your employees strikes another employee with a keyboard. The local media hear about the incident and broadcast/publish stories about it under the title "Computer-related attack."

    In this circumstance, who would likely be prosecuted?

    A. Your organization

    B. The attacker

    C. The victim

    D. You, as the manager of both parties

59. _____ is the legal concept that describes the actions and processes a cloud customer uses to ensure that a reasonable level of protection is applied to the data in their control.

   A. Due care

   B. Due diligence

   C. Liability

   D. Reciprocity

60. Which of the following aspects of virtualization make the technology useful for evidence collection?

   A. Hypervisors

   B. Pooled resources

   C. Snapshotting

   D. Live migration

61. Which of the following practices can enhance both operational capabilities and forensic readiness?

   A. Highly trained forensic personnel

   B. Regular full backups

   C. A highly secure data archive

   D. Homomorphic encryption

62. Which of the following practices can enhance both operational capabilities and configuration management efforts?

   A. Regular backups

   B. Constant uptime

   C. Multifactor authentication

   D. File hashes

63. Which of the following is probably the *most* volatile form of data that might serve a forensic purpose?

   A. Virtual instance RAM

   B. Hardware RAM

   C. Hypervisor logs

   D. Drive storage

64. You are the security representative of a small company doing business through a cloud provider. Your company comes under investigation by law enforcement for possible wrongdoing. In performing e-discovery activity so as to comply with a court order, the cloud provider offers to ship a piece of hardware, a storage drive, from their data center to you for inspection/analysis.

What should probably be your response?

A. Yes. You want it because it gives you the most granular and comprehensive view of the pertinent data.

B. Yes. You want to be able to inspect it before law enforcement has the opportunity to review it.

C. No. You don't want the liability of possibly disclosing someone else's privacy data.

D. No. You don't want the liability of possibly damaging someone else's property.

65. The Reporting phase of forensic investigation usually involves presenting findings to _____.

A. Senior management

B. Regulators

C. The court

D. Stakeholders

66. When presenting forensic evidence in court as testimony, you should include, if at all possible, _____.

A. Your personal opinion

B. A clear, concise view of your side of the case

C. Alternative explanations

D. Historical examples that have bearing on the circumstances of the current case

67. When collecting digital evidence for forensic purposes, it is important to compare the integrity value for any copied material against _____.

A. The original

B. The backup

C. Another copy

D. The industry standard

68. Who should be responsible for ensuring the state, security, and control of all evidence, from the time it's collected until it is presented in court?

A. The data controller

B. The evidence custodian

C. The security manager

D. The IT director

69. When you're accessing an electronic storage file for forensic purposes, it is a best practice to use _____.

A. Gloves

B. A trusted computing base

C. Sysadmin access

D. A write-blocker

70. Which of the following should *not* be true about any tests performed during forensic analysis?

   A. Tests should be repeatable by opposing attorneys.

   B. Tests should be standard to the forensics industry.

   C. Tests should be performed by trained, certified professionals.

   D. Tests should be tailored and customized for specific purposes.

71. Which of the following pieces of data is considered personally identifiable information (PII) in the European Union (EU) but *not* in the United States?

   A. Name

   B. Home address

   C. Birth date

   D. Mobile phone number

72. The Privacy Shield program allows U.S. companies to collect and process privacy information about European Union (EU) citizens. The program is included in which law?

   A. Federal Information Security Management Act (FISMA)

   B. The EU General Data Protection Regulation (GDPR)

   C. Health Information Portability and Accountability Act (HIPAA)

   D. Sarbanes-Oxley Act

73. You are the security manager for a U.S.-based company that has branches abroad, including offices in Germany, Italy, and Brazil. If your company wants to process European Union (EU) citizen personally identifiable information (PII) data, one of the options is to use standard contractual clauses (also known as model contracts, or binding rules).

   If you choose this option, your company will have to get approval from _____.

   A. Privacy officials in Italy

   B. Privacy officials in Brazil

   C. Privacy officials in Italy and Germany

   D. Privacy officials in Italy, Germany, and Brazil

74. Using cloud storage is considered _____ under most privacy frameworks and laws.

   A. Illegal

   B. Data collection

   C. Opt-in

   D. Processing

75. Which U.S. federal government entity is in charge of administering the Privacy Shield program?

    A. State Department

    B. Privacy Protection Office

    C. Federal Trade Commission (FTC)

    D. Department of Health and Human Services (HHS)

76. In deciding which cloud provider to use, one of the characteristics you may want to determine about the provider is their level of professionalism. Which of the following tools could be used to determine the thoroughness, detail, and repeatability of the processes and procedures offered by a cloud provider?

    A. The Cloud Security Alliance (CSA) Security, Trust, and Assurance Registry (STAR) certification program

    B. The Risk Management Framework (RMF)

    C. The Capability Maturity Model (CMM)

    D. The EuroCloud Star Audit Certification

77. Service Organization Control (SOC) 2 reports were intended to be _____.

    A. Released to the public

    B. Only technical assessments

    C. Retained for internal use

    D. Nonbinding

78. To receive a Service Organization Control (SOC) 2 Type 2 report from a potential provider, the provider may require you to perform/provide a(n) _____.

    A. Security deposit

    B. Nondisclosure agreement (NDA)

    C. Cloud Security Alliance (CSA) Security, Trust, and Assurance Registry (STAR) certification application

    D. Act of fealty

79. The Generally Accepted Privacy Principles described by the American Institute of Certified Public Accountants (AICPA) are very similar to the privacy principles described by _____.

    A. The Organisation for Economic Cooperation and Development (OECD) and European Union (EU) General Data Protection Regulation (GDPR)

    B. National Institute of Standards and Technology (NIST) and European Union Agency for Network and Information Security (ENISA)

    C. Health Information Portability and Accountability Act (HIPAA) and Gramm–Leach–Bliley Act (GLBA)

    D. The Federal Trade Commission (FTC) and the U.S. State Department

80. The Payment Card Industry Data Security Standard (PCI DSS) requires that all merchants who want to process credit card transactions be compliant with a wide variety of security control requirements. Approximately how many controls are listed in the PCI DSS?

  A. Around a dozen

  B. About 20

  C. About 100

  D. Over 200

81. The Payment Card Industry Data Security Standard (PCI DSS) requires that all merchants who want to process credit card transactions be compliant with a wide variety of security control requirements. Merchants are assigned different tier levels under PCI DSS, based on _____.

  A. Availability

  B. Redundancy

  C. Location of their corporate headquarters

  D. Number of transactions per year

82. The Payment Card Industry Data Security Standard (PCI DSS) requires that all merchants who want to process credit card transaction be compliant with a wide variety of security control requirements. The different merchant tier requirements will dictate _____.

  A. Different types of audits each must conduct

  B. Different amounts of audits each must conduct

  C. Different control sets based on tier level

  D. Different cost of controls based on tier level

83. _____ are required to use *only* cryptographic modules that are compliant with Federal Information Processing Standard (FIPS) 140-2.

  A. Americans

  B. Cloud providers

  C. Infrastructure as a service (IaaS) providers

  D. U.S. federal agencies

84. In performing vendor management and selection, one of the questions you, as the potential cloud customer, might ask is, "Does it seem as if this vendor is subject to any pending acquisitions or mergers?" In gathering data to answer this question, what are you trying to avoid?

  A. Vendor lockout

  B. Due care

  C. Third-party dependencies

  D. Regulatory oversight

Chapter

7

Practice Exam 1

1. You work for a government research facility. Your organization often shares data with other government research organizations. You would like to create a single sign-on experience across the organizations, where users at each organization can sign in with the user ID/authentication issued by that organization, then access research data in all the other organizations. Instead of replicating the data stores of each organization at every other organization (which is one way of accomplishing this goal), you instead want every user to have access to each organization's specific storage resources.

   What is the term for this kind of arrangement?

   A. Public-key infrastructure (PKI)

   B. Portability

   C. Federation

   D. Repudiation

2. You work for a government research facility. Your organization often shares data with other government research organizations. You would like to create a single sign-on experience across the organizations, where users at each organization can sign in with the user ID/authentication issued by that organization, then access research data in all the other organizations. Instead of replicating the data stores of each organization at every other organization (which is one way of accomplishing this goal), you instead want every user to have access to each organization's specific storage resources.

   You want to connect your organization to 13 other organizations. You consider using the cross-certification model but then decide against it. What is the *most* likely reason for declining that option?

   A. It is impossible to trust more than two organizations.

   B. If you work for the government, the maximum parties allowed to share data is five.

   C. Trying to maintain currency in reviewing and approving the security governance and configurations of that many entities would create an overwhelming task.

   D. Data shared among that many entities loses its inherent value.

3. You work for a government research facility. Your organization often shares data with other government research organizations. You would like to create a single sign-on experience across the organizations, where users at each organization can sign in with the user ID/authentication issued by that organization, then access research data in all the other organizations. Instead of replicating the data stores of each organization at every other organization (which is one way of accomplishing this goal), you instead want every user to have access to each organization's specific storage resources.

   In order to pass the user IDs and authenticating credentials of each user among the organizations, what protocol, language, or technique will you *most* likely utilize?

   A. Representational State Transfer (REST)

   B. Security Assertion Markup Language (SAML)

   C. Simple Object Access Protocol (SOAP)

   D. Hypertext Markup Language (HTML)

4. You work for a government research facility. Your organization often shares data with other government research organizations. You would like to create a single sign-on experience across the organizations, where users at each organization can sign in with the user ID/authentication issued by that organization, then access research data in all the other organizations. Instead of replicating the data stores of each organization at every other organization (which is one way of accomplishing this goal), you instead want every user to have access to each organization's specific storage resources.

   If you don't use cross-certification, what other model can you implement for this purpose?

   A. Third-party identity broker

   B. Cloud reseller

   C. Intractable nuanced variance

   D. Mandatory access control (MAC)

5. You work for a government research facility. Your organization often shares data with other government research organizations. You would like to create a single sign-on experience across the organizations, where users at each organization can sign in with the user ID/authentication issued by that organization, then access research data in all the other organizations. Instead of replicating the data stores of each organization at every other organization (which is one way of accomplishing this goal), you instead want every user to have access to each organization's specific storage resources.

   If you are in the United States, one of the standards you should adhere to is

   _____.

   A. National Institute of Standards and Technology (NIST) 800-53

   B. Payment Card Industry (PCI)

   C. ISO 27014

   D. European Union Agency for Network and Information Security (ENISA)

6. You work for a government research facility. Your organization often shares data with other government research organizations. You would like to create a single sign-on experience across the organizations, where users at each organization can sign in with the user ID/authentication issued by that organization, then access research data in all the other organizations. Instead of replicating the data stores of each organization at every other organization (which is one way of accomplishing this goal), you instead want every user to have access to each organization's specific storage resources.

   If you are in Canada, one of the standards you will have to adhere to is

   _____.

   A. FIPS 140-2

   B. PIPEDA

   C. HIPAA

   D. EFTA

7. You are the security policy lead for your organization, which is considering migrating from your on-premises, traditional IT environment into the cloud. You are reviewing the Cloud Security Alliance Cloud Controls Matrix (CSA CCM) as a tool for your organization.

   Which of the following benefits will the CSA CCM offer your organization?

   A. Simplifying regulatory compliance

   B. Collecting multiple data streams from your log files

   C. Ensuring that the baseline configuration is applied to all systems

   D. Enforcing contract terms between your organization and the cloud provider

8. You are the security policy lead for your organization, which is considering migrating from your on-premises, traditional IT environment into the cloud. You are reviewing the Cloud Security Alliance Cloud Controls Matrix (CSA CCM) as a tool for your organization.

   Which of the following regulatory frameworks is *not* covered by the CCM?

   A. ISACA's Control Objectives for Information and Related Technologies (COBIT)

   B. Canada's Personal Information Protection and Electronic Documents Act (PIPEDA) privacy law

   C. The ALL-TRUST framework from the environmental industry

   D. The U.S. Federal Risk and Authorization Management Program (FedRAMP)

9. You are the security policy lead for your organization, which is considering migrating from your on-premises, traditional IT environment into the cloud. You are reviewing the Cloud Security Alliance Cloud Controls Matrix (CSA CCM) as a tool for your organization.

   Which tool, also available from the CSA, can be used in conjunction with the CCM to aid you in selecting and applying the proper controls to meet your organization's regulatory needs?

   A. The Consensus Assessments Initiative Questionnaire (CAIQ)

   B. The Open Web Application Security Project (OWASP) Top Ten

   C. The Critical Security Controls (CSC) list

   D. National Institute of Standards and Technology (NIST) Federal Information Processing Standard (FIPS) 140-2

10. You are the security policy lead for your organization, which is considering migrating from your on-premises, traditional IT environment into the cloud. You are reviewing the Cloud Security Alliance Cloud Controls Matrix (CSA CCM) as a tool for your organization.

    What is probably the *best* benefit offered by the CCM?

    A. The low cost of the tool

    B. Allowing your organization to leverage existing controls across multiple frameworks so as not to duplicate effort

   C. Simplicity of control selection from the list of approved choices

   D. Ease of implementation by choosing controls from the list of qualified vendors

11. You are the IT security subject matter expert for a hobbyist collective that researches and archives old music. Your collective is set up in such a way that the members own various pieces of the network themselves, pool resources and data, and communicate and share files via the Internet. This is an example of what cloud model?

   A. Hydrogenous

   B. Private

   C. Public

   D. Community

12. You are the IT security subject matter expert for a hobbyist collective that researches and archives old music. Your collective wants to create a single sign-on experience for all members of the collective, where assurance and trust in the various members are created by having each member review all the others' policies, governance, procedures, and controls before allowing them to participate. This is an example of what kind of arrangement?

   A. Security Assertion Markup Language (SAML)

   B. Cross-certification federation

   C. Third-party certification federation

   D. JavaScript Object Notation (JSON)

13. You are the IT security subject matter expert for a hobbyist collective that researches and archives old music. Your collective exchanges music files in two forms: images of written sheet music and electronic copies of recordings. Both of these are protected by what intellectual property legal construct?

   A. Trademark

   B. Copyright

   C. Patent

   D. Trade secret

14. You are the IT security subject matter expert for a hobbyist collective that researches and archives old music. If you create a federated identity management structure for all the participants in the collective using a third-party certification model, who would be the federated service provider(s) in that structure?

   A. The third party

   B. A cloud access security broker (CASB)

   C. The various members of the collective

   D. The cloud provider

15. You are the IT security subject matter expert for a hobbyist collective that researches and archives old music. You receive a Digital Millennium Copyright Act (DMCA) takedown notice from someone who claims that your collective is hosting music that does not belong to you. You are fairly certain the complaint is not applicable and that the material in question does not belong to anyone else. What should you do in order to comply with the law?

   A. Take the material down, do an investigation, and then repost the material if the claim turns out to be unfounded.

   B. Leave the material up, do an investigation, and post the results of the investigation alongside the material itself once the investigation is complete.

   C. Ignore the complaint.

   D. Leave the material up until such time as the complainant delivers an enforceable governmental request, such as a warrant or subpoena.

16. You are the IT security subject matter expert for a hobbyist collective that researches and archives old music. You receive a Digital Millennium Copyright Act (DMCA) takedown notice from someone who claims that your collective is hosting music that does not belong to you. Upon investigation, you determine that the material in question is the sheet music for a concerto written in 1872. What should you do in order to comply with the law?

   A. Contact the current owners of the copyright in order to get proper permissions to host and exchange the data.

   B. Nothing. The material is so old it is in the public domain, and you have as much right as anyone else to use it in any way you see fit.

   C. Apply for a new copyright based on the new usage of the material.

   D. Offer to pay the complainant for the usage of the material.

17. Bob is designing a data center to support his organization, a financial services firm. What Uptime Institute tier rating should Bob try to attain in order to meet his company's needs without adding extraneous costs?

   A. 1

   B. 2

   C. 3

   D. 4

18. Bob is designing a data center to support his organization, a financial services firm. Bob's data center will have to be approved by regulators using a framework under which law?

   A. Health Industry Portability and Accountability Act (HIPPA)

   B. Payment Card Industry (PCI)

   C. Gramm–Leach–Bliley Act (GLBA)

   D. Sarbanes–Oxley Act (SOX)

19. Bob is designing a data center to support his organization, a financial services firm. Which of the following actions would *best* enhance Bob's efforts to create redundancy and resiliency in the data center?

    A. Ensure that all entrances are secured with biometric-based locks.

    B. Purchase uninterruptible power supplies (UPSs) from different vendors.

    C. Include financial background checks in all personnel reviews for administrators.

    D. Make sure all raised floors have at least 24 inches of clearance.

20. Bob is designing a data center to support his organization, a financial services firm. How long should the uninterruptible power supply (UPS) provide power to the systems in the data center?

    A. 12 hours

    B. An hour

    C. 10 minutes

    D. Long enough to perform graceful shutdown of the data center systems

21. You are the IT security manager for a video game software development company. For your company, minimizing security flaws in the delivered product is *probably* a
    _____.

    A. Functional requirement

    B. Nonfunctional requirement

    C. Regulatory issue

    D. Third-party function

22. You are the IT security manager for a video game software development company. In order to test your products for security defects and performance issues, your firm decides to use a small team of game testers recruited from a public pool of interested gamers who apply for a chance to take part. This is an example of _____.

    A. Static testing

    B. Dynamic testing

    C. Code review

    D. Open source review

23. You are the IT security manager for a video game software development company. In order to test your products for security defects and performance issues, your firm decides to use a small team of game testers recruited from a public pool of interested gamers who apply for a chance to take part. To optimize this situation, the test will need to involve
    _____.

    A. Management oversight

    B. A database administrator

    C. A trained moderator

    D. Members of the security team

24. You are the IT security manager for a video game software development company. In order to test your products for security defects and performance issues, your firm decides to use a small team of game testers recruited from a public pool of interested gamers who apply for a chance to take part. Of the parties listed, who should *most* be excluded from the test?

   A. Management

   B. Security personnel

   C. Billing department representatives

   D. The game developers

25. You are the IT security manager for a video game software development company. In order to test your products for security defects and performance issues, your firm decides to use a small team of game testers recruited from a public pool of interested gamers who apply for a chance to take part. It is absolutely crucial to include _____ as part of this process.

   A. Managerial oversight

   B. Signed nondisclosure agreements

   C. Health benefits

   D. The programming team

26. You are the IT security manager for a video game software development company. Which of the following is *most* likely to be your primary concern on a daily basis?

   A. Health and human safety

   B. Security flaws in your products

   C. Security flaws in your organization

   D. Regulatory compliance

27. You are the IT security manager for a video game software development company. Which type of intellectual property protection will your company likely rely upon for legally enforcing your rights?

   A. Trademark

   B. Patent

   C. Copyright

   D. Trade secret

28. You are the IT security manager for a video game software development company. In order to test your products for security defects and performance issues, your firm decides to use a small team of game testers recruited from a public pool of interested gamers who apply for a chance to take part. Gamers are notorious for attempting to perform actions that were never anticipated or intended by the programmers. Results gathered from this activity are _____.

   A. Useless

   B. Harmful

   C. Desirable

   D. Illegal

29. You are the IT security manager for a video game software development company. In order to test your products for security defects and performance issues, your firm decides to use a small team of game testers recruited from a public pool of interested gamers who apply for a chance to take part. Gamers are notorious for attempting to perform actions that were never anticipated or intended by the programmers. Trying to replicate this phenomenon in a testbed environment with internal testing mechanisms is called

_____.

   A. Source code review

   B. Deep testing

   C. Fuzz testing

   D. White-box testing

30. You are the IT security manager for a video game software development company. Your development team hired an external game development lab to work on part of the game engine. A few weeks before the initial release of your game, the company that owns the lab publishes a strikingly similar game, with many of the features and elements that appear in your work. Which of the following methods could be used to determine if your ownership rights were violated?

   A. Physical surveillance of their property and personnel

   B. Communications tapping of their offices

   C. Code signing

   D. Subverting insiders

31. You are the IT security manager for a video game software development company. Your development team hired an external game development lab to work on part of the game engine. A few weeks before the initial release of your game, the company that owns the lab publishes a strikingly similar game, with many of the features and elements that appear in your work. Which of the following legal methods are you likely able to exercise to defend your rights?

   A. Criminal prosecution

   B. Public hearings

   C. Civil court

   D. Arrest and detention

32. You are the IT security manager for a video game software development company. In order to test the functionality of online multiplayer game content, your testing team wants to use a cloud service independent from the internal production environment. You suggest that a(n) _____ service model will best meet this requirement.

   A. IaaS

   B. PaaS

   C. SaaS

   D. TaaS

33. You are the IT security manager for a video game software development company. In order to test the functionality of online multiplayer game content, your testing team wants to use a cloud service independent from the internal production environment. You remind them that it is absolutely crucial that they perform _____ before including any sample player or billing data.

   A. Vulnerability scans

   B. Intrusion detection

   C. Masking

   D. Malware scans

34. Which of the following is not an essential element defining cloud computing?

   A. Broad network access

   B. Metered service

   C. Off-site storage

   D. On-demand self-service

35. Which of the following is not an essential element defining cloud computing?

   A. Rapid elasticity

   B. Pooled resources

   C. On-demand self-service

   D. Immediate customer support

36. In what cloud computing service model is the customer responsible for installing and maintaining the operating system?

   A. IaaS

   B. PaaS

   C. SaaS

   D. QaaS

37. Your company is considering migrating its production environment to the cloud. In reviewing the proposed contract, you notice that it includes a clause that requires an additional fee, equal to six monthly payments (equal to half the term of the contract) for ending the contract at any point prior to the scheduled date. This is best described as an example of _____.

   A. Favorable contract terms

   B. Strong negotiation

   C. Infrastructure as a service (IaaS)

   D. Vendor lock-in

38. There are two general types of smoke detectors. Which type uses a small portion of radioactive material?

    A. Photoelectric

    B. Ionization

    C. Electron pulse

    D. Integral field

39. You are the privacy data officer for a large hospital and trauma center. You are called on to give your opinion of the hospital's plans to migrate all IT functions to a cloud service. Which of the following Uptime Institute tier-level ratings would you insist be included for any data center offered by potential providers?

    A. 1

    B. 2

    C. 3

    D. 4

40. What is the *most* important factor when considering the lowest temperature setting within a data center?

    A. System performance

    B. Health and human safety

    C. Risk of fire

    D. Regulatory issues

41. Storage controllers will typically be involved with each of the following storage protocols *except* _____.

    A. Internet Small Computer Systems Interface (iSCSI)

    B. RAID

    C. Fibre Channel

    D. Fibre Channel over Ethernet

42. When you're using a storage protocol that involves a storage controller, it is very important that the controller be configured in accordance with _____.

    A. Internal guidance

    B. Industry standards

    C. Vendor guidance

    D. Regulatory dictates

43. What is the importance of adhering to vendor guidance in configuration settings?

    A. Conforming with federal law

    B. Demonstrating due diligence

    C. Staying one step ahead of aggressors

    D. Maintaining customer satisfaction

44. Which of the following is a true statement about the virtualization management toolset?

  A. It can be regarded as something public facing.

  B. It must be on a distinct, isolated management network (virtual local area network [VLAN]).

  C. It connects physically to the specific storage area allocated to a given customer.

  D. The responsibility for securely installing and updating it falls on the customer.

45. In order to ensure proper _____ in a secure cloud network environment, consider the use of Domain Name System Security Extensions (DNSSEC), Internet Protocol Security (IPSec), and Transport Layer Security (TLS).

  A. Isolation

  B. Motif

  C. Multitenancy

  D. Signal modulation

46. Domain Name System Security Extensions (DNSSEC) provides all of the following *except* _____.

  A. Payload encryption

  B. Origin authority

  C. Data integrity

  D. Authenticated denial of existence

47. All of the following are activities that should be performed when capturing and maintaining an accurate, secure system baseline *except* _____.

  A. Updating the OS baseline image according to a scheduled interval to include any necessary security patches and configuration modifications

  B. Starting with a clean installation (hardware or virtual) of the desired OS

  C. Including only the default account credentials and nothing customized

  D. Halting or removing all unnecessary services

48. All of the following are activities that should be performed when capturing and maintaining an accurate, secure system baseline *except* _____.

  A. Removing all nonessential programs from the baseline image

  B. Excluding the target system you intend to baseline from any scheduled updates or patching used in production systems

  C. Including the baseline image in the asset inventory and configuration management database

  D. Configuring the host OS according to the baseline requirements

49. All of the following are activities that should be performed when capturing and maintaining an accurate, secure system baseline, *except* _____.

   A. Auditing the baseline to ensure that all configuration items have been included and applied correctly

   B. Imposing the baseline throughout the environment

   C. Capturing an image of the baseline system for future reference, versioning, and roll-back purposes

   D. Documenting all baseline configuration elements and versioning data

50. You are the IT director for a small contracting firm. Your company is considering migrating to a cloud production environment. Which service model would *best* fit your needs if you wanted an option that reduced the chance of vendor lock-in but also did not require the highest degree of administration by your own personnel?

   A. IaaS

   B. PaaS

   C. SaaS

   D. TanstaafL

51. You are the data manager for a retail company; you anticipate a much higher volume of sales activity in the final quarter of each calendar year than the other quarters. In order to handle these increased transactions, and to accommodate the temporary sales personnel you will hire for only that time period, you consider augmenting your internal, on-premises production environment with a cloud capability for a specific duration and will return to operating fully on-premises after the period of increased activity. This is an example of _____.

   A. Cloud framing

   B. Cloud enhancement

   C. Cloud fragility

   D. Cloud bursting

52. You are the data manager for a retail company; you anticipate a much higher volume of sales activity in the final quarter of each calendar year than the other quarters. In order to handle these increased transactions, and to accommodate the temporary sales personnel you will hire for only that time period, you consider augmenting your internal, on-premises production environment with a cloud capability for a specific duration, and will return to operating fully on-premises after the period of increased activity. Which facet of cloud computing is *most* important for making this possible?

   A. Broad network access

   B. Rapid elasticity

   C. Metered service

   D. Resource pooling

53. You are the data manager for a retail company; you anticipate a much higher volume of sales activity in the final quarter of each calendar year than the other quarters. In order to handle these increased transactions, and to accommodate the temporary sales personnel you will hire for only that time period, you consider augmenting your internal, on-premises production environment with a cloud capability for a specific duration, and will return to operating fully on-premises after the period of increased activity. Which deployment model best describes this type of arrangement?

A. Private cloud

B. Community cloud

C. Public cloud

D. Hybrid cloud

54. You are the security manager for a research and development firm. Your company does contract work for a number of highly sensitive industries, including aerospace and pharmaceuticals.

Your company's senior management is considering cloud migration and wants an option that is highly secure but still offers some of the flexibility and reduced overhead of the cloud. Which of the following deployment models do you recommend?

A. Private cloud

B. Community cloud

C. Public cloud

D. Hybrid cloud

55. You are the IT director for a small engineering services company. During the last year, one of your managing partners left the firm, and you lost several large customers, creating a cash flow problem. The remaining partners are looking to use a cloud environment as a means of drastically and quickly cutting costs, migrating away from the expense of operating an internal network.

Which cloud deployment model would you suggest to best meet their needs?

A. Private cloud

B. Community cloud

C. Public cloud

D. Hybrid cloud

56. You run an online club for antique piano enthusiasts. In order to better share photo files and other data online, you want to establish a cloud-based environment where all your members can connect their own devices and files to each other, at their discretion. You do not want to centralize payment for such services as Internet service provider (ISP) connectivity, and you want to leave that up to the members.

Which cloud deployment model would best suit your needs?

A. Private cloud

B. Community cloud

C. Public cloud

D. Hybrid cloud

57. Full isolation of user activity, processes, and virtual network segments in a cloud environment is incredibly important because of risks due to _____.

   A. Distributed denial of service (DDoS)

   B. Unencrypted packets

   C. Multitenancy

   D. Insider threat

58. You are the security manager for a small European appliance rental company. The senior management of your company is considering cloud migration for the production environment, which handles marketing, billing, and logistics.

   Which cloud deployment model should you be *most* likely to recommend?

   A. Private cloud

   B. Community cloud

   C. Public cloud

   D. Hybrid cloud

59. You are the security manager for a data analysis company. Your senior management is considering a cloud migration in order to use the greater capabilities of a cloud provider to perform calculations and computations. Your company wants to ensure that neither the contractual nor the technical setup of the cloud service will affect your data sets in any way so that you are not locked in to a single provider.

   Which of the following criteria will probably be *most* crucial for your choice of cloud providers?

   A. Portability

   B. Interoperability

   C. Resiliency

   D. Governance

60. Migrating to a cloud environment will reduce an organization's dependence on _____.

   A. Capital expenditures for IT

   B. Operational expenditures for IT

   C. Data-driven workflows

   D. Customer satisfaction

61. Firewalls, DLP (data loss prevention or data leak protection) and digital rights management (DRM) solutions, and security information and event management (SIEM) products are all examples of _____ controls.

   A. Technical

   B. Administrative

   C. Physical

   D. Competing

62. Fiber-optic lines are considered part of Layer _____ of the Open Systems Interconnection (OSI) model.

    A. 1

    B. 3

    C. 5

    D. 7

63. It is probably fair to assume that software as a service (SaaS) functions take place at Layer _____ of the OSI model.

    A. 1

    B. 3

    C. 5

    D. 7

64. Because of the nature of the cloud, all access is remote access. One of the preferred technologies employed for secure remote access is _____.

    A. VPN

    B. HTML

    C. DEED

    D. DNS

65. You are the security manager for a small retailer engaged in e-commerce. A large part of your sales is transacted through the use of credit and debit cards.

    You have determined that the costs of maintaining an encrypted storage capability in order to meet compliance requirements are prohibitive. What other technology can you use instead to meet those regulatory needs?

    A. Obfuscation

    B. Masking

    C. Tokenization

    D. Hashing

66. Which of the following mechanisms *cannot* be used by a data loss prevention or data leak protection (DLP) solution to sort data?

    A. Labels

    B. Metadata

    C. Content strings

    D. Inverse signifiers

67. You are the security manager for an online marketing company. Your company has recently migrated to a cloud production environment and has deployed a number of new cloud-based protection mechanisms offered by both third parties and the cloud provider, including data loss prevention or data leak protection (DLP) and security information and event management (SIEM) solutions.

After one week of operation, your security team reports an inordinate amount of time responding to potential incidents that have turned out to only be false-positive reports. Management is concerned that the cloud migration was a bad idea and that it is too costly in terms of misspent security efforts. What do you recommend?

A. Change the control set so that you use only security products not offered by the cloud provider.

B. Change the control set so that you use only security products offered by the cloud provider.

C. Wait three weeks before making a final decision.

D. Move back to an on-premises environment as soon as possible to avoid additional wasted funds and effort.

68. In a cloud context, who determines the risk appetite of your organization?

A. The cloud provider

B. Your Internet service provider (ISP)

C. Federal regulators

D. Senior management

69. You are the security manager for a small application development company. Your company is considering the use of the cloud for software testing purposes.

Which of the following traits of cloud functionality is probably the *most* crucial in terms of deciding which cloud provider you will choose?

A. Portability

B. Interoperability

C. Resiliency

D. Governance

70. You are the security manager for a small application development company. Your company is considering the use of the cloud for software testing purposes. Which cloud service model is *most* likely to suit your needs?

A. IaaS

B. PaaS

C. SaaS

D. LaaS

71. ISO 31000 is most similar to which of the following regulations, standards, guidelines, and frameworks?

   A. NIST 800-37

   B. COBIT

   C. ITIL

   D. GDPR

72. Which of the following entities publishes a cloud-centric set of risk-benefit recommendations that includes a "Top 8" list of security risks an organization might face during a cloud migration, based on likelihood and impact?

   A. National Institute of Standards and Technology (NIST)

   B. International Organization for Standardization (ISO)

   C. European Union Agency for Network and Information Security (ENISA)

   D. Payment Card Industry (PCI)

73. Which standards body depends heavily on contributions and input from its open membership base?

   A. National Institute of Standards and Technology (NIST)

   B. International Organization for Standardization (ISO)

   C. Internet Corporation for Assigned Names and Numbers (ICANN)

   D. Cloud Security Alliance (CSA)

74. In regard to most privacy guidance, the data subject is _____.

   A. The individual described by the privacy data

   B. The entity that collects or creates the privacy data

   C. The entity that uses privacy data on behalf of the controller

   D. The entity that regulates privacy data

75. In regard to most privacy guidance, the data controller is _____.

   A. The individual described by the privacy data

   B. The entity that collects or creates the privacy data

   C. The entity that uses privacy data on behalf of the controller

   D. The entity that regulates privacy data

76. In regard to most privacy guidance, the data processor is _____.

   A. The individual described by the privacy data

   B. The entity that collects or creates the privacy data

   C. The entity that uses privacy data on behalf of the controller

   D. The entity that regulates privacy data

77. In most privacy-regulation situations, which entity is *most* responsible for deciding how a particular privacy-related data set will be used or processed?

   A. The data subject

   B. The data controller

   C. The data steward

   D. The data custodian

78. In most privacy-regulation situations, which entity is *most* responsible for the day-to-day maintenance and security of a privacy-related data set?

   A. The data subject

   B. The data controller

   C. The data steward

   D. The data custodian

79. You are the compliance officer for a medical device manufacturing firm. Your company maintains a cloud-based list of patients currently fitted with your devices for long-term care and quality assurance purposes. The list is maintained in a database that cross-references details about the hardware and some billing data.

In this situation, who is likely to be considered the data custodian, under many privacy regulations and laws?

   A. You (the compliance officer)

   B. The cloud provider's network security team

   C. Your company

   D. The database administrator

80. Which of the following is probably *least* suited for inclusion in the service-level agreement (SLA) between a cloud customer and cloud provider?

   A. Bandwidth

   B. Jurisdiction

   C. Storage space

   D. Availability

81. Which of the following items, included in the contract between a cloud customer and cloud provider, can best aid in reducing vendor lock-in?

   A. Data format type and structure

   B. Availability

   C. Storage space

   D. List of available OSs

82. Which of the following contract terms *most* incentivizes the cloud provider to meet the requirements listed in the service-level agreement (SLA)?

    A. Regulatory oversight

    B. Financial penalties

    C. Performance details

    D. Desire to maintain customer satisfaction

83. Which of the following contract terms *most* incentivizes the cloud customer to meet the requirements listed in the contract?

    A. Financial penalties

    B. Regulatory oversight

    C. Suspension of service

    D. Media attention

84. Which of the following is *not* a reason for conducting audits?

    A. Regulatory compliance

    B. Enhanced user experience

    C. Determination of service quality

    D. Security assurance

85. Which of the following is a tool that can be used to perform security control audits?

    A. Federal Information Processing Standard (FIPS) 140-2

    B. General Data Protection Regulation (GDPR)

    C. ISO 27001

    D. Cloud Security Alliance Cloud Controls Matrix (CSA CCM)

86. Which of the following dictates the requirements for U.S. federal agencies operating in a cloud environment?

    A. ISO 27002

    B. NIST SP 800-37

    C. ENISA

    D. FedRAMP

87. Which of the following common aspects of cloud computing can aid in audit efforts?

    A. Scalability

    B. Virtualization

    C. Multitenancy

    D. Metered self-service

88. Which of the following does *not* typically represent a means for enhanced authentication?

    A. Challenge questions

    B. Variable keystrokes

    C. Out-of-band identity confirmation

    D. Dynamic end-user knowledge

89. Which of the following is *not* a common identity federation standard?

    A. WS-Federation

    B. OpenID

    C. OISame

    D. Security Assertion Markup Language (SAML)

90. Multifactor authentication typically includes two or more of all the following elements *except* _____.

    A. What you know

    B. Who you know

    C. What you are

    D. What you have

91. Which of the following aspects of cloud computing can enhance the customer's business continuity and disaster recovery (BC/DR) efforts?

    A. Multitenancy

    B. Pooled resources

    C. Virtualization

    D. Remote access

92. Which of the following aspects of cloud computing can enhance the customer's business continuity and disaster recovery (BC/DR) efforts?

    A. Rapid elasticity

    B. Online collaboration

    C. Support of common regulatory frameworks

    D. Attention to customer service

93. Which of the following aspects of cloud computing can enhance the customer's business continuity and disaster recovery (BC/DR) efforts?

    A. On-demand self-service

    B. Pooled resources

    C. Virtualization

    D. The control plane

94. What functional process can aid business continuity and disaster recovery (BC/DR) efforts?

   A.   The software development lifecycle (SDLC)

   B.   Data classification

   C.   Honeypots

   D.   Identity management

95. Which common security tool can aid in the overall business continuity and disaster recovery (BC/DR) process?

   A.   Honeypots

   B.   Data loss prevention or data leak protection (DLP)

   C.   Security information and event management (SIEM)

   D.   Firewalls

96. Which of the following aspects of cloud computing can enhance the customer's business continuity and disaster recovery (BC/DR) efforts?

   A.   Geographical separation of data centers

   B.   Hypervisor security

   C.   Pooled resources

   D.   Multitenancy

97. Which of the following is *not* typically used as an information source for business continuity and disaster recovery (BC/DR) event anticipation?

   A.   Open source news

   B.   Business threat intelligence

   C.   Egress monitoring solutions

   D.   Weather monitoring agencies

98. Which of the following aspects of the business continuity and disaster recovery (BC/DR) process poses a risk to the organization?

   A.   Premature return to normal operations

   B.   Event anticipation information

   C.   Assigning roles for BC/DR activities

   D.   Preparing the continuity-of-operations plan

99. Which of the following aspects of the business continuity and disaster recovery (BC/DR) process poses a risk to the organization?

   A.   Threat intelligence gathering

   B.   Preplacement of response assets

   C.   Budgeting for disaster

   D.   Full testing of the plan

100. In container virtualization, unlike standard virtualization, what is *not* included?

  A. Hardware emulation

  B. OS replication

  C. A single kernel

  D. The possibility for multiple containers

101. Which of the following is *not* typically a phase in the software development lifecycle (SDLC)?

  A. Define

  B. Test

  C. Develop

  D. Sanitization

102. An application programming interface (API) gateway can typically offer all of the following capabilities *except* _____.

  A. Rate limiting

  B. Access control

  C. Hardware confirmation

  D. Logging

103. Cloud customers in a public cloud managed services environment can install all the following types of firewalls *except* _____.

  A. Provider operated

  B. Host-based

  C. Third party

  D. Hardware

104. The Transport Layer Security (TLS) protocol creates a secure communications channel over public media (such as the Internet). In a typical TLS session, who initiates the protocol?

  A. The server

  B. The client

  C. The certifying authority

  D. The Internet service provider (ISP)

105. The Transport Layer Security (TLS) protocol creates a secure communications channel over public media (such as the Internet). In a typical TLS session, what is the *usual* means for establishing trust between the parties?

  A. Out-of-band authentication

  B. Multifactor authentication

  C. Public-key infrastructure (PKI) certificates

  D. Preexisting knowledge of each other

106. The Transport Layer Security (TLS) protocol creates a secure communications channel over public media (such as the Internet). In a typical TLS session, what form of cryptography is used for the session key?

A. Symmetric key

B. Asymmetric key pairs

C. Hashing

D. One asymmetric key pair

107. DevOps is a form of software development that typically joins the software development team with _____.

A. The production team

B. The marketing team

C. The security office

D. Management

108. The Agile Manifesto for software development focuses largely on _____.

A. Secure build

B. Thorough documentation

C. Working prototypes

D. Proper planning

109. When a program's source code is open to review by the public, what is that software called?

A. Freeware

B. Malware

C. Open source

D. Shareware

110. Why is Simple Object Access Protocol (SOAP) used for accessing web services instead of the Distributed Component Object Model (DCOM) and the Common Object Request Broker Architecture (CORBA)?

A. SOAP provides a much more lightweight solution.

B. SOAP replaces binary messaging with XML.

C. SOAP is much more secure.

D. SOAP is newer.

111. How does representational state transfer (REST) make web service requests?

A. XML

B. SAML

C. URIs

D. TLS

112. Representational state transfer (REST) outputs often take the form of
_____.

    A. JavaScript Object Notation (JSON)

    B. Certificates

    C. Database entries

    D. WS-Policy

113. "Sensitive data exposure" is often included on the list of the Open Web Application Security Project (OWASP) Top Ten web application vulnerabilities. In addition to programming discipline and technological controls, what other approach is important for reducing this risk?

    A. Physical access control to the facility

    B. User training

    C. Crafting sophisticated policies

    D. Redundant backup power

114. During maintenance mode for a given node in a virtualized environment, which of the following conditions is *not* accurate?

    A. Generation of new instances is prevented.

    B. Admin access is prevented.

    C. Alerting mechanisms are suspended.

    D. Events are logged.

115. How are virtual machines (VMs) moved from active hosts when the host is being put into maintenance mode?

    A. As a snapshotted image file

    B. In encrypted form

    C. As a live instance

    D. Via portable media

116. Which of the following is *not* a typical mechanism used by intrusion detection system (IDS) and intrusion prevention system (IPS) solutions to detect threats?

    A. Signature-based detection

    B. User input

    C. Statistical-based detection

    D. Heuristic detection

117. When you're deploying a honeypot/honeynet, it is best to fill it with
_____ data.

    A. Masked

    B. Raw

    C. Encrypted

    D. Useless

118. The cloud provider should be required to make proof of vulnerability scans available to all of the following *except* _____.

    A. Regulators

    B. The public

    C. Auditors

    D. The cloud customer

119. You are the security director for a chain of automotive repair centers across several states. Your company uses a cloud software as a service (SaaS) provider for business functions that cross several of the locations of your facilities, such as ordering of parts, logistics and inventory, billing, and marketing.

The manager at one of your newest locations reports that there is a competing car repair company that has a logo that looks almost exactly like the one your company uses. This intellectual property is likely protected as a _____.

    A. Copyright

    B. Trademark

    C. Patent

    D. Trade secret

120. You are the security director for a chain of automotive repair centers across several states. Your company uses a cloud software as a service (SaaS) provider for business functions that cross several of the locations of your facilities, such as ordering of parts, logistics and inventory, billing, and marketing.

The manager at one of your newest locations reports that there is a competing car repair company that has a logo that looks almost exactly like the one your company uses. This conflict will *most* likely have to be resolved with what legal method?

    A. Breach of contract lawsuit

    B. Criminal prosecution

    C. Civil suit

    D. Military tribunal

121. You are the security director for a chain of automotive repair centers across several states. Your company uses a cloud software as a service (SaaS) provider for business functions that cross several of the locations of your facilities, such as ordering of parts, logistics and inventory, billing, and marketing.

The manager at one of your newest locations reports that there is a competing car repair company that has a logo that looks almost exactly like the one your company uses. What will *most likely* affect the determination of who has ownership of the logo?

    A. Whoever first used the logo

    B. The jurisdiction where both businesses are using the logo simultaneously

    C. Whoever first applied for legal protection of the logo

    D. Whichever entity has the most customers who recognize the logo

122. Which Statement on Standards for Attestation Engagements (SSAE) 18 audit report is simply an attestation of audit results?

   A. Service Organization Control (SOC) 1

   B. SOC 2, Type 1

   C. SOC 2, Type 2

   D. SOC 3

123. Which Statement on Standards for Attestation Engagements (SSAE) 18 report is purposefully designed for public release (for instance, to be posted on a company's website)?

   A. Service Organization Control (SOC) 1

   B. SOC 2, Type 1

   C. SOC 2, Type 2

   D. SOC 3

124. Which of the following countries has a national privacy law that conforms to European Union (EU) legislation?

   A. The United States

   B. Australia

   C. Jamaica

   D. Honduras

125. Which of the following countries has a national privacy law that conforms to European Union (EU) legislation?

   A. Japan

   B. Alaska

   C. Belize

   D. Madagascar

Chapter

8

Practice Exam 2

1. You are the IT director for an automotive parts supply distribution service; your
    company wants to operate a production environment in the cloud. In reviewing provider
    options, management considers an offer from Cloud Services Corp., who has contracts
    with several cloud providers and data centers and has offered to tailor a package of
    services for your company's needs. In this case, Cloud Services Corp. is considered a
    _____.

    A. Cloud provider

    B. Cloud customer

    C. Cloud reseller

    D. Cloud database

2. You are the IT director for an automotive parts supply distribution service; your company
    wants to operate a production environment in the cloud. Management has expressed
    a concern that any cloud provider the company chooses will have your company at a
    disadvantage—that your company will be at great risk because the provider will have
    your data and operational capability, and that the provider could hold the data "hostage"
    in order to raise the price of the service dramatically at the end of the contract term. To
    address management's concerns, you should try to find a cloud offering that places a great
    deal of emphasis on the _____ trait of cloud computing.

    A. Resource pooling

    B. Scalability

    C. Portability

    D. Metered service

3. You are the IT director for an automotive parts supply distribution service; your company
    wants to operate a production environment in the cloud. As you consider possible
    providers, you are careful to check that they each offer the essential traits of cloud
    computing. These include all of the following *except* _____.

    A. Broad network access

    B. Metered service

    C. On-demand self-service

    D. Automatic anti-malware and intrusion prevention

4. You are the IT director for an automotive parts supply distribution service; your company
    wants to operate a production environment in the cloud. Your company wants to install
    its own software solutions in a managed environment to decrease the cost of purchasing
    and maintaining the hardware of a data center. You should *most* likely be considering a(n)
    _____ offering.

    A. IaaS

    B. PaaS

    C. SaaS

    D. Hybrid

5. If a company wanted to retain some of its own internal traditional hardware but use the cloud as a means of performing software testing functions, which service and deployment models should it probably use?

    A. PaaS, hybrid

    B. IaaS, private

    C. PaaS, community

    D. SaaS, hybrid

6. A company wants to absolutely minimize their involvement in administration of IT; which combination of cloud service model and deployment should it consider?

    A. IaaS, private

    B. PaaS, private

    C. SaaS, private

    D. SaaS, public

7. During a cost–benefit analysis, your company determines that it spends a disproportionate amount of money on software licensing and administration. Which cloud model may best help your company to reduce these costs?

    A. IaaS

    B. PaaS

    C. SaaS

    D. Hybrid

8. Your company does not have a well-trained, experienced IT staff and is reluctant to spend more money on training personnel (in recent company history, personnel have received training and then immediately quit the company to work for competitors). If senior management considers cloud migration, which deployment model would probably best suit their needs?

    A. Public

    B. Private

    C. Community

    D. Hybrid

9. Your company operates under a high degree of regulatory scrutiny. Senior management wants to migrate to a cloud environment but is concerned that providers will not meet the company's compliance needs. Which deployment model would probably best suit the company's needs?

    A. Public

    B. Private

    C. Community

    D. Hybrid

10. Your company operates in a highly competitive market, with extremely high-value data assets. Senior management wants to migrate to a cloud environment but is concerned that providers will not meet the company's security needs. Which deployment model would probably best suit the company's needs?

    A. Public

    B. Private

    C. Community

    D. Hybrid

11. Your company operates in a highly cooperative market, with a high degree of information sharing between participants. Senior management wants to migrate to a cloud environment but is concerned that providers will not meet the company's collaboration needs. Which deployment model would probably best suit the company's needs?

    A. Public

    B. Private

    C. Community

    D. Hybrid

12. Your company maintains an on-premises data center for daily production activities but wants to use a cloud service to augment this capability during times of increased demand (cloud bursting). Which deployment model would probably best suit the company's needs?

    A. Public

    B. Private

    C. Community

    D. Hybrid

13. A company is considering a cloud migration to a platform as a service (PaaS) environment. Which of the following factors might make the company *less* likely to choose the cloud environment?

    A. The company wants to reduce overhead costs.

    B. The company operates proprietary software.

    C. The company hopes to reduce energy costs related to operation of a data center.

    D. The company is seeking to enhance its business continuity and disaster recovery (BC/DR) capabilities.

14. Which mechanism *best* aids to ensure that the cloud customer receives dependable, consistent performance in the cloud environment?

    A. Audits

    B. Service-level agreement (SLA)

    C. Regulators

    D. Training

15. What is the business advantage of shifting from capital expenditure in an on-premises environment to the operating expenditures of a cloud environment?

    A. Reduces the overall cost

    B. Reduces tax exposure

    C. Reduces cash flow risks

    D. Increases profit

16. A host-based firewall in a virtualized cloud environment might have aspects of all the following types of controls *except* _____.

    A. Administrative

    B. Deterrent

    C. Corrective

    D. Preventive

17. A virtual network interface card (NIC) exists at Layer _____ of the OSI model.

    A. 2

    B. 4

    C. 6

    D. 8

18. Which technology is *most* associated with tunneling?

    A. IPSec

    B. GRE

    C. IaaS

    D. XML

19. Secure Shell (SSH) tunneling can include all of the following services *except* _____.

    A. Remote log-on

    B. Content filtering

    C. Port forwarding

    D. Command execution

20. Transport Layer Security (TLS) is a session encryption tool that uses _____ encryption to create a _____ session key.

    A. Symmetric, symmetric

    B. Asymmetric, symmetric

    C. Asymmetric, asymmetric

    D. Symmetric, asymmetric

21. Which of the following architecture frameworks was designed for service delivery entities, from the perspective of how they serve customers?

    A. SABSA (Sherwood Applied Business Security Architecture)

    B. ITIL

    C. COBIT (Control Objectives for Information and Related Technologies)

    D. TOGAF (The Open Group Architecture Framework)

22. The Cloud Security Alliance (CSA) created the Trusted Cloud Initiative (TCI) to define principles of cloud computing that providers should strive for in order to foster a clear understanding of the cloud marketplace and to enhance that market. Which of the following is not one of the CSA's TCI fundamental principles?

    A. Delegate or federate access control when appropriate.

    B. Ensure the [trusted cloud] architecture is resilient, elastic, and flexible.

    C. Ensure the [trusted cloud] architecture addresses and supports multiple levels of protection.

    D. Provide economical services to all customers, regardless of point of origin.

23. Data loss prevention or data leak protection (DLP) solutions typically involve all of the following aspects *except* _____.

    A. Data discovery

    B. Tokenization

    C. Monitoring

    D. Enforcement

24. A typical data loss prevention or data leak protection (DLP) tool can enhance the organization's efforts at accomplishing what legal task?

    A. Evidence collection

    B. Delivering testimony

    C. Criminal prosecution

    D. Enforcement of intellectual property rights

25. Which of the following activities can enhance the usefulness and abilities of a data loss prevention or data leak protection (DLP) solution?

    A. Perform emergency egress training for all personnel.

    B. Require data owners, stewards, and custodians to properly classify and label data at time of creation or collection.

    C. Require senior management to participate in all security functions, including initial, recurring, and refresher training.

    D. Display security guidance in a variety of formats, including a web page, banner, posters, and hard-copy material.

26. Data archiving can also provide what production capability?

   A. Enhanced database mechanisms

   B. Near-term data recovery

   C. New data-driven business workflows

   D. Greater management insight into productivity

27. Data archiving can be required for regulatory compliance as a legal mandate. What other business function is also often tied to archiving?

   A. Marketing

   B. Business continuity and disaster recovery (BC/DR)

   C. Personnel development

   D. Intellectual property protection

28. Which of the following is probably *most* important to include in a data archiving policy?

   A. Data format and type

   B. Data classification

   C. Encryption procedures and standards

   D. Data audit and review processes

29. The destruction of a cloud customer's data can be required by all of the following *except* _____.

   A. Statute

   B. Regulation

   C. The cloud provider's policy

   D. Contract

30. Which of the following data storage types is most associated with software as a service (SaaS)?

   A. Content delivery network (CDN)

   B. Databases

   C. Volume storage

   D. Data warehousing

31. You are the security manager for a bookkeeping firm that is considering moving to a cloud-based production environment. In selecting a cloud provider, your company is reviewing many criteria. One of these is enhancing the company's business continuity and disaster recovery (BC/DR) capabilities. You want to ensure that the cloud provider you select will allow for migration to an alternate provider in the event of contingencies. The provider you choose should be able to support a migration to an alternate provider within _____.

   A. 24 hours

   B. 1 hour

   C. Your company's recovery time objective (RTO)

   D. Your company's recovery point objective (RPO)

32. In which phase of the cloud secure data lifecycle does data leave the production environment and go into long-term storage?

   A. Store

   B. Use

   C. Share

   D. Archive

33. In which phase of the cloud secure data lifecycle should classifications and labels be assigned to data?

   A. Create

   B. Store

   C. Use

   D. Share

34. Which of the following is *not* included in the Open Web Application Security Project (OWASP) Top Ten web application security threats?

   A. Injection

   B. Cross-site scripting

   C. Internal theft

   D. Sensitive data exposure

35. Your organization is developing software for wide use by the public. You have decided to test it in a cloud environment, in a platform as a service (PaaS) model. Which of the following should be of particular concern to your organization for this situation?

   A. Vendor lock-in

   B. Backdoors

   C. Regulatory compliance

   D. High-speed network connectivity

36. Which of the following management risks can make an organization's cloud environment unviable?

   A. Insider trading

   B. Virtual machine (VM) sprawl

   C. Hostile takeover

   D. Improper personnel selection

37. You are the security manager for a company that is considering cloud migration to an infrastructure as a service (IaaS) environment. You are assisting your company's IT architects in constructing the environment. Which of the following options do you recommend?

   A. Unrestricted public access

   B. Use of a Type I hypervisor

   C. Use of a Type II hypervisor

   D. Enhanced productivity without encryption

38. Your company uses a managed cloud service provider to host the production environment. The provider has notified you, along with several other of the provider's customers, that an engineer working for the provider has been using administrative access to steal sensitive data and has been selling it to your competitors. Some of this sensitive data included personally identifiable information (PII) related to your employees. Your company's general counsel informs you that there are at least three jurisdictions involved that have laws requiring data breach notification for PII. Who has *legal* liability for the costs involved with making the required notifications?

   A. The cloud provider

   B. Your company

   C. The Internet service provider (ISP)

   D. Your regulators

39. Which of the following techniques is *not* recommended for privileged user management?

   A. Increased password/phrase complexity

   B. More frequent password/phrase changes

   C. More detailed background checks

   D. Less detailed audit trail

40. You are the security officer for a company operating a production environment in the cloud. Your company's assets have a high degree of sensitivity and value, and your company has decided to retain control and ownership of the encryption key management system. In order to do so, your company will have to have which of the following cloud service/deployment models?

   A. Public

   B. Infrastructure as a service (IaaS)

   C. Hybrid

   D. Software as a service (SaaS)

41. Which security principle dictates that encryption key management and storage should be isolated from the data encrypted with those keys?

   A. Least privilege

   B. Two-person integrity

   C. Compartmentalization

   D. Separation of duties

42. Which cloud data storage technique involves encrypting a data set, then splitting the data into pieces, splitting the key into pieces, then signing the data pieces and key pieces and distributing them to various cloud storage locations?

   A. RAID

   B. Secret sharing made short (SSMS)

   C. Homomorphic encryption

   D. Asymmetric encryption

43. Which theoretical technique would allow encrypted data to be manipulated without decrypting it first?

    A. RAID

    B. Secret sharing made short (SSMS)

    C. Homomorphic encryption

    D. Asymmetric encryption

44. Which theoretical technology would allow superposition of physical states to increase both computing capacity and encryption keyspace?

    A. All-or-nothing-transform with Reed-Solomon (AONT-RS)

    B. Quantum computing

    C. Filigree investment

    D. Sharding

45. In a virtualized environment, suspended virtual machine (VM) instances at rest are subject to increased risk because _____.

    A. There is no way to encrypt instances at rest

    B. Insider threats are greater for data storage locations than processing locations

    C. The instances are saved as image snapshots and highly portable

    D. They are unprotected unless multifactor authentication is required

46. In a virtualized cloud environment, the management plane is usually responsible for provisioning virtual machine instances with all of the following resources *except* _____.

    A. CPU

    B. Memory

    C. User interface

    D. Permanent storage

47. Which of the following business continuity and disaster recovery (BC/DR) testing methodologies is least intrusive?

    A. Walk-through

    B. Simulation

    C. Tabletop

    D. Full test

48. In order for an organization to determine if its backup solution is adequate for meeting the recovery point objective (RPO), what *must* be done?

    A. Conduct full backups at least daily.

    B. Use a data mirroring solution.

    C. Put all backups in the cloud.

    D. Practice a restore from backup.

49. Which common characteristic of the cloud data center also serves customer business continuity and disaster recovery (BC/DR) needs?

    A. Multitenancy

    B. Virtualization

    C. Redundancy

    D. Software-defined networking

50. Which phase of the business continuity and disaster recovery (BC/DR) process can result in a second disaster?

    A. Event anticipation

    B. Creating BC/DR plans and policy

    C. Return to normal operations

    D. Incident initiation

51. Which process artifact aids an organization in determining the critical assets and functions that need to continue operations during a business continuity and disaster recovery (BC/DR) contingency?

    A. Service Organization Control (SOC) 2, Type 2

    B. Business impact analysis (BIA)

    C. Qualitative risk analysis report

    D. Annual loss expectancy (ALE) calculation

52. In general, a cloud business continuity and disaster recovery (BC/DR) solution will be _____ than a physical solution.

    A. Slower

    B. Less expensive

    C. Larger

    D. More difficult to engineer

53. Which of the following is not a common federation technology?

    A. WS-Federation

    B. OWASP

    C. OpenID

    D. OAuth

54. Which of the following is an audit report on the design of an organization's controls?

    A. Service Organization Control (SOC) 1

    B. SOC 2, Type 1

    C. SOC 3

    D. SOC 4

55. Which of the following is not usually suitable for inclusion in a service-level agreement (SLA) for managed cloud services?

    A. Service availability

    B. Number of users and virtual machines

    C. Background checks for provider personnel

    D. Amount of cloud storage

56. Which of the following is *not* a typical physical access control mechanism in the cloud data center?

    A. Cage locks

    B. Video surveillance

    C. Rack locks

    D. Fire suppression

57. Which of the following cloud environment accounts should only be granted on a temporary basis?

    A. Remote users

    B. Senior management

    C. Internal users

    D. External vendors

58. Which of the following attack vectors is new to the cloud environment and was not typically found in on-premises, legacy environments?

    A. Distributed denial of service (DDoS)

    B. Guest escape

    C. Internal threats

    D. Inadvertent disclosure

59. Which of the following is a file server that provides data access to multiple, heterogeneous machines and users on the network?

    A. Storage area network (SAN)

    B. Network-attached storage (NAS)

    C. Hardware security module (HSM)

    D. Content delivery network (CDN)

60. You are the security manager for a retail company that is considering cloud migration to a public, software as a service (SaaS) solution both for your current internal production environment (an on-premises data center) and to host your e-commerce presence. Which of the following is a new concern you should bring up to senior management for them to consider before the migration?

    A. Regulatory compliance for your credit card processing transactions

    B. Inadvertent disclosure by internal (company) personnel

    C. Data disclosure through insufficiently isolated resources

    D. Malicious intrusion by external entities

61. When a data center is configured such that the backs of the devices face each other and the ambient temperature in the work area is cool, it is called _____.

    A. Hot aisle containment

    B. Cold aisle containment

    C. Thermo-optimized

    D. Heating, ventilation, and air conditioning (HVAC) modulated

62. Disciplined cable management is crucial for cloud data centers because it provides greater assurance of only authorized lines operating in the environment and _____.

    A. Reduces unproductive heating, ventilation, and air conditioning (HVAC) activity

    B. Reduces the risk of slip, trip, and fall hazards

    C. Greatly reduces the environmental footprint

    D. Ensures regulatory compliance

63. To optimize airflow within a data center according to industry standards, a raised floor used as an air plenum must have at least _____ of clearance.

    A. One foot

    B. One meter

    C. 24 inches

    D. 30 inches

64. Raised flooring can serve as both an air plenum and _____.

    A. A convenient location for RAID arrays

    B. Cool storage for data center personnel meals

    C. A conduit for running cable

    D. Disaster shelter locations

65. Typically, when raised flooring is used as an air plenum, _____ air is directed through it.

    A. Warm

    B. Cold

    C. Bleed

    D. Exhaust

66. There are two general types of smoke detectors. One type uses a light source to detect the presence of particulate matter resulting from a fire, and the other uses _____.

    A. Electric pulses

    B. Small amounts of radioactive material

    C. Fiber-optic mechanisms

    D. A water-pressure plate

67. Fire suppression systems are often linked to a detection system. Common detection systems include all of the following *except* _____.

   A. Heat

   B. Pressure

   C. Flame

   D. Smoke

68. FM-200 has all the following properties *except* _____.

   A. It's nontoxic at levels used for fire suppression

   B. It's gaseous at room temperature

   C. It may deplete the earth's ozone layer

   D. It does not leave a film or coagulant after use

69. FM-200 has all the following properties *except* _____.

   A. It is colorless

   B. It leaves a faint chemical residue after use

   C. It is liquid when stored

   D. It is nonconducive

70. Dynamic Host Configuration Protocol (DHCP) servers in a network will provide the clients with all of the following *except* _____.

   A. A temporary IP address

   B. Encryption protocols

   C. A default gateway

   D. Time server synchronization

71. You are the security officer for a cloud deployment. In order to secure data in transit, you can choose to implement all of the following techniques and technologies *except* _____.

   A. DNSSEC

   B. TLS

   C. IDS/IPS

   D. IPSec

72. All of the following techniques are used in OS hardening *except* _____.

   A. Removing default accounts

   B. Disallowing local save of credentials

   C. Removing unnecessary services

   D. Preventing all administrative access

73. You are performing an audit of the security controls used in a cloud environment. Which of the following would *best* serve your purpose?

    A. The business impact analysis (BIA)

    B. A copy of the virtual machine (VM) baseline configuration

    C. The latest version of the company's financial records

    D. A Service Organization Control (SOC) 3 report from another (external) auditor

74. In a cloud environment, prior to putting a node into maintenance mode, all of the following actions should be taken *except* _____.

    A. Prevent any new users from logging on or creating any new instances

    B. Migrate any existing guest virtual machines (VMs) to another node

    C. Disable alerts from host-based intrusion detection systems (IDSs), intrusion prevention systems (IPSs), or firewalls

    D. Disable logging functions and tools

75. A cloud provider conducting scheduled maintenance of the environment should do all the following *except* _____.

    A. Notify any customers who may be affected

    B. Require reverification of all user accounts

    C. Follow approved change-management procedures and processes

    D. Confirm that remaining resources are sufficient to manage the minimum load as dictated by service-level agreements (SLAs)

76. Which of the following is characterized by a set maximum capacity?

    A. A secret-sharing-made-short (SSMS) bit-splitting implementation

    B. A tightly coupled cloud storage cluster

    C. A loosely coupled cloud storage cluster

    D. A public-key infrastructure

77. Which of the following is an open source cloud-based software project characterized by a toolset that includes components called Nova, Neutron, Heat, Ironic, and Cinder?

    A. OWASP

    B. OAuth

    C. OpenStack

    D. Mozilla

78. You are the security director for a call center that provides live support for customers of various vendors. Your staff handles calls regarding refunds, complaints, and the use of products customers have purchased. To process refunds, your staff will have access to purchase information, determine which credit card the customer used, and identify specific elements of personal data. How should you best protect this sensitive data and still accomplish the purpose?

    A. Encrypt the data while it is at rest but allow the call center personnel to decrypt it for refund transactions.

    B. Encrypt the data while call center personnel are performing their operations.

C. Mask the data while call center personnel are performing their operations.

D. Have the call center personnel request the pertinent information from the customer for every refund transaction.

79. Which of the following is *not* typically included as a basic phase of the software development lifecycle (SDLC)?

A. Define

B. Design

C. Describe

D. Develop

80. What is the most important input to the software development lifecycle (SDLC)?

A. Senior management direction

B. Legislation/regulation

C. Investor oversight

D. Business requirements

81. Which of the following can be included in the cloud security architecture as a means to identify and reject hostile SQL commands?

A. Web application firewall (WAF)

B. Application programming interface (API) gateway

C. Data loss prevention or data leak protection (DLP)

D. Database activity monitor (DAM)

82. You are the security manager for a software development firm. Your company is interested in using a managed cloud service provider for hosting its testing environment. Which cloud service or deployment model would probably best suit your needs?

A. Infrastructure as a service (IaaS)

B. Platform as a service (PaaS)

C. Software as a service (SaaS)

D. Community

83. You are the security manager for a software development firm. Your company is interested in using a managed cloud service provider for hosting its testing environment. Which of the following tools, technologies, or techniques may be very useful for your purposes?

A. Data loss prevention or data leak protection (DLP)

B. Digital rights management (DRM)

C. Sandboxing

D. Web application firewall (WAF)

84. You are the security manager for a software development firm. Your company is interested in using a managed cloud service provider for hosting its testing environment. Previous releases have shipped with major flaws that were not detected in the testing phase; leadership wants to avoid repeating that problem. What tool, technique, or technology might you suggest to aid in identifying programming errors?

    A. Vulnerability scans

    B. Open source review

    C. Service Organization Control (SOC) audits

    D. Regulatory review

85. You are the security manager for a software development firm. Your company is interested in using a managed cloud service provider for hosting its testing environment. Previous releases have shipped with major flaws that were not detected in the testing phase; leadership wants to avoid repeating that problem. It is important to prevent _____ from being present during the testing.

    A. Senior management

    B. Marketing department personnel

    C. Finance analysts

    D. Programmers who worked on the software

86. You are the security manager for a software development firm. Your company is interested in using a managed cloud service provider for hosting its testing environment. Management is interested in adopting an Agile development style. When you explain what impact this will have, you note that _____ may be decreased by this option.

    A. Speed of development

    B. Thoroughness of documentation

    C. Availability of prototypes

    D. Customer collaboration

87. You are the security manager for a software development firm. Your company is interested in using a managed cloud service provider for hosting its testing environment. Management is interested in adopting an Agile development style. In order for this to happen, the company will have to increase the involvement of _____.

    A. Security personnel

    B. Budget and finance representatives

    C. Members of the user group

    D. Senior management

88. You are the security manager for a software development firm. Your company is interested in using a managed cloud service provider for hosting its testing environment. Management is interested in adopting an Agile development style. This will be typified by which of the following traits?

  A. Reliance on a concrete plan formulated during the Define phase

  B. Rigorous, repeated security testing

  C. Isolated programming experts for specific functional elements

  D. Short, iterative work periods

89. You are the security manager for a software development firm. Your company is interested in using a managed cloud service provider for hosting its testing environment. Management is interested in adopting an Agile development style. This will be typified by which of the following traits?

  A. Daily meetings

  B. A specific shared toolset

  C. Defined plans that dictate all efforts

  D. Addressing customer needs with an exhaustive initial contract

90. You are the security manager for a software development firm. Your company is interested in using a managed cloud service provider for hosting its testing environment. The backend of the software will have the data structured in a way to optimize XML requests. Which API programming style should programmers most likely concentrate on for the frontend interface?

  A. Simple Object Access Protocol (SOAP)

  B. Representational state transfer (REST)

  C. Security Assertion Markup Language (SAML)

  D. Data loss prevention or data leak protection (DLP)

91. You are the security manager for a software development firm. Your company is interested in using a managed cloud service provider for hosting its testing environment. You recommend the use of STRIDE threat modeling to assess potential risks associated with the software. Which of the following is *not* addressed by STRIDE?

  A. External parties presenting false credentials

  B. External parties illicitly modifying information

  C. Participants able to deny a transaction

  D. Users unprepared for secure operation by lack of training

92. You are the security manager for a software development firm. Your company is interested in using a managed cloud service provider for hosting its testing environment. Management has decided that the company will deploy encryption, data loss prevention or data leak protection (DLP), and digital rights management (DRM) in the cloud environment for additional protection. When consulting with management, you explain that these tools will most likely reduce _____.

   A. External threats

   B. Internal threats

   C. Software vulnerabilities

   D. Quality of service

93. You are the security manager for a software development firm. Your company is interested in using a managed cloud service provider for hosting its testing environment. Your company has, and wishes to retain, ISO 27034 certification. For every new application it creates, it will also have to create a(n) _____.

   A. Organizational normative framework (ONF)

   B. Application normative framework (ANF)

   C. Intrinsic normative framework (INF)

   D. Service Organization Control (SOC) 3 report

94. You are the security manager for a software development firm. Your company is interested in using a managed cloud service provider for hosting a customer-facing production environment. Many of your end users are located in the European Union (EU) and will provide personal data as they use your software. Your company will not be allowed to use a cloud data center in which of the following countries?

   A. Japan

   B. Australia

   C. Belgium

   D. Chile

95. You are the security manager for a software development firm. Your company is interested in using a managed cloud service provider for hosting a customer-facing production environment. Many of your end users are located in the European Union (EU) and will provide personal data as they use your software. Your company will not be allowed to use a cloud data center in which of the following countries?

   A. Argentina

   B. Israel

   C. South Korea

   D. Switzerland

96. You are the security manager for a software development firm. Your company is interested in using a managed cloud service provider for hosting a customer-facing production environment. Many of your end users are located in the European Union (EU) and will provide personal data as they use your software. Your company will not be allowed to use a cloud data center in which of the following countries?

A. Canada

B. Singapore

C. France

D. Kenya

97. Which of the following is not a core principle included in the Organisation for Economic Cooperation and Development (OECD) privacy guidelines?

A. The individual must have the ability to refrain from sharing their data.

B. The individual must have the ability to correct errors in their data.

C. The individual must be able to request a purge of their data.

D. The entity holding the data must secure it.

98. Who is the entity identified by personal data?

A. The data owner

B. The data processor

C. The data custodian

D. The data subject

99. What is the current European Union (EU) privacy legislation that restricts dissemination of personal data outside the EU?

A. The EU Data Directive

B. Privacy Shield

C. The General Data Protection Regulation (GDPR)

D. Sarbanes–Oxley (SOX)

100. In order for American companies to process personal data belonging to European Union (EU) citizens, they must comply with the Privacy Shield program. The program is administered by the U.S. Department of Transportation and the _____.

A. U.S. State Department

B. Fish and Wildlife Service

C. Federal Trade Commission (FTC)

D. Federal Communication Commission (FCC)

101. In addition to the Privacy Shield program, what other means can non–European Union (EU) companies use to be allowed to process personal data of EU citizens?

A. Enhanced security controls

B. Standard contractual clauses

C. Increased oversight

D. Modified legal regulation

102. Which entity is legally responsible for the protection of personal data?

   A. The data subject

   B. The data controller

   C. The data processor

   D. The data steward

103. When a company is first starting and has no defined processes and little documentation, it can be said to be at level _____ of the Capability Maturity Model (CMM).

   A. 1

   B. 2

   C. 3

   D. 4

104. Which of the following standards addresses a company's entire security program, involving all aspects of various security disciplines?

   A. ISO 27001

   B. ISO 27002

   C. National Institute of Standards and Technology (NIST) 800-37

   D. Statement on Standards for Attestation Engagements (SSAE) 18

105. A cloud provider might only release Service Organization Control (SOC 2), Type 2 reports to _____.

   A. Regulators

   B. The public

   C. Potential customers

   D. Current customers

106. A cloud provider's Service Organization Control (SOC) 1 report may not be useful to customers interested in determining the provider's security posture because the SOC 1 report contains only information about _____.

   A. Sales projections

   B. Financial reporting

   C. Previous customer satisfaction

   D. Process definition

107. The Payment Card Industry (PCI) Data Security Standard requires different levels of activity based on participants' _____.

   A. Number of personnel

   B. Branch locations

   C. Number of transactions per year

   D. Preferred banking institutions

108. Which IT product review framework is intended to determine the accuracy of vendor claims regarding security functions of the product?

    A.   Underwriters Laboratories (UL)

    B.   Federal Information Processing Standard (FIPS) 140-2

    C.   Payment Card Industry (PCI) Data Security Standard (DSS)

    D.   Common Criteria

109. What is the lowest level of cryptographic security for a cryptographic module, according to the Federal Information Processing Standard (FIPS) 140-2 standard?

    A.   1

    B.   2

    C.   3

    D.   4

110. What is the highest level of the Cloud Security Alliance Security, Trust, and Assurance Registry (CSA STAR) certification program for cloud service providers?

    A.   1

    B.   2

    C.   3

    D.   4

111. Every cloud service provider that opts to join the Cloud Security Alliance Security, Trust, and Assurance Registry (CSA STAR) program registry must complete a _____.

    A.   Service Organization Control (SOC) 2, Type 2 audit report

    B.   Consensus Assessment Initiative Questionnaire (CAIQ)

    C.   National Institute of Standards and Technology (NIST) 800-37 Risk Management Framework (RMF) audit

    D.   ISO 27001 information security management system (ISMS) review

112. The term *cloud carrier* most often refers to _____.

    A.   The cloud provider

    B.   The cloud customer

    C.   An Internet service provider (ISP)

    D.   A cloud manager

113. In a centralized broker identity federation, which entity typically creates and sends the Security Assertion Markup Language (SAML) token?

    A.   The cloud provider

    B.   The Internet service provider (ISP)

    C.   The broker

    D.   The cloud customer

114. Which of the following tools incorporates and references the requirements listed in all the others?

  A. ISO 27001

  B. Cloud Security Alliance (CSA) Cloud Controls Matrix (CCM)

  C. Federal Risk and Authorization Management Program (FedRAMP)

  D. European Union Agency for Network and Information Security (ENISA)

115. Which of the following is an example of true multifactor authentication?

  A. Having a login that requires both a password and a personal identification number (PIN)

  B. Using a thumbprint and voice recognition software for access control

  C. Presenting a credit card along with a Social Security card

  D. Signing a personal check

116. Which of the following is appropriate to include in a service-level agreement (SLA)?

  A. That the provider deliver excellent uptime

  B. That the provider host the customer's data only within specific jurisdictions

  C. That any conflicts arising from the contract be settled within a particular jurisdiction

  D. The specific amount of data that can be uploaded to the cloud environment in any given month

117. Which of the following standards is typically used to convey public key information in a public-key infrastructure (PKI) arrangement?

  A. Security Assertion Markup Language (SAML)

  B. X.400

  C. X.509

  D. 802.11

118. In working with various networking technologies such as Frame Relay, ATM, and Ethernet, the capability of the network to provide better service to selected traffic is called _____.

  A. QaS

  B. ASP

  C. OLA

  D. QoS

119. Which type of networking model is optimized for cloud deployments in which the underlying storage and IP networks are combined so as to maximize the benefits of a cloud workload?

  A. Software-defined networking model

  B. Enterprise networking model

  C. Converged networking model

  D. Legacy networking model

120. Which type of law consists of a body of rules and statutes that define prohibited conduct and is set out to protect the safety and well-being of the public?

    A. Tort

    B. Criminal

    C. Civil

    D. Contract

121. What is the primary reason for the use of SSDs in the cloud today?

    A. They are faster than traditional spinning drives.

    B. They last longer than traditional spinning drives.

    C. They are easier to replace than traditional spinning drives.

    D. They can be replaced quickly.

122. Which of the following are risks associated with virtualization?

    A. Loss of governance, snapshot and image security, and sprawl

    B. Public awareness, snapshot and image availability, and sprawl

    C. Increased cost, snapshot and image security, and sprawl

    D. Loss of data

123. Which of the following is the core of any system handling all input/output (I/O) instructions?

    A. Central processing unit (CPU)

    B. Hypervisor

    C. User interface

    D. Supervising application

124. Which of the following is an international organization of network designers and architects who work together in establishing standards and protocols for the Internet?

    A. Internet Assigned Numbers Authority (IANA)

    B. International Organization for Standardization (ISO)/ International Electrotechnical Commission (IEC)

    C. National Institute of Standards and Technology (NIST)

    D. Internet Engineering Task Force (IETF)

125. _____ is a symmetric block type of cipher used to encrypt information and is currently the standard for the U.S. government in protecting sensitive and secret documents.

    A. MD5

    B. Secure Socket Layer (SSL)

    C. Blowfish

    D. Advanced Encryption Standard (AES)

Appendix

Answers to Review Questions

Chapter 1: Domain 1: Cloud Concepts, Architecture, and Design

1. **A.** PaaS will allow her developers to create and design their software on a variety of operating systems (OSs), increasing the breadth of the market she can sell to. Also, she can use geographically dispersed programmers to work on projects concurrently, and the provider will be responsible for maintaining and updating the OSs as necessary. IaaS is a less attractive option because it would retain the need for Alice's company to administer the OSs in addition to building their software; it might be less expensive in terms of paying the cloud provider, but the time and effort and personnel necessary to maintain the OSs would offset that cost, probably in a net-negative way. SaaS is not an option; Alice wants her company to build software, not rent it or buy it. Backup as a Service (BaaS) would not be useful for creating, designing, or deploying Alice's company's software.

2. **A.** Of these four options, multitenancy poses the greatest risk to software developers in the cloud, because developers need to be concerned with two things: protecting their intellectual property (the software they're making) and protecting resource calls their software makes to the underlying infrastructure (which, if detectable by other cloud customers, could provide information that constitutes a side-channel attack). Metered service doesn't pose much of a security risk. The SLA might include some security aspects (such as response time), but it's usually more of a performance-ensuring tool, and this choice is not as good as option A. Remote access, in this particular case, provides more benefit than risk: Alice can utilize work from developers located across the country or across the planet. While she does have to consider the risks inherent in all remote access, those risks are not as significant as the risks due to multitenancy, so option A is still preferable.

3. **C.** Turnstiles are a physical security barrier to prevent piggybacking/tailgating (an unauthorized person coming through an entrance behind someone who is authorized), but they don't really present much protection for intellectual property in this case. Egress monitoring (often referred to as "DLP" solutions) is a great way to reduce the likelihood of intellectual property leaving the owner's control in an unexpected/unapproved manner. Likewise, strong encryption is useful in the cloud to reduce the impact of theft either from leakage to other cloud tenants or from insider threats (such as malicious admins in the employ of the cloud provider). Finally, digital watermarks aid protection of intellectual property by proving original ownership, which is essential for enforcing intellectual property rights (in the case of software design, mainly copyright protections).

4. **D.** While all of these are traits of cloud computing and will likely benefit Alice's company, from her position as senior manager of the organization she is likely to consider the financial benefit first and foremost.

5. **A.** With infrastructure as a service (IaaS), the customer (data owner) will administer the OS and applications. In PaaS, the provider will manage the underlying hardware and the OS. In an on-premises enterprise, the data owner is also the system owner and will be responsible for everything. In an SaaS environment, the cloud provider will handle all aspects of processing, except for adding and manipulating the production data.

6. B. PCI DSS requires that the CCV (or, sometimes, "CVV" for "card verification value") only be used in the transaction, not stored. The data described in all the other options may be stored after the transaction is complete.

7. A. The four merchant levels in PCI are distinguished by the number of transactions that merchant conducts in a year. The dollar value of transactions per year, geographic location, and jurisdiction are not attributes that are evaluated for PCI DSS tier levels.

8. C. Technically, BC efforts are meant to ensure that critical business functions can continue during a disruptive event, and DR efforts are supposed to support the return to normal operations. However, in practice, the efforts often coincide, use the same plans/personnel, and have many of the same procedures.

Option A is incorrect; both BC and DR use the RTO and RPO as metrics to determine success.

Option B is incorrect; BC and DR efforts are not specific to the cause of a disruptive event.

Option D is incorrect; health and human safety should be paramount in all security efforts, with very few exceptions.

9. D. The contract between the cloud customer and current cloud provider has no bearing on what the customer will have to pay to a new provider; that will be governed by the contract between the customer and the new provider.

All the other options are topics that should be addressed in the contract between the current cloud provider and the cloud customer in order to properly address BCDR needs.

10. A. The customer will have to pay for the costs of modification requested by the customer, regardless of purpose.

All the other options are simply incorrect, especially option D, which is never true.

11. D. The brand associated with the cloud provider should not influence the cost–benefit analysis; the cloud provider's brand (and even which cloud provider an organization uses) will most likely not even be known to the consumers who have a business relationship with the organization.

The provider does not absorb the cost when the customer's requests a modification of the SLA. Though an even split of the cost between customer and provider may seem fair, the customer pays for all costs associated with modifications to the SLA by the customer. Finally, customer modifications to their SLA are chargeable expenses that will almost certainly be paid for by the customer.

12. C. The timing of recurring payments to the provider will probably not be a significant factor in the cost–benefit analysis.

All the other options are topics that are more important to review when an organization is considering cloud migration.

13. B. In a traditional environment, enterprise software costs can be exorbitant, and the price of licensing doesn't even reflect the hidden costs associated with licensing, such as managing the license library. In a cloud arrangement, especially software as a service (SaaS), the customer pays only the contract fee to the cloud provider, and it is the provider's responsibility to arrange for software licensing and to manage those licenses.

Option A is incorrect because the number of users should not be affected whether the organization is operating in the cloud or a legacy environment. The exception would be the reduced number of privileged users, because the cloud provider will be handling more administrative tasks in the environment; however, because "privileged" was not specified, option B is still a better answer.

Option C is incorrect because that may or may not be true of an organization's migration to the cloud.

Option D is incorrect because the organization certainly hopes it is not going to lose clientele by moving to the cloud!

14. **A.** Cloud providers are purchasing utilities (power, water, Internet connectivity) at such a massive rate that they can realize per-unit cost savings that would far exceed any smaller organizations' pricing for individual data centers. In this case, economies of scale are very much in favor of the larger entity.

Option B may or may not be true, depending on the degree of sensitivity and value of the organization's data and what controls the organization will request/contract for in the cloud.

Options C and D are not influenced by cloud migration in any way and are wholly dependent on other factors within the organization.

15. **C.** Constant reinvestment in IT assets (which are almost always obsolete by the time they're marketed, much less by the time they're deployed in operational environments) is plagued with sunk costs; money spent on hardware devices or software licenses is unlikely to be recovered. Avoiding expenditures for IT systems by moving to the cloud means reducing these costs considerably.

Option A is incorrect; cloud migration should not affect the need for personnel training; employees will just need to be trained in a different manner.

Options B and D should not be affected by cloud migration in any way; whether your organization has a high personnel turnover rate or risk from internal threat is not based on whether the IT environment is owned or leased.

16. **B.** Every security process, tool, and behavior entails a related cost, both financially and operationally. Although a "base price" cloud service might appear extremely affordable compared to the traditional environment, add-ons such as encryption, digital rights management (DRM), security incident/event management (SIM/SEM/SIEM), and intrusion detection/prevention systems (IDS/IPS) may all come with additional cost and may degrade performance, thus reducing the cost savings compared to the cost of operations prior to migration. This is extremely important for the organization to consider before migration, especially if the organization exists in a highly regulated industry.

Option A is incorrect because the altitude of the cloud data center does not translate into a reduction of the actual financial benefit the organization would realize in moving to the cloud environment.

Option C is wrong because it should be the opposite of the actual case: losing ownership of the IT assets, and paying only for the use of those assets, should lead directly to a savings over the costs of a traditional IT environment, if compared on a seat-to-seat basis.

Option D should not be true; the cost of connecting users to the Internet should not be significantly greater if the organization operates in the cloud or with an on-premises data center—if the cost is considerably greater, the organization should never have migrated in the first place.

17. C. ISO 27001 mandates an ISMS; organizations can be certified according to compliance with 27001.

National Institute of Standards and Technology (NIST) SP 800-53 is the list of security controls approved for use by U.S. government agencies and a means to map them to the Risk Management Framework.

The Payment Card Industry Data Security Standard (PCI DSS) is the payment card industry's framework of compliance for all entities accepting or processing credit card payments.

NIST SP 800-37 is the Risk Management Framework.

18. D. The ISO 27001 standard is designed to be product agnostic. The other answers suggest ISO 27001 favors a type of technology, and are therefore incorrect.

19. C. The ISO standards are almost universally accepted and recognized, and they're even mandated for certain industries/locales.

They are not, however, cheap, fast, or easy to adopt, implement, and audit against, so all the other answers are incorrect.

20. A. The NIST standards are not particularly easy or fast to implement (in fact, they require continual improvement), and they are not widely recognized or mandated outside of the U.S. government federal sector.

However, they are in the public domain, so an organization would not have to pay for the standards material if the organization chose to use NIST standards.

21. A. ISO 27002 is used for choosing security controls in order to comply with the ISMS, which is contained in ISO 27001.

PCI DSS is the payment card industry's framework of compliance for all entities accepting or processing credit card payments.

NIST SP 800-37 is the Risk Management Framework.

HIPAA is the U.S. law regarding patient data privacy in the medical sector.

22. B. SSAE 18 is the current AICPA audit standard, as of 2018.

All the other options are distractors: SABSA is an IT architecture framework, Biba is an access control model, and NIST SP 800-53 contains guidance for selecting security controls in accordance with the Risk Management Framework.

23. D. GLBA is a U.S. federal law pertaining to financial and insurance customer information.

NIST 800-53 is a standard, not a law, so option A is incorrect.

Health Insurance Portability and Accountability Act (HIPAA) is a U.S. federal law concerning medical information, so option B is incorrect.

SOX affects publicly traded corporations, making option C incorrect.

24. C. The SSAE 18 is an audit standard, and the SOC reports were specifically designed to report on the suitability of organizations that provide services. This is not to say that SOC reports are not used to assess other types of organizations—they are, but they were not designed for that purpose, so all the other answers are incorrect.

25. C. The SOC 2, Type 2 report will provide details on IT security controls used by the target and how well those controls function.

The SOC 1 report provides information about financial reporting mechanisms of the target only and is of little interest to the IT security professional, so option A is incorrect.

The SOC 2, Type 1 report describes IT security controls designed by the target only but not how effectively those controls function, so option B is incorrect.

The SOC 3 report is only an attestation that the target was audited and that it passed the audit, without detail, so option D is incorrect.

26. A. The SOC 1 report provides information about financial reporting mechanisms of the target only. Although this information may be of little use to the IT security professional, it may be of great use to potential investors, if for nothing other than providing some assurance that reporting is valid and believable.

The SOC 2, Type 1 report describes IT security controls designed by the target only but not how effectively those controls function. While of some interest to the IT security professional, this is of little interest to the investor, so option B is incorrect.

The SOC 2, Type 2 report will provide details on IT security controls used by the target and how well those controls function. While of great interest to the IT security professional, this is of little interest to the investor, so option C is incorrect.

The SOC 3 report is only an attestation that the target was audited and that it passed the audit, without detail, so option D is incorrect.

27. D. The SOC 3 report is an attestation that the target was audited and that it passed the audit, without detail; you could use the SOC 3 reports to quickly narrow down the list of possible providers by eliminating the ones without SOC 3s.

The SOC 1 report provides information about financial reporting mechanisms of the target only. This information may be of little use to the IT security professional and won't help you choose a cloud vendor, so option A is incorrect.

The SOC 2, Type 1 report describes IT security controls designed by the target only but not how effectively those controls function. While of some interest to the IT security professional, it is more comprehensive and detailed than a SOC 3 report, so it would take more time; option B is incorrect.

The SOC 2, Type 2 report will provide details on IT security controls used by the target and how well those controls function. While of great interest to the IT security professional, it is very detailed and comprehensive and wouldn't be a speedy tool to narrow the field. Option C is incorrect.

28. D. PCI DSS applies only to those entities that want to engage in the business of taking or processing credit card payments, which would include options A, B, and C. A counseling service is not engaged in commerce involving credit cards and therefore is under no obligation to adhere to the PCI DSS.

29. B. Because PCI DSS is strictly voluntary, and the PCI Council is not a government body but a consortium of private interests, they cannot detain or imprison anyone.

They can, however, assess fees, suspend processing privileges, and require more auditing, so the other answers are true and therefore incorrect.

30. B. The PCI merchant levels are based on how many transactions a compliant entity engages in over the course of a year.

All the other options are incorrect because the dollar value of transactions and location of the merchant or processor are not the criteria used for determining PCI DSS merchant levels. Only the transactions a compliant entity engages in over the course of a year is the correct answer.

31. A. Merchant level 1 is for the merchants that engage in the most transactions per year (six million or more). It carries with it the requirement for the most comprehensive, detailed, and repeated security validation actions.

It may be tempting to choose the highest number when choosing an answer for the highest merchant level. It may be counterintuitive to think that level 1 would be a higher level than a level 4. However, level 1 is the highest merchant level and is the correct answer to this question.

32. C. The Payment Card Industry Data Security Standard (PCI DSS) requires multiple kinds of technical and nontechnical security requirements (including specific control types) for those entities that choose to subscribe to the standard.

Option A is partially correct and partially incorrect. While the security requirements are partially technical, some requirements are also nontechnical. Therefore, option A is incorrect.

Option B is also partially correct and partially incorrect. While the security requirements are partially nontechnical, some requirements are technical. Therefore, option B is incorrect.

Option C is incorrect because the requirements are technical and nontechnical, not neither technical nor nontechnical.

33. D. The Payment Card Industry Data Security Standard (PCI DSS) allows for cardholder information at rest to be secured with either tokenization or encryption, but use of one is mandatory.

The other options are distractors and not dictated by PCI DSS. They can, however, be useful in fulfilling certain credit card support services, such as customer support, where the personnel engaged in the activity (customer support agents, for instance) may need access to a limited set of the cardholder's account information (for instance, name, mailing address, and date of the payment) but do not have a need to know other elements of that data set (particularly, the full credit card number); masking and obfuscation can satisfy that business need without putting data unduly at risk.

34. B. The Payment Card Industry Data Security Standard (PCI DSS) disallows the storage of the CVV for any length of time; the CVV may only be used during the payment transaction, and not saved.

The other options may be stored for future transactions with the same merchant. However, unlike the CVV they may be stored by the merchant.

35. B. The EAL is a measure of how thoroughly the security features the product vendor claims the product offers have been tested and reviewed, and by whom.

The EAL does not offer any true measure of how well those security features will work in a production environment so options A and C are incorrect. Whether those features are preferable to other features offered by competing products, or whether the product is "good." Therefore, option D is incorrect.

36. A. EAL 1 is for functionally tested products. Option B is incorrect because EAL 3 is for solutions that have been methodically tested and checked.

Option C, EAL 5 is incorrect because that is for solutions that have been semi-formally designed and tested.

Option D is incorrect because EAL 7 is for solutions that have been formally verified design and tested.

37. D. EAL 7 is for those products that have undergone independent third-party testing and verification of security feature design. All other options are distractors and incorrect.

EAL 1 is for functionally tested products.

EAL 3 is for solutions that have been methodically tested and checked.

EAL 5 is for solutions that have been semi-formally designed and tested.

38. B. The vendor/manufacturer of a given product will pay to have it certified, with the premise that certification costs are offset by premium prices that certified products command and that customers won't purchase uncertified products.

NIST does not certify products for Common Criteria. NIST is a U.S. government organization.

Option C is incorrect because the cloud customer does not pay to have IT products certified.

Option D is incorrect because the end user is an individual and individuals do not pay to have IT products certified.

(Note: Of course, the manufacturer/vendor is going to amortize the cost of the certification process across the price of the products they sell, so the customers who purchase the product will eventually "pay" for the certification, but that's a very oblique and abstract way of reading the question.)

39. D. NIST publishes the list of validated crypto modules. The other choices are government or non-government organizations that are not involved with publishing the list of cryptographic modules that meet FIPS 140-2 requirements.

40. C. Vendors seeking HSM certification under FIPS 140-2 send their products to independent laboratories that have been validated as Cryptographic Module Testing Laboratories under the National Voluntary Laboratory Accreditation Program (the Accreditation Program is run by NIST, which approves the laboratories). As of this writing, 21 labs in the United States and Canada are accredited.

Option A is incorrect because NIST does not perform the review process. NIST approves the independent laboratories that perform the review process.

Option B is incorrect. Of all the activities that the NSA does perform, reviewing the process for Hardware Security Modules in accordance with FIPS 140-2 is certainly not one of them.

Option D is incorrect because the ENISA is a European Union organization that supports European Union institutions and stakeholders.

41. D. The highest security level a product can reach is 4. Option A is incorrect because Level 1 is the lowest level of security. Option B is incorrect because Level 2 simply improves upon the physical security of Level 2. Option C is incorrect because Level 3 improves upon Level 2 certification and adds tamper-detection/response capabilities.

42. B. The security levels acknowledge different levels of physical protection offered by a crypto module, with 1 offering crypto functionality and no real physical protection and 4 offering tamper-resistant physical features and automatic zeroization of security parameters upon detection of tamper attempts.

The question asks what distinguishes the security levels for cryptographic modules. Option A focuses on the sensitivity of the data being protected. The sensitivity of the data that is being protected is important when it comes to the cryptographic module being used, but that is not the distinction between the security levels in FIPS 140-2.

Option C is incorrect because the size of the IT environment the cryptographic module is protecting is not what distinguishes the different levels.

Option D is not correct because whether the cryptographic module is or is not allowed in a certain geographic location has no bearing on whether or not it works. The cryptographic module either works or it does not, regardless of its location.

43. A. FIPS 140-2 is only for SBU data. Options B, C, and D are incorrect because FIPS 140-2 certifies cryptographic modules for unclassified data. Secret, Top Secret, and Sensitive Compartmentalized Information all are categorized as classified information when it refers to their sensitivity level.

44. B. Vendors who want their products certified under FIPS 140-2 must pay the laboratory that performs the evaluation.

Option A is incorrect because the U.S. government is not in the business of paying for cryptographic module certifications. The U.S. government can require the use of cryptographic modules in certain situations.

Certification laboratories receive funds for certifying cryptographic modules. They do not pay to have them certified. Therefore, option C is incorrect.

Option D is incorrect. Users do not pay to have solutions certified.

45. B. Most of the items on the Top Ten could be addressed with strong coding practices and by adhering to strict internal management processes (on the part of the organization involved in development). A good number of the items that continually appear on the list, such as injection, cross-site scripting, insecure direct object references, security misconfiguration, missing function-level access control, use of components with known vulnerabilities, and unvalidated redirects and forwards, can all be addressed by basic development practices, such as bounds checking/input validation, code validation/ verification protocols, and informed oversight of the project.

Strangely, option A is not correct in this case. Social engineering is perhaps the aspect of information security that is least understood (by users) and easiest to exploit, and it is the attack tactic most likely to succeed. Social engineering training could probably reduce the greatest number of overall security threats in our field today. However, this specific question is all about application security, and the element of social engineering is negligible.

Option C is not correct because source code testing is only one aspect of code review and would not address as many items on the Top Ten as option B would.

Option D is not correct for much the same reason option A is incorrect; this question is specifically about application security, and the physical protection element is very minor.

46. C. In injection attacks (a large percentage of which are called SQL injection, for the prevalence with which attackers target databases with this attack), the attacker enters a string of command code into a user-facing field in an attempt to get the application to run the command. This results in a process that the attacker can leverage or puts the software into a fail state that might negate some of the security controls that are present in normal operation.

Option A is incorrect; this is a description of social engineering.

Option B is incorrect; SQL injection does not typically involve malware.

An attack that allows someone to penetrate a facility is a physical attack. The attacker has to physically be at the facility itself. Option D is incorrect.

47. C. Attackers attempting injection put command code into a data entry field; if the application has suitable input validation (that is, refusing code strings and confirming that input conforms to field value types), it will block those attacks.

Injection attacks target applications, not users, so user training has little to do with preventing injection, making option A incorrect.

The OS usually has little to do with injection attacks, which usually target user-facing web apps that ride on the OS, so option B is not correct.

Injection attacks are logical, not physical, so locks won't aid the security effort in this case, making option D incorrect.

48. A. This answer requires a bit of thought and knowledge of common practices. Throughout the IT industry, many developers attempt to design and implement their own authentication schema. According to OWASP, this approach is almost always a bad idea because of the many vulnerabilities such custom schemes may fail to address. Using approved, tested authentication implementations is a way to avoid this problem.

Authentication schema should be transparent to users, who will have little or (preferably) no control over that element of communication. Thus, training is not applicable in this case, making option B wrong.

Input validation is used to counter injection attacks and has no efficacy in authentication implementations, making option C incorrect.

The X.400 standards are for email communication and are not applicable to session authentication; thus, option D is wrong.

49. D. HIPAA is the U.S. federal law governing medical information; it has nothing to do with authentication or session management. Failure to follow HIPAA leads to regulatory noncompliance (for those covered by it).

All the other options are practices that can enhance an attacker's ability to compromise authentication implementations and sessions.

50. C. As breaking authentication and session management is a logical attack, lack of physical controls don't affect such attacks.

All the other options are practices that can enhance an attacker's ability to compromise authentication implementations and sessions.

51. D. In many cases, HTML documents are meant to be seen by the public or new users who do not yet have trust associations (accounts) with the organization, so encrypting every HTML document would be counter to the purpose. Moreover, total encryption of everything, even material that is not particularly sensitive or valuable, incurs an additional cost with no appreciable benefit.

The other options are all actions that OWASP recommends for reducing the risk of XSS attacks: www.owasp.org/index.php/XSS_(Cross_Site_Scripting)_Prevention_Cheat_Sheet.

52. B. Option B is a incorrect because the answer narrows the risk for only the identity assertions and does not address XSS attack risks. All the other options are actions recommended by OWASP for reducing XSS attack risks.

This question is particularly difficult as it delves into a level of detail that may or may not appear on the actual exam; however, all source documents listed in the *Candidate Information Bulletin*, including the OWASP Top Ten, are fair game for the test, so it is best to have at least an understanding of these sources.

53. A. The URL in option A reveals a location of specific data as well as the format for potential other data (such as other authors' pages/accounts); this is a classic example of an insecure direct object reference.

Option B is a DoS program string; C is a SQL database command line (which wouldn't reveal any information on its own; it would prompt for a password); and option D is just an email address.

54. B. Untrusted sources calling a direct reference should be authenticated to ensure that the source has authorization to access that object.

Option A will not aid in insecure direct object risks; this is not a user issue, usually, but a programming issue. Option C is for physical security, while insecure direct object references are logical attacks. Option D does not reduce the risk of insecure direct object references because classification and categorization are not protections themselves but need to be paired with proper control sets in order to provide protection.

55. C. Default accounts are a continual security problem in the InfoSec space, and one that is relatively easy to address. Any new systems should be checked for default accounts, which should be stripped out before deployment.

Untrusted users should not have encryption keys, so this is not a misconfiguration; therefore, option A is incorrect.

A public-facing website can be extremely useful for marketing purposes and is not necessarily a security issue in and of itself, so option B is incorrect.

Option D might or might not be true; both turnstiles and mantraps are physical security controls, and we can't be sure whether one or the other is preferable in any given situation, so we don't know if this is a misconfiguration or a proper configuration. Option C is therefore preferable.

56. A. Any software with out-of-date builds can be considered misconfigured.

Option B is bad security practice but not considered a misconfiguration.

Data owners are supposed to classify/categorize the data under their control, so option C is not a correct answer.

Preventing users from reaching untrusted resources may be a proper control in a given environment, so option D is not a misconfiguration, and not a correct answer.

57. B. This question requires some thought. All the options are examples of good security practices and could therefore arguably be ways to reduce misconfiguration risks. However, option B is the best answer for this specific question: it is a method for reducing risks due to misconfiguration—a repeatable process for hardening systems/software that addresses other bad practices and is itself a good practice. This is the best answer.

58. C. All the options are examples of good security practices and could therefore arguably be ways to reduce misconfiguration risks. However, option C is the best answer for this specific question. The other three options are personnel/administrative/managerial controls, where the security misconfiguration is more a technical issue, which requires a technical solution.

59. B. All the options are examples of good security practices and could therefore arguably be ways to reduce misconfiguration risks. However, option B is the best answer for this specific question. The other three options are personnel/administrative/managerial controls, where the security misconfiguration is more a technical issue, which requires a technical solution.

60. D. All of these are good security practices, but only option D is a method for detecting and addressing misconfigurations.

61. A. Users are the most likely source of sensitive data exposure, particularly inadvertently. Ensuring that users know how to handle material properly is an excellent means for addressing the issue.

Option B is incorrect because firewalls that inspect inbound traffic only will not notice data exposed accidentally or maliciously as it travels outbound.

Option C is incorrect because it has nothing to do with data disclosure and is instead about business continuity and disaster recovery (BC/DR).

Option D is incorrect because it has nothing to do with data disclosure and is instead about physical security.

62. B. Data needs to be categorized according to its value/sensitivity; avoiding accurate categorization is just as troublesome, from a security perspective, as not categorizing the data or overcategorizing it (putting it in a higher category than it deserves).

All the other options are ways of reducing the risk of sensitive data disclosure. Option A reduces the possibility of disclosure by reducing the amount of data on hand (from the OWASP: "Data you don't have can't be stolen"). Option C reduces the chance of disclosing keys, which leads to disclosing the data. Option D reduces the possibility that the form will disclose sensitive data to someone filling it out by prompting with an entry that should be protected.

63. A. Setting the default to denying access forces all resource requests to be verified, thus ensuring that no particular function may be run without explicitly ensuring that it was called by an authorized user.

Option B is used to deter cross-site scripting attacks, so it is incorrect.

Option C is correct but insufficient; option A includes a more restrictive mode, so is therefore a better choice.

Option D is used to deter the possibility of insecure direct object references, so it is incorrect.

64. A. The method in option A will help you determine if there are functions that regular users should not have access to and thereby demonstrate that you are missing necessary controls.

According to the OWASP, "automated tools are unlikely to find these problems," so option B is incorrect.

Option C is incorrect because it is the exact opposite of what you're trying to accomplish; this is an example of what happens when function-level access controls are missing.

Option D in no way addresses the problem of missing function-level access controls, which is a technical problem, not a user issue.

65. D. Having the user authenticate the intentional request is a way to reduce the automated, forged requests attackers might submit as part of CSRF; CAPTCHA is a great way to reduce the likelihood of success for automated attacks.

Option A is incorrect because HTTP requests are usually made by the browser, without the user's knowledge; the user has no perspective of such requests, so this wouldn't be a useful mechanism in prevention.

Option B is incorrect because it's unrealistic. Removing all browsers would decrease the utility of the systems to the point where productivity would be negligible.

Option C is incorrect for similar reasons; the danger from CSRF is not because of links to the target website but because of the browser behavior.

66. D. This is a description of social engineering, not CSRF, which is a browser-based attack.

All the other options are possible exploits an attacker might try to accomplish with a CSRF attack.

67. B. This is the option OWASP recommends as the very least form of protection. Having a unique, unpredictable token for each session reduces the likelihood an attacker will be able to reuse tokens known by the browser or craft tokens that can be used in future attacks.

Option A is not optimal or sensible because it would inhibit all web traffic and remote access.

Option C is not optimal or sensible because it would severely limit your online capabilities.

Option D is not sensible because all browsers use stored tokens/cookies, and no browser is preferable for the purpose over others.

68. B. This is not an easy question and requires an understanding of how component libraries are used in software design.

Option B is preferable to the others because, according to the OWASP, publishers of component libraries do not often patch old components but rather issue the fixed component(s) as a new version. This is also why option D is incorrect.

Options A and C are two ways of stating the same thing, and not optimal; trying to use this method would require every one of your software packages to be wholly written by your programmers, which is actually not more secure than using published component libraries because the risk of additional human error and lack of review is introduced to the process.

69. B. This is not an easy question and requires an understanding of how component libraries are used in software design.

Option B makes the most sense; some vulnerabilities are known to exist only when a component is used in a specific way or with specific services; if the programmers are not including that way of using the component or the risky service, then the vulnerability would not pose a threat to the software they are creating and may therefore be acceptable.

Option A is not correct because an underwriter would be unlikely to cover a claim resulting solely from negligence; using a component with a known vulnerability and putting the product/user at risk knowingly would probably invalidate any insurance policy.

Option C might conceivably be considered correct in a fashion; different countries have different legislation/regulations, and a vulnerability that could cause noncompliance in one country might not in another. However, this is a rather tortured reading of the question, requiring some convoluted reasoning, and this option is therefore not the best answer.

Option D is not correct because a hidden vulnerability, by definition, is not a known vulnerability.

70. B. Staying current with published vulnerabilities for your component is crucial. This might not be simple as there are many versions of design components, and nomenclature is not always uniform.

Option A is incorrect because even standard libraries are subject to vulnerabilities, so you have to review notifications about those as well.

Option C is not correct; this is a method for reducing the risk of cross-site scripting (XSS) attacks.

Option D will not work as users have no influence or effect on which components are used in software design.

71. B. Oddly enough, this may be a good topic to explain during user training; when an attacker is trying to conduct an attack by exploiting unvalidated redirects and forwards, it is often in conjunction with a social engineering/phishing aspect. Users trained to recognize social engineering/phishing indicators might be able to avoid susceptibility to these attacks.

Option A is not correct; this is a method for reducing the risk of cross-site scripting (XSS) attacks.

Option C is not correct; it is ridiculous and would result in preventing all remote access.

Option D is not correct; audit logging would only track activity, not prevent a user from being directed/forwarded to an attack site.

72. A. Basic as it may seem, not including redirects and forwards within your software is an easy way to avoid the problem altogether, and redirects/forwards are not necessary for efficient usage.

Option B is a incorrect because this type of attack is not aimed at stored credentials.

Options C and D are both incorrect because neither of those types of solutions detect or prevent this type of attack.

73. A. This is the definition of cloud migration interoperability challenges. Portability is the measure of how difficult it might be to move the organization's systems/data from a given cloud host to another cloud host. Stability has no specific meaning here and is just a distractor. Security might be an element of this challenge but is not the optimum answer; the question posed a concern about functionality, not disclosure or tainting the information.

74. B. This is the definition of cloud migration portability, the measure of how difficult it might be to move the organization's systems/data from a given cloud host to another cloud host. Interoperability issues involve whether the cloud customer's legacy services/data will interface properly with the provider's systems. Stability has no specific meaning here and is just a distractor. Security might be an element of this challenge, but it is not the optimum answer; the question posed a concern about functionality, not disclosure or tainting the information.

75. D. This is the definition of a regulatory issue. Option B might also be a factor in this kind of issue, but because the subject of privacy or any specific related topic (such as personally identifiable information [PII], the European Union General Data Protection Regulation) was not mentioned, option D is the better answer. Resiliency issues involve the provider's ability to handle disruptive externalities, such as natural disasters, system failures, and utility outages. Performance issues address the ability of the provider to meet the customer's IT needs.

76. D. This is not an easy question. In the context of the question, the cloud customer is trying to ascertain whether they are getting what they're paying for; that is, a way for them to audit the cloud provider and the service as a whole. This is not a regulatory issue, as it concerns the contractual agreement between the provider and the customer, not a third party performing oversight. It is also not a privacy issue (primarily; privacy concerns might be part of the contract, but it's not the prevailing aspect of the issue here). Resiliency issues involve the provider's ability to handle disruptive externalities, such as natural disasters, system failures, or utility outages.

77. B. Encryption consumes processing power and time; as with all security controls, additional security means measurably less operational capability—there is always a trade-off between security and productivity. Option A is gibberish and only a distractor. Option C is incorrect because vendor lock-out does not result from encryption; it is what might happen if the cloud provider goes out of business while holding your data. Data subjects are the individuals whose personally identifiable information (PII) an organization holds; usually, they will not know or care if something is encrypted (unless there is a breach of that PII, and then investigators will want to determine how that PII was protected) and would probably welcome total encryption, even though that might mean a decrease in operational capability.

78. C. Security should be commensurate with asset value, as determined by management; putting extra security on everything in an environment is usually not cost effective. The other options don't make sense. For example, encryption doesn't affect the potential for physical theft, encryption can be implemented organization-wide, and access controls can be placed on encrypted information as well as unencrypted.

79. C. Discretion is not an element of identification and has no meaning in this context. All the other options are aspects of the identification portion of IAM.

80. B. Of these options, HR is most likely to participate in identity provisioning; HR will usually validate the user's identity against some documentation (driver's license, passport, etc.) as part of the user's initial employment process and then pass confirmation of validation along to whatever entity issues system sign-on credentials. None of the other entities usually takes part in user identification.

81. B. Unused accounts that remain open can serve as attack vectors. All the other options are not associated with identity and access management.

82. D. Job performance is not a germane aspect of account review and maintenance; that is a management concern, not an access control issue. All the other options are legitimate access control concerns.

83. A. This is not an easy question. The best answer to the question does not appear on the list; that would be the data owner, because the data owner should be the ultimate arbiter of who has what access to the data under the owner's control. However, of these options, A is the best; the user's manager will have the greatest amount of insight into the role of the user within the organization and therefore will understand best which data the user needs to access. The security manager does not have this insight, and the task of reviewing all access for all users within the organization would be far too large an undertaking for that position. Accounting and incident response play no part in reviewing ongoing user account applicability.

84. C. LDAP is used in constructing and maintaining centralized directory services, which are vital in all aspects of IAM. SSL and IPSec are used to create secure communication sessions—important, but not most applicable for IAM. AADT is a fictitious term used as a distractor.

85. D. The additional capabilities of privileged users make their activities riskier to the organization, so these accounts bear extra review. The number of encryption keys a user has is meaningless out of context; the amount of risk is the issue, not the number of keys. The user's type (regular versus privileged) is not an indicator, itself, of trustworthiness. Additional review activity for privileged users is an extra control we place on privileged users, not a reason for doing so.

86. D. The efficacy of frisking administrators and managers is doubtful, and the harm to morale and disparity of enforcement likely outweighs any security benefit. All the other options could and should be included in privileged account review.

87. C. Which bank branch a privileged user frequents is unlikely to be of consequence. Too much money can indicate that the privileged user is accepting payment from someone other than the employer, which can be an indicator of malfeasance or corruption. Too little money can indicate that the privileged user is subject to undue financial stress, which might be the result of behavior that makes the privileged user susceptible to subversion, such as a drug habit, family problems, or excess gambling. Specific senders and recipients of personal funds can indicate untoward activity on the part of the privileged user.

88. D. There is no specific rule for the timeliness of privileged user account reviews. However, as a matter of course, privileged user accounts should be reviewed more often than the accounts of regular users because privileged users can cause more damage and therefore entail more risk.

89. A. Privileged users should have privileged access to specific systems/data only for the duration necessary to perform their administrative function; any longer incurs more risk than value. The other options are not associated with appropriate privilege access management.

90. C. The CSA points out that data breaches come from a variety of sources, including both internal personnel and external actors. Although breaches might be overt or covert, or large or small, we don't usually think of them in these terms, and the CSA doesn't discuss them that way, so options A and D aren't correct. Option B is just incorrect because subterranean is not associated with the CSA's Notorious Nine list of common threats.

91. A. Data breach notification laws are plentiful; organizations operating in the cloud are almost sure to be subject to one or more such laws. Option B is incorrect because the CSA does not suggest that an organization that operates in the cloud environment and suffers a data breach may be required to reapply for cloud service. Option C is unlikely because most cloud customers won't have physical access to/control of devices; moreover, a breach does not always entail sanitization. Option D does not make sense, either; regulations are imposed on organizations, as legal mandates, and an organization does not get to choose which regulations affect it.

92. D. The cost of detection exists whether or not the organization suffers a breach. All other options are costs an organization will likely face as the result of a breach.

93. C. This question requires a bit of thought. Option C is correct because an organization is not required to subscribe to all standards but instead only the standards it selects (or are imposed on it through regulation). However, most cloud customers will have to comply with multiple state laws (at the very least, the laws of the states where the customer's organization resides, where the data center resides, and where its end clientele reside); any contractual requirements (between the cloud customer and its consumers, vendors, or service providers, such as, for example, Payment Card Industry Data Security Standard [PCI DSS]); and any federal regulations that govern that cloud customer's industry.

94. A. Data loss can be the result of deliberate or accidental behavior. The other options are less correct than option A.

95. B. Bad policy won't explicitly lead to data loss, but it might hinder efforts to counter data loss. However, misplaced crypto keys can result in a self-imposed denial of service, bad backup procedures can result in failure to retain data (a form of data loss), and accidental overwrites occur all the time—hence the need for proper backups.

96. D. All. Service traffic hijacking can affect all portions of the CIA triad. Through hijacking, an attacker could eavesdrop on legitimate communication (breaching confidentiality), insert inaccurate/incorrect data into legitimate communication (damaging integrity), and/or redirect legitimate users from valid services (making the legitimate sources unavailable). Although all of the answers are correct, option D is the most comprehensive and therefore the best answer.

97. B. Users sharing account credentials is a fairly common (although undesirable) practice and one that can lead to significant misuse of the organization's resources and greatly increase risk to the organization. Although ending all user activity would make our IT environments so much more secure and defensible, it would also make them utterly useless from a productivity standpoint, so option A is incorrect. Option C is incorrect because the CSA recommends multifactor authentication as a means to reduce the risk of hijacking. Though not documented on the CSA's website, the CSA most certainly does not recommend the prohibition of interstate commerce in order to diminish the likelihood of account/service traffic hijacking. Therefore, option D is an incorrect answer.

98. C. Cloud computing users are especially susceptible to hijacking attacks because all of their use is contingent on remote access; users in a traditional internal environment are not passing as much traffic over untrusted infrastructure (the Internet), and the type of traffic is often different (where identity credentials are passed only to servers/systems that are locally, physically connected to the user's device).

Scalability might be seen as an attribute of cloud computing that increases the potential for hijacking attacks because a proliferation of users means more attack surface. But even that aspect is contingent on the users accessing cloud resources remotely, so option C is still a better answer than A.

The metered service nature of cloud computing has nothing to do with a hijacking threat; metered service indicates that the customer pays only for those resources users consume.

Cloud customers pool resources might be of concern when considering hijacking attacks because poorly configured cloud environments could leave one cloud customer subject to attack by another tenant in that same environment. But, again, hijacking is predicated on attacking data in transit, so it is the remote access aspect that is the best answer for this question.

99. A. Because a significant percentage of cloud customer interactions with the cloud environment will utilize APIs, the threat of insecure APIs is of great concern in cloud computing.

Option B is incorrect because APIs are not inherently insecure and it is unlikely that the CSA has stated that they are.

Option C is incorrect because it is predicated on the inaccurate notion that all APIs are inherently insecure and that the vulnerabilities of all known APIs have been published.

Lastly, option B is inaccurate because APIs are not known carcinogens. To be a carcinogen, the carcinogen needs to be a substance that causes cancer in living tissue. As far as we know, APIs do not cause cancer.

100. A. The continuous modification of APIs issued/designed by cloud providers introduces the potential for vulnerabilities to be created in interfaces that were previously thought to be vetted and secure. Increased complexity necessarily means increased potential for vulnerability. And third-party modifications may lead to user credentials being unknowingly exposed to those third parties.

Automation is not inherently a source of threats/vulnerabilities, so option B is not correct.

Options C and D are not true.

101. B. APIs will be used for many tasks that could have a significant negative impact on the organization, so any vulnerabilities are of great concern.

Not all API interaction involves administrative access, so option A is wrong.

APIs may or may not be cursed.

Secure code practices can be used to design robust APIs, so option D is incorrect.

102. C. If users can't access the cloud provider, then the operational environment is, for all intents and purposes, useless. DoS attacks that affect availability of cloud services are therefore a great concern.

A lot of attackers/criminals operate internationally; this has no bearing on whether an organization operates in the cloud or otherwise. Option A is incorrect.

There are laws prohibiting DoS attacks, so option B is incorrect.

The volume of DoS traffic necessary to disrupt modern cloud providers is rather significant, so these types of attacks are not simple. Option D is incorrect.

103. D. Denial-of-service attacks staged from multiple machines against a specific target is the definition of a DDoS. All the other options are either fictitious or are not typically associated with the definition of DDoS.

104. B. In a managed cloud service context, one malicious cloud administrator could ostensibly victimize a great number of cloud customers, making the impact much greater than a sole insider in the legacy environment.

The other options are not applicable to the insider threat.

105. A. Because users in cloud customer organizations often do not pay directly for cloud services (and are often not even aware of the cost of use), scalability can be a significant management concern; individuals, offices, or departments within the organization can create dozens or even hundreds of new virtual systems in a cloud environment, for whatever purpose they need or desire, and the cost is realized only by the department in the organization that is charged with paying the bill. This type of abuse hinges on the immense scalability of cloud services and is frequently not associated with any malicious intent but is instead an inadvertent result of well-intentioned or careless behavior.

The other options are not applicable to the threat of abuse of cloud services.

106. D. The cloud customer will not have any insight into the personnel security aspects of the cloud provider; when an organization contracts out a service, the organization loses that granular level of control.

It is imperative that the cloud customer determine whether any application dependencies exist in the legacy environment before migrating to the cloud.

Reviewing the contract between the cloud customer and provider is an essential element of due diligence.

Determining the long-term financial viability of a cloud provider is a way to avoid losing production capability/data in the cloud.

107. B. This is the definition of vendor lockout.

Vendor lock-in is when data portability is limited, either through unfavorable contract language or technical limitations.

Vendor incapacity and unscaled are not meaningful terms in the context of cloud computing.

108. D. A hub is a (mostly archaic) network device that simply connects physical machines together; it cannot serve the purpose of network segmentation.

All the other options are segmentation methods/tools. Option C may be perceived as a viable answer because bridges connect network segments (allowing a segmented network, but not really creating segmentation), but option D is a better choice for this question.

109. A. Knowing exactly where and what your assets are, from an IT security professional's perspective, allows you to better apply uniform and ubiquitous governance and controls across the environment. Without these clear demarcations, that task becomes more difficult.

Nothing is impossible; these tasks may become more challenging, but not impossible. So options B and C are incorrect.

Option D is not true because lack of physical endpoints may actually reduce the threat of physical theft/damage.

110. A. PaaS customers should never be given shell access to underlying infrastructure because any changes by one customer may negatively impact other customers in a multitenant environment.

All the other options are simply incorrect.

111. B. Mass permissions assigned to multiple instances may be susceptible to inadvertent authorization creep and permission inheritance over time as users shift roles and responsibilities and are assigned to new tasks and teams and as new users come into the existing, fluid environment.

All the other options are just wrong, with at least one nonsensical element in each.

112. C. Organizational policies dictate rules for access entitlement.

International standards do not apply to every organization's internal needs and individual user roles, so option A is incorrect.

Not all organizations are bound by all (or any) federal regulations, but all organizations should have policies regarding user access rules, so option B is incorrect.

Option D is a nod to Star Trek and also incorrect.

113. A. Authentication is verifying that the user is who they claim to be and assigning them an identity assertion (usually a user ID) based on that identity.

Authorization is granting access based on permissions allocated to a particular user/valid identity assertion.

Nonrepudiation is the security concept of not allowing a participant in a transaction to deny that they participated.

Regression is a statistical concept not relevant to the question in any way.

114. B. This is the definition of authorization.

Authentication is verifying that the user is who they claim to be and assigning them an identity assertion (usually a user ID) based on that identity.

Nonrepudiation is the security concept of not allowing a participant in a transaction to deny that they participated.

Regression is a statistical concept not relevant to the question in any way.

115. B. In access management, the user is first authenticated (their identity verified and validated as correct), then authorized (permissions granted based on their valid identity), and given access.

116. B. PaaS environments are attractive for software development because they allow testing of software on multiple operating systems that are administered by the cloud provider. Software developers routinely use backdoors as development and administrative tools in their products; these backdoors, if left in software when it ships, are significant vulnerabilities.

All cloud environments, including PaaS, rely on virtualization, have multitenancy, and are scalable, so those options are not correct.

117. C. Backdoors that were used legitimately during the development process can sometimes be left in a production version of the delivered software accidentally, when developers forget to remove them. Sometimes, these products ship with backdoors purposefully placed there for administrative and customer service functions as well.

Option A is incorrect as backdoors are not a control.

Option B is incorrect because backdoors don't serve as DoS protection in any way.

Option D is incorrect because backdoors are not distractions for attackers, but means for attack.

118. C. This is an example of typical SQL injection. All the other options are also attacks listed in the Open Web Application Security Project (OWASP) Top Ten, but they do not have the characteristics as the one contained in the question.

119. A. This is the definition of a cross-site scripting attack. Options B and C are also attacks listed in the Open Web Application Security Project (OWASP) Top Ten. Option D is not in the Top Ten and is made up as a fictitious option.

120. D. This is likely a security misconfiguration, as crypto keys must not be disclosed or the cryptosystem does not provide protection; most successful attacks on cryptosystems have been configuration/implementation attacks, not mathematical or statistical. The other options are all also in the Open Web Application Security Project (OWASP) Top Ten.

121. B. In the cloud environment, it is very easy for a user to generate a new virtual instance; that is one of the advantages of the cloud. However, this can pose a problem for management, as users might generate many more instances than expected because the users don't usually realize (or have to pay) the per-instance costs associated with doing so. However, the organization will have to pay the full price of many more instances at the end of each billing cycle, and exceeding the allotted amount dictated by the contract can be quite expensive. In the traditional environment, this would not pose a risk because the number of possible instances is limited by the resource capacity within the organization and additional instances don't have attendant direct costs. All the other options are not cloud-specific risks; they also exist in the traditional environment.

122. D. A Type 2 hypervisor is run on top of an existing operating system, greatly increasing the potential attack surface.

Option A does not make logical sense; a Type 1 hypervisor is not more straightforward than other hypervisors. Option A is not the correct answer.

Option B is not true. A Type 1 hypervisor has a smaller attack surface, not a larger one.

Option C is not true in general. Type 2 hypervisors are not necessarily less protected than other hypervisors. Option C is not the correct answer.

123. B. Option B is the only element that lends itself well to a discrete, objective metric; the other options might be something the customer is interested in but will often have little control over; if the customer is insistent on those points, they should be included in the contract, not the SLA.

124. B. Usually, when a provider does not meet the terms specific in the SLA, the provider will not be paid for a period of service; this is the strongest, most immediate tool at the customer's disposal. The other options simply are not true.

125. D. In an IaaS configuration, the customer still has to maintain the OS, so option D is the only answer that is not a direct benefit for the cloud customer.

126. C. This is the textbook definition of an incident versus event. However, this question is not easy, because many sources in the IT security field define incidents differently; it's common to think of incidents as events that have an adverse impact, or incidents are something that require response. However, option C is the correct answer.

127. D. Elasticity is a beneficial characteristic in that it supports the management goal of matching resources to user needs, but it does not provide any security benefit.

128. B. Cloud customers can test different hardware/software implementations in the cloud without affecting the production environment and use this information to make decisions before investing in particular solutions. Option A is not true because the cloud does not store physical assets. Option C is not accurate because production data in the cloud must still be secured. And option D is not true because cloud hosting is not free; there is some cost (even if that cost is less than it would be for comparable on-premises hosting).

129. D. The American Institute of Certified Public Accountants publishes the SSAE 18 standard. NIST is a U.S. government entity that publishes many standards for federal agencies, so option A is incorrect. ENISA is a European Union (EU) standards body, so option B is incorrect. The GDPR is an EU law about privacy data, so option C is incorrect.

130. D. SOC reports are the audit reporting mechanisms dictated by SSAE 18. SOX is a federal law targeting publicly traded corporations in the United States. SSL is a way to conduct secure online transactions. SABSA is an architecture framework.

131. C. The SOC 1 audit report is not for security controls; it is for financial reporting controls. The AICPA SOC 2 Type 1 audit report reviews the controls an organization has selected and designed. Both the CAIQ and the CCM are tools created by the CSA to review an organization's controls across several frameworks, regulations, and standards.

132. C. The SOC 2 Type 2 reviews the implementation of security controls. The SOC 1 reviews financial reporting controls, not security controls. The SOC 2 Type 1 reviews the design and selection of security controls, not implementation. The SOC 3 is only an attestation of an audit, so option C is better.

133. A. Due care is the minimal level of effort necessary to perform your duty to others; in cloud security, that is often the care that the cloud customer is required to demonstrate in order to protect the data it owns. Due diligence is any activity taken in support or furtherance of due care. This answer, then, is optimum: the due care is set out by the policy, and activities that support the policy (here, auditing the controls the policy requires) are a demonstration of due diligence.

The General Data Protection Regulation (GDPR) and GLBA are both legislative mandates; these might dictate a standard of due care, but they are not the due care or due diligence, specifically.

Door locks and turnstiles are physical security controls; they both might be examples of due care efforts, but neither demonstrates due diligence.

Due care and diligence can be demonstrated by either internal or external controls/processes; there is no distinction to be made based on where the control is situated.

134. B. The distinguished name (DN) is the nomenclature for all entries in an LDAP environment.

A domain name is used to identify one or more IP addresses. For instance, `Microsoft.com` and `google.com` are domain names. Option A is incorrect.

A directory name is typically associated with a file system structure and not something related to LDAP. Option C is incorrect.

"Default Name" is not a common term, and is made up. Option D is not the correct answer.

135. B. Inversion is not part of the IAM process at all and has no meaning in this context. All the other options are elements of identification.

136. C. By creating a need for two identity assertions or authentication elements to access assets, two-person integrity prevents a single person from gaining unauthorized access and forces a would-be criminal to join up with at least one other person to conduct a crime. This reduces the possibility of the crime taking place.

All the other options are simply untrue and are therefore exceedingly poor choices for answers to CCSP test questions.

137. D. The PCI DSS is a voluntary standard, having only contractual obligation. All the other options are statutes, created by lawmaking bodies.

138. C. Because the cloud customer will retain ownership of some elements of hardware, software, or both at the customer's location (for instance, security hardware modules [HSMs]), client-side key management could be considered a hybrid cloud model.

Option A is incorrect because the scenario stated in the question does not identify a threat.

Option B is incorrect because the scenario stated in the question does not identify a risk. Allowing the customer to retain their own encryption keys is actually less risky than sharing their encryption keys with the provider.

Option D is incorrect because the provider does not have a right to the customer's encryption keys, so, there cannot be an infringement on the provider's rights.

139. C. With a private cloud deployment, the customer gets to dictate governance requirements, which is a significant benefit for customers in highly regulated industries.

Private clouds typically cost more than public cloud deployments, so option A is incorrect.

Performance is not necessarily enhanced (or decreased) by any of the cloud deployment models, so option B is incorrect.

Retaining a higher degree of control over the cloud environment will necessarily require the cloud customer to have more maintenance capability, not less, so option D is incorrect.

140. B. In SaaS, the cloud provider might license and deliver commercially available software for the customer, via the cloud (hosted application management), or provide the customer access to the provider's proprietary software (software on demand).

All the other options are incorrect. The options contain legitimate words put together to form gibberish.

141. D. The cloud customer is ultimately responsible for all legal repercussions involving data security and privacy; the cloud provider might be liable for financial costs related to these responsibilities, but those damages can only be recovered long after the notifications have been made by the cloud customer.

All the other options are incorrect because they do not correctly identify who is required to make data breach notifications in accordance with all applicable laws. That responsibility rests with the cloud customer.

142. D. An IaaS service model allows an organization to retain the most control of their IT assets in the cloud; the cloud customer is responsible for the operating system, the applications, and the data in the cloud. The private cloud model allows the organization to retain the greatest degree of governance control in the cloud; all the other deployment models would necessitate giving up governance control in an environment with pooled resources.

143. C. With SaaS, the cloud customer is responsible only for the data in the cloud; the cloud provider is responsible for the underlying IT infrastructure, the operating system, and the applications; maintenance for this service model will be minimal, compared to the others. A public cloud deployment will reduce costs even more, as it is the least expensive of the options—with the least amount of control for the cloud customer.

All the other options would include some degree of administration of the cloud resources on the part of the cloud customer and so are not as optimal as option C.

Chapter 2: Domain 2: Cloud Data Security

1. C. In application-level encryption, the application will encrypt data before it is placed in the database. In transparent encryption, the entire database is encrypted. Symmetric-key encryption is a kind of encryption and not truly indicative of a strategy used in database encryption. Homomorphic encryption is an experimental, theoretical process that might allow processing encrypted information without the need to decrypt it first.

2. C. Because the tool will require at least some installation and reporting capability within the cloud environment, it is essential to coordinate with the cloud provider to ensure that the solution you choose will function properly and is allowed by the provider. Option A is true, but not a major concern; that is a benefit of SIEM/SEM/SIM tools. Option B is not true because dashboards can often misconstrue pertinent reporting data when they are used to chase management goals instead of distilling raw data appropriately. Option D is not true because management should not be involved in such granular decisions.

3. C. In crypto-shredding, the purpose is to make the data unrecoverable; saving a backup of the keys would attenuate that outcome because the keys would still exist for the purpose of recovering data. All other steps outline the crypto-shredding process.

4. A. Cloud customers are allowed to encrypt their own data and manage their own keys; crypto-shredding is therefore possible. Degaussing is not likely in the cloud because it requires physical access to the storage devices and because most cloud providers are using solid-state drives (SSDs) for storage, which are not magnetic. Physical destruction is not feasible because the cloud customer doesn't own the hardware and therefore won't be allowed to destroy it. Overwriting probably won't work because finding all data in all aspects of the cloud is difficult and the data is constantly being backed up and securely stored, so a thorough process would be very tricky.

5. A. Crypto-shredding is for secure sanitization, not portability. The other methods all enhance portability.

6. D. The owner of intellectual property will not change whether the material is stored in the cloud or in a legacy environment. Moving into the cloud will probably result in more use of personal devices, requiring users to install local DRM agents, so option A is true, making it not a suitable answer to this question. Options B and C are also true, due to the nature of cloud computing, and are therefore also not suitable for this question.

7. A. Option A creates a conflict of interest and does not enforce separation of duties.

The best practice is to not store cryptographic keys with the data they encrypt, to avoid a potential conflict of interest and to enforce separation of duties. Each of the other choices is a reasonable choice and therefore not the answer to this question.

8. D. A long-term storage facility may or may not be located underground; the security of that facility (and the data contained therein) is not dependent on this aspect. Option A is a security concern because loss of the keys may result in losing the data (by losing access to the data), and keeping the keys with the data they protect increases risk. Both the format of the data and the media on which it resides (options B and C) are important to bear in mind, as either (or both) may be outmoded by the time the data might need to be retrieved from the archive; data and formats do not age well.

9. B. Data dispersion is basically RAID in the cloud, with data elements parsed and stored over several areas/devices instead of stored as a unit in a single place. RAID (and data dispersion) does aid in BC/DR activities by increasing the robustness and resiliency of stored data, but BC/DR is a much more general discipline, so it is not the optimum answer for the question. SDN is used for abstracting network control commands away from production data, and CDN is usually used for ensuring quality of streaming media.

10. A. Where RAID used data striping across multiple drives, with data dispersion this technique is referred to as "chunking," or sometimes "sharding" when encryption is also used. The other options are not common data dispersion terms used in cloud computing and have no meaning in this context.

11. C. Erasure coding is the practice of having sufficient data to replace a lost chunk in data dispersion, protecting against the possibility of a device failing while it holds a given chunk; parity bits serve the same purpose in a traditional RAID configuration. The other options are not common data dispersion terms used in cloud computing and have no meaning in this context.

12. D. Data dispersion can't aid in inadvertent loss caused by an errant user; if the user accidentally deletes/corrupts a file, that file will be deleted/corrupted across all the storage spaces where it is dispersed. The technique does, however, protect against the other risks. It enhances confidentiality because an attacker gaining illicit access to a single storage space will only get a chunk of the data, which is useless without the other chunks. This same aspect also protects loss when law enforcement seizes a specific storage device/space when they are investigating another tenant at the same cloud provider your organization uses. And loss of availability due to single device failure is probably the primary reason for having data dispersion (like RAID before it).

13. B. Volume storage allows all the functions described in the question. Object storage has data arranged in a file structure, and databases arrange data in tables and relational schemes; neither of these options offers the functions described in the question. Synthetic is not a cloud memory configuration option.

14. A. Object storage is usually arranged in a file hierarchy. Volume storage has data with no defined structure (only memory space), and databases ar-range data in tables and relational schemes; neither of these options offers the functions described in the question. Synthetic is not a cloud memory con-figuration option.

15. B. Egress monitoring solutions (often referred to as DLP tools, where DLP stands for data loss protection or data leak prevention, or some combination of these terms) require the organization to appropriately inventory and classify data assets so the tool knows what to protect. DLP does not aid in protections for DDoS or natural disasters, which affect availability, not confidentiality (DLP only enhances confidentiality efforts). Option C is not a benefit of implementing an egress monitoring solution.

16. C. Egress monitoring solutions (often referred to as DLP tools, where DLP stands for data loss protection or data leak prevention, or some combination of these terms) will often include a discovery function, which will locate data assets according to criteria defined by the organization. DLP solutions cannot arbitrate contract breaches or perform personnel evaluations. Usually, DLPs also do not apply additional access controls; that is typically a characteristic of a digital rights management (DRM) solution.

17. C. Egress monitoring solutions (often referred to as DLP tools, where DLP stands for data loss protection or data leak prevention, or some combination of these terms) will often include an agent that resides on client devices in order to inspect data being shared/sent by end users. DLP tools do not inspect incoming packets, with or without stateful inspection; this is the job of firewalls. DLP solutions do not typically use biometrics in any way.

18. B. DRM is mainly designed to protect intellectual property. It can also sometimes be used for securing PII, but intellectual property is a better answer here. Plans and policies aren't usually protected in this manner, and marketing material is usually meant to be disseminated, so it does not require protection.

19. D. DRM is often deployed to ensure that copyrighted material (frequently software) is only delivered to and used by licensed recipients. Patents are more complicated and not often distributed to a mass market, so DRM does not assist in that way. Trademarks are representations of a brand and meant to be distributed, so DRM does not protect them. PII is not typically a type of intellectual property.

20. A. Persistence is the trait that allows DRM protection to follow protected files wherever they might be stored/copied. The other options are not characteristics associated with DRM solutions.

21. A. Automatic expiration is the trait that allows DRM tools to prevent access to objects when a license expires or to remove protections when intellectual property moves into the public domain. The other options are not characteristics associated with DRM solutions.

22. C. Continuous audit trail is the trait that allows DRM tools to log and exhibit all access to a given object. The other options are not characteristics associated with DRM solutions.

23. A. Mapping to existing access control lists (ACLs) is the trait that allows DRM tools to provide additional access control protections for the organization's assets. The other options are not characteristics associated with DRM solutions.

24. A. The Cloud Secure Data Lifecycle phases are, in order, Create, Store, Use, Share, Archive, Destroy (a good mnemonic might be CSU-SAD).

Options B and D are phases of CSU-SAD but do not immediately follow Create.

Option C is not a phase of CSU-SAD.

25. C. The Cloud Secure Data Lifecycle phases are, in order, Create, Store, Use, Share, Archive, Destroy (a good mnemonic might be CSU-SAD).

Options A and B are phases of CSU-SAD but do not immediately precede Share.

Option D is not a phase of CSU-SAD.

26. D. The Cloud Secure Data Lifecycle phases are, in order, Create, Store, Use, Share, Archive, Destroy (a good mnemonic might be CSU-SAD). This is not truly a cycle because data does not continue after the destroy phase (that is to say, the same data or process does not go back to create after destroy).

Option A might be considered true because the CSU-SAD cycle is not unique to $(ISC)^2$, but this is not the best answer; option D is preferable because it is not truly a cycle.

Options B and C are incorrect because activity in each of the phases involves security aspects and all phases relate to how data is involved in the cloud.

27. A. The Cloud Secure Data Lifecycle phases are, in order, Create, Store, Use, Share, Archive, Destroy (a good mnemonic might be CSU-SAD). The best practice for categorizing/classifying data is to do so when it is first created/collected so that the proper security controls can be applied to it throughout the rest of the cycle.

Options B and D are phases of the CSU-SAD but are not the proper times to be applying classification/categorization; that would be too late in the cycle.

Option C is not a phase of CSU-SAD.

28. B. The Cloud Secure Data Lifecycle phases are, in order, Create, Store, Use, Share, Archive, Destroy (a good mnemonic might be CSU-SAD). Crypto-shredding (also called cryptographic erasure) is the preferred method of data sanitization for a cloud environment; this should take place in the final phase of the cycle, destroy.

Option A is incorrect because data dispersion is a means of making data more resilient and secure; in the final phase of the cycle, we want to get rid of the data, not make it resistant to loss.

Option C is incorrect because *cryptoparsing* is a made-up term and used here as a distractor.

Option D is incorrect because cryptosporidium is a microorganism and is not associated with InfoSec.

29. D. The Cloud Secure Data Lifecycle phases are, in order, Create, Store, Use, Share, Archive, Destroy (a good mnemonic might be CSU-SAD). Archiving (the fifth phase) is the process of moving data out of the production environment and into long-term storage.

The other phases in the options are create, store, and share and are therefore incorrect.

30. D. Object storage stores data as objects (hence the name), often arranged in a hierarchical structure.

Volume storage is not a hierarchal cloud storage structure and is therefore an incorrect answer for this question.

Option B is incorrect because databases are applications in both traditional and cloud computing.

A CDN is a geographically distributed network of proxy servers and their data centers. Option C is incorrect because it is not a form of cloud storage.

31. A. In volume storage, the user is assigned a logical drive space into which anything (such as raw data, objects, or applications) may be saved or installed, similar to a mounted drive on a traditional network.

Databases store data in an arrangement of characteristics and values, not in an unstructured drive space, so option B is incorrect.

CDNs are for distributing data with less chance of quality loss, so option C is incorrect.

Object storage arranges data as objects in a structured hierarchy, so option D is incorrect.

32. C. CDNs are often used to place large stores of multimedia data in a location geographically near to the end users who will consume that data; this approach is designed mostly to accomplish a reduction in data degradation due to distance between resource and user.

Volume storage assigns a logical, unstructured drive space to the user, so option A is incorrect.

Databases store data in an arrangement of characteristics and values, so option B is incorrect.

Neutral storage is not a form of cloud storage, so option D is incorrect.

33. B. The PaaS model allows the cloud customer to install and run applications in the cloud environment. With a database, the cloud customer can store data in a database administered by the cloud provider but can then tailor applications and services for reaching into and manipulating that database.

Ephemeral and long-term storage take place in the software as a service (SaaS) model, and there is no such thing as "nefarious data storage," so the other options are incorrect.

34. B. Data dispersion is the cloud version of using RAID arrays, protecting data by spreading it across multiple volumes/devices.

Options A and C are terms that have no meaning in this context.

Crypto-shredding is a form of device/media sanitization utilizing cryptography and has nothing to do with RAID, so option D is incorrect.

35. C. Similar to parity bits in RAID, erasure coding is used in cloud data dispersion implementations to create a situation where data can still be recovered even if a segment or portion of the dispersed data is lost (due to drive failure, disaster, etc.).

Options A and B have no meaning in this context.

Transposition is a cryptographic technique and does not relate to RAID in any way, so option D is also incorrect.

36. A. DLP, also referred to as egress monitoring, is used to detect and prevent sensitive data from leaving the organization's control without proper approval.

Because it is designed to prevent the egress of only certain data sets, options B and C are not correct.

Controlling data outside the reach of the organization is difficult at best. While there are some mechanisms that might accomplish this, DLP is not specifically designed for that purpose, so option D is incorrect.

37. D. Commercial DLP products that monitor speech in real time and censor conversations are not yet widely available.

A proper DLP solution will monitor all the technologies in the other options, so those are incorrect.

38. B. Inference is an attack technique that derives sensitive material from an aggregation of innocuous data; DLP tools, thus far, do not have this capability.

All the other techniques listed may be used by DLP solutions to detect sensitive data before it leaves the control of the owner.

39. C. A cloud customer can install applications on a PaaS environment, usually as they see fit and without prior coordination with the provider.

If you are introducing hardware into the cloud environment, you will need permission from your cloud provider, regardless of the deployment model you use. Therefore, option A is incorrect (and unlikely to occur, as permission is probably not going to be granted).

Although the provider may offer an egress monitoring function as an add-on service, which would be permissible for you to use, the use of an outside vendor's product may have to be reviewed by the provider before implementation, based on a number of other variables (such as the other possible answers). Option C is preferable, so option B is incorrect.

Affecting all images on a host may impact other customers in a multitenant environment, so option D is not the correct answer.

40. B. All security functions come with an attendant negative productivity effect: the most secure environment will be the least productive, and the most productive will be the least secure. Egress monitoring tools will have an overhead cost in terms of production impact and loss of efficiency and speed. This may affect the cost savings that were realized in a cloud migration from the legacy environment, and senior management needs to understand this trade-off.

Implementing an egress monitoring solution should not incur any additional risks of external attack, so option A is incorrect.

Because the tool has already been purchased, explaining the purchase price is irrelevant at this point, so option C is incorrect.

If it was germane (and it was likely not), you should have explained how the tool works before purchasing it; explaining at this point might be interesting but is not as important as option B, so option D is incorrect.

41. A. In order to "train" the egress monitoring solution properly, you'll need to inform it as to which data in your organization is sensitive…and, in order to do that, you'll need to determine what information your data owners deem sensitive; a survey is a way to do that.

A proper egress monitoring solution should not affect or be affected by the firewalls, routers, or hypervisors, so options B, C, and D are incorrect.

42. B. It will take a while for the tool to "learn" the particulars of your environment and to be conditioned properly. A significant number of false-positive indications will be expected in the near term, until you can hone the responses to properly meet your organization's needs.

The tool will not work optimally immediately upon implementation, so option A is incorrect.

Egress monitoring tools do not affect morale or revenues, so options C and D are incorrect.

43. B. It's unlikely that any egress monitoring tools will be able to detect sensitive data captured, stored, and/or sent as graphic image files, which is the usual form of screenshots.

A proper egress monitoring tool should be able to detect all the other types of activity, so the other options are incorrect.

44. A. This is a tricky question. In the cloud environment, we know that all users will be entering the environment through remote access; in many cases, this will include the use of their personal devices. In order for egress monitoring solutions to function properly, all devices accessing the production environment must have local agents installed, and that requires signed user agreements.

It would be unnecessary (and intrusive, and cumbersome) to install agents on all assets in the cloud data center, which includes not only your organization's assets but also those of all the other cloud tenants in that data center. This might even be illegal. Option B is incorrect.

Assuming you could install (or even know) all the routers between your users and the cloud data center is ridiculous; option C is incorrect.

Getting your customer to install an egress monitoring client would be nice, in theory... but also pointless. Your customers don't work for you; they are outside your organization. Egress monitoring tools are used to prevent sensitive data from leaving your environment; by the time it has reached a customer, sensitive information is far outside your control and the egress monitoring tool would be of no use. Option D is therefore incorrect.

45. A. Egress monitoring tools combined with DRM and SIEM enhance the security value of each because you create in-depth/layered defense.

Project management software does not really have anything to do with security, so option B is incorrect.

Insurance is a risk transfer mechanism and does not aid in risk mitigation efforts; egress monitoring is for risk mitigation, so option C is incorrect.

The Tier certification program is for the cloud provider and is not used by the cloud customer, so option D is incorrect.

46. C. These are all possible settings for a modern egress monitoring solution. However, the best option, in light of the question, is to query the user as to their intent; this aids the user in understanding and knowing when sensitive data might be leaving the organization accidentally, through a mistake on the user's part. The other options are more severe and restrictive; these will enhance security but reduce productivity and are management and technological controls instead of awareness tools, so they are incorrect answers for this question.

47. B. The fact that cloud data centers are designed with multiple redundancies of all systems and components won't really have any bearing on your decision and implementation of your egress monitoring solution.

Because data will move across nodes in the data center and will take different forms (such as live data in a virtualized instance or snapshotted data saved in a file store when a virtual machine is not being used at a specific moment), you will have to determine how the tool will function in that environment, and whether it was designed for cloud usage. Option A is incorrect.

Option C is true for any environment, not just the cloud; all security functions necessarily negatively impact operations and production. Option B is a better answer.

Option D is also correct; without administrative privileges to the underlying hardware (which customers should not have), the customer may not be able to install monitoring agents everywhere necessary for those tools to work properly.

48. A. Egress monitoring solutions do not facilitate access control efforts in any way.

Egress monitoring tools do, however, provide all the functions listed in the other options, so those are incorrect.

49. D. The term *data of relief* doesn't really mean anything and is therefore the correct answer for this question.

Encryption is used in all other aspects of cloud data.

50. A. The user is not really an aspect of an encryption deployment, although it may be argued that the user will need to refrain from disclosing their own key(s) to anyone else.

The other three options are the components of an encryption deployment.

51. B. An authorized user will still be able to access and decrypt the data for which they've been granted permissions, so encryption will not offer any protections for that threat.

Volume storage encryption will, however, protect against all the other threats, because any outsider (that is, a person who does not have access to the volume operating system) will be able to steal only encrypted data, which they should not be able to decrypt in a timely fashion. Therefore, all the other options are incorrect.

52. D. TLS is encryption used in a communication session, not a storage volume.

All the other options are examples of object storage encryption options, so they are incorrect.

53. B. SSL is encryption used in a communication session, not a storage volume.

All the other options are examples of database encryption options, so they are incorrect.

54. A. The application contains the encryption engine used in application-level encryption.

The operating system is responsible for providing the resources an application needs and for running the applications. The operating system does not do application-level encryption, so option B is incorrect.

Option C is incorrect because application-level encryption is performed by the application that interfaces with the database.

The application-level encryption engine may or may not reside in the same volume as the database engine, so option D is incorrect.

55. B. Encrypting specific tables within the database is one of the options of transparent encryption; this is not true of the other options, so they are incorrect.

56. C. Application-level encryption involves encrypting the data before it enters the fields of the database; it is much more difficult to search and review data that has been encrypted, so this reduces the functionality of the database.

All the other options are incorrect because they are not database encryption techniques.

57. D. Best practice is to not keep the encryption keys alongside the data they've been used to encrypt.

Options A and B are both viable but not as good as option D, which is more general and includes them both.

Option C is clearly incorrect because it is counter to the best practice advice offered by (ISC)².

58. C. Data retention periods should be established in policy regardless of the projected lifetime of the media the data resides on. All the other options do/should influence data retention periods.

59. A. Event monitoring tools can help detect external hacking efforts by tracking and reporting on common hack-related activity, such as repeated failed login attempts and scanning. It is unlikely that these tools could predict physical device theft; they could, of course, report on a device that is no longer connected to the environment after it has been removed by noting a lack of event activity, but that's not quite the same thing. Event monitoring tools don't aid in data classification/categorization; egress monitoring and digital rights management tools might provide that function, though. Social engineering attacks are mostly transparent to the majority of logical tools (the exception being social engineering efforts combined with IT traffic, such as phishing, which might be detected by email filters and sophisticated firewalls).

60. B. Event monitoring tools can be used to predict system outages by noting decreases in performance; repeated performance issues can be an indicator a device is failing. While an event monitoring tool might be able to detect a user who continually conducts unproductive activity or fails to complete certain functions, it is impossible to determine if the source of the problem is lack of training. These tools in no way serve to detect conflict of interest or enforce mandatory vacation, which are managerial/administrative controls.

61. C. Event monitoring tools can detect repeated performance issues, which can be used by administrators and architects to enhance performance/productivity. These tools don't aid in the managerial function of noting individual workload, nor do they reduce log file sizes (indeed, they might add to the size of log files) or have anything to do with lighting.

62. A. Event monitoring tools can detect repeated performance issues, which can be indicative of improper temperature settings in the data center; also, some system monitoring metrics, such as CPU temperature, can directly indicate inadequate HVAC performance. These tools do not aid in cloud migration (which is the task of architects and administrators) nor in risk decisions (which is the task of senior management); they also don't provide any kind of assistance with fire.

63. C. Event logs are used to reconstruct a narrative of activity; they tell the story of what happened, how it happened, and so forth. This is crucial for evidentiary purposes. Event logging tools do not aid in any of the other options (especially acoustic dampening, which is gibberish in this context).

64. D. The manual element of log review is tedious and necessarily slow because it requires a trained, knowledgeable person to perform the task; these tools can greatly increase the amount of log data that can be reviewed, in a much shorter amount of time. These tools do not, however, aid in any of the other options.

65. B. Public keys have to be shared in order for asymmetric cryptography to function properly; that is their purpose. Private keys, on the other hand, must remain secret, known only to the individuals to whom they are assigned.

Seeding key generation processes with pseudorandom numbers makes decryption that much more difficult and is a desired practice, so option A is incorrect.

Losing keys to encrypted data means that the data stays encrypted, which is a way of applying a denial-of-service attack on yourself, so option C is incorrect.

Symmetric keys, known as shared secrets, ought to be transmitted to recipients over a different medium than the mode of communication intended for the encrypted traffic. If the users intend to use encrypted email, for instance, they should pass the keys via telephone. Option D is therefore incorrect.

66. B. The customer service representative may need to see a partial version of the customer's SS number to verify that the customer is who they claim to be, but that representative does not need to see the full number, which would create an unnecessary risk.

The shipping department definitely needs the customer's address in order to send things to the customer, so option A is not correct.

The billing department needs the customer's full credit card number to process payments, so option C is incorrect.

HR needs the employee's full license number in order to verify and validate the employee's identity, so option D is not correct.

67. D. Conflation is not a masking technique and is meaningless in this context. All the others are suggested as possible masking techniques.

68. C. While deletion is a very good way to avoid the possibility of inadvertently disclosing production data in a test environment, it also eliminates the usefulness of the data set as a plausible approximation of the production environment, greatly reducing the quality of the testing.

The other options modify the raw production data into something that approximates the real environment without disclosing real data, to a greater or lesser extent; some are better than the others, but they are all better than deletion for testing purposes.

69. A. Static masking involves modification of an entire data set, all at once. This would be a good method to create a sample data set for testing purposes.

Static testing for customer service use would be overkill; replicating all the customer accounts at once so that the fraction of customers who contact customer service may receive assistance is inefficient and cumbersome, and customer account information is likely to change between static updates, making it less useful. Therefore, option B is incorrect.

Neither regulators nor shareholders need to see masked data, so both options C and D are incorrect.

70. B. Dynamically masking a user's account information each time a customer service representative accesses that data is an efficient, secure means of masking data as necessary.

Trying to mask each data element as it is called by an application in a test environment would be unwieldy and not likely to provide accurate test data, so option A is incorrect.

Neither incident response nor BC/DR purposes need masked data, so both options C and D are incorrect.

71. C. Using an algorithm to mask data suggests that the same algorithm, if learned or reverse-engineered by an aggressor, could be used on the masked data to reveal the production data.

Algorithmic masking causes no more risk to production data than the other masking methods, so option A is incorrect.

Accidental disclosure *might* be interpreted as the same thing as determining the original data from the masked set, so option B might be considered accurate, but option C is a better way of stating the risk, so B is incorrect.

Option D is about the use of the deletion technique for masking, not algorithmic, so it is incorrect.

This is not an easy question, and it involves some abstract thought to arrive at the correct answer.

72. B. The user's name is a direct identifier, explicitly stating who that person is. The user's age is not a direct identifier because it doesn't specify a certain person, but it is a piece of demographic information that could be used to narrow down the user's identity from a group of users of different ages, so it is an indirect identifier.

Username and password are identity assertions and authentication credentials, not identifiers. The username might be a direct identifier, but the password is neither a direct nor an indirect identifier (especially if it is kept secret, as it should be). Option A is thus incorrect.

Option C is incorrect because both elements could be considered direct identifiers (depending on the jurisdiction) if the user's machine is considered a legal representation of the user.

Option D is incorrect because both elements are indirect identifiers.

73. D. Anonymization is the process of removing identifiers from data sets so that data analysis tools and techniques cannot be used by malicious entities to divine personal or sensitive data from nonsensitive aggregated data sets.

All the other answers are incorrect because they are not part of the anonymization process.

74. B. PCI requires that credit card numbers and other cardholder data be obscured when stored for any length of time. Encryption is one approved method; tokenization is another.

GLBA, COPA, and SOX do not specifically require obscuring stored data, so those options are incorrect.

75. B. Tokenization will require, at a minimum, a database for the tokens and another for the stored sensitive data.

One database will not suffice; a single database holding both the tokens and the sensitive data they represent would not be in compliance with any standard requiring data to be obscured. Option A is thus incorrect.

Option C might be an answer some readers choose; it is easy to overthink this question. You might consider that the data requires two databases (one for tokens, one for sensitive data), and that access control would require a third database (for authentication credentials); however, the tokenization methodology does not strictly require that access be controlled through an authentication server. Option C is therefore incorrect. Be sure not to read more into the question than appears at face value.

Option D is incorrect; that's just too many databases.

76. B. Inference is an attack strategy, not a reason for implementing tokenization.

All the other options are good reasons to implement tokenization, and they are therefore not correct.

77. A. In the traditional environment, a RAID array is a set of disks/drives on which data is spread to enhance the availability, security, and resiliency of the data. In the cloud, bit-splitting/data dispersion performs this same function in much the same way.

All the other options have nothing to do with spreading data across multiple storage areas.

78. B. Bit-splitting involves chopping data sets up into segments and storing those segments in multiple places/devices. An attacker getting access to one segment won't be gaining anything of value because one segment of the data set would most likely make no sense out of context.

Bit-splitting may or may not function as an access control method; option B is preferable to A.

Bit-splitting may or may not move data across jurisdictions, which may or may not be useful to the data owner; option B is preferable to C.

Bit-splitting does not, in itself, provide access logs; option D is incorrect.

79. A. When law enforcement entities wish to seize assets (including data), they must cooperate with other law enforcement agencies in other jurisdictions if the data is not contained fully within their own. This may aid a data owner who is concerned about the risk of losing their data in a multitenant environment if another tenant conducts illicit activity and law enforcement seizes an entire data storage device as part of an investigation, accidentally collecting data belonging to innocent parties.

Attackers are jurisdiction-agnostic; they don't care where data is stored or what laws apply. Option B is thus incorrect.

Authorized users can access bit-split data regardless of the location and can disclose information worldwide; option C is incorrect.

Bit-splitting does not pertain to types of access roles; option D is incorrect.

80. C. Bit-splitting, as with many security methods/technologies, carries a significantly greater overhead than data sets that don't use this method. Bit-splitting, in particular, takes an extensive amount of processing to perform.

Bit-splitting should make a data set more secure and decrease the chance of unauthorized access, so options A and B are incorrect.

It is unlikely that bit-splitting would violate regulatory standards; even if that were to be the case, it is *always* true that bit-splitting carries greater overhead, so option C is preferable to D.

81. A. This is not a simple question and requires the reader to think through the situation suggested by each answer. Option A is correct because the data owner may opt to perform bit-splitting across multiple cloud services to enhance security (not all the "eggs" will be in one "basket"). When this is the case, the data owner will have additional dependencies: all the vendors involved in storing the various data elements.

There should be no additional management concern; if bit-splitting is not compliant with the data owner's policy, it won't be adopted. Option B is incorrect.

Bit-splitting implementations should be transparent to users; option C is incorrect.

There are plenty of vendors offering bit-splitting solutions; option D is incorrect.

82. C. Ironically, data dispersion can lead to some additional risk of loss of availability, depending on the method/breadth of the dispersion. If the data is spread across multiple cloud providers, there is a possibility that an outage at one provider will make the data set unavailable to users, regardless of location. However, there are methods for attenuating this threat, and bit-splitting usually provides greater availability of data over traditional storage without dispersion.

   Data dispersion should have no effect on physical theft risks and would actually serve to minimize the opportunity for an attacker to acquire useful sensitive data as the data would be on several geographically disparate devices. Option A is incorrect.

   Bit-splitting should have no effect on public image whatsoever; option B is incorrect.

   Bit-splitting does not have an attendant fire risk; option D is incorrect.

83. B. This is the definition of homomorphic encryption.

   All the other answers are incorrect.

84. B. Real-time analytics allows for reactive and predictive operations (such as recommending other, related products) based on customers' current and past shopping behavior.

   All the other answers are data discovery approaches but not used for this particular application (options C and D are two names for the same thing).

85. D. The Agile approach to data analysis offers greater insight and capabilities than previous generations of analytical technologies.

   Options B and C are other data discovery technologies, but neither is the correct answer.

   Option A is incorrect because obverse polyglotism is just a made up term that does not have any relevance as an answer to the question.

86. D. *Data hover* is a made up term which is not a data discovery technique. All the other answers are actual data discovery techniques.

87. A. This is the definition of metadata: data about data, usually created by systems (hardware and/or software) when the data is captured/collected.

   Options B and C are also data discovery techniques, but not involving metadata.

   Data hover is a made up term and is therefore, not a data discovery technique, so option D is incorrect.

88. C. The data owners, presumably the personnel closest to and most familiar with the data, should be the ones labeling it.

   The other answers are incorrect because they are not the data owners.

89. C. For the most efficient classification/categorization process, and to streamline the application of proper controls, data labeling should be performed when the data is first being collected/created.

Options A and B are incorrect because they are not part of a data labeling process.

Option D is incorrect because the discovery tools need to have the data labeled to work properly.

90. A. Egress monitoring tools (often referred to as DLP) are specifically designed to seek out and identify data sets based on content; this is part of how they operate. They can be used for or in conjunction with content-based data discovery efforts.

Digital rights management (DRM) is an additional access control solution for objects, so option B is incorrect.

Internet Small Computer System Interface (iSCSI) allows storage controller commands to be sent over a Transmission Control Protocol (TCP) network and has nothing to do with data discovery; thus, option C is incorrect.

Fibre Channel over Ethernet (FCoE) is a standard for approaching fiber-media speeds of data transfer on an Ethernet network; it has nothing to do with data discovery, so option D is incorrect.

91. D. Inheritance has nothing to do with content analysis; it is usually referring to object-oriented traits derived from originating objects.

All the other answers are characteristics of content that can be used in content-analysis methods of data discovery.

92. B. Because dashboards are often used for management purposes (graphical representations of technical data), management pressures often result in skewed data dashboarding ("no red!"), which can lead to the "data" being used for fallacious decisions.

All the other answers are not affected by dashboarding at all and are incorrect.

93. D. A data discovery effort can only be as effective as the veracity and quality of the data it addresses. Bad data will result in ineffective data discovery.

All the other answers do not impact data discovery efforts and are only distractors. (Poor bandwidth might slow down data discovery, but it won't have true negative impact, so option D is still better.)

94. C. Label assignment is a task of the data owner—the cloud customer, not the provider.

All the other answers are requirements for the cloud provider to meet the data discovery needs of the customer and should be negotiated before migration.

95. D. The cloud customer will have to determine which levels of performance/responsibilities on the part of the provider will be necessary to meet the customer's needs for data discovery. These should be codified in the contract/service-level agreement (SLA).

The other answers are general regulations and standards; they will not contain specific guidance for every customer's needs and are only distractors.

96. D. This is a difficult question and requires insight on the practice of classifying data and a good understanding of the material. While the determination of what sorts of data need to be protected may come from external sources (laws, standards, regulations, etc.), the classification of data for each data owner/cloud customer will be specific to that entity. Therefore, the cloud customer will have to impose data classification schema on itself and its own data.

The other answers represent external entities, some of whom might require that certain information be handled with a certain duty or care (such as Payment Card Industry [PCI] mandates for cardholder information). However, these entities will not impose a classification scheme on the data owner or cloud customer; that responsibility falls on the data owner or cloud customer to do for itself and the data under its control.

97. D. This is a difficult, and somewhat tricky, question. Each organization has to decide, for itself, how to classify its own data. With that said, many factors bear on this determination: external regulations and drivers, the type of industry in which the organization operates, and so forth. But the kinds of data the organization uses, and how that data is sorted, will differ for every organization, and each must make its own determination on how to best sort that data.

All the other answers are factors that an organization might consider when creating a classification scheme, but they are not mandatory for every organization. Option D is still the best answer for this question.

98. B. This is another difficult question. Classification of data is an element of labeling, insofar as labeling is the grouping of data into discrete categories and types. Labels must be affixed to objects and data sets in accordance with an overall policy that lists objective criteria to guide the data owner(s) in assigning the appropriate label; this is a form of classification.

Option A might be considered apt, as labeling and classification fall generally under the auspices of "security," but option B is more specific and therefore correct.

Classification is not considered a facet of data control or data markup. Therefore, options C and D are incorrect.

99. B. An organization could implement an automated tool that assigns labels based on certain criteria (location of the source of the data, time, creator, content, etc.), much like metadata, or the organization could require that data creators/collectors assign labels when the data is first created/collected, according to a policy that includes discrete, objective classification guidance.

Option A is incorrect because even though the word pair may seem pretty technical, together they are meaningless with respect to data classification.

It may be true that data classification can be correct or incorrect, however, option C is not as good of an answer as option B. The goal for the data owner is to correctly classify the data and not to incorrectly classify the data. So, option C is incorrect.

It is difficult to imagine data classification that only takes place at a certain time of day. Therefore, it is not likely to be the correct answer and certainly option D is not as good an answer as option B.

100. A. Color is unlikely to be a characteristic for which data is classified, much less reclassified. Although some exceptions might exist (motion picture production, satellite imagery, paint vendors, etc.), those would be far from the norm, and the other answers are much more general cases and would apply to many more organizations. Therefore, color is the correct answer (in the negative), and the rest are incorrect (because they are true).

101. C. The purposes of classifying/categorizing data is to create proper associated control sets for each data type and aid the efficiency and cost-effectiveness of applying those controls to that data.

While dollar value may be a good metric for assessing data type in many organizations, it is not the only such trait, and not for all organizations; option C is still a better answer, so A is wrong.

Metadata may or may not be used in a classification/categorization scheme; option B is incorrect.

Policies are not assigned to data types; a policy will dictate how data classifications/categories are assigned to data. Option D is incorrect.

102. B. Data transforming from raw objects to virtualized instances to snapshotted images back into virtualized instances and then back out to users in the form of raw data may affect the organization's current classification methodology; classification techniques and tools that were suitable for the traditional IT environment might not withstand the standard cloud environment. This should be a factor of how the organization considers and perceives the risk of cloud migration.

Multitenancy should be a consideration of cloud migration for the potential risks of data leakage and disclosure but not because of data transformation. Option A is not correct.

Remote access and physical distance should not include aspects of data transformation that are not already considered in the traditional IT environment, so options C and D are incorrect.

103. D. The cloud customer, as the PII data owner, is ultimately legally responsible for all losses of PII data. The customer may be able to recoup some of the costs of damages related to the breach by placing *financial* liability on the provider through the use of strong contract terms and conditions, but all *legal* responsibility falls on the customer, in all cases.

The other options are parties that may have some partial or contributory responsibility for the breach (especially, in this case, the provider, who was negligent), but the ultimate responsibility lies with the customer.

104. D. The subject is the human being to whom the PII applies.

The other answers are not data subjects, and are therefore incorrect.

105. B. In a PII context, the processor is any entity that processes data on behalf or at the behest of the data owner. In the case of most managed cloud service arrangements, that will be the cloud service provider. (The cloud customer may also process its own data, but the customer is the data owner/controller.)

Options A, C, and D are all incorrect. The cloud customer provides the subject's PII to the cloud provider for processing. The regulator ensures that the PII is protected properly and the individual is the data subject. So, options A, C, and D are incorrect answers.

106. A. In a PII context, the controller is the entity that creates/collects, owns, or manages the data—that is, the data owner. In a managed cloud service arrangement, that would be the cloud customer.

Options B, C, and D are all incorrect. The cloud provider is the entity that processes the PII data. The regulator ensures that the PII is protected properly and the individual is the data subject.

107. B. This is not a simple question, and it requires a bit of insight into uses of data. The most suitable answer here is "viewing," as it is entirely passive; the viewer is not performing any action on the data. "Processing," in a PII context, is any manipulation of the data, to include securing or destroying it, in electronic or hard-copy form. In a "viewing" action, the processor would be displaying the data to the viewer, while the viewer is only receiving it, not storing it or using it. Note that the answer did not involve "using," which definitely would be a processing action.

All the other answers are examples of processing and therefore not correct.

108. B. The United States has some federal PII laws that apply to specific sectors (the government itself [Privacy Act], medical providers [Health Information Portability and Accountability Act], financial and insurance vendors [Gramm-Leach-Bliley Act], etc.), but not a single, overarching federal law that addresses PII in a uniform, nationwide manner.

All the other options list countries that have such laws, and those options are therefore incorrect.

109. A. Under HIPAA, the subject must opt in to information sharing—that is, the subject (the patient) must explicitly state, in writing and with a signature, who the vendor is allowed to share personal information with, such as family members, spouses, parents, and children. (Under HIPAA, this personal information is referred to as electronic private health information [ePHI].) The vendor is prohibited from sharing the patient's data with anyone else.

Under HIPAA, the patient does not have to opt out of information sharing; the default situation is to not share patient data. Option B is incorrect.

HIPAA does not require any kind of screening or template, so Options C and D are incorrect.

110. B. Under GLBA, financial and insurance vendors are allowed to share account holders' personal data with other entities (including other businesses owned by the same vendor) unless the account holder explicitly states, in writing, that the vendor is not allowed to do so. The vendor is required to provide a form for opting out of data sharing when the account holder creates the account and annually every subsequent year.

Option A is incorrect; under GLBA, the default situation allows banks and insurance providers (owned by the same entity) to share customer data—the customer must opt out of this arrangement if the customer doesn't want information shared.

Options C and D are incorrect because they do not relate to the sharing of PII data by a bank or insurer.

111. B. The EU is probably at the forefront of global efforts to sanctify and enshrine personal privacy; the current statutes and precedents based on court decisions have clearly denoted Europe's intent to treat individual privacy as a human right.

Options A and D are simply incorrect.

It is very possible to consider option C as correct because European businesses are held to strict standards regarding the privacy data under their control. However, option B has more significance and is more general, so it is the proper selection among this list.

112. B. The EU regulations associated with personally identifiable information (PII) belonging to EU citizens prohibit that data to be utilized in any way in any country that does not have a national privacy law commensurate with the EU regulations. Of this list, only the United States has no such law. Indeed, the EU regulations might very well be taken to be aimed directly at the United States, and probably for good reason; the United States has not proven to be a good steward of or even recognize the importance of personal privacy.

113. C. The right to be forgotten is the EU's codification of an individual's right to have any data store containing their own personal data purged of all personally identifiable information (PII). There are, of course, some obvious exceptions (such as law enforcement databases).

The other answers are not as accurate; "the right to be forgotten" is a very well-known and important aspect of the GDPR.

114. B. Under current laws and regulations, ultimate liability for the security of privacy data rests on the data controller—that is, the cloud customer. A PLA would require the cloud provider to document expectations for the cloud customer's data security, which would be an explicit admission of liability. There is little motivation for cloud providers to take on this additional liability (and the costs associated with it) with no mandate or market force pushing them to do so.

Option A is wrong because the provider's liability is already limited under current legal schemes; the PLA would not enhance that limitation.

Options C and D are wrong because agreements (as contracts) are both binding and enforceable, and even if they were not, those are not reasons.

115. C. The CMM is not included in the CSA CCM and, indeed, is not even a security framework.

All the other options are included in the CSA CCM and are therefore not correct answers for this question.

116. D. The DMCA deals with intellectual property and not specifically with personal privacy. It is not included in the CSA CCM.

All the other answers are laws that are included in the CSA CCM and are therefore not correct answers for this question.

117. A. DRM solutions are mainly designed to protect intellectual property assets (and mainly those covered by copyright, hence the name), but they can also be used to provide enhanced protection to other electronic information. All the other options are forms of electronic information, while option A is a piece of hardware; DRM does not enhance hardware security, so this is the correct answer.

118. A. Deploying DRM usually requires installing a local agent on each device intended for use in that environment; with BYOD, that means getting all users to agree and install that agent because they own the devices.

DRM *is* an enhanced security protocol, so option B is incorrect.

The cloud is not specifically necessary for DRM implementations, even in BYOD environments, so option C is incorrect.

Any DRM solution involving a BYOD environment must be suitable for all devices, not just a certain selection, because the organization can't easily mandate which devices are used (otherwise, it's not BYOD). Option D is incorrect.

119. B. In a BYOD environment, users might bring any number of devices/operating systems to the network, and any DRM solution selected for the purpose must interact well with all of them.

The organization cannot dictate specific packages in a BYOD environment—otherwise it is not BYOD—so option A is incorrect.

Turnstiles are for physical access control and have no bearing on BYOD or DRM, so option C is incorrect.

BYOD and DRM should have no effect on BC/DR vendors (or the numbers thereof), and vice versa, so option D is incorrect.

120. D. The CSA CCM does not deal with whether security controls are feasible or correct from a business perspective, only whether they are applicable to an organization under certain regulations.

All the other answers are incorrect because they are too specific and not required by any regulation/legislation. Therefore, options A, C, and D are poor choices and also incorrect answers.

121. B. For DRM to work properly, each resource needs to be outfitted with an access policy so that only authorized entities may make use of that resource.

All the other answers are distractors.

122. B. DRM and DLP work well to address complementary security issues—namely, asset classification/categorization and discovery, along with access and dissemination of those assets.

RIS is a made-up term, so option A is not correct.

Adjusting BIOS settings is not particularly relevant to DRM in any way, so option C is incorrect.

TEMPEST is a program for harvesting data from electromagnetic emanations, so option D is not correct.

123. C. Access rights following the object in whatever form or location it might be or move to is the definition of persistence, one of the required traits for a DRM solution of any quality.

All the other answers are traits that should be included in DRM solutions but do not match the definition in the question, so they are incorrect.

124. A. Capturing all relevant system events is the definition of a continuous audit trail, one of the required traits for a DRM solution of any quality.

All the other answers are traits that should be included in DRM solutions but do not match the definition in the question, so they are incorrect.

125. D. The question describes dynamic policy control, one of the required traits for a DRM solution of any quality.

All the other answers are traits that should be included in DRM solutions but do not match the definition in the question, so they are incorrect.

126. C. The question describes automatic expiration, one of the required traits for a DRM solution of any quality.

All the other answers are traits that should be included in DRM solutions but do not match the definition in the question, so they are incorrect.

127. B. The question describes support for existing authentication security infrastructure, one of the required traits for a DRM solution of any quality.

All the other answers are traits that should be included in DRM solutions but do not match the definition in the question, so they are incorrect.

128. D. This is not an easy question and requires some interpretation and abstract thought. All of the elements listed are extremely important aspects of the data retention policy. However, using proper data retrieval procedures is the one without which all the others may become superfluous. An organization can perform thorough backups in a timely manner and secure them properly at an excellent location, but if those backups can't be used to restore the operational environment, they are pointless.

All the other options are important, but option D is probably the most important.

129. B. The question states the definition of archiving.

Deletion involves using the operating system or an application to obscure the location of an object or file, so option A is wrong.

Crypto-shredding is a secure sanitization technique using cryptographic techniques, so option C is wrong.

Storing is a general term covering all retention of data, so option B is a better answer than option D.

130. A. Not all policies are temporary or have expected durations; usually, policy is an enduring piece of governance that will continue until such time as it is revoked.

All the other options are elements that should usually be included in policies.

131. D. Secure sanitization is intended to ensure that there is no possible way for the data to be recovered; a backup copy would defeat the entire purpose.

All the other answers are goals of secure sanitization.

132. C. Deletion, using basic system assets (usually the operating system), mainly involves removing pointers to and addresses of the files or objects that are the targets of deletion. This leaves the raw data remaining on the storage resource, and it could be recovered later.

Options A and B both include secure destruction methods, but they are not exclusive (obviously, because there are two of them), so therefore they are untrue and also incorrect.

Option D does not make practical sense; if users could not delete files/objects, common workplace activity would become burdensome and difficult.

133. C. The preferred methods of secure sanitization require physical access to (and control of) the hardware on which the data is stored; in the cloud, this belongs to the cloud provider, and the cloud customer will not be allowed to perform destructive procedures.

Options A, B, and D are incorrect because the question is about the difficulty of performing data destruction in the cloud computing environment. Often, the only reliable form of data destruction is to destroy the hardware where it is stored. None of these options address that question the way that option C does.

134. A. One of the benefits of using managed cloud services is that most providers are constantly performing backup and preservation activities in order to ensure that customers do not lose data. This can make it complicated for customers to even locate all their stored data, much less permanently destroy it.

Delete commands are certainly allowed in the cloud. Otherwise, cloud providers would eventually run out of storage space. Option B is incorrect.

Option C is incorrect because ISPs do not have the authority to prohibit the destruction of data by data owners.

It may be unclear who the "end client" is in option D. If the end client is the individual, then it does not make sense that the individual would prohibit the destruction of data by the cloud provider, given that the cloud provider owns the hardware itself.

135. D. Secure sanitization would affect storage resources where more than one customer stores their data; truly secure destructive measures would likely result in destroying data belonging to someone else.

Law enforcement can destroy their own data, however, law enforcement is not permitted to destroy data that belongs to other individuals. Option A is therefore incorrect.

Option B is incorrect because data destruction is required from time to time in the cloud as part of system maintenance.

Fortunately, option C is incorrect. If data renewed itself automatically in the cloud then cloud providers would eventually run out of storage space.

136. C. Destroying the drive, disk, and media where the data resides is the only true, complete method of data destruction.

Options A and B are also good methods for data destruction, but neither is the best method.

Option D is incorrect because a legal order is not a secure method of data destruction and therefore it cannot be the correct answer.

137. B. Cloud data storage likely uses solid-state drives (or disks), which are not affected by degaussing because they don't use magnetic properties to store data.

Option A is incorrect because it is untrue. A gauss is a unit of magnetism. Not all data storage devices in the cloud are magnetic. Some storage space does not require magnetism to work. Solid State Drives (SSDs) are an example of a type of storage space that does not rely on magnetism to store data.

Federal law does not prohibit degaussing of magnetic media in the United States so option C is incorrect.

Option D is incorrect because process of degaussing magnetic media does not produce a blast and therefore it does not produce a blast radius.

138. D. Overwriting is the practice of filling the entire storage of the target data with randomized characters (usually involving multiple passes and a final pass with a single, repeated character). In the cloud, this is untenable for many reasons, including the fact that cloud data is constantly moving from one storage resource to another and is not kept in a single, identifiable logical location for an extended period of time (which is actually a security benefit). Without you knowing which storage resources to overwrite, overwriting is impossible.

All the other options are only distractors. Options A and C describe elements of the overwriting process but not reasons why it's challenging in the cloud. Option B is true, but overwriting does not require physical access, so the option is incorrect.

139. B. Regulators do not disapprove of secure sanitization; it is an acceptable form of secure data destruction if implemented properly.

All the other answers are actual reasons overwriting is not a viable secure sanitization method in the cloud.

140. A. Crypto-shredding relies on the eventual destruction of the final keys; if keys are not under the management of the customer, they may be replicated or difficult to dispose of.

The lack of physical access to the cloud environment should not affect the crypto-shredding process, so option B is incorrect.

External attackers should not affect the crypto-shredding process, so option C is incorrect.

Crypto-shredding should not require input or activity from users, so option D is incorrect.

141. B. The proper procedure for crypto-shredding requires two cryptosystems: one to encrypt the target data, the other to encrypt the resulting data encryption keys.

All the other answers are wrong and just distractors.

142. D. If users inadvertently erase or modify data, an archived backup copy could be useful for restoring the original, correct version.

All the other answers are incorrect; archiving does none of those things.

143. B. An archived data set could be useful for investigative purposes, especially if it covers a significant period of time and includes multiple copies. The archived versions may be used as a reference to determine when a certain malicious activity occurred, which is useful during an investigation.

All the other answers are incorrect; archiving does not aid in these functions.

144. A. Archiving may be required by regulation, and archived versions of the environment or data may be used to create deliverables for auditors, especially if the archive included event logs.

Archived data is not an optimum gauge of performance because it is not "live" data—that is, the archived data is no longer in the operational environment and so is not a useful indicator of how well that environment currently operates. Option B is therefore incorrect.

Archiving has nothing to do with investment; option C is incorrect.

Archiving may occur as the result of policy but is not an enforcement tool; thus, option D is incorrect.

145. D. Many cloud providers will offer archiving services as a feature of the basic cloud service; realistically, most providers are already performing this function to avoid inadvertent loss of customer data, so marketing it is a logical step. However, because the customer is ultimately responsible for the data, the customer may elect to use another, or an additional, archive method. The contract will stipulate specific terms, such as archive size, duration, and so on.

Either the cloud customer or provider (or *both*) may perform archiving, depending on the contract terms, so options A and B are incorrect.

Regulators do not perform archiving; option C is incorrect.

146. A. The policy for data archiving and retention must include guidance on the length of time data is expected to remain stored.

Describing or prescribing the physical specifications of a secure archive facility is probably beyond the responsibility or requirements of a data owner (and belowground storage is not a requirement for archiving and retention), so option B is incorrect.

Although it is important to task and train personnel to take part in data restoration from archived data, naming the specific personnel in the policy is not an optimum or useful practice, so option C is incorrect.

Although management is responsible for publishing and promulgating policy and governance, the name of the specific manager is not the essential element (but their office or position is). Regulators don't personally approve internal policies of the organizations they oversee, so option D is incorrect.

147. B. It is important to indicate the data format and media type for long-term storage in order to ensure restoration capability; outdated or obsolete data formats and media may not be useful for restoration of data to the operational environment several years after it has been stored.

Options A and C are not correct because specific names don't belong at the policy level of governance; the specific names (or identification credentials) of allowed third-party recipients should be included at the process/procedure level of governance, and a list of *offices* or *departments* whose data will be archived can be included in the policy.

Option D is not correct because the particular ISP should not have any bearing on the archiving policy.

148. C. Once the policies have been published and put into force, the names and contact information of the people who crafted them are no longer useful or germane.

All the other options represent entities that the organization may want to contact in the event of a security incident or breach and so should be included in security procedure documentation.

149. B. This is a question that requires some thought. All the answers are processes or elements that should be included in the security operations' procedures except for option B; the cloud customer will not get to select, or probably even know, what tools and devices the cloud provider has put into place, so this will not be included in the customer's procedures.

150. D. Option D is the definition of nonrepudiation.

Option A is a description of confidentiality.

Option B is an element of the Atomicity, Consistency, Isolation, Durability (ACID) test to enhance the utility and security of a database.

Option C is a technique to reduce the likelihood of nonrepudiation but not the definition of the term.

Chapter 3: Domain 3: Cloud Platform and Infrastructure Security

1. C. It's best to have your backup at another cloud provider in case whatever causes an interruption in service occurs throughout your primary provider's environment; this will be more complicated and expensive, but it provides the best redundancy and resiliency. Using the same provider for production and backup is not a bad option, but it entails the risk of the same contingency affecting both copies of your data. Having either the backup or the production environment localized does not provide the best protection, so neither option B nor option D is desirable.

2. B. A trained and experienced moderator can guide the participants through the activity, enhancing their training and noting pitfalls and areas for improvement. Option A is not preferable because having the participants gathered together ensures their full attention and provides interaction that remote participation might not yield. Option C is a baseline; all participants should have copies of the policy as a matter of course. Option D is not useful in a tabletop exercise; only critical participants in the organization should take part in the tabletop.

3. B. This is a difficult question that requires a great deal of thought. Option B is correct because appropriate cloud data security practices will require encrypting a great deal of the data, and having the keys will be necessary during contingency operations in order to access the backup; without the keys, you won't be able to access your data. Option A is not correct because using the cloud for BC/DR will allow personnel to access the backup from anywhere they can get broadband connectivity, not specifically a recovery site. Option C is not correct because the customer will rarely have physical access to servers in the cloud environment. Option D is not correct because forensic analysis is not a significant consideration in BC/DR; it is much more important for incident response.

4. A. A full test will involve both the production environment and the backup data; it is possible to create an actual disaster during a full test by ruining the availability of both. Therefore, it is crucial to have a full backup, distinct from the BC/DR backup, in order to roll back from the test in case something goes horribly wrong. Option B is incorrect because not all personnel will have tasks to perform; most personnel will have to evacuate from the facility only during a full test. Option C is incorrect because the cloud provider should not initiate the test, and the test should not take place at a random moment. Option D is not correct because the regulators' presence will not add any value to the test.

5. A. Security Assertion Markup Language (SAML) is based on XML. HTTP is used for port 80 web traffic; HTML is used to present web pages. ASCII is the universal alphanumeric character set.

6. A. Option A is the definition of the term;the other answers are not.

7. C. The administrative offices of a cloud data center rarely are part of the critical functions of the operation; a data center could likely endure the loss of the administrative offices for a considerable length of time, so redundancy here is probably not cost effective.

All the other items *are* part of the critical path and need redundancies.

8. D. Option D is the definition of a cloud carrier, from National Institute of Standards and Technology (NIST) Special Publication (SP) 500-292.

All the other options are incorrect, as defined by NIST SP 500-292.

9. B. The question describes a software-defined network (SDN).

A VPN is used for creating an encrypted communications tunnel over an untrusted medium, so option A is incorrect.

ACLs are used as centralized repositories for identification, authentication, and authorization purposes, so option C is incorrect.

RBAC is an access control model used to assign permissions based on job functions within an organization, so option D is incorrect.

10. B. The NBI usually handles traffic between the SDN controllers and SDN applications.

Options A and C are incorrect because neither of those options lists any of the SDN infrastructure, be that the controllers or the applications. Option D may be *arguably* correct, as there might be an NBI handling that traffic between those nodes, but option B is more specific and always true for this definition, so it is the better choice.

11. D. Option D is really a definition of a CDN (content delivery network).

All the other options are aspects of SDNs.

12. B. The question describes an HSM.

KMB is a nonsense term used as a distractor, so it is incorrect.

TGT is a term associated with Kerberos single sign-on systems and is incorrect.

The TCB includes the elements of hardware and software (usually in the operating system) that ensure that a system can only be controlled by those with the proper permissions (i.e., admins with root control), so it is also incorrect.

13. C. The compute nodes of a cloud data center can be measured in terms of how many central processing units (CPUs) and how much random access memory (RAM) is available within the center.

Option A is incorrect because routers would be considered a part of the networking of a data center (and because option C is a better answer).

Option B involves applications and how traffic flows between them and storage controllers; it has nothing to do with the compute nodes and is therefore wrong.

Option D might obliquely be considered correct because it's technically true (compute nodes will include both virtual and hardware machines), but option C is a much better and more accurate choice.

14. C. *Cancellations* is not a term used to describe a resource allotment methodology. All of the other options are such terms.

15. A. The question is the definition of reservations.

Options B and D are also resource apportioning methods, but they do not fall under the definition described in the question.

Option C is incorrect because it has no meaning in this context.

16. D. The question describes limits.

Options A and B are also resource apportioning methods, but they do not fall under the definition described in the question.

Option C is because it has no meaning in this context.

17. B. The question describes shares.

Options A and D are also resource apportioning methods, but they do not fall under the definition described in the question.

Option C is incorrect because it has no meaning in this context.

18. A. A bare-metal hypervisor is a Type 1 hypervisor.

Option B describes another type of hypervisor; the other options are incorrect because there is no such thing as a Type 3 or Type 4 hypervisor.

19. B. The question describes a Type 2 hypervisor.

Option A describes another type of hypervisor; the other options are incorrect because there is no such thing as a Type 3 or Type 4 hypervisor.

20. B. A Type 2 hypervisor relies on the underlying operating system (OS) to operate properly; the underlying OS offers a large attack surface for aggressors.

A Type 1 hypervisor boots directly from the hardware; it's much easier to secure a machine's Basic Input/Output System (BIOS) than an entire OS, so option B is better than option A.

Options C and D are incorrect because there is no such thing as a Type 3 or Type 4 hypervisor.

21. D. VMs are snapshotted and simply stored as files when they are not being used; an attacker who gains access to those file stores could ostensibly steal entire machines in highly portable, easily copied formats. Therefore, these cloud storage spaces must include a significant amount of controls.

Options A and C are simply untrue.

Option B is untrue when crypto-shredding is utilized.

22. C. While options A and B are both also true, C is the most significant reason cloud data centers use VMs. If the cloud provider had to purchase a new box for every user, the cost of cloud services would be as much as running a traditional environment (or likely cost even more), and there would be no reason for any organization to migrate to the cloud, especially considering the risks associated with disclosing data to a third party.

Option D is simply untrue. VMs are not easier to operate than actual devices.

23. D. The question describes what the hypervisor does. (Note that the answer "operating system" would also work here but was not one of the options.)

Option A is incorrect; the allocation of resources is not performed manually.

The router directs traffic between networks; it does not apportion resources. Therefore, option B is incorrect.

A VM makes resource calls; option C is incorrect.

24. B. Object storage is, literally, a means of storing objects in a hierarchy such as a file tree.

All the other options are terms used to describe cloud storage areas without file structures.

25. B. Snapshotted VM images are usually kept in object storage, as files.

All the other options are incorrect and option C is not a type of storage.

26. C. Only the most trusted administrators and managers will have access to the cloud data center's management plane. These will usually be cloud provider employees, but some cloud customer personnel may be granted limited access to arrange their organization's cloud resources.

Regulators do not operate a customer's management plane, so option A is incorrect.

Option B is ambiguous. However, a consumer of data is unlikely to have been given the elevated privileges necessary of operate the management plane in a cloud environment. Option B is incorrect.

Option D is also an ambiguous answer. Only the most trusted administrators and managers have access to the cloud data center's management plane. A privacy data subject is neither a most trusted administrator nor a trusted manager. Therefore, option D is incorrect.

27. D. The contract is probably the cloud customer's best tool for avoiding vendor lock-in; contract terms will establish how easy it is to migrate your organization's data to another provider in a timely, cost-effective manner.

Options A and B are also important ways to avoid vendor lock-in, but D is the best answer.

Option C is incorrect and will not aid in avoiding vendor lock-in.

28. C. The regulator(s) overseeing your industry/organization will make the final determination as to whether your cloud configuration is suitable to meet their requirements. It is best to coordinate with your regulator(s) when first considering cloud migration.

Cloud providers, cloud customers, and ISPs are not particularly concerned about whether an organization's migration is satisfactory from a compliance perspective. The words, "compliance perspective" should automatically bring to mind regulator(s). Options A, B, and D are therefore incorrect answers.

29. D. Vendor lock-out occurs when the provider suddenly leaves the market, as during a bankruptcy or acquisition. The risks associated with lock-out include denial of service, because of total unavailability of your data. The best way to handle these risks is to have another, full backup of your data with another vendor and the ability to reconstitute your operating environment in a time frame that doesn't exceed your recovery time objective (RTO).

The other options do not aid in addressing vendor lock-out.

30. A. Because the cloud provider owns and operates the cloud data center, the provider will craft and promulgate the governance that determines the control selection and usage. This is another risk the cloud customer must consider when migrating into the cloud; the customer's governance will no longer have direct precedence over the environment where the customer's data is located.

Both the cloud customer and the regulator(s) may have specific control mandates that might require the customer to deploy additional security controls (at the customer side, within the data, as agents on the user devices, or on the provider side or in application programming interfaces [APIs] as allowed by the service model or contract), so options B and C are also partially true, but A is a better answer as it is more general.

Option D untrue because the end user does not determine which controls are selected for the cloud data center and how they are deployed. That is the responsibility of the cloud provider.

31. B. The question describes a guest escape.

Options A and C are other risks of operating in the cloud. Option D can lead to A or B, but B describes the more specific situation and therefore the correct answer.

32. A. The question describes host escape.

Options B and C are other risks of operating in the cloud. Option D can lead to A or B, but A is the more specific situation and therefore the correct answer.

33. D. Because most cloud users don't see direct costs in creating new VM instances (the bills usually go to a single point of contact in the organization, not the user or the user's office), they may tend to create additional VMs at a significant rate, without realizing the attendant cost. This is largely because it is so easy to do and has no apparent cost, from their perspective.

All the other options do not cause virtualization sprawl.

34. C. Sprawl needs to be addressed from a managerial perspective because it is caused by allowed user actions (usually in a completely authorized capacity).

Options A and D mean the same thing and could be considered as contributing to sprawl because the technological capabilities of virtualization create the ease of use that can cause sprawl. However, option C is a better answer.

Option B is incorrect; sprawl occurs within the organization.

35. D. Because all cloud access is remote access, the risks to data in transit are dramatically heightened in the cloud.

The other options exist in both the traditional environment and the cloud but are probably actually reduced in the cloud because cloud providers can use economies of scale to invest in means to reduce those risks in ways that individual organizations would not be able to.

36. B. Defense in depth, or layered defense, is perhaps the most fundamental characteristic of all security concepts.

Options A and C are security aspects of some environments, and option A is likely to be a necessary trait of managed cloud services, but they are not fundamentals—they are specifics.

Option D is specifically an administrative control; the question is looking for a fundamental aspect of security. Option B is more general (it applies to all types of security, in all industries and uses) and therefore is the correct choice for this question.

37. B. A secure baseline configuration, applied and maintained automatically, ensures the optimum security footprint with the least attack surface.

All the other options are benefits of automated configuration but are not specifically security enhancements.

38. B. The Security Assertion Markup Language (SAML) is probably the most common protocol being used for identity federation at the moment.

Options A and C are not identity federation protocols.

Option D is a federation specification, but it also uses SAML tokens.

39. C. This is a very popular function of federated identity.

Single sign-on (SSO) is similar to federation, but it is limited to a single organization; federation is basically SSO across multiple organizations. Option A is incorrect.

Options B and D are threats listed in the Open Web Application Security Project (OWASP) Top Ten; they are incorrect.

40. A. The cross-certification federation model is also known as a *web of trust*.

Proxy is another model for federation, so option B is incorrect.

Single sign-on is similar to federation, but it is limited to a single organization; option C is incorrect.

Option D does not have relevance in this context and therefore incorrect as an answer.

41. B. In the proxy federation model, the third party acts on behalf of the member organizations, reviewing each to ensure that they are all acceptable to the others.

Cross-certification is another model for federation, so option A is incorrect.

Single sign-on is similar to federation, but it is limited to a single organization; option C is incorrect.

Option D does not have relevance in this context and is therefore incorrect as an answer.

42. A. In a web of trust federation model, all of the participating organizations are identity providers; each organization will assign identity credentials to its own authorized users, and all the other organizations in the federation will accept those credentials.

A trusted third party, regulators, and clientele are not involved in the web of trust model, so the other options are incorrect.

43. A. In a web of trust model, each member organization usually supplies both the access/identification credentials and the resources that the users want to access, so the organizations are both the identity providers and service providers in a web of trust federation model.

A trusted third party, regulators, and clientele are not involved in the web of trust model, so the other options are incorrect.

44. D. While it's likely the participating organizations will be subject to other federal regulations, HIPAA covers electronic patient information, so it will definitely be applicable in this case.

GLBA covers financial and insurance service providers, so option A is incorrect.

FMLA dictates how employers give vacation time to employees, so option B is not correct.

PCI DSS is a contractual, not regulatory, standard, so option C is incorrect.

45. C. The question describes authorization.

Options A and B are part of the overall identity and access management (IAM) process, as is option C, but they do not specifically describe granting access to resources.

Federation is a means of conducting IAM across organizations; option C is more specific, so D is incorrect.

46. D. Redacting is an editorial process of excising sensitive information from disclosed data. All the other options are elements of identity management.

47. C. This is a complicated question and requires thinking through the portions of the identification process.

Identification of personnel is usually verified during the hiring process, when HR checks identification documents (such as a passport or birth certificate) to confirm the applicant's identity, often as part of a tax registration process.

Options A and B include offices that may play a role in the identification process, but it is usually HR that does the actual verification.

Option D, "Sales" is untrue. If a Sales department exists in an organization, it does not perform the verification part of the provisioning element of the identification process.

48. C. Cloud providers may be reluctant to grant physical access, even to their customers, on the assumption that allowing access would disclose information about security controls. In some cases, cloud customers won't even know the location(s) of the data center(s) where their data is stored.

The other options are all untrue. Data in the cloud and controls in the cloud can most certainly be audited. So, options A and B are incorrect. D is untrue; there are regulators for all industries, including those that operate in the cloud.

49. D. In many circumstances, a cloud audit will depend on which information a cloud provider discloses, which makes auditing difficult and less trustworthy.

Option A is incorrect because cryptography is sometimes present in traditional environments and audits still take place.

Option B is incorrect; auditors' opinions are not relevant.

Option C is untrue; equipment does not resist auditing—it is inanimate and unfeeling.

50. A. Because cloud audits are often the result of third-party assertions, recipients of cloud audit reports may be more skeptical of the results than they would have been of traditional audits, in which the recipients may have performed firsthand.

Option B is untrue. The difficulty of standards is not a hindrance to audit.

Option C is untrue. Paperwork does not hinder audits.

Option D is not only untrue, but also hilarious. If you have ever been involved in an audit, you know that there are plenty of auditors to go around.

51. B. The "sensitive information," in this case, is whatever knowledge of the data center's security controls and processes might be gathered by physically visiting the data center. Even though a cloud customer cannot get access to the facility, this also means that other cloud customers (some of whom may be inimical to another customer's interests) also will not have access, so none would have advantage over the other(s).

Option A is incorrect because qualified personnel are still required whether a cloud environment has limited access to their data center or not. In fact, security may be degraded by having unqualified personnel rather than qualified personnel working in the cloud data center.

Option C is incorrect because reducing jurisdictional exposure does not enhance security.

There may be a correlation between ensuring statutory compliance and enhancing security as it applies to limiting access to the cloud data center. However, option B is a better answer because it is certainly true. Therefore, option D is not the best answer to the question.

52. B. Because VMs don't take updates when they are not in use (snapshotted and saved as image files) and updates may be pushed while the VMs are saved, it's important to ensure that they receive updates when they are next instantiated.

A physical tracking mechanism won't be of much aid for virtual devices because they aren't physically stolen like hardware boxes, so option A is incorrect.

Having an ACL in the image baseline would create a situation where every user from every cloud customer could access every VM in the data center; option C is incorrect.

Write protection is used in forensic analysis of machines (virtual or otherwise); it would not be useful in an operational baseline. Option D is incorrect.

53. A. Version control can be difficult in a virtual environment because saved VMs don't receive updates. Ensuring that each VM is the correct version is a function of configuration management (CM), and CM controls can be built into the baseline.

Each organization will have its own training and awareness program, and there is no one-size-fits-all solution that is appropriate; this does not belong in the baseline. Option B is incorrect.

Having a baseline that cannot be copied is pointless; option C is incorrect.

Keystroke loggers will create a huge volume of detailed, stored data that will pose more of a security risk (and may actually be a violation of customer privacy regulations) than any benefit it offers; option D is incorrect.

54. C. Event logging is essential for incident management and resolution; this can be set as an automated function of the CM tools.

Not all systems need or can utilize biometrics; option A is incorrect.

Usually, *tampering* refers to physical intrusion of a device; since the question is about VMs, it is probably not applicable. Option B is incorrect.

Hackback is illegal in many jurisdictions; option D is incorrect.

55. B. A specified configuration built to defined standards and with a controlled process can be used to demonstrate that all VMs within an environment include certain controls; this can greatly enhance the efficiency of an audit process.

The VM's image has very little to do with physical security or training; options A and C are incorrect.

Baseline images are the opposite of customization; option D is incorrect.

56. C. The baseline will contain the suite of security controls applied uniformly throughout the environment.

A VM image audit is unlikely to involve any form of physical security; A is incorrect.

Baselines won't predictively show malicious activity; B is incorrect.

Baselines also do not have anything to do with user training and awareness; option D is incorrect.

57. B. Having an additional backup with a different provider means that if your primary provider becomes unusable for any reason (including bankruptcy or unfavorable contract terms), your data is not held hostage or lost.

Custom VMs may or may not work in a new environment; this is actually a risk when porting data out of the production environment; option A is incorrect.

Performance probably will not increase if data is replicated to another cloud provider; in fact, you will probably lose some load balancing capability you might have had if you kept the data and backups together. Option C is incorrect.

Having two providers will always be more costly than a single provider; option D is incorrect.

58. D. Having the backup within the same environment can allow easy rollback to a last known good state or to reinstantiate clean VM images after minor incidents (e.g., a malware infection in certain VMs).

Ease of compliance will not be determined by the location of the backup, so option A is incorrect.

Traveling should not be a major cost for cloud usage; option B is incorrect.

The location of the backups won't have any effect on user training; option C is incorrect.

59. D. Having your data backed up and accessible in the cloud eliminates any need for having a distinct hot site/warm site separate from your primary operating environment; instead, your personnel can recover operations from anywhere with a good broadband connection.

Cloud BC/DR capability does not remove the necessity of security personnel and appropriate policies; both options A and B are incorrect.

Option C makes no sense as an answer to the question. It is unclear how you can cut costs by eliminating your old access credentials. In fact, it is difficult to imagine how that is a true statement. Therefore, option C is a poor choice and option D is the best choice.

60. D. Without ISP connectivity, nobody will be able to use the Internet and, thus, the cloud. Of course, realistically, without Internet connectivity not much business will get done anyway, for most organizations, regardless of whether they were operating in the cloud or on-premise.

Option A is incorrect because the loss of any, single, cloud administrator is unlikely to gravely affect your organization's RTO.

The loss of a specific VM will probably not gravely affect your organization's RTO. VMs can be reinstantiated with ease. Option B is incorrect.

The loss of your policy and contract documentation cannot gravely affect your organization's RTO. Option C is untrue.

61. C. Health and human safety is always paramount in all security activity.

All the other options are assets that should be protected, but nothing is as important as option C, so they are incorrect answers for this question.

62. B. The recovery point objective (RPO) is a measure of data that can be lost in an outage without irreparably damaging the organization. Data replication strategies will most affect this metric, as the choice of strategy will determine how much recent data is available for recovery purposes.

Recovery time objective (RTO) is a measure of how long an organization can endure an outage without irreparable harm. This may be affected by the replication strategy, but not as much as the RPO. Option A is incorrect.

The maximum allowable downtime (MAD) is how long an organization can suffer an outage before ceasing to be an organization. This is not dependent on the RPO, and the data replication strategy won't have much effect on it at all. Option C is incorrect.

The mean time to failure (MTTF) is a measure of how long an asset is expected to last (usually hardware), as determined by the manufacturer/vendor. The data replication strategy will have no bearing on this whatsoever. Option D is incorrect.

63. D. A data backup/archive can offer your organization an operational "reachback" capability, where admins can assist users in recovering data lost by accident or carelessness.

The backup/archive does not aid in any of the areas in the other options. So, options A, B, and C are incorrect.

64. B. When using two different cloud providers, a cloud customer runs the risk that data/software formats used in the operational environment can't be readily adapted to the other provider's service, thus causing delays during an actual failover.

Risks of physical intrusion are neither obviated nor enhanced by choosing to use two cloud providers; option A is incorrect.

Using a different cloud provider for backup/archiving actually reduces the risks of outages due to vendor lock-in/lock-out and natural disasters, so options C and D are not correct.

65. B. Theoretically, all the options are possibly true. However, option B is the most likely to occur and is fairly common in practice; the cost and risk of moving operations from one environment/provider to another is sizable, so staying with the secondary provider (making them the new primary) is a good way to reduce some of the risk involved in returning to normal.

66. A. The business requirements will determine the crucial aspects of BC/DR.

All the other options may constitute some input that will influence the BC/DR, but they are not the prevailing factors, so are incorrect.

67. C. The business impact analysis (BIA) is designed for this purpose: to determine the critical path of assets/resources/data within the organization. It is a perfect tool to use in shaping the BC/DR plan.

The risk analyses options and the risk appetite option may provide input for the BIA, but they are not what is used to determine the critical assets necessary to protect in the BC/DR activity. So, options A, B, and D are incorrect.

68. D. If the contingency operation will last for any extended period of time, it is important to know whether all the same service expectations can be met by the backup provider as were available in the production environment.

All the other questions are important, but not as crucial as option D, so they are incorrect.

69. C. BC/DR responsibilities must be negotiated and codified in the contract; initiation could be something performed by provider or customer, depending on circumstances, so the parties must agree before those circumstances are realized.

It is exceedingly unlikely that "any user" in a managed cloud services arrangement can invoke a BC/DR action. Option D is therefore a poor choice for the answer to the question.

70. C. Without a full test, you can't be sure the BC/DR plan/process will work the way it is intended.

Audits are good, but they will not demonstrate actual performance the way a test will, so options A and B are incorrect.

It is important that the BC/DR capacity and performance be included in the contract, but that will not truly ensure that the functionality exists; a test is required, so option D is incorrect.

71. A. All of these are important, but without regular updates, the information will soon become outdated and a lot less useful.

72. C. This is not an easy question, because *every* plan/policy should include mention of the governance documents that drive the formation of the plan/policy; however, these can be included by reference only—you don't need to include full copies of these governance documents.

All the other options should be included in the BC/DR plan/policy.

73. D. This question is difficult. You want your BC/DR plan/process to include sufficient detail such that it could be followed by someone with the right background (perhaps IT for certain roles, security for others, etc.) but without any experience or specific training in that role. This is because a contingency of the scope that would require initiation of BC/DR activities might involve dramatic, significant external forces to the point where the personnel normally tasked with BC/DR actions are not available (for instance, natural disasters, fire, civil disruption, etc.), so the tasks may need to be completed by whoever is available at the time.

The BC/DR plan/process should be written and documented in such a way that someone with the requisite skills can use it. It is unlikely that typical users or regulators have the requisite skills to perform many of the BC/DR activities. Therefore options A and C are poor choices for answers to the question.

It is tempting to choose option B, however, option D is a better answer because it ensures that someone with the requisite skills will be able to read the BC/DR plan and perform the activities they document. Having to rely on essential BC/DR team members being present and available to follow the plan is risky. So option B is incorrect.

74. C. A premature return to normal operations can jeopardize not only production, but personnel; if the contingency that caused the BC/DR action is not fully complete/addressed, there may still be danger remaining.

The BC/DR plan/process should take into account both the absence of essential personnel and telecommunications capabilities, so options A and D are incorrect.

Option B does present a serious problem for the organization, but C is still a greater risk, so B is incorrect.

75. C. Not returning to normal operations in a timely fashion can cause you to exceed the RTO and the MAD.

During a contingency, some of the requirements your organization faces may relax somewhat; for instance, if a life-threatening natural disaster occurs, regulators will likely understand if some of the normal compliance activities/controls are not fully incorporated while personnel and assets are moved to safety (depending on the nature of the industry, of course). Options A and B are therefore incorrect; option C poses a greater risk.

Option D is a distractor; not all organizations need encrypted communications during contingencies.

76. A. Depending on your industry and the nature of your data, moving information into another jurisdiction may affect or invalidate your regulatory compliance.

Cloud providers, wherever they are located, should compensate for environmental and physical security factors, so this should have no impact on your potential risk; options B and C are incorrect.

Option D is incorrect because it is blanket statement that is not always true. In fact, for some organizations, the physical location where their data is stored can have serious regulatory consequences.

77. C. ENISA's approach to cloud risk assessments does not specifically address this type of assurance, probably because of the wide variety of possible regulators and the difficulty in crafting a risk assessment that would address them all.

All the other options are assurance efforts that ENISA's cloud risk assessment is meant to enhance, so they are incorrect answers for this question.

78. D. ENISA includes "programmatic management" as a defining trait of cloud computing, even specifying "through WS API." This is not included in the definition published by (ISC)^2 (or by NIST).

All the other characteristics are included in the (ISC)^2 (and NIST) definitions.

79. D. The only reason organizations accept any level of risk is because of the potential benefit also afforded by a risky activity.

Profit is not the hallmark of every opportunity (or every organization—many organizations are nonprofit or government-based), so option A is incorrect.

Likewise, not all risky activities offer a chance to enhance performance, so option B is incorrect.

Cost is not a benefit, so that doesn't even make sense in the context of the question; option C is not correct and a distractor.

80. D. The cloud greatly enhances opportunities for collaboration between organizations, mostly by giving external parties some limited access to the owner's data in the cloud. While there is risk in this situation, the truly comparable risk in the traditional environment would result from sending data outside the organization to external collaborators. (Furthermore, the organization has to balance this risk against the cost of business of not being able to collaborate, if data is never shared with third parties.)

Option A is ridiculous; data should be secured whether it is in an on-premise environment or in the cloud.

Option B does not create a true equivalence; disclosing data under controlled conditions is not the same as public disclosure.

Option C is not equivalent to the costs/benefits of the other forms of collaboration; it would be too cumbersome for the organization to truly benefit from collaboration in a modern business environment.

81. C. Under current legal frameworks, some risks (such as legal liability for privacy data breaches) cannot be transferred to a contracted party, so the data owners (that is, cloud customers) will still retain those risks.

Option A is ridiculous; risks can and should be mitigated, even in the cloud.

Option B is not correct; cloud migration will require some risk acceptance, but that is true for everything except avoided risk.

Option D is incorrect; cloud providers can choose not to offer services or not to accept certain clients.

82. C. As the models increase in level of abstraction and service, the customer's control over the environment decreases.

83. B. Sharing resources with other, unknown customers (some of whom may be competitors of or even hostile to the organization) is a risk not faced by organizations that maintain their own, on-premise data centers.

All the other answers are threats that exist in both environments and are therefore incorrect.

84. D. Because supply chain dependencies can affect service, the cloud customer will need assurance that any third-party reliance is secure.

Regulators and end users do not provide security to the enterprise, so options A and B are incorrect.

The vendors used for on-premise security will no longer affect the data, so option C is incorrect.

85. D. It is possible that a cloud provider will be unable to handle an increased load during contingency situations where *all* its customers are demanding additional resources far beyond their usual contracted rate. While this is unlikely (many cloud providers, especially the major operators in the market, have resources that greatly exceed any possible demand by their customers), it could conceivably occur if a significant number of customers experience an immediate and dramatic need for capacity, such as during a major BC/DR event (a region-wide natural disaster or a physical attack on a city). This is not something that would affect an on-premise solution; your organization's data center is not affected by others' demand for resources (although the on-premise environment may be affected by the same contingency that causes cloud resource exhaustion, of course).

All the other options portray risks faced by both cloud and on-premise environments.

86. B. Guest escape (a malicious user leaving the confines of a VM and able to access other VMs on the same machine) is less likely to occur and to have a significant impact in an environment provisioned for and used by a single customer.

In a public cloud, this is more likely and would be more significant, so option A is incorrect.

The service model doesn't specifically dictate the likelihood of occurrence or impact (both PaaS and IaaS could be in a private or public cloud, which is the more important factor), so both options C and D are incorrect.

87. B. Because of multitenancy and shared resources in the cloud, law enforcement may seize a cloud customer's assets (a physical device, a data set, etc.) and inadvertently capture assets belonging to another, unsuspected/innocent organization. This could not happen in a situation where all individual organizations only kept their own assets on their own premises.

All the other options include risks that exist in the traditional, on-premise environment, as well as the cloud, so they are incorrect.

88. C. This is not an easy question; the simple answer seems to be option A, which is true for data stored/saved/migrated to the cloud (and property that already has been created in the cloud), but for new intellectual property created in the cloud, strong contract language in favor of the customer's rights is very necessary. Without clear-language support about the customer's ownership of all intellectual property created in the cloud data center, the cloud provider could, ostensibly, make a claim on such property, as the provider's resources were used in a collaborative effort to create that property.

Options B and D are security controls used to protect all sorts of assets, including intellectual property, but they are not as specifically addressing the creation of new intellectual property in the cloud the way explicit contract clauses would, so option C is still the better answer.

89. B. While it is possible that one guest VM seeing the resource calls of another VM could possibly allow one guest to see the other's data, it's much more likely that a user seeing another user's use of resources, rather than raw data, would allow the viewer to infer something about the victim's behavior/usage/assets.

Likewise, it may be possible for the viewer to leverage knowledge of this usage as part of a social engineering attack, but that would be subsequent to the inference itself; option B is still better than C.

Lack of resource isolation does not affect physical intrusions, which is just a distractor here.

90. B. Social factors should not/don't affect the level of entropy in a random number generator.

However, all the other factors listed in the other answers *do*, and that means that a malicious user in the cloud would be more likely (statistically) to guess/predict the random number used to create/seed an encryption key made in that same cloud environment. Cloud customers should take this into account when designing/planning their cloud configuration.

91. C. Without uniformity of data formats and service mechanisms, there is no assurance that a customer would be able to easily move their cloud operation from one provider to another; this can result in lock-in.

All the other options are not affected by lack of standards.

92. A. Many cloud providers prohibit activities that are common for administrative and security purposes but can also be construed/used for hacking; this includes port scanning and penetration testing. These restrictions can reduce the customer's ability to perform basic security functions.

While geographical dispersion of cloud assets might make securing those assets more difficult in the notional sense (customer administrators can't physically visit the devices that host their data), remoteness does not necessarily inhibit good security practices, which can be performed at a remove. This is not as detrimental as rules against port scanning/pen testing, so option B is incorrect.

There are no rules against user training or laws against securing your own assets, in the cloud or otherwise; options C and D are incorrect.

93. A. Brewer-Nash was specifically created for managed services arrangements, where an administrator for a given customer might also have access to a competitor's data/environment; the model requires that administrators not be assigned to competing

customers. In the modern cloud provider model, a cloud data center administrator will almost definitely have access to many customers from the same industry (i.e., competitors) but probably won't even know it.

All the other options are access control security models; cloud administrators will not (or should not) be assigning access rights, so all these options are wrong.

94. B. Administrative and support staff are usually not part of the critical path of a data center; they are nonfunctional-requirement elements, not functional requirements.

All the other options are mission-critical elements of the cloud data center and must have redundancy capabilities.

95. B. To avoid a situation where severing a given physical connection results in severing its backup as well (such as construction/landscaping, etc.), have redundant lines enter on different sides of the building.

For health and human safety, multiple egress points from each facility is preferred (and often required by law); option A is incorrect.

Emergency lighting should receive power regardless of their proximity to the power source, and parking vehicles near generators is a bad idea from a safety perspective; option C is incorrect.

Not all facilities need to withstand earthquakes; this may be true of data centers in California, but not in Sydney, so it is not an industry-wide best practice. Option D is incorrect.

96. D. People entering the facility can be vectored through a single security checkpoint as a means of enhancing access control; multiple lines of ingress are not necessary (although multiple lines of *egress* are essential to ensure health and human safety).

All the other options are facility elements that require redundancy.

97. C. A recovery from backup into the production environment carries the risk of failure of both data sets—the production set and the backup set. This can cause cataclysmic harm to the organization.

Recovering in the primary facility would probably be cheaper than having a different test facility, so option A is incorrect.

A proper test is worth the financial expenditure, so option B is incorrect.

Option D is incorrect because any BCDR plan would account for sufficient personnel workspace.

98. B. Assuming your facility is not available during contingency operations allows you to better approximate an emergency situation, which adds realism to the test.

Though option A is an act of benevolence on the part of the organization towards the community, option B is still a better answer for the question.

Option C is an act of benevolence on the part of the organization towards the employee, option B is still a better answer for the question.

Option D is incorrect because it makes assumptions that cannot be counted upon. Regulatory oversight should not be avoided, and should always be assumed.

99. B. In an infrastructure as a service (IaaS) model, the provider is only responsible for provisioning the devices and computing/storage capacity; the customer is responsible for everything else, including the security of the applications.

All the other answers are incorrect because those individuals/organizations do not accept responsibility for securing cloud-based applications.

100. A. According to ENISA, custom IAM builds can become weak if not properly implemented.

Strong contract language in favor of the customer is always desirable for the customer, so option B is incorrect.

Training for specific conditions is always advisable, so option C is incorrect.

There is nothing wrong with having encryption take place before data is sent to the cloud, so option D is incorrect.

101. D. With strong contract terms, the cloud customer may be able to recover monetary damages (and even penalties) from the cloud provider as a result of a loss suffered by the customer; however, legal liability remains with the cloud customer.

The other answers are not relevant in this context.

102. B. Revoking credentials that might be lost when a device goes missing is a way to mitigate the possibility of those credentials being used by an unauthorized person.

Punishing a user and notifying law enforcement does not prevent data from being disclosed; options A and C are incorrect.

Tracking devices may assist recovery efforts, but it won't protect against data disclosures during the period the device is not under the organization's control; option D is incorrect.

103. B. Of all these options, only B is not something that will reveal untoward behavior.

104. D. Multifactor authentication offers additional protections for assets that are critical to the organization.

All logins should utilize strong passwords, whether they are critical or not, so option A is incorrect.

Some form of physical perimeter security is useful, but not necessarily chain-link fences, and not only for critical assets (perimeter security will protect all assets on the campus), so option B is incorrect.

Homomorphic encryption is a theoretical technology; option C is incorrect.

105. A. An asset that is not tracked will not be maintained properly, and an improperly maintained asset provides an avenue for attack.

Options B and D are management issues, not security issues; option A is preferable to both of them.

Option C is incorrect; users don't care if their devices are catalogued and annotated. Option C is a poor choice for an answer to the question.

106. A. Data formatted in a manner that allows its reuse in other environments is essential for portability.

None of the other options are relevant to the issue of data portability.

107. B. Testing is a great way to enhance assurance that applications will work in the new environment.

None of the other options are relevant to the issue of application portability.

108. C. The RTO must always be less than the MAD.

It is good to know that services will operate in the alternate environment and that first response contact info is current, but neither determines the speed with which services and data will be available during contingency operations; options A and B are incorrect.

Regulators will usually not dictate MAD/RTO for a given organization; option D is incorrect.

109. D. Of the listed options, knowing how other customers feel about a provider may be the most valuable data point; it is the most realistic depiction of whether an organization realized projected/anticipated benefits after a migration.

Options A and B are just marketing materials and should not, by themselves, be all that convincing for making a migration decision.

Option C is a good factor to consider, but it is only a very small piece of what migration entails; D is still a much better option.

110. C. Because cloud access is remote access, pen tests will be remote tests; it doesn't really matter what the physical origin of the simulated attack is.

All the other options are items the provider will want to know before the customer launches the test.

111. D. Performing live deception and trickery against employees of the cloud provider (or its suppliers/vendors) could be construed as unethical and possibly illegal, especially without their knowledge and/or consent. Social engineering probably won't be involved in penetration tests run by customers.

All the other options are legitimate activities a customer might perform during a penetration test (with provider permission).

112. D. In most jurisdictions, the activity involved in penetration testing would be considered criminal, and quite serious, and the provider would be justified in seeking law enforcement involvement and prosecution.

None of the other answers make sense with respect to the question.

113. B. Because all penetration tests launched by the customer require notifying the provider beforehand (and getting permission), the simulation loses quite a bit of realism. In the traditional environment, where the organization had full control over its own assets, penetration tests could involve double-blind status, which was much more realistic.

Everyone uses remote access for cloud activity, so option A is incorrect.

Cloud customers will not be able to deploy malware as part of a test because that is a crime, so option C is wrong.

Regulators are not involved in penetration tests, so option D is incorrect.

114. D. Virtualization allows for the scalability and cost reduction available in managed cloud services.

All the other options are incorrect because they do not cite the technology that creates most of the cost saving in the cloud environment. Only virtualization provides this cost savings.

115. D. In the traditional environment, the cloud customer must pay for a device for every user, which requires additional capacity that is almost never fully used; this represents a cost with no associated benefit. Moving into a virtualized environment allows the organization to only pay for resources that are utilized and not for underutilized or unused capacity.

The risks and regulatory requirements for an organization do not go away when the organization moves into the cloud, so there is no cost savings associated with these elements. Therefore, all of the other options are incorrect.

116. C. An organization operating in the cloud should not need as many IT personnel as would be required to operate a traditional enterprise with the same level of services for users; this can represent a significant cost savings.

Moving into the cloud reduces neither risk nor data; options A and D are incorrect.

Arguably, the cloud customer may realize some cost savings through cloud migration because the customer will not be solely responsible for acquiring, deploying, and managing security controls. However, security controls still exist—they are, instead, the responsibility of the cloud provider, and the price of applying them is enclosed in the cost of the cloud service. Moreover, this savings is not nearly as significant as the savings realized through reduction in personnel, so option C is still preferable.

117. B. Because virtual machine images are stored as imaged files, an attacker able to access the stored files would have a much easier time transporting those files than transporting actual drives/machines.

Option A actually represents a risk in the physical environment that is reduced by the use of virtual machines and is incorrect.

VMs are not any more or less susceptible to malware or EMP, so options C and D are incorrect.

118. C. Both the hypervisor and the OS orchestrate access to resources (the hypervisor coordinates requests from VMs, and the OS coordinates requests from applications).

Option A is incorrect because the CPU in a traditional environment performs calculations, while the operating system manages resources and performs process scheduling.

The security team in a traditional environment has a narrow and focused role, not like the operating system that manages the entire system and its resources.

Pretty Good Privacy is an application that performs a specific, limited role. Option D is incorrect.

119. D. Solid-state drives (SSDs) are currently the most efficient and durable storage technology, so cloud providers will favor them.

All the other options are older technologies that employ magnetic media in one form or another, while SSD employs electronic circuitry to store data.

120. C. In object storage, data objects/files are saved in the storage space along with relevant metadata such as content type and creation date.

Options A and B are different names for the same type of storage arrangement and incorrect.

Option D has no meaning in this context.

121. C. NIST's definition of *cloud carrier* is "an intermediary that provides connectivity and transport of cloud services from Cloud Providers to Cloud Consumers."

Of the choices, option C best represents this definition.

122. D. The hypervisor orchestrates assignment of resources and is responsible for avoiding and resolving contention.

The router manages traffic flow, which might be considered as resolving contention issues for resource requests outside the local device (for example, from a given device to the storage cluster) but wouldn't handle resource requests inside a given device (such as a VM on the device making a request to the device CPU), so option D is a better answer.

An emulator virtualizes programs, not machines, and is not responsible for orchestrating resource calls, so option B is incorrect.

Regulators do not manage resources, so option C is incorrect.

123. D. Security controls operating on a guest VM OS are only active while the VM is active; when the VM is stored, it is snapshotted and saved as a file, so those controls won't be active either.

All user access to the VMs will be done remotely; option A is simply incorrect.

Security controls on OSs that are not scanned or subject to version control may be out of date or not optimized, but they will still function (just not as well), so option D is still preferable to B and C.

124. A. Solid-state drives (SSDs) are usually more expensive, per drive, than their counterparts. However, as the industry matures, this is changing rapidly. Moreover, cloud providers are usually buying devices at such a scale and under such a budget that individual price differentials for device types is not the main criteria for making purchase decisions.

Size and shape are not defining criteria of SSDs or tapes; options B and C are irrelevant (and also somewhat wrong).

The physical nature of the drive does not affect its vulnerability to malware; option D is incorrect.

125. B. SSD technology offers a great increase in speed and efficiency.

SSDs are not typically more difficult to install or administer than traditional technology, nor are they more likely to fail than other storage devices, so all the other options are incorrect.

126. B. Because SSDs do not use magnetic properties to store data, degaussing is not a suitable means of sanitizing SSDs.

All the other options are untrue and are therefore inappropriate answers.

127. C. Theoretically, all combinations of security controls are preferable to any one security control used by itself (this is the principle of layered defense). All of the potential responses are therefore true. However, of this list, the pairing that makes the most sense is option C, because encrypting the data while also spreading it across multiple storage devices/ locations increases the protection each one offers against certain common threats (in this case, physical theft of a storage device, failure of a device, legal seizure of a device in a multitenant environment, etc.).

128. C. Theoretically, all combinations of security controls are preferable to any one security control used by itself (this is the principle of layered defense). All of the potential responses are therefore true. However, of this list, the pairing that makes the most sense is option C, because adding another layer of access control on objects while also detecting outbound motion of objects increases the protection each one offers against certain common threats (in this case, internal threats, escalation of privilege, unauthorized or inadvertent dissemination of data, etc.).

129. C. Every organization is responsible for performing its own risk assessment for its own particular business needs.

Cloud providers will not perform risk assessments on behalf of their customers.

Regulatory bodies and legislative entities do not perform risk assessments.

130. C. The best method for avoiding vendor lock-in is to have strong contract language favorable to the customer; the entity best equipped to craft contracts is the office of the general counsel.

Senior management can assist the organization to avoid vendor lock-in by tasking the correct resources (offices/personnel) to perform vendor selection activities, but option A is not as accurate as C.

Security personnel will have the technical skills and knowledge to properly determine the organization's IT needs and can inform general counsel as to what services/resources will best meet the organization's needs, but these entities are not as adept and trained at crafting contract language as the attorneys. Options B and D are not preferable to C.

131. B. Using distinct cloud providers for production and backup ensures that the loss of one provider, for any reason, will not result in a total loss of the organization's data.

None of the other options address vendor lock-out and are therefore unsuitable as answers.

132. C. Users in a cloud environment may not realize the attendant costs that come along with creating many new virtual instances, and the ease with which new instances are created allows users to do so without much effort.

While DDoS and phishing may include an element of user gullibility and ignorance, at least one party (the attacker) is not engaged in inadvertent activity—their behavior is very purposeful. Options A and B are incorrect.

While inadvertent action can often result in incidents, disasters are usually at a much greater scale and aren't as likely to be the result of unknowing action; option D is incorrect.

133. B. Management plane breach allows an attacker to gain full control of the environment and can affect all aspects of the CIA triad.

DDoS and physically attacking the utility lines, options A and D, only affect availability, which is a significant negative impact but not as bad as option B, which can affect integrity and confidentiality as well.

Guest escape is a breach limited to a specific device and the virtual machines on that device; this is not as much impact as breaching the management plane, which gives full access to the entire environment.

134. A. Controlling access is optimized by minimizing access.

All the other options are incorrect.

135. D. Usually, mantrap areas control access to sensitive locations within a facility, not an entrance to the facility.

None of the other options address vendor lock-out and are therefore unsuitable as answers.

136. C. Health and human safety is a paramount goal of security; all facilities must have multiple emergency egress points.

All the other options are distractors as they are included in option C.

137. B. In the traditional environment, when all resources are owned, controlled, and used by the organization's personnel, loss of isolation will only expose data to other members of the organization; isolation failure in the cloud environment may expose data to people outside the organization, a more significant impact.

All the other options are risks that have similar likelihoods and impacts in the cloud and traditional environments and are therefore incorrect.

138. B. Security and productivity/operations are always trade-offs.

Option A is a generalization that may or may not be true depending on several variables. Some security controls are inexpensive to implement.

Senior management approval may be required before security controls can be implemented, however, some may not need prior approval. It depends on the organization and how it is managed. Option C is incorrect.

Option D is another generalization that may or may not be true. Whether a security control will work in the cloud environment as well as they worked in the traditional environment depends on the control and how it is implemented. Option B is a better choice.

139. A. Because cloud providers may use data centers that span state (or even national) borders, new legal risks may be introduced to the customer's organization after cloud migration.

All the other options are risks faced by organizations in both the cloud and traditional environments and are therefore incorrect.

140. A. In the traditional environment, if DDoS prevented the organization's connectivity with the Internet or other organizations, users still had access to their own data but simply could not share it or use it in external transactions; this hampered productivity, but not availability. In the cloud, without connectivity outside the organization, users cannot reach their data, which is an availability issue.

DDoS does not affect value, confidentiality, or liability; all the other options are incorrect.

141. D. DDoS prevents all these things except for data integrity. DDoS only prevents communication; it does not usually result in modified data.

142. C. In some instances, more virtualized machines will entail a relative increase in the number of software seat licenses, which can be a significant expense.

Typically, cloud customers do not pay extra for additional consumption of floor space or power usage for the number of virtual machines; these costs are rolled into the per-instance price, so options A and B are incorrect.

Option D is incorrect; users don't require more training if they have more virtual assets.

143. D. When performing BC/DR tests, it is useful to create scenarios that are unpredictable and vary from previous tests so as to better approximate conditions of an actual disaster.

All the other answers represent elements that should avoid variables as much as possible and are incorrect.

Chapter 4: Domain 4: Cloud Application Security

1. A. The ONF lists all the controls used in all the applications within an organization; each ANF lists the particular controls used in each application the organization has. Standard Application Security is a made-up term therefore options C and D are incorrect.

2. D. Each application will have its own ANF, derived from the organization's ONF. This can be a difficult question because there are many ANFs in the organization, but only one for each application. The reader needs to examine the question carefully.

3. C. SOAP necessarily uses XML.

HTML is a language used to tag text files so that they can be displayed with different fonts, colors, graphics and hyperlinks. HTML is not used in SOAP. Option A is incorrect.

Option B is incorrect because X.509 is a standard and the question is about a programming language.

Option D is incorrect because HTTP is protocol and the question is about a programming language.

4. B. Generally, a REST interaction involves the client asking the server (through an application programming interface [API]) for data, sometimes as the result of processing; the server processes the request and returns the result. In REST, an enduring session, where the server has to store some temporary data about the client, is not necessary.

These interactions obviously involve servers and clients, so options C and D are not correct.

Using REST does not eliminate the need for credentials, so option A is not correct.

5. B. Roy Fielding, the author of the PhD dissertation that created REST, was also the author of HTTP, so it's no surprise the command set is the same.

All the other options are incorrect because the REST APIs do not use HTML, XML or ASCII as protocol verbs.

6. C. The web is mainly HTTP, which is a RESTful protocol.

All the other options are incorrect because they do not answer the question about the architecture of the World Wide Web.

7. A. Servers can return REST requests to clients in a number of formats, including XML and JSON.

X.509 certificates are used for passing session encryption information, not data requests, so option B is incorrect.

Servers usually return data requests in some sort of display format, not plain text or ASCII, so option C is incorrect.

HTML responses would simply be an entire web page, not specific data, so option D is incorrect.

8. D. All the other options are simply words used in other contexts. They are incorrect.

9. B. All the other options are risks that exist in the traditional environment as well as the cloud.

10. C. In order for developers to properly create and secure applications, they will need to understand the extent of resource sharing (public/private/hybrid/community) and level of control (infrastructure as a service [IaaS], platform as a service [PaaS], software as a service [SaaS]) the organization will expect in the cloud environment.

Each of the other options includes at least one element that programmers don't need to know (specifically, the native language, Internet service provider [ISP], country code) and is therefore incorrect.

11. B. A trial run in the cloud will reveal any functionality/performance loss before a permanent cloud migration.

Option A doesn't reduce any risk for a specific application; it trades the risk of one application not operating correctly with the risk of another application not working correctly. This answer is wrong.

All applications should be reasonably patched and updated, whether it is in the traditional environment or the cloud. Option C is incorrect.

An emulator won't reduce the risk of degraded performance; it will probably result in degraded performance. Option D is incorrect.

12. D. Not all programs (or organizations) will require database access, or even use databases, and hashing is not a common requirement.

All the other functions are expected in the majority of cloud operations.

13. A. In PaaS, the customer is responsible for the administration (and security) of applications.

Neither regulators nor programmers are responsible for the security of the applications in the production environment. That is the responsibility of the cloud customer.

It may appear as though the cloud provider should be responsible for application security, however, as the cloud customer acquires more responsibility for their cloud environment, the cloud provider assumes less responsibility. Option B is incorrect.

14. D. Performance and security both need to be reviewed for adequacy.

In this context, *quality* would be synonymous with *performance* and *requirements*, so D is a better answer than A or C.

Brevity is not a trait we look for in testing, even though it may be desirable in programming, so B is incorrect.

15. A. In the Define phase, we're trying to determine the purpose of the software, in terms of meeting the users' needs; therefore, we may solicit input from the user community in order to figure out what they really want.

Options B and C are other phases of the SDLC, but not all SDLC models incorporate user input in these phases, so the options are not correct.

Option D is not a phase of the SDLC and is incorrect.

16. D. Disposal is the only phase concerned with the sanitization of media or destruction of data.

All the other options are also SDLC phases, however, crypto-shredding is much more likely to be used in the disposal phase.

17. B. Design is the correct answer, as this is where the requirements gathered during the Define phase are mapped to system designs.

All the other options are SDLC phases where requirements are not mapped to software construction.

18. D. Function is usually *the* functional requirement, describing what action the tool/process satisfies.

All the others are usually nonfunctional requirements. Exceptions to this are when the characteristic listed is the actual desired function. For instance, if the product is a tool that enunciates text so that a blind user can hear the words, then sound would be the functional requirement. If the product is a security tool such as a firewall or data loss prevention (DLP) solution, then security would be a functional requirement. Otherwise, these are nonfunctional requirements for standard products.

19. C. Traditional apps won't usually require encryption in all phases of the data lifecycle because data is protected in several stages in the traditional environment without the need for additional controls. In the cloud environment, however, data exposed at any point in the lifecycle might constitute an inadvertent disclosure, so cloud apps require encryption for data at rest and in motion (and usually in use as well).

Even traditional apps require IAM and field validation functions, so options A and D are incorrect.

Most anti-DDoS activity will be performed by hardware and communication software run by the cloud provider or Internet service provider (ISP); developers should not typically need to include anti-DDoS elements in their programs. Option B is incorrect.

20. A. Because the cloud is a multitenant environment, one of the concerns that developers should consider is how well the application prevents other applications/users from observing its operation and resource calls. In the traditional environment, this is not usually required because the organization owns the underlying infrastructure (as a single tenant) and there is very little risk in exposing the application's functionality.

Inference framing is a nonsense term, used here only as a distractor.

Software should include known secure components, and testing should include known bad data (fuzz testing), whether it is going to be used in the cloud or in a traditional environment, so options C and D are incorrect.

21. D. The cloud provider may have controls that restrict logging, or the delivery of log data, in the environment; this can make it complicated for cloud developers to include that functionality/security element in cloud apps.

    All the other options are things that can (and should) be done with software whether the application is being used in traditional or cloud environments, so those options are incorrect.

22. D. Using only known secure libraries and components in software design may slow down development efforts but shouldn't impact how the application runs.

    All the other options are security controls that will degrade performance because they require additional overhead; these options are incorrect.

23. D. This is the definition of escalation of privilege (sometimes referred to as "elevation of privilege").

    Inversion is a nonsense term in this context and just a distractor.

    Options B and C are threat modeling elements but are not correct answers for this question.

24. A. The STRIDE threat model does not deal with business continuity and disaster recovery (BC/DR) actions.

    All the other options are elements of STRIDE (escalation of privilege, repudiation, and spoofing, respectively) and are therefore not correct.

25. D. Users in the production environment will leverage whatever tools and techniques they can in order to get their job done in a better, faster way, often regardless of whether this complies with security policies.

    All the other options are untrue and therefore cannot be the correct answer. For test-taking purposes, be very suspicious of words like, "constantly" and "can't ever" in answer choices.

26. B. Because many programs are currently constructed from "building block" components found in code libraries, any security issues within specific components may not be understood or identified by coders who don't know the code inside the component.

    Option A is an unfair generalization.

    Option C is another broad generalization that may or may not be true. Option B is a better answer.

    Option D does not relate to the question about the SDLC and is therefore a poor choice for an answer.

27. D. Obviously, using multiple forms of code review will produce more secure results than any one form of review, in the same way that having multiple forms of security controls (physical, logical, administrative, etc.) will provide better security than just one type.

The question is which is the "most" secure form of code testing and review. That would be the most extensive. Since the correct answer is a combination of open source and proprietary, the least secure would be least extensive. Option A is strictly open source so that is incorrect. Option C is neither open source nor proprietary, which is even less extensive. Option C is incorrect. Proprietary/internal is also less extensive than Option D. So Option B is incorrect.

28. B. This is the textbook definition of these terms. All the other options are incorrect answers.

29. B. Business needs and risk acceptable to senior management should drive all organizational decisions, including access. Specific user or object access will, of course, be delegated down from senior management to a manageable layer of the organization, but the principle applies.

This decision, however, should be informed by pertinent externalities, which include regulatory mandates (option A), user requirements and management requests (option C), and, to some degree, the trade-off of performance and security (option D, and both characteristics should also be dictated by senior management as an aspect of acceptable risk). While these externalities and options all play a part in determining appropriate access, they are all subordinate to business needs and acceptable risk, which are paramount; B is still the best answer to this question.

30. C. The data owner is responsible for the disposition of the data under their control; this includes access decisions.

The cloud provider is not typically the data owner; option A is incorrect.

Ostensibly, senior management is the data owner (the organization, as a whole, is the legal owner of the data, and the senior managers are the legal representatives of the organization). However, in practice, this responsibility can be (and usually is) delegated down to a manageable level, where the data owner for a given data set understands it best and can provide a sufficiently granular control of that data set. This is rarely senior management and is more likely department heads, branch managers, or some other form of middle management. Option C is preferable to B.

System administrators will usually be the literal granters of access, insofar as admins will modify access control systems that allow or disallow access for specific individuals or roles. However, the sysadmin does not make the decision of who is granted access and instead responds to direction from data owners (middle management); again, option C is preferable to D.

31. D. PGP is an email encryption tool, not an identity federation standard. All the other options are federation standards.

32. B. OpenID Connect is a federation protocol that uses representational state transfer (REST) and JavaScript Object Notation (JSON); it was specifically designed with mobile apps in mind, instead of only web-based federation.

WS-Federation is a federation protocol that is part of the WS-Security family of standards and reliant on Simple Object Access Protocol (SOAP), so option A is incorrect.

Option C is incorrect; SOC 2 is a type of Statement on Standards for Attestation Engagements (SSAE) 18 audit report, not a federation standard.

OWASP is a volunteer group of and for web app developers, not a federation standard or protocol, so option D is incorrect.

33. B. Because there is no transitive property of identification and authentication, knowing a trusted entity is not sufficient for validating an identity assertion.

All the other options are typical authentication mechanisms and so are incorrect.

34. A. At the ATM, the customer will use the card (something you have) and enter a PIN (something you know). This is true multifactor authentication.

A password and PIN are both something you know, so option B is incorrect.

Using a voice sample and fingerprint are two forms of something you are, so option C is incorrect.

A birth certificate and credit card are both something you have, so option D is incorrect.

35. B. Multifactor authentication should be considered for operations that have a significant risk or that deal with highly sensitive data (for instance, privileged user logins or when handling financial transactions).

Requiring multifactor authentication for every transaction is an undue burden on both the users and the systems and is a needless addition of extra overhead, so option A is incorrect.

All cloud access will entail remote login; this is a common operation, so adding multifactor authentication is an unnecessary burden in most cases. Option C is incorrect.

The decision to use multifactor authentication should be based on the risk of the operation and the sensitivity of the data, not on whether it takes place in the traditional or online environment, so option D is incorrect.

36. C. A WAF is a Layer 7 tool.

All the other options are incorrect.

37. D. WAFs recognize HTTP traffic and can respond to traffic that matches prohibited rulesets or conditions.

Option A is technically correct; a WAF can be given a ruleset that recognizes certain forms of attack traffic. However, this answer is too general, and D is a much better response for this question.

Options B and C are protocols not usually inspected by WAFs and are therefore incorrect.

38. D. WAFs can be used to attenuate the possibility that cross-site scripting attacks will be successful.

WAFs do not protect against social engineering or physical attacks in any way, so options A and B are incorrect.

Option C is a nonsense term and is therefore incorrect.

39. C. A DAM is a Layer 7 tool.

All the other options are incorrect.

40. A. DAMs can be used to reduce the possibility that SQL injection attacks will be successful.

DAMs do not protect against cross-site scripting, insecure direct-object reference, or social engineering attacks in any way, so options B, C, and D are incorrect.

41. C. The XML gateway can provide this functionality; it acts as a reverse proxy and can perform content inspection on many traffic protocols.

The WAF and DAM are also security tools that inspect traffic but do not usually handle SFTP content, so options A and B are incorrect.

Option D, single sign-on, concerns authentication functions, not communications traffic, and is only a distractor in this context.

42. B. An API gateway translates requests from clients into multiple requests to many microservices and delivers the content as a whole via an API it assigns to that client/session.

XML gateways, WAFs, and DAMs are also tools used frequently in cloud-based enterprises, but they do not handle microservice requests in a meaningful way.

43. B. While it would be wonderful, for security purposes, to know the identity of attackers before or while they're making an attack, this is information the attacker doesn't usually share.

All the other options are methods firewalls can use to recognize attacks.

44. C. TLS maintains the confidentiality and integrity of communications, often between a web browser and a server.

In this context, *privacy* and *security* mean much the same thing; *privacy* is synonymous with *confidentiality*, which is a subset of the overall topic of security. Therefore, option A is repetitive and not correct.

TLS does not optimize performance or add any sort of enhancement, so options B and D are incorrect.

45. A. TLS uses symmetric key crypto for each communications session in order to secure the connection; the session key is uniquely generated each time a new connection is made.

Options B and C are names for another type of encryption. Asymmetric encryption is also used in establishing a secure TLS connection; however, the keys used in this portion of the process will not change from session to session, and therefore these options are incorrect.

Option D is a nonsense term and is therefore incorrect.

46. B. A VPN is a temporary, synthetic encrypted tunnel between two endpoints (often a client and a server).

Option A is subtly misleading; the VPN secures the connection *between* two endpoints, not the ends of the connection. This option is incorrect.

Option C is not correct; VPN is not used for encrypting databases—it is used for encrypting communications.

Option D is incorrect; the symmetric key used in VPN is shared only between two parties (the endpoints), and the elements of the asymmetric key pair are either held by only one party (the owner of each private key) or by anyone at all (public key).

47. C. Users may not offer enough coverage for larger software products that have a great deal of functionality; it can be useful to also use automated agents to checks paths that users might not often attempt or utilize.

The developers should not be involved in any form of testing the software as they have an inherent conflict of interest, so options A and B are incorrect.

Dynamic testing does not involve social engineering; option D is incorrect.

48. C. This is the definition of "conflict of interest."

All the other answers are incorrect.

49. C. A sandbox can be used to run malware for analysis purposes as it won't affect (or infect) the production environment; it's worth noting, though, that some malware is sandbox-aware, so additional anti-malware measures are advisable.

Options A, B, and D are not correct because the sandbox should be completely disconnected (air-gapped) from the production environment so that users can't perform productive activity there.

50. C. Software that has either been purchased from a vendor or developed internally can be tested in a sandboxed environment that mimics the production environment in order to determine whether there will be any interoperability problems when it is installed into actual production.

All the other options aren't uses for sandboxes and are incorrect.

51. A. Virtualized applications can run on platforms that wouldn't otherwise allow them to function, such as running Microsoft apps on a Linux box.

Because the virtualization engine encapsulates the application from the native runtime environment, patches can't be applied through virtualized programs; option B is incorrect.

Virtualization really doesn't have anything to do with access control; option C is incorrect.

The overhead of running a software virtualization engine will actually add to system overhead, not decrease it, so option D is incorrect.

52. D. Application virtualization allows the software to run on a simulated environment on the device without the need to install it on the device.

Virtualization really doesn't have anything to do with access control; option A is incorrect.

Virtualization neither detects nor responds to DDoS; option B is incorrect.

Virtualization does not replace encryption; if data needs to be secure within the virtualization environment, encryption may still have to be utilized. Option C is incorrect.

53. B. ISO 27034 dictates that an organization will have a collection of security controls used for all software within that organization; this collection is called the ONF.

All the other options are distractors and incorrect.

54. B. Each application in an organization compliant with ISO 27034 will be assigned an Application Normative Framework (ANF), which lists all the controls assigned to that application.

Technically, the controls for each application within an organization compliant with ISO 27034 will be listed in the Organizational Normative Framework (ONF), because the ONF is the list of all controls for all applications; however, for a given application, only the controls used for that application are listed in an ANF, so option B is a preferable answer to A.

TTF (time to failure) has no meaning in this context, so option C is incorrect.

FTP (File Transfer Protocol) is a protocol for transferring files and not applicable here; option D is incorrect.

55. A. SAST is often referred to as white-box testing.

Black-box testing does not include access to source code, which is required for SAST. Option B is therefore incorrect.

Option C is a combination of black-box and white-box testing so option C is an incorrect answer for this question.

Option D has no meaning in this context.

56. D. In SAST, testers review the source code of an application in order to determine security flaws and operational errors.

While determining "software outcomes" may be considered a possible goal of SAST, "source code" is a much better answer as it is more specific and applicable to the question. Option D is still preferable.

SAST does not check user performance or system durability; options B and C are incorrect.

57. B. DAST is often referred to as black-box testing.

White-box testing requires the tester to have access to source code, which is not provided in DAST. Option A is therefore incorrect.

Option C is a combination of black-box and white-box testing so option C is an incorrect answer for this question.

Option D has no meaning in this context.

58. B. DAST is performed while the application is running.

Software testing should *not* take place in the production environment; option A is incorrect.

DAST, like other forms of testing, may or may not take place in the cloud and is not confined to any particular service model (although it is unlikely to occur in software as a service [SaaS] environments); options C and D are incorrect.

59. B. Vulnerability scans use signatures of known vulnerabilities to detect and report those vulnerabilities.

Vulnerability scans do not typically require administrative access to function; option A is incorrect.

Both malware libraries and forensic analysis of existing vulnerabilities may be used to create the signatures that vulnerability scanning tools utilize to detect and report vulnerabilities; however, these answers are too specific (limiting the answer), making option B a better answer than either C or D.

60. D. Because vulnerability scanning tools require vulnerability signatures to operate effectively, unknown vulnerabilities that might exist in the scanned system won't be detected (no signature has been created by vendors until a vulnerability is known). User errors are not detected by vulnerability scans; option A is incorrect. Scans can't tell you whether you've picked the optimum security controls for your environment; option B is incorrect. Vulnerability scanning tools may or may not detect cloud-based vulnerabilities, depending on the tool used, the level of access to the target environment, and the settings applied to the scanner; option C is less accurate than option D.

61. A. A penetration test requires the tester to analyze the security of an environment from the perspective of an attacker; this also includes actually taking action that would result in breaching that environment.

Penetration tests may or may not be comprehensive, depending on the intended scope and area of analysis. Option B is incorrect.

While it's nice to think of any security assessment as *total*, that is an extreme term, like *all* or *never*; such terms can rarely be used in security because there are no absolutes when dealing with risk, and it has no meaning in this context. Option C is not correct.

Although the cost of a penetration test will vary according to a vast range of variables, it will rarely be considered inexpensive, especially relative to other forms of security testing. Option D is not correct.

62. D. Also called fuzz testing, dynamic testing methods should include known bad inputs in order to determine how the program will handle the "wrong" data (will it fail into a state that is less secure than normal operations, etc.).

Source code review is not part of dynamic testing; option A is incorrect.

For accurate quality testing, user familiarity with the target software should be minimal and should not be assessed; option B is not correct.

Penetration includes active steps to overcome security measures; this is rarely the purpose of software testing; option C is not the best answer.

63. B. User surveys are not an element of active security testing, although they might be used in acceptance testing. All of the other options are included in the OWASP guide to active security testing.

64. D. Privacy review testing is not included in the OWASP guide to active security testing, although it might be included as an aspect of compliance testing (for organizations in highly regulated industries). All of the other options are included in the OWASP guide to active security testing.

65. A. While session management testing is included in the OWASP guide to active software security testing, session initiation is not. All of the other options are included in the OWASP guide to active security testing.

66. C. Intuition testing is not part of the OWASP guide to active security testing. All of the other options are included in the OWASP guide to active security testing.

67. C. This metric is usually expressed as a percentage of lines of code. For example, "SAST covered 90% of the source code."

The number of testers involved means very little when discussing testing coverage; this is a distractor and not correct.

In some cases, testing reports might include a statistic representing the number of flaws discovered in the code; however, this is usually not a pertinent metric (undetected flaws can't be measured, so counting the ones that have doesn't add to your surety the code is secure), and code coverage is used more often. Option C is preferable to option B.

Testing should first occur in an environment where the software has not even been exposed to the possibility of malware infection. Option D is incorrect.

68. C. In dynamic software security testing, the objective is to test a significant sample of the possible logical paths from data input to output.

User coverage is a distractor and has no real meaning in this context; option A is incorrect.

Code coverage is the metric used in static testing, making option B incorrect.

While it would be nice to test each and every data pathway through an application, with both known good and known bad data, that could be unrealistic, depending on the number of possible branches in the application; this goes up exponentially every time another option/choice is added to the program. Total coverage is not a metric—it's a hope. Option D is incorrect.

69. D. Known good data is used to determine if the software fulfills the business requirements for which it was acquired. Known bad data tests the ability of the software to handle inputs and conditions that might put it into a fail state; these inputs and conditions can be invoked either purposefully (by attackers) or inadvertently (by users who make mistakes).

Testing does not attempt to mimic managers, regulators, or vendors, so the other answers are incorrect.

70. B. This is not a simple question, and more than one answer could be construed as correct, but option B is the best answer. Tracking and monitoring personnel training is absolutely vital in order to demonstrate regulatory requirements (and many, if not all, organizations are obligated to comply with some regulation that mandates user training) and legal requirements (as an element of due diligence in the modern workplace).

Option A is the other answer that could be perceived as accurate, but there is a bit of nuance that makes it less preferable than B. Security is a business requirement—it may not be a *functional* requirement, but it is a requirement nonetheless. Therefore, these two terms are repetitive; security requirements are just a subset of business requirements. Option B is still the better answer.

Options C and D do not make sense in this context.

71. B. Training is usually a formal process involving detailed information. This is for those personnel who are involved with the specific topic or task for which the training is intended (for example, personnel involved in business continuity and disaster recovery [BC/DR] activities should get specific, detailed training on how to perform those actions).

Option A incorrect because not all personnel require task-centric training. Training required for all personnel in an organization cannot be task-centric training, by definition (not all personnel perform the same tasks).

Options C and D are incorrect because they would only answer a subset of the question. Management personnel would receive management training and HR personnel would receive HR training. The correct answer is task-centric training is for specific personnel.

72. A. Awareness efforts are usually intended to reach as wide an audience as possible within the organization, for generalized information. For instance, fire drills are awareness exercises; everyone in the facility needs to know how to get out and where to go.

    Specific personnel, management personnel, and HR personnel would all receive task-centric training in addition to the awareness instruction that all personnel receive. Options B, C, and D are incorrect.

73. D. Modern developers usually aren't writing code—they are recombining library components in novel ways to create new functionality. They may not understand the security risks associated with their work, especially for the cloud environment, which entails a different set of challenges from the traditional environment, which the developers might be more familiar with.

    Options A and B are actually the same concept, reworded, which is patently untrue: depending on the cloud deployment and service models the organization chooses to use, software developers may or may not be crucial (for instance, in a software as a service [SaaS] public cloud, many organizations won't even need internal development teams).

    Option C is just wrong: security controls *can* be added to software after it has been fielded. This is just not a best practice, as it is usually less effective and more expensive (in terms of both money and overhead).

74. B. Because cloud operations are so dependent on encryption protections in all data life-cycle phases, developers will have to accommodate the additional overhead and interoperability encryption requires.

    The hacking threat (foreign or otherwise) does not change whether the target is the cloud or the (connected) traditional environment; option A is incorrect.

    Likewise, the threat of DDoS attacks does not increase; if anything, it may decrease, because the cloud provider may be more resistant to such attacks than individual organizations would be. Option C is not correct.

    Regulatory requirements may or may not change when moving into the cloud. Moreover, developers are not likely to be the ones interpreting and responding to these new mandates; that is a level of abstraction above developer insight into software requirements. Option D is not preferable to B.

75. D. Because shared resources in the cloud may mean increased opportunity for side-channel attacks, developers will have to design programs to function in a way that ensures process isolation.

    Management oversight should not change from a policy perspective, regardless of where the processing is taking place; option A is incorrect.

    There is no additional workload resulting from cloud migration; in fact, the load should decrease, because the cloud customer cannot impose governance on the cloud provider. Option B is wrong.

    Malware threat does not increase or decrease in the cloud environment; option C is incorrect.

76. B. Masking allows customer service representatives to review clients' sales and account information without revealing the entirety of those records (for instance, obscuring credit card numbers except for the last four digits).

Anonymization strips out identifying information from a record. This would not aid in limiting customer service personnel from viewing sensitive data, but it would make it impossible for customer service personnel to know who they were communicating with and leave them unable to identify customers, which would defeat the purpose of their existence. Option A is incorrect.

Encryption of sales/account records would not limit customer service personnel in their review of account records. It would either disallow them to see the records at all or allow them to see the entirety of the records (depending on whether the representatives were given keys to that encrypted data). Option C is incorrect.

Training does not limit access; option D is incorrect.

77. A. While some development models allow for user involvement in the entirety of the process, user input is most necessary in the Define phase, where developers can understand the business/user requirements—what the system/software is actually supposed to produce, in terms of function and performance. All the other options are beneficial phases to gauge user input, but not as crucial as option A.

78. A. The earlier security inputs are included in the project, the more efficient and less costly security controls are overall. The Define phase is the earliest part of the SDLC. All the other options are later phases and incorrect.

79. D. During testing, getting outside perspective is invaluable, for both performance and security purposes; internal development and review capabilities are enhanced by augmentation from external parties.

All the other phases are not normally appropriate for external participation.

80. A. Once the system is deployed operationally, continuous security monitoring, including periodic vulnerability assessments and penetration testing, is recommended. All the other options are security functions that should take place in phases prior to the system's deployment.

81. C. Security and operations are always inversely related; excessive controls necessarily degrade performance.

Excessive use of controls should not lead to more data breaches; if anything, it may reduce their occurrence. However, it is more likely that there will be no effect. Option A is incorrect.

Many controls don't affect the electromagnetic spectrum in any way. Option B is incorrect.

Regulations don't usually mandate a maximum set of controls but rather a minimum. Option D is incorrect.

82. D. From a simple financial perspective (which is often the managerial perspective), money spent on excessive *anything* is money wasted; spending to no good effect is detrimental.

Overuse of controls should not result in greater risks of DDoS, malware, or environmental threats in any way. Options A, B, and C are incorrect.

83. A. If excessive controls impact the user/customer experience to the extent that system response speeds and results are delayed significantly, and performance is degraded to the point where competitors' systems are far superior, customer dissatisfaction can be a severe problem.

Some security controls (particularly physical controls) can affect health and human safety, such as if extraneous fencing/walls/barriers are put in place to control access/egress, and this hinders emergency escape from facilities. However, not all security controls pose this risk, so option B is a bit too specific; option A is still preferable.

Security controls should not affect stock price or, in and of themselves, negate insurance needs (risk mitigation does not automatically offset the benefits of risk transference). Options C and D are incorrect.

84. D. The problem in this case is not so much that policies have been violated or that, in a more literal sense, the unapproved APIs are being used to access the data, the problem is that the violations are so pervasive and extensive that taking any immediate direct action (such as the responses in options A, B, and C) might interfere with business activity in a drastic and potentially harmful way. Because of this, the matter needs to be dealt with as a business decision and requires that senior management make a determination before action is taken.

85. A. Again, before taking any action that might impact operations, it would probably be best to figure out the actual user needs being met by the unapproved APIs, and the severity of impact if they were removed from service, before performing the actions described in options B, C, and D.

86. D. It's hard to argue with success; operational capability and security are always a trade-off, but this kind of productivity increase with little attendant cost is probably too good to pass up. It also seems evident that the existing policy is far too restrictive and limiting and that it is not being accepted by a significant number of users; trying to mandate its acceptance, and enforcing it with punitive measures, especially in the face of the overwhelming success of the violations, is most likely counter to the company's overall interests. It is best to revisit the policy itself, determine why it didn't meet user needs originally, and modify it so as to meet the demands of *both* the users *and* senior management (as well as whatever other externalities may have been the foundation of the policy). Options A, B, and C may be attractive, but they are all less preferable than D.

87. D. APIs chosen by users may or may not have integral security and probably weren't chosen according to how secure they are; because the company will continue to be exposed to additional risks from these (and future) APIs, additional security controls are absolutely necessary.

However, personnel actions and draconian enforcement efforts at this point would be pointless and vindictive, and probably counter to the company's interests. Options A, B, and C are incorrect.

88. B. Because untrusted APIs may not be secured sufficiently, increased vigilance for the possibility of introducing malware into the production environment is essential.

It is impossible to encrypt devices that don't belong to the organization. Option A is incorrect.

Securing access to user-owned devices is admirable, but it has no effect at all on securing the device (or production environment) from risks due to installed APIs; option C is incorrect.

This is a security question, and option D addresses performance; this is incorrect.

89. A. In order to detect possible erroneous or malicious modification of the organization's data by unauthorized or security-deficient APIs, it's important to take representative samples of the production data on a continual basis and perform integrity checks.

Additional personnel security measures will not, in this case, yield any relevant security benefit; options B and D are not correct.

It is always good to refer to regulations in policies; this isn't something to be performed in response to the policy change but should have been included when the policy was created. Option C is incorrect.

90. C. Additional user training would be helpful in this situation, particularly any information that helps users understand the reasons APIs from unknown sources might be less secure and the potential impacts from using them.

All the other answers are incorrect; securing the connection between endpoints and the cloud is irrelevant in protecting against risks caused by software installed on the client devices.

91. B. Cryptography for the two main types of APIs is required; this is TLS for representational state transfer (REST) and message-level encryption for Simple Object Access Protocol (SOAP).

SSL has been deprecated because of severe vulnerabilities; this eliminates options A and C. Whole drive encryption protects against loss or theft of a device but does not secure API access to the data, which eliminates option D.

92. D. Accountability is the end purpose of all IAM efforts; all the other options are the elements of IAM that support this effort.

93. A. Regulatory compliance has historically driven IAM efforts. All the other options can to some extent drive IAM efforts, however, they do not have as much influence as regulatory factors. Therefore options B, C, and D are incorrect answers.

94. C. Both physical and logical controls are possible (and necessary) to implement in both environments.

Options A and B are really only feasible if the organization is using a cloud service (or other managed service); the terms *managed* and *provider* suggest this. This makes these options less desirable for a question that also includes the traditional environment.

It is not reasonable to expect that the organization can impose administrative controls in a cloud environment (for the provider environment), so option D is not correct.

95. B. The data owner is most familiar with the risks and impacts associated with the data sets under their control.

The data subject may grant permission for a data owner to have the subject's data but will not govern the granular assignment of access rights. Option A is incorrect.

The data processor does not have the right to grant data access and must only act at the direction of the data owner. Option C is incorrect.

Regulators dictate how data must be secured, and possibly in what manner, but do not supervise explicit access to that data. Option D is incorrect.

96. C. Performance should not determine who gets access to which data; all the other options are the factors for making this determination.

97. D. Federation allows users from multiple member organizations to access resources owned by various members.

All the other answers are simply not correct.

98. C. Federation allows ease of use for access to multiple resource providers; this provides a transparent user mechanism.

The goal of federation is to enhance the user experience, the exact opposite of making the environment more hostile to them. Option A is incorrect.

Option B is incorrect because it is meaningless in this context.

Option D is incorrect. Users typically do not pay for the organization's IT environment.

99. C. WAFs apply rulesets to web traffic, which uses HTTP. All the other answers are incorrect.

100. C. These are both Layer 7 tools. All the other answers are incorrect.

101. B. Aside from encryption, PCI DSS allows for tokenization as a means to protect account and cardholder data at rest.

Tokenization is not encryption; there is no encryption engine and no key involved in the process. Option A is incorrect.

Tokenization does not necessarily enhance or detract from the user experience; option C is incorrect.

Management is not allowed any additional oversight into any particular function by tokenization; option D is incorrect.

102. A. By offloading privacy data to a tokenizing third party, merchants can free themselves of the contractual burdens for protecting cardholder data at rest.

The data owner is the merchants themselves, and the data subject is the person to whom the privacy data applies, so privacy data cannot be outsourced to either of these, and options B and C are incorrect.

The PCI Council is the body that promulgates and enforces the PCI DSS; they will not process data on behalf of any merchant. Option D is incorrect.

103. C. This answer requires some thought about how the original data is displayed and its properties.

Option A masks only one letter in a four-letter string; this is not sufficient because the original string could be identified with a very low-work factor, brute-force attack of only 26 possible combinations.

Option B is likewise easy to break; it only reverses the content of the string, which is very simple to determine, and would allow easy recovery of any other similar strings in the data set.

Option D mixes numeric characters into what was originally only an alphabetic string; this may detract from the utility of the string if the masked version is to be used for software testing.

Option C completely obscures the original content but retains the qualities of the original (all alphabetic characters). It may affect the use of the string by mixing uppercase and lowercase, but this is still the best choice of the four possible answers.

104. D. Installing malware on systems owned by someone else may be illegal in many jurisdictions. While on-premises sandboxes are fine for this purpose, it may be a felony if performed in the cloud.

All the other options are good uses of cloud-based sandboxes.

105. C. It is important to verify and validate the program at each stage of the SDLC.

Adding functionality at each stage of the SDLC is the definition of scope creep, which is what we'd like to avoid. Option A is incorrect.

Management should not have to shepherd software through the development process; this is the process of the development team. Option B is incorrect.

Option D is a distractor and makes no actual sense.

106. A. It is important to verify and validate the program at each stage of the SDLC.

Adding functionality at each stage of the SDLC is the definition of scope creep, which is what we'd like to avoid. Option A is incorrect.

Management should not have to shepherd software through the development process; this is the process of the development team. Option B is incorrect.

Option D makes no sense: you can't repurpose something that has just been developed.

107. A. When security is created as an aspect of the software itself, there is less need to acquire and apply additional security controls to mitigate risks after deployment. Option B is also wrong for this same reason.

Options C and D are incorrect because the inclusion of security aspects in software design should not affect interoperability in any significant way.

108. C. ISO 27034 addresses the sets of controls used in software throughout the environment.

800-37 is the Risk Management Framework, which is about the organization's overall security, not software development, so option A is incorrect.

The AICPA is a standards-making body, not a standard itself, so option B is incorrect.

HIPAA deals with health care privacy, so option D is incorrect.

109. D. It is important to consider software development as having a defined process and an eventual endpoint for the useful life of the product.

Not every organization is a software development company. Even in software development companies, not everyone participates in development (there are other departments/offices, such as sales, accounting, etc.). Option A is a poor choice.

Option B is only a correct answer if the organization is a software development company. Otherwise, it is not a correct answer. Option B is incorrect.

If software development poses the most significant risk to your organization, you probably shouldn't be doing software development. Option C is incorrect.

110. A. Running the software and allowing users to operate it is a great form of dynamic testing, which simulates both known good and known bad inputs.

Dynamic testing does not involve source code review or social engineering; options B and C are incorrect.

Penetration tests occur in the production environment, not on pre-deployment software; option D is incorrect.

Chapter 5: Domain 5: Cloud Security Operations

1. D. This is not an easy question; different industries and different organizations will have differing goals. Each organization will determine for itself what the primary goal of incident response will be, and this may even differ from incident to incident, depending on the nature of the incident itself (in other words, a given organization may set priorities such that the primary goal of incident response in a disaster is continuity of operations, while the goal in responding to unauthorized access may be halting data disclosure).

2. D. The minimum recommended height of a raised floor in a data center is 24 inches. All other options are incorrect.

3. B. The raised floor in a data center will serve as an air plenum (usually for cold air) and a wiring chase. All the other options are incorrect.

4. D. The preferred method is cold aisle containment (hot aisle containment, where the inlets on racks face each other, is all right too). Options A and B are the same incorrect answer, just worded differently; if the exhaust fans on one rack face into the inlet vents on another rack, you would end up blowing warm air into the components, defeating the purpose of airflow management. Perpendicular racks will not optimize your airflow.

5. C. All activity in the environment can be considered events. Any event that was not planned or known is an incident. In the security industry, we often ascribe negative effects to the term *incident*, but incidents are not always malicious; they are only unscheduled.

All the other options are incorrect.

6. A. This is a difficult, nuanced question. Options A–C are true; each element would affect the design of a cloud data center (D is not something that should be included in data center design). But the physical location of the data center would include legal constraints (based on jurisdiction), geological/natural constraints (based on altitude, proximity to water formations/flooding, climate, natural disaster, etc.), price, and other variables. Therefore, location would most likely have the greatest impact on the design of the facility.

7. D. Language of the customers is irrelevant, assuming they can pay. All the other options are factors that must be considered in data center design.

8. B. This is not an easy question. All the options are correct except C. Option B is the most correct because it will lead to maximizing performance, value, and profitability.

9. D. The goal of automating service enablement is probably paramount for any cloud service provider (of the qualities listed), because it allows for the most scalability and offers the most significant reduction in costs (which mainly come from personnel) and therefore the most profitability. The details of "public cloud," "IaaS," and "North America" are distractors in this context as they are irrelevant—this answer would be true for any cloud provider offering any type of services.

Options A and B are not true because most cloud providers of any appreciable size are purchasing hardware on a scale that makes the per-unit failure rate fairly irrelevant; the bulk nature of IT purchases by cloud providers makes differences in MTTR and MTBF between vendors and products statistically insignificant.

Option C is incorrect because RTO is a quality involving business continuity and disaster recovery (BC/DR) planning, not IT architecture.

10. C. Network segmentation allows providers to create zones of trust within the cloud environment, tailoring the available services to meet the needs of a variety of clients and markets.

SDN does not really involve monitoring outbound traffic (that is done by egress monitoring solutions) or inbound traffic (that is usually performed by firewalls and routers), nor does it really prevent DDoS attacks (nothing can prevent such attacks, and risk reduction is usually done by routers), so all the other options are incorrect.

11. B. The ability to log activity is useful for many security purposes (such as monitoring and forensics); having that purposefully included in SaaS applications reduces the need to have a different tool added to the environment to achieve that same goal and reduces the possibility that any additional interface won't perform optimally.

The other options are all about enhancing the customer's ability to perform business function or meeting the customer's business needs. Although this is paramount from the customer's perspective and may tangentially fulfill some security purpose (increased processing capacity may, for instance, allow the use of additional encryption, where the overhead may otherwise deter the use of that tool), these are not direct security purposes and therefore are not correct answers to this specific question.

12. D. California is known for suffering massive destruction from earthquakes, and physical design is the means with which this risk is addressed.

All the other options either involve a nonphysical risk (DRM will be necessary, because the entertainment industry relies heavily on copyrighted material) or a method other than physical design to address a risk (floods are physical threats, but insurance is an administrative control for risk transfer), so D is the best choice of these options.

13. A. For the purposes described in the question, a Tier 1 data center should suffice; it is the cheapest, and you need it only for occasional backup purposes (as opposed to constant access). The details of location and market are irrelevant.

Tiers 3 and 4 would be much more expensive, and they are not necessary for your business purposes; options B and C are thus incorrect.

There is no Tier 8 in the Uptime Institute system.

14. C. If your company is involved in e-commerce, you are most likely using credit cards for online transactions; if you're using credit cards, you are almost certainly constrained by the Payment Card Industry Data Security Standard (PCI DSS) or one of the other contractual standards like it. Because of this, you will be required to encrypt or tokenize all stored cardholder data, and for long-term storage, encryption is the cheaper, more durable process.

DDoS and mirroring are availability protections, and availability is not your company's main concern for cloud services from the question description; long-term storage is not focused on availability. Options A and B are thus incorrect.

Hashing is an integrity protection, and though hashes may be useful in this case (to determine whether stored data is accurate), they won't be as important as compliance with credit card standards. Option C is the preferable answer compared to D.

15. C. ISO is the only truly international standard on this list of choices; all the rest are either American laws or standards (options A and D) or European (option B).

16. B. The changing nature of your business will require a much more stringent set of operating standards, to include an increase in Uptime Institute tier levels; because you're no longer just using the cloud for backup and long-term storage and are now using it in direct support of health and human safety, Tier 4 is required.

Fully automated security controls are useful from the provider's perspective (allowing more profitability and scalability), but this is not a major concern of the customer. Option A is incorrect.

Global remote access and reducing the risk of malware infections (to include ransomware) are basic functions of almost all cloud providers; these functions aren't useful discriminators when choosing cloud providers because all cloud providers have them. Options C and D are thus incorrect.

17. C. Backup power does not have to be delivered by batteries; it can be fed to the data center through redundant utility lines or from a generator.

All the other elements are necessary for safe and secure data center operations, for both the personnel and the equipment within the data center.

18. A. This answer is mostly arrived at through a process of elimination.

Option B is not optimum because of the potential for vendor lock-in, restrictions on build-out, and privacy concerns.

Option C is not optimum because Tier 2 is not sufficient for medical uses.

Option D is not optimum because there was obviously a reason to consider a new option.

We are therefore left with option A, which is the most expensive of the choices but allows the greatest amount of control and security.

19. D. In any large metropolitan area, government restrictions on development and construction can severely limit how you use your property; this can be a significant limiting factor in building a data center.

The size of the plot may or may not matter, depending on if you are allowed to build up or dig down to make use of additional space—these options will be limited by municipal building codes, so option D is preferable to option A.

Utilities and personnel are usually easy to acquire in an urban setting, so options B and C are incorrect.

20. C. In a rural location, the positioning and depth of first responders (fire, law enforcement, paramedics, etc.) may be severely limited in comparison to an urban setting.

    Natural disasters affect all locations, rural or urban, so a rural setting is not any more or less limiting in planning accordingly; option A is incorrect.

    Oddly enough, because of the very limited need for personnel within modern data centers with significant automation, recruiting and placing the number of people necessary to serve the purpose should not be too difficult; option B is not correct.

    One of the appeals of a rural setting is that building codes are often rudimentary or non-existent. Option D is incorrect.

21. C. All the other options are incorrect.

22. A. The range suggested by the ASHRAE Technical Committee 9.9 is 64 to 81 degrees Fahrenheit. All the other options are distractors (although D is particularly distracting, because it is *lower* than the recommended range, but that is not what the question is asking).

23. D. Being damp does not make people more susceptible to trickery.

    Moisture in the air can, however, create mold/mildew, short circuits, and rust, so all the other options are incorrect.

24. B. The return air temperature will be slightly higher than anywhere else inside the data center because the air has been warmed by passing through the equipment (thus cooling the equipment but warming the air). Using this as a temperature set point will result in much cooler air feeding the server inlets, which takes more energy, which will be more expensive.

    Options A and C are incorrect because that air is already cold; using these locations as set points will not consume as much energy and may result in somewhat warmer air entering the servers. This will be less expensive than option B.

    Option D is an outlying distractor; if you set your heating, ventilation, and air conditioning (HVAC) controls to respond to the temperature outside the data center, your HVAC units are responding to temperatures that have nothing to do with the internal environment. In effect, you'd be trying to adjust the temperature of the outside world, which is ridiculous.

25. D. The HVAC system is a heat exchange, swapping warm internal air from the data center to the outside world and drawing fresh air through the HVAC chillers to feed the internal environment.

    All the other options are incorrect because they will have the opposite effect by pushing warm air into those areas that cools air is supposed to be.

26. D. When cables come up through a raised floor used as a cold air feed, we don't want cold air bleeding around the cables in an unplanned manner; this can cause inefficiencies in airflow control. Gaskets are required at all points where cable comes through the floor, to restrict airflow and reduce the possibility of cold air escaping.

    All the other options are incorrect because we want to minimize obstructions in under-floor plenums we use for airflow. Options A, B, and C do not accomplish this.

27. D. While minimizing equipment in the operational environment can aid in many efforts, including cable management, it is not strictly an aspect of cable management, so this is the best choice from those available. All the other options are definitely aspects of cable management.

28. B. Cable management is an ongoing process. All the other options are incorrect because they are time based intervals rather than continuous.

29. C. It shouldn't matter which design you use as long as airflow is managed. Neither hot nor cold aisle containment is preferable to the other, so options A and B are incorrect. Airflow does need to be managed, though, so option D is incorrect as well.

30. B. This is a difficult question because almost all of the options are true—they will all have an effect on the cost of running HVAC systems.

    Because HVAC operates as a heat exchange, the outside environment will dictate how much power is needed to force warm air out of the data center. The warmer the climate in the location of the data center, the more energy it will take to exchange the heat, and the more costly the HVAC operation. This is the most significant factor.

    Option A is incorrect and it is the only choice that does not affect energy costs; hot and cold aisle containment should be equivalent in terms of operational costs.

    The initial cost of the HVAC units themselves will probably have an effect on operational costs because better equipment will cost more money, but it will also be more efficient and therefore less expensive to operate than cheaper alternatives. However, the effect still won't be as significant as the external climate, so option C is still not as good as option B.

    Good cable management will make airflow more efficient and therefore make HVAC less expensive, but this will not be as dramatic in impact on operating costs as the external environment. Once again, option B is preferable to option D.

31. D. Usually, different political regions are served by different utility providers; placing your data center on such a boundary may make it feasible to have redundant, overlapping power providers.

    Municipalities typically limit selection of power providers by granting an artificial monopoly to a single provider; option A is incorrect.

    Rural settings are often only served by a single provider because the demand is not sufficient to support competition; option B is incorrect.

    Coasts do not affect the availability of multiple power providers; option C is a distractor.

32. B. While maintaining a library of software licenses is important, it is not part of the practice we ordinarily consider "hardening."

    The other options are all aspects of software hardening.

33. C. Audits usually aren't considered an element of hardening. Hardening is the process of provisioning a specific element (in this case, a host) against attack. Audits don't protect against attack; they only detect and direct response to attacks.

All the other options are aspects of host hardening.

34. B. Users are not an aspect of configuration management.

All the other options are elements of secure configuration management.

35. A. HTTPS is not a storage protocol. All the other options are.

36. B. Virtual switches are widely used in virtualized networks. Unlike physical switches, which only lose one connection if a connecting cable is lost, virtual switches can be connected to multiple virtual machines via a single cable; if a cable is lost in a virtualized network, that can affect tens or dozens of devices. In this context, the benefits offered by scalability come with attendant risks.

The other options are characteristics that don't cause additional risk to the environment; in fact, redundancy reduces risk.

37. A. It is possible to route multiple VLANs through a switch port (physical or virtual) with proper frame tagging. However, to optimize isolation of subnets and processes in a virtual network environment, it is better to use different ports instead.

iSCSI traffic should be encrypted as another layer of defense within the environment; option B is wrong.

HIDSs may or may not be cost-effective, depending on the value and sensitivity of the data on each guest; the additional overhead may not justify their use. Option C is incorrect.

Firewalls should be hardened regardless of the nature of the network whether virtual or physical.

38. B. The management systems control the entirety of the virtual environment and are therefore extremely valuable and need to be protected accordingly. When possible, isolating those management systems, both physically and virtually, is optimum.

All the other options are incorrect because they imply that virtual and physical cannot coexist when in fact they need to coexist to work correctly.

39. A. When an active virtual machine is moved from a given host to another (for instance, when the host is going into maintenance state), it is passed along the network without encryption. Theoretically, an insider threat observing the line along which the virtual machine is moving could capture/copy it in its entirety.

All the other options are not risks specific to a virtualized environment and are therefore incorrect.

40. D. In a pooled environment, law enforcement may acquire physical or logical assets (drives, data stores, etc.) that include your organization's data, even if your organization was not the target of the investigation.

All the other options are not risks due to pooled resources; they exist in all environments. These options are not correct.

41. C. The cost of each device is spread across many machines in the data center; unlike a desktop-based environment, where every user and every machine need their own KVM setup, just a few devices can serve an entire data center.

While the cloud provider may generate a great deal of revenue, no company likes to throw away money unnecessarily; option A is incorrect.

Cloud providers are not typically invested in KVM vendors. Option B is incorrect.

Option D is simply incorrect.

42. D. The range suggested by the ASHRAE Technical Committee 9.9 is 64 to 81 degrees Fahrenheit. All the other options are incorrect (although A is particularly distracting, because it is *higher* than the recommended range, but that is not what the question is asking).

43. A. Secure KVMs support drastically isolated operations; they cut down on the possibility of data being inadvertently shared from one customer to another.

Option B is incorrect because devices will not leave the cloud data center simply because they are not managed by secure KVMs.

Option C is incorrect because using secure KVMs will not have an effect on physical inventories.

Option D does contain enough information to be the correct answer. "Audit purposes" is ambiguous.

44. A. Referred to as "break before make," these devices often take the form of manual pushbutton controls; as the button is pushed, the current connection is forced to physically separate, and when the button is fully engaged, the new connection is made.

Options B and C have more to do with risks of electromagnetic emanations than with air-gapped selectivity; even air-gapped devices can leak data through emanations.

Option D is incorrect because portability is not a property we seek in device selectors.

45. D. The production activities will make full use of pooled resources, so they will not be isolated (unless the customer is paying for that specific characteristic of service).

All the other options are functions that should take place on isolated networks/segments.

46. B. Broadcast packets sent by machines outside the VLAN will reach machines outside the VLAN that are on the same network/segment.

All the other options are characteristics of a VLAN.

47. A. Gateway devices enforce the VLAN rules and can allow or deny outbound traffic.

Communications traffic from a VLAN may or may not be encrypted; option B is incorrect.

Repeaters are used to enhance signals along a line over a certain distance; they have nothing to do with VLANs. Option C is incorrect.

Option D makes no sense in this context.

48. B. TLS uses X.509 certificates to establish a connection and create a symmetric key that lasts for only one session.

SAML is used for federation authentication/identification; option A is incorrect.

802.11 is the suite of wireless standards; option C is incorrect.

Diffie-Hellman uses asymmetric key pairs to create a symmetric key; option D is incorrect.

49. B. This question is an outlier because it is one of the few such questions where the answer is *not* that it poses a threat to health and human safety (although, in fact, it does; option A is true, but incorrect). Halon was not prohibited because of this property. Halon was outlawed because it, like other CFCs (chlorofluorocarbons), was blamed for depleting the earth's ozone layer. Halon is still allowed in some very specialized cases (such as fire-suppression systems on aircraft), but this is an exception.

Options C and D are incorrect and untrue.

50. B. User interaction with the cloud is not described in this term. All the other options are characteristics of cloud computing mentioned in *ping, power, pipe*.

51. C. The penetration test is not part of the site survey, which is one of the initial steps in securing/auditing a facility. The penetration test will, however, probably make use of the site survey information later.

All the other options are goals of the site survey.

52. B. There is no such thing as zero risk; there will always be *some* chance of service interruption, no matter how minimized.

All the other options are capabilities allowed by redundancy.

53. D. Before flooding an enclosed space with a gas that will displace oxygen, it is important to ensure that all personnel are out of the area. While this requires personnel training, such training is ineffective without a system to support this capability. Option C is true, but not as accurate as option D.

Options A and B are incorrect because they do not make senses given the question is about a system that displaces oxygen in the facility.

54. A. The logical design should come before the physical design; function dictates form. Audit and revision come after creation.

55. C. While physical controls that inhibit movement affect personnel, they are not regarded as personnel controls. All the other options are examples of personnel controls.

56. C. Because updating the virtualization toolset may require server downtime, it is essential to have a sufficient amount of redundant machines to roll out the update over the environment without significant disruption of operations.

Option A assumes that there isn't already enough of whatever the infusion of capital will purchase. Option A is incorrect.

Thankfully, option B is incorrect. It would be costly to obtain an alternate data center each time the virtual machine management tools are updated.

Peer review is not required when updating virtual machine management tools. Option D is incorrect.

57. B. It is important to limit access to the virtualization toolset to those administrators, engineers, and architects who are vital for supporting the virtualized environment and nobody else.

The other options are incorrect because they do not restrict access to the virtualization management tool set as specifically as role-based access control does. If someone's role changes and they no longer require access, then their access should be terminated.

58. C. Toolset vendors will specify secure configurations of their products; these must be followed in order to fulfill due care requirements.

Standards and laws don't usually specify builds for products or brands, so options A and B are incorrect.

Expert opinion, while useful, is not sufficient to demonstrate due care in many cases; option D is not the best response.

59. B. In order to understand, optimize, and re-create your secure baseline, proper and full documentation is absolutely essential.

Personnel training is important for secure system use, but it is not an element of baselining. Option A is incorrect.

A secure baseline for a given system may include HIDS and/or encryption, but they are not essential elements, so options C and D are incorrect.

60. A. An image of the baseline should be stored securely, preferably in more than one location (to include the archive, the disaster kit, and any alternate site, to name a few). It is essential to have a copy on hand for reconstructing the environment during contingency operations, and it is also useful for audit/review purposes.

Option B is incorrect because planned modifications are not yet part of the actual baseline.

Option C may be a good answer in some situations; however, it is not essential, and option A is still a better answer.

Option D is incorrect because every environment (and, therefore, the baseline used in that environment) should be exclusively tailored for the organization using that environment.

61. D. In order to ensure timely application of patches, patching may receive blanket approval and only be reviewed by the committee or board after the fact for final approval.

Requiring normalized processing for patching may delay patching and expose the organization to undue risk; option A is thus incorrect.

Patching still needs to involve testing and confirmation to avoid interoperability and additional security problems, making option B incorrect.

Third parties can identify security problems as well as vendors; external patches need to be considered as well as vendor patches. Option C is thus incorrect.

62. D. Clustering does not preclude the time and diligence necessary to perform patching or updates.

All the other options are attributes provided by host clustering.

63. C. Tokenization is a method for obscuring or protecting data using two distinct databases, not a resource allocation method.

All the other options are methods for allocating shared resources.

64. D. In a loosely coupled storage cluster, each node acts as an independent data store that can be added or removed from the cluster without affecting other nodes. This, however, means that the overall cluster's performance/capacity depends on each node's own maximum performance/capacity.

The physical backplane can be a limiting factor in a tightly coupled architecture but has less effect in a loosely coupled cluster; option A is incorrect.

Because each node in a loosely coupled cluster has its own limitations, the number of nodes will not affect overall performance. Option B is incorrect.

Option C is incorrect because "usage demanded" is not a factor in performance and capacity of a loosely coupled storage cluster.

65. B. Auditing is probably even more important during maintenance mode than normal operation because administrator activity is almost always involved.

All the other options are necessary measures for maintenance mode.

66. D. Almost invariably, stand-alone hosting will cost more than pooled resources and multitenancy.

All the other options are characteristics of stand-alone hosting.

67. D. In many cases, the customer will no longer *have* an on-premises environment after a cloud migration.

All the other options are methods cloud providers use to achieve "high availability" environments.

68. B. Behavioral detection looks for activity beyond the norm of the organization's usual traffic. Unique attacks would most likely fall into this category.

Unique attacks would not be detected by signature matching because no signatures exist for unique attacks; option A is incorrect.

Content filtering is less a means of detection and more a means of controlling traffic that users/systems are exposed to; while it may be useful for mitigating the possibility of malware infection, it's less suited to the purpose posed in the question. Option C is incorrect.

Firewalls don't work with biometrics; option D is a distractor.

69. C. Internet service providers don't usually offer firewall services.

All the other options are locations/ways to implement firewalls.

70. B. It is very important to distinguish the purpose of the honeypot. It is *not* for luring in attackers; a lure is an invitation, and inviting an attack decreases the organization's ability to have the attacker prosecuted or conduct successful litigation against the attacker.

All the other options are purposes of a honeypot.

71. D. The honeypot is used to gather information about the attacker, the attacker's tools, and the attacker's techniques.

The honeypot should not contain anything of value; all the other options are incorrect.

72. C. It's preferable to have compartmentalized zones of trust within the production environment and not allow total access with one set of credentials.

All the other options are aspects that should be used in cloud access.

73. B. Historically, when encryption had been used as a security mechanism, it was not defeated by attacking the encryption directly but rather by subverting the encryption implementation.

All the other options are actual methods for breaking encryption but are not the best answer for this question.

74. D. Cloud vendors do not typically assign individual administrators permanently to specific accounts. All the other options (A–C) *are* methods used to reduce risks associated with privileged accounts.

75. C. All the options are useful for enhancing the security and efficacy of the BC/DR effort, but only option C ensures that the BC/DR has a likely chance of success.

76. B. Patches can, and often do, *create* interoperability problems.

All the other options are functions offered by patching.

77. B. In many cases, patches are released to deal with an imminent vulnerability/risk. Some organizations will give blanket preapproval for applying these patches and having the formal change management process approve the patch after the fact.

All the other options are activities that should take place with patching.

78. B. Not all patches are necessary for all environments. Automated patching won't always account for variations in organizations and could cause interoperability problems in some.

Users don't usually apply patches and aren't involved in automatic patching; option A is incorrect.

It is rare that an automated patch tool will be exploited to install malware; option C is incorrect.

Automated patching is faster and more efficient than manual patching; option D is incorrect.

79. A. When a VM instance is inactive, it is saved as a snapshot image in a file; patches can't be applied until the instance is running. Automated patching set to a certain scheduled time may miss inactive VMs.

Patches can be applied remotely or locally; option B is not true or correct.

Patching may be the responsibility of the cloud customer or provider, depending on the service model, type, and contract. Option C is incorrect.

Cloud service providers should apply patches ubiquitously throughout their service environment; option D is incorrect.

80. A. Because a multitenant environment may have a variety of different configurations for various customers, a given patch might interfere with a certain number of customers due to interoperability problems.

Option B is untrue. Patches do work with SaaS models. Option B is incorrect.

Option C is untrue. Patches do work with private cloud builds. Option C is incorrect.

On the contrary, vendors do issue patches to cloud providers. Option D is incorrect.

81. C. Manual patching requires a significant degree of effort and time and is simply not feasible in a large enterprise, much less in the vast environment of the cloud.

Manual patching is slower than automated patching. Option A is incorrect.

Option B is incorrect; this is true in both traditional and cloud environments.

Option D is incorrect; users should not be performing patching.

82. D. Patching is a mundane, repetitive process, and people have trouble focusing on such tasks, especially for the number of times necessary to patch a cloud environment. Automation can aid in addressing this aspect of patching.

With human involvement in patching, there is an opportunity to be aware of imminent patch impacts and to determine applicability of the patch before it is applied; options A and B are incorrect.

Option C is a risk involved with all patching and not limited to manual patching; option D is preferable as it is specific to the question.

83. C. It is perfectly reasonable to not want to use the first version of a patch as there may be interoperability problems or even additional vulnerabilities contingent with its implementation. However, for as long as your environment remains unpatched, you are subject to attack through that new vulnerability.

All the other options are untrue.

The cloud provider will not suspend your access or sue your organization if you delay patching because of concerns about interoperability afterwards. Options A and B are incorrect.

Option D is incorrect. The opposite may actually be true. Your end clients may appreciate that you delay or test the patch before installing it on production systems.

84. B. If your organization doesn't apply a patch for a known vulnerability, regulators may claim the organization was not performing adequate due diligence and penalize it accordingly.

None of the other entities listed in the other options can assess penalties, so they are incorrect. (End clients may try to recover damages realized from an attack through a known vulnerability, but those penalties will be imposed by a court if the end clients conduct successful litigation.)

85. C. If patches are rolled out across an environment where users are operating virtual machines (VMs) at different times, there is a possibility that VMs will not be patched uniformly, which could lead to data disruption.

Option A is incorrect. Users should not be performing patching.

Option B is incorrect; a contract specifying who is responsible for specific patching activities actually reduces risk by enhancing the probability of proper patch application.

Option D is incorrect; attacker activity should be irrelevant to the patch process.

86. B. RUM harvests information from actual user activity, making it the most realistic depiction of user behavior.

Synthetic monitoring approximates user activity but is not as exact as RUM; option A is incorrect.

SIEM monitors more than web applications, so option C is not ideal for this question.

DAM is an OSI Layer 7 tool for monitoring database activity, specifically, so it is not the ideal answer for this question.

87. C. Depending on the jurisdiction, RUM may entail unlawful surveillance, so the practitioner must take this into account and plan accordingly.

Option A is incorrect. False positives are typical for real-user monitoring systems.

Option B has no relevance in this context. Option B is incorrect.

Sandboxed environments are not a concern when using real-user monitoring for web application activity analysis. Option D is incorrect.

88. C. Synthetic agents can simulate user activity in a much faster, broader manner and perform these actions 24/7 without rest.

All the other options are incorrect; synthetic agents may cost more than RUM, are less accurate than actual user activity, and both can take place on the cloud.

89. B. Logging should suffice for the purpose of reconstructing the pertinent information (who, what, where, when, etc.) necessary to form a narrative of what transpired. This will be different for every organization and environment (so option D is incorrect). You will have to make this determination for your organization.

Logging everything would result in log storage that exceeds the amount of data in the production environment and would actually make it more difficult to locate pertinent information. Option A is incorrect.

Option C is incorrect. Logging data after the fact is impossible.

90. D. It is important for the log review to be performed by someone who understands the normal operations of the organization so that they can discern between regular activity and anomalous behavior. This person also needs a security background so they can recognize common attack patterns/activity.

Option A sounds great, but the better answer is option D. A person with knowledge of the operation is a better fit than someone who is trained to review logs.

Options B and C are incorrect. Auditors are not the ones who should be reviewing logs for an organization.

91. C. The clock needs to be synched throughout the environment so that all activity can be contextualized and mapped and a true narrative of events can be reconstructed later.

All the other options are incorrect because they are simply IT terms. When it comes to useful logs, having the correct time relevant to all logged activity is vital.

92. B. Response to anomalous activity detected by the SIEM tool will still require human involvement.

All the other options are functions that the SIEM system can perform on its own as automated tasks.

93. B. Because the logs are essential to reconstructing a record of what occurred within the environment, they are a valuable target for attackers. They therefore need a sufficient level of protection commensurate with the data/systems they are about.

We don't want to have less protection on the logs than on the systems they monitor; the controls on those systems were chosen according to what threats and risks they may be exposed to—the level of security provided by those controls are, at a minimum, required for the log data. Option A is incorrect.

Encryption may or may not be used for securing log data, depending on the level of sensitivity of the systems/data they are protecting; option C is too specific and thus incorrect.

NIST guidelines are not suitable for all organizations and uses; option D is too broad and incorrect.

94. D. While historical information, especially that specific to the organization's industry, can be useful in assessing threats, risk must be considered independently from other occurrences; whether something has occurred elsewhere does not necessarily directly affect the likelihood it will or will not occur for a certain target.

All the other options are elements typically considered in the risk context.

95. D. We usually do not evaluate our customer base as an aspect of risk management. All the other options are aspects of common risk management practices.

96. B. While all the options are somewhat true, because all of that information can be used to provide the most comprehensive risk picture, the *best* answer among those listed is money; it is a discrete, numeric metric that can be used both for comparison to countermeasure/control cost and for recompense efforts (insurance claims, lawsuits, etc.).

97. B. Qualitative risk assessments are preferable in situations where the organization has personnel who understand the IT environment but may not have a lot of experience with risk functions and where the organization does not have a great deal of time or money to spend on the project.

A quantitative risk assessment requires a significant budget of time and money as well as well-trained, experience personnel familiar with risk; option A is not correct.

Options C and D are incorrect; these are not types of risk assessments.

98. B. The monetary value of the asset is the most objective, discrete metric possible and the most accurate for the purposes of SLE determination.

The other options are factors that may bear on how you determine the dollar value of the asset but are not as useful as option B.

99. B. While previous activity is not a great predictor of future outcomes (especially in the field of IT security), it is the best source we have.

Threat intelligence information is useful but not as good as historical data in predicting ARO; option A is not as good as option B.

Vulnerability scans and aggregation do not really aid in predicting rate of occurrence at all; options C and D are incorrect.

100. A. The threat vector is the multiplier involved in determining exposure factor; of the options listed, this is the best answer (and, other than C, the only one that actually has bearing on EF).

101. C. Absent any other information about a total physical loss, we can consider the rate of occurrence as 1: We would not expect the plant to burn down more than once in a year. In fact, we would expect that unless the plant was involved in some particularly flammable activity, the ARO would be less than 1 (that is, a fire is not expected every year) due to controls involved in the planning and building process of the plant (location of flammable material, fire-resistant construction techniques, etc.).

Options B and D are incorrect. The ARO is a number, not a dollar amount.

It is unlikely that the plant would burn down 12 times a year or every month. Option A is incorrect.

102. D. What we can't determine from the available information is the actual annualized loss expectancy (ALE); the cost of the physical plant itself is not the actual value of the asset, so it's impossible to determine the ALE and therefore impossible to compare the ALE against the cost of possible controls and countermeasures.

All the other options are incorrect; we can't make a suitable choice from the available information.

103. D. Unless this number is being used to determine the measures of options A or B, or we're trying to better estimate the cost of the impact of the first occurrence (i.e., including the value of lost product in the single loss expectancy [SLE]), the *amount* of product the plant creates is not as important as the attendant revenue that amount generates for the company.

All the other options are factors we need to know: The amount of revenue and the pace at which it is generated by the plant and the duration of downtime for the plant in the event of fire (so as to calculate possible lost revenue) will help us arrive at the annualized loss expectancy (ALE). In fact, additional information would also be useful, such as potential loss of market share if product was not delivered for the duration of the downtime, etc.

104. B. The fire suppression system is the most cost-effective, reasonable means of dealing with the risk, if we use the formula for determining annualized loss expectancy (ALE).

First, we need to determine the single loss expectancy (SLE) and annualized rate of occurrence (ARO). ARO can be assumed to be 1; absent any other information about the plant, we don't expect more than one fire per year (and perhaps less, but we don't have that information, either). The SLE is $36 million ($24 million for the cost of rebuilding the plant, assuming no increase in costs over the previous construction, plus $2 million per month of lost revenue, for the six months it will take to rebuild).

Therefore, the ALE is $36 million (36 [SLE] × 1 [ARO]).

Either the fire suppression system or the insurance policy would be appealing, from a strictly financial standpoint, if we only compared the ALE to the annualized cost of the countermeasure ($15 million for the suppression system, $12 million for the insurance policy).

However, other factors have a bearing on this consideration too. For instance, fire poses a threat to health and human safety; obviating such risks should be a paramount concern to senior management. An insurance policy doesn't truly protect people, it only offsets the damages people experience through loss. Also, the insurance policy would be a recurring, continual cost; it costs less than the fire suppression system in the *first year* of the plant's operation ($12 million for insurance versus $15 million for the system), but once the system is purchased, though it may need upkeep and maintenance, we can assume it won't cost the same amount in future years, and it probably won't cost anywhere near as much as the continual costs of the insurance.

All the other options are not as good as B.

105. A. Because risk can never be mitigated to zero (there is no such thing as "no risk" or "perfect security"), there will always be some residual risk after risk mitigation; this residual risk must be accepted.

Risk mitigation does not *always* involve risk transfer, or risk avoidance. "Risk attenuation" is not an industry-standard term associated with risk management Options B, C, and D are incorrect.

106. B. Secondary risk is any risk resulting from enacting a control/countermeasure to the original risk. In this case, a fire suppression system that displaces oxygen is a means to mitigate the original risk (fire) but adds a new risk (suffocating people).

All the other options are not causes of secondary risk (except if we draw out unreasonable conclusions from the most extreme, ridiculous cases, for example, "the secondary risk is the risk that the control doesn't work").

107. D. The best means to address risk is completely dependent on the business needs of the specific entity and process. Mitigation may or may not be the optimum choice.

All the other options are true statements about risk mitigation.

108. D. A risk assessment may, indeed, be an estimate of a moving target, but it is invaluable in terms of measuring risk at any given point in time.

109. D. In the certification/accreditation model of system approval, certification is the fundamental step.

All other options are incorrect because certification comes first in the certification/accreditation model of system approval.

110. C. The RMF is based on perceived risk as opposed to threats (threats may factor into risk assessment but are not the driver for the RMF).

All the other options are true regarding the RMF.

111. D. In symmetric encryption, a single key is used to both encrypt and decrypt a message. This is often referred to as a shared secret.

Two key pairs are not used in symmetric encryption; option A is incorrect.

Parties most often must be known to each other using symmetric encryption; option B is incorrect.

Certificates require public-private key pairs, which is not an element of symmetric encryption; option C is incorrect.

112. B. In symmetric encryption, the key must usually be passed through a different medium than will be used for sending and receiving the encrypted messages.

DH is usually used for asymmetric encryption, to establish a temporary symmetric key; option A is incorrect.

Option C describes asymmetric encryption and is therefore incorrect.

Option D describes hashing and is therefore incorrect.

Chapter 6: Domain 6: Legal, Risk, and Compliance

1. C. The Statement on Standards for Attestation Engagements (SSAE) 18 is the current AICPA (American Institute of Certified Public Accountants) audit standard.

   ISO 27001 is an international audit standard.

   The Sarbanes-Oxley Act (SOX) is a U.S. law pertaining to publicly traded corporations.

   There is no such thing as the IEC 43770 standard.

2. B. The STAR program has three tiers.

3. A. Tier 1 is the lowest tier of the STAR program, involving only self-assessment.

4. C. The Diffie-Hellman key exchange process is designed to allow two parties to create a shared secret (symmetric key) over an untrusted medium. RADIUS is an outmoded access control service for remote users. RSA is an encryption scheme. TACACS is a network access protocol set used through a centralized server.

5. C. A party who does not perform sufficient due diligence in choosing a contractor can be held accountable for the actions made by that contractor. In current privacy and data laws, this is usually the government's perspective regarding wrongdoing on the part of cloud providers.

   All the other options are incorrect because they are simply legal terms that do not correctly answer the question.

6. D. An affidavit is only a form of formal testimony presented to the court. All the other options are enforceable governmental requests.

7. D. *Streamlining* is a nonsense term in this context. All the other options represent normal ways of addressing risk. Mitigation is the use of controls to attenuate the impact or likelihood (or both) of risk, acceptance is allowing the business to function with no further action, and avoidance is halting the business function.

8. B. The collection limitation principle requires any entity that gathers personally identifiable information (PII) about a person to restrict data collection to only information that is necessary for the transaction, and only with the knowledge and permission of the individual. The other options are meaningless in this context.

9. A. The data quality principle requires any entity that gathers personally identifiable information (PII) about a person to ensure that the data remains valid and accurate and allows for corrections by the data subject. The other answers are meaningless in this context.

10. D. The purpose specification principle requires any entity that gathers personally identifiable information (PII) about a person to clearly state the explicit purpose for which the PII will be used. The other answers are meaningless in this context.

11. A. The use limitation principle requires any entity that gathers personally identifiable information (PII) about a person to restrict the use of that PII to that which was permitted by the data subject and the reason given when it was collected. The other answers are meaningless in this context.

12. B. The security safeguards principle requires any entity that gathers personally identifiable information (PII) about a person to protect that data against unauthorized access and modification. The other answers are meaningless in this context.

13. D. The openness principle requires any entity that gathers personally identifiable information (PII) about a person to allow that person to access the information. The other answers are meaningless in this context.

14. B. The EU crafted first the EU Data Directive and then the General Data Protection Regulation largely according to the OECD guidelines. The US Congress has (at the time of this writing) made no broad federal privacy law and instead has treated personal privacy on an industry-by-industry basis. The Politburo no longer exists. The ISO is not a lawmaking body.

15. B. The General Data Protection Regulation prohibits entities within a country that has no nationwide privacy law from gathering or processing privacy data belonging to EU citizens. Entities can be allowed to do so if the following conditions are met:

- Their own country has nationwide laws that comply with the EU laws.

- The entity creates contractual language that complies with the EU laws and has that language approved by each EU country from which the entity wishes to gather citizen data.

- The entity voluntarily subscribes to its own nation's Privacy Shield program.

There is no process for the entity to appeal to the EU for permission to do so, however.

16. A. The Privacy Shield program is for non-EU entities that also do not exist in a country with a nationwide privacy law; no entity is required to join the program, but those who don't are prevented from collecting and processing EU citizen privacy data. Entities within the EU are already subject to the EU General Data Protection Regulation law and therefore are not eligible or benefited by the Privacy Shield program.

17. B. The United States does not have a general nationwide privacy law that complies with the EU privacy statutes; it instead has created industry-specific privacy laws. Canada has a law (Personal Information Protection and Electronic Documents Act) that conforms with the EU laws, as does Switzerland and Japan.

18. D. Brazil does not yet have federal privacy laws sufficient to be considered acceptable for EU compliance. Israel, Australia, and Argentina all do.

19. D. The Department of Commerce manages the Privacy Shield program in the United States; the Departments of State and Interior do not. There is no Department of Trade.

20. A. SOX is only applicable to publicly traded corporations, not all companies. HIPAA may be applicable to the data you work with as a medical student, if you work with patient data. Your payment and personal data is governed by PCI DSS. FERPA protects your personal student information.

21. B. The FedRAMP standard dictates that American federal agencies must retain their data within the boundaries of the United States, including data within cloud data centers.

FISMA is the federal law requiring agencies to comply with National Institute of Standards and Technology (NIST) guidance; option A is broader than B, so B is better in this case.

Options C and D are not American laws and therefore not applicable.

22. B. Level 2 of the CSA STAR program requires third-party assessment of the provider.

Level 1 is a self-assessment; option A is incorrect.

Level 3 requires continual monitoring by a third party; option C is incorrect.

There is no Level 4 of the STAR program.

23. A. This is an example of due care.

Due diligence is the processes and activities used to ensure that due care is maintained; option B is incorrect.

Liability is the measure of responsibility an entity has for providing due care; option C is incorrect.

Option D has no meaning in this context.

24. D. The CCSP candidate is probably most familiar with the European Union's (EU's) Data Directive and General Data Protection Regulation in this regard. The directive allows every member country to create its own law that is compliant with the directive; the regulation mandates that all countries comply with the regulation itself.

Both directives and regulations can be enforced by either member states or EU international tribunals; option A is not correct.

Both directives and regulations are statutory; option B is not correct.

Both directives and regulations deal with both internal EU matters and those that extend outside Europe; option C is not correct.

25. C. A government service provider is not allowed to refuse service if an individual refuses to participate in data collection.

Option A is incorrect. There is no requirement for hardcopy.

Option B is incorrect because the provider is a government agency.

Option D is incorrect. The scenario in the question is illegal whether or not the visitor is asked about their nationality.

26. C. All the other options are incorrect.

27. D. The GDPR describes requirements for data collection by and transfers to data controllers and processors.

All the other options are incorrect.

28. B. This is the definition of shadow IT: unplanned costs from uncontrolled user activity.

This does not constitute a data breach because no data has been disclosed to unauthorized entities; option A is incorrect.

This is not an intrusion because no external entity has gained access to the environment; option C is incorrect.

While shadow IT may be considered a particular kind of insider threat, we usually consider insider threats as malicious, and shadow IT is typically the result of benign intentions. Option B is better than option D.

29. D. The ISO 27001 certification is for the information security management system (ISMS), the organization's entire security program.

The SAS 70 and SSAE 18 are audit standards for service providers and include some review of security controls but not a cohesive program (and the SAS 70 is outdated); options A and B are not correct.

The SOC reports are how SSAE 18 audits are conducted; option C is incorrect.

30. B. This is what a SOC 2, Type 1 report is for.

The SOC 1 is for financial reporting; the SOC 2, Type 2 is to review the implementation (not design) of controls; and the SOC 3 is just an attestation that an audit was performed. All these options are incorrect.

31. B. This is the definition of a gap analysis.

SOC reports are specific kinds of audits; option A is incorrect.

The scoping statement is a pre-audit function that aids both the organization and the auditor to determine what, specifically, will be audited. Option C is incorrect.

Federal guidelines are government recommendations on how something should be done. Option D is incorrect.

32. C. The 27002 standard contains sets of controls to be used in order to allow the organization to match the security program created for the organization with 27001.

The SAS 70 and SSAE 18 are audit standards for service providers and include some review of security controls but not a cohesive program (and the SAS 70 is outdated); options A and B are not correct.

NIST SP 800-53 allows the organization to craft a set of controls to meet the requirements created for and by the organization when using NIST SP 800-37; option D is incorrect.

33. D. While the auditor is not a law enforcement entity, they will likely have an ethical, if not legal, requirement to report illicit activities discovered during the audit.

All the other options are incorrect as they are all facets of audit scoping.

34. B. Auditors may find it necessary to speak to particular individuals in order to locate artifacts and understand the environment. Although there may be some limitation on particular points of contact and nature of interviews, there cannot be a total prohibition.

All the other options are incorrect as they are all facets of audit scoping.

35. D. The ECSA is designed as a cloud service certification motif for organizations located in Europe.

NIST (which also administers FedRAMP) is designed specifically for federal agencies in the United States and is not applicable for European providers, so options A and B are incorrect.

ISO 27034 deals with an organization's use of security controls for software; while this may be pertinent to your organization, it is not a comprehensive view of cloud services and is not as beneficial or equivalent to the CSA STAR or Uptime Institute certifications. Option D is preferable to option C.

36. C. Perspectives gained from people outside the audit target are invaluable because they may see possibilities and opportunities revealed by the audit, whereas the personnel in the target department may be constrained by habit and tradition.

Options A and B are incorrect because this poses a conflict of interest.

Option D is incorrect. Audits often reveal sensitive information that does not need to be shared with an external audit body that was not part of the original audit.

37. A. An IT security audit is not intended to locate financial fraud; it may, however, lead to such revelations unintentionally. There are specific other audits that exist for this purpose.

All the other options are incorrect because they are intended goals for IT security audits.

38. D. ISO 27018 describes privacy requirements for cloud providers, including an annual audit mandate.

Option A is incorrect because NIST SP 800-37 describes the Risk Management Framework and is not an international privacy standard.

The Personal Information Protection and Electronic Documents Act is a Canadian law relating to data privacy. Option B is incorrect.

Option C is incorrect because the PCI DSS is specifically for merchants who accept credit cards, not cloud providers (while cloud providers may process credit cards, and therefore must follow PCI DSS, option D is preferable, and a better answer).

39. D. Aside from industry-specific legislation, the United States does not have any federal laws outlining how citizens' privacy data should be treated.

All the other entities have published such guidance, and those options are therefore incorrect.

40. B. With rare exceptions, digital forensics does not include creation of data (other than the forensic reports regarding the analysis of data). While this could arguably be considered an aspect of digital forensics as well, the other options are more suited to describing digital forensics, so this is the best negative answer.

41. D. This is the definition of extradition.

Applicable law is the regulation/legislation affecting a certain circumstance. Option A is incorrect.

Judgments are legal conclusions or decisions. Option B is incorrect.

Option C is incorrect because criminal law is the body of law that pertains to crime.

42. A. Civil courts (for example, in a breach of contract case) are held to the "preponderance of evidence" standard.

All the other options are incorrect because they do not hold to the preponderance of the evidence requirement.

43. D. Except in jurisdictions where contributory negligence is a factor in the proceedings, civil courts use a standard of "preponderance of evidence," so the entity that has a simple majority of fault (51 percent or more) is responsible for the full weight of the breach. Because the question did not specify the case was in contributory negligence jurisdiction, option D is the best answer because it is the most likely outcome.

Options A, B, and C are incorrect because they are 25%, 75% and 0% of the full weight of the breach.

44. B. The silver platter doctrine allows law enforcement entities to use material presented voluntarily by the owner as evidence in the prosecution of crimes, without a warrant or a court order.

The doctrine of plain view allows law enforcement to act on probable cause when evidence of a crime is within their presence; option A is incorrect.

The GDPR is a European Union (EU) privacy law and not applicable here; option C is incorrect.

FISMA is the American law requiring federal agencies to adhere to National Institute of Standards and Technology (NIST) standards; option D is incorrect.

45. B. As of May 2018, the GDPR is the law throughout all EU member states, superseding any existing local laws.

Belgian law will be superseded at that point, and the GDPR has primacy over Belgian law. Option A is incorrect.

Options C and D are an American standard and law, respectively, and are not applicable to companies in the European Union (EU), so they are therefore incorrect.

It's important to note that the GDPR covers all entities that are located and/or operate in the EU, regardless of other details such as where the business entity stores the data or where the customers are located.

46. A. A litigation hold notice is required to prevent possible destruction of pertinent evidence that may be used in the case.

An audit scoping letter outlines the parameters for an audit engagement; option B is incorrect.

Options C and D do not have meaning in this context.

47. A. *Spoliation* is the term used to describe the destruction of potential evidence (intentionally or otherwise); in various jurisdictions, it can be a crime, or the grounds for another lawsuit.

Destroying evidence is not fraud; fraud can be a crime or tort on its own, but option B is incorrect.

Jurisdiction describes the geographical area over which a court has power; option C is incorrect.

Recompositing is a made-up word and has no meaning in this context. Option D is incorrect.

48. A. In an SaaS model, the customer has little insight into event logs and traffic analysis useful for evidentiary purposes. The customer will largely be reliant on the cloud provider to locate, collect, and deliver this information for e-discovery.

Regulators do not take part in e-discovery; option B is incorrect.

In this situation, your company is the cloud customer and will not have a great deal of access to event logs, which may be a crucial element of e-discovery; options C and D are incorrect.

49. B. Multitenancy in the cloud is a direct result of sharing resources; many customers use the same underlying hardware infrastructure. A seizure of hardware assets by law enforcement investigating another cloud customer could conceivably result in the seizure of your company's data because it happened to be residing on the same hardware when that hardware was seized.

The other options are aspects of cloud computing but do not have anything to do with the risk of unauthorized disclosure due to seizure by law enforcement.

50. D. Your company will not be allowed to destroy any data for the duration of the legal case because that might constitute tampering with potential evidence.

All the other aspects of software development may continue as long as no destructive measures or methods are utilized; all the other options are incorrect.

51. D. While e-discovery may be a painful, monotonous, expensive process, a vast data dump of the organization's entire data store would entail massive risk and liability.

The other options are simply incorrect.

52. B. Typically, a discovery tool is a primary component of a DLP solution. This might be employed for purposes of identifying and collecting pertinent data.

All the other options describe important facets of an overall organizational security program but are not especially helpful in e-discovery efforts.

53. C. Courts can issue seizure orders for anything and everything.

All the other options are either incorrect because they are too limited (A and B) or just absurd (D).

54. C. In order to deliver credible, believable expert testimony, it's important that your personnel have more than an amateur's understanding and familiarity with any forensic tools they use to perform analysis. Formal training and certification are excellent methods for creating credibility.

Scripting testimony is usually frowned on by the court; coaching witnesses how to perform and what to expect in court is all right, but it does not lead to credibility. Option A is incorrect.

Your expert witnesses are not allowed to withhold any evidence from their testimony if it is pertinent to the case, even if that evidence aids the other side. Option B is incorrect.

You should pay your employees for their time, regardless of whether they're performing on the job site or in a courtroom, but this has nothing to do with enhancing credibility. Option D is incorrect.

55. B. There are certain jurisdictions where forensic data/IT analysis requires licensure (the American states of Texas, Colorado, and Michigan, for example); it is important for you to determine whether this is the case in your jurisdiction before proceeding with any forensic efforts.

It is important for forensic investigators to have proper training, background checks, and approved tools in every jurisdiction, so all the other options are incorrect as they are not specific enough.

56. B. All forensics processes and activity should be documented with extreme scrutiny. It is very important for your actions to be documented and repeatable in order for them to remain credible.

Evidence is only inadmissible if it has no probative value—that is, if it has no bearing on the case. Modified data is still admissible, as long as the modification process was documented and presented along with the evidence. Option A is incorrect.

Option C is ambiguous as to its meaning and is therefore an incorrect choice for an answer.

Option D is true if the data modification process is not documented and presented in detail.

57. C. The battery is a crime and may be prosecuted as such, and the act may also result in the victim suing the attacker for damages.

Options A and B are not sufficient compared to C.

Option D is a distractor in this case; battery is not a form of racketeering, unless linked to a larger pattern of crimes.

58. B. The attacker is the one who committed the crime and is therefore likely to be prosecuted (*prosecuted* denotes a criminal trial, as opposed to a civil suit).

It is unlikely that the company would be prosecuted for causing the crime because the company did not engage in the wrongful behavior; in this case, there was a very specific attacker and victim. Option A is incorrect.

The victim does not get prosecuted for crimes committed against them. Option C is incorrect.

If you had ordered the attack, or somehow caused it to occur, you might be prosecuted, but this is not detailed in the question and is an unlikely circumstance; option D is incorrect.

59. B. This is an example of due diligence.

Due care is the duty owed by one entity to another, in terms of a reasonable expectation; option A is incorrect.

Liability is the measure of responsibility an entity has for providing due care; option C is incorrect.

Answer D has no meaning in this context; option D is incorrect.

60. C. Snapshotting an entire virtual machine or memory device is an excellent method for capturing its current data and settings at a specific moment.

Hypervisors do not particularly aid in evidence collection, although they may provide log data; option C is still preferable to option A.

Pooled resources actually complicate evidence collection; option B is quite wrong.

Live migration does not aid in evidence collection; option D is incorrect.

61. B. Backups can serve to provide excellent forensics about incidents that have already occurred and also serve to provide an operational reach-back capability for users that have accidentally lost data or modified it incorrectly.

While highly trained forensic personnel will be very useful in forensic activities, that is not usually an operational benefit. Option A is incorrect.

The more secure the data archive, the less useful it is for operational purposes; option C is not as good as option B.

Option D is wrong because homomorphic encryption is still theoretical and currently serves no actual purpose.

62. D. File hashes can serve as integrity checks for both configuration management (to determine which systems are not configured to the baseline) and audit purposes (as artifacts/common builds of systems for audit review).

Backups and constant uptime may aid in availability efforts for operational purposes, but they don't really help in configuration management; options A and B are incorrect.

Multifactor authentication provides neither configuration management nor forensic benefits; option C is wrong.

63. A. Because RAM is inherently volatile, and virtual resources are simulated only for limited time periods, virtual RAM is probably the most volatile data store.

Hardware RAM is probably as volatile as virtual RAM, but the virtualization aspect of option A may make it a more suitable answer for this particular question.

Log data and drive storage should both be durable and not volatile at all, so options C and D are incorrect.

64. C. In a multitenant environment, it is quite likely that any particular piece of hardware will contain data from many customers. In this case, your company may become liable for violating privacy laws for accessing privacy data belonging to another cloud customer, which would increase your company's exposure (something that could be disastrous because the company is already under investigation).

None, some, or all of the other options might be true, however, the liability of possibly disclosing someone else's privacy data is an overwhelming business risk; therefore, option C is the best answer.

65. C. This is a very difficult question as all the options are correct. However, the ultimate recipient of all forensic evidentiary collection and analysis—the entity getting the reports— will be the court, in order to make a final determination of its merits and insights.

66. C. It's important to present a full view of the evidence, including any alternative findings that were considered but eliminated through reason. This serves many purposes, not the least of which is strengthening your case in the minds of those who hear your testimony.

Your professional opinion is vital, but your personal opinion should not have bearing on the case; option A is incorrect.

Option B is only incorrect because it limits the presentation to your side of the case, where C is broader and more accurate.

Unless instructed by counsel, bringing up similar past activity is not germane to the current case; option D is incorrect.

67. A. An integrity check comparing the copy to the original is essential so that the report can demonstrate that none of the data was lost or tampered with before analysis begins.

All the other options are simply incorrect for integrity check purposes.

68. B. The evidence custodian is the person designated to maintain the chain of custody for the duration of the investigation. All the other options could be roles of people who are tasked with custodianship.

69. D. It is important that any changes to the data only be made in purposeful, specific ways; a write-blocker helps to ensure that extraneous changes aren't made to the data.

The other options are not necessary for accessing an electronic storage file for forensic purposes. Options A, B, and C are incorrect.

70. D. You do *not* want to have unique testing techniques used in your analysis, because those may not be repeatable or accepted by other experts (or the court).

All the other options are traits of forensic testing we *do* want our tests to include.

71. D. U.S. laws do not, for the most part, consider cell phone numbers an element of PII; in the EU, they are.

All the other options are PII elements under both jurisdictions.

72. B. The GDPR contains the provisions under which the Privacy Shield program was implemented.

All the other options are all U.S. law and therefore incorrect.

73. C. The EU General Data Protection Regulation (GDPR) requires that multinationals using standard contractual clauses get those clauses approved by the privacy office in every EU member state where the company will operate. Italy and Germany are both EU member states; Brazil is not.

74. D. Processing includes any manipulation, use, movement, or alteration of data—pretty much anything that can be done with or to data is "processing" (including making and manipulating hard-copy versions of data).

Storing data in the cloud is not illegal in most jurisdictions (as long as certain rules are followed, for specific industries and data sets); option A is incorrect.

Storing often happens at or soon after the time of collection, but they are not the same function; option B is incorrect.

Opt-in is the concept under which a data subject must give clear consent to personally identifiable information (PII) data collection and use; option C is incorrect.

75. C. The FTC is in charge of the Privacy Shield program.

The State Department is involved with controlling some exports, under the International Traffic in Arms Regulations (ITAR) regulations; option A is incorrect.

There is no Privacy Protection Office; option B is meaningless term and is incorrect.

HHS is in charge of managing the Health Information Portability and Accountability Act (HIPAA); option D is incorrect.

76. C. The CMM is a way of determining a target's maturity in terms of process documentation and repeatability.

The CSA STAR and EuroCloud Star programs are certifications based on applicable control sets and compliance with standards and regulations, not process maturity; options A and D are incorrect.

The RMF is National Institute of Standards and Technology (NIST) guidance on how to assess risk in an environment; option B is incorrect.

77. C. SOC 2 reports were not designed for dissemination outside the target organization.

All the other options are incorrect.

78. B. In order to protect extremely sensitive material that is discussed in the SOC 2, Type 2, the provider may request that you sign an NDA and limit distribution.

The provider is the entity that should be seeking CSA STAR certification, not the customer; option C is incorrect.

Be wary of any provider that asks for security deposits and/or acts of fealty; options A and D are incorrect.

79. A. The AICPA, the OECD, and the EU have all outlined certain basic expectations for entities that are privacy data controllers; these expectations are extremely similar in the documentation produced by all three.

All the other options are forms of legislation or regulators that do have some content that addresses privacy; however, option A is the most specific and preferable answer because the privacy principles of the AICPA, OECD, and EU are so very similar.

80. D. The PCI DSS is extremely thorough and wide-reaching.

All the other options are just wrong.

81. D. The different merchant tiers are based on the number of transactions a specific merchant conducts annually.

All the other options are incorrect.

82. B. Merchants at different tiers are required to have more or fewer audits in the same time frame as merchants in other tiers, depending on the tier.

All PCI DSS–compliant merchants must meet all the control and audit requirements of the standard; options A and C are incorrect.

PCI DSS does not dictate costs of controls; option D is wrong.

83. D. U.S. federal entities are prohibited from using cryptosystems that are not compliant with FIPS 140-2.

All the other options are incorrect because they are not related to FIPS 140-2.

84. A. Vendor lock-out can occur when your provider no longer offers the service for which you contracted; it is possible that a merger or acquisition of your provider might lead to this circumstance.

All the other options are incorrect because they are not relevant in terms of the question.

Chapter 7: Practice Exam 1

1. C. This is the definition of federation. PKI is used to establish trust between parties across an untrusted medium, portability is the characteristic describing the likelihood of being able to move data away from one cloud provider to another, and repudiation is when a party to a transaction can deny having taken part in that transaction.

2. C. In the cross-certification model, every participating organization has to review and approve every other organization; this does not scale well, and once the number of organizations gets fairly substantial, it becomes unwieldy.

Option A is incorrect because it is possible to trust more than two organizations.

Option B is not true. There is no law/rule that limits the government to sharing data to five or less parties.

Option D is incorrect. Sharing data does not automatically affect the value of the data.

3. B. SAML 2.0 is currently the standard used to pass security assertions across the Internet. REST and SOAP are ways of presenting data and executing operations on the Internet, and HTML is a way of displaying web pages.

4. A. A third-party identity broker can serve the purpose of checking and approving all participants to the federation so that the participants don't have to perform that task. A cloud reseller is an entity that sells cloud services without maintaining its own data centers. Option C is gibberish. MAC is used to define access relationships between subjects and objects.

5. A. NIST Special Publication 800-53 pertains to U.S. federal information systems, guiding the selection of controls according to the Risk Management Framework. PCI is a contractual standard for commercial entities that take credit card payments, not applicable to the government. ENISA publishes a European standard, which is also not applicable to the United States. ISO is not required for government systems in the United States.

6. B. The Personal Information Protection and Electronic Documents Act (PIPEDA) is a Canadian law governing protection of personal information. The Federal Information Processing Standard (FIPS) 140-2 standard certifies cryptologic components for use by American federal government entities. The Health Information Portability and Accountability Act (HIPAA) is an American law regulating patient information for medical providers. The European Free Trade Association (EFTA) is not a standard; it is a group of European countries.

7. A. The CSA CCM will aid you in selecting and implementing appropriate controls for various regulatory frameworks. The CCM does not aid in collecting log files; that is the function of a security information and event management (SIEM), search engine marketing (SEM), or security information management (SIM) tool. The CCM will not help ensure that the baseline is applied to systems; automated configuration tools are available for that purpose (although this answer might be interpreted as desirable; the CCM will help you select appropriate controls for your baseline, but it won't check to see if those are applied). Contract terms are not enforced by the CCM; the service-level agreement (SLA) should be the mechanism for that task.

8. C. Option C is a nonsense term made up as a distractor. All the other frameworks are addressed in the CCM.

9. A. The CAIQ is a self-administered tool propagated by the CSA for the purpose of aiding organizations in selecting the necessary controls. The OWASP Top Ten is used to indicate trends in poor design of web applications. The CSC may be a useful tool for choosing and implementing appropriate controls, but it comes from the Center for Internet Security (CIS), not the CSA. The FIPS 140-2 lists only approved cryptographic tools and is published by NIST.

10. B. The CCM allows you to note where specific controls (some of which you might already have in place) will address requirements listed in multiple regulatory and contractual standards, laws, and guides. Option A is a misnomer because the CCM is free of charge. Options C and D are incorrect because the CCM does not list either specific controls or vendors.

11. D. This is a community cloud, because various parties own different elements of it for a common purpose. A private cloud would typically be owned by a single entity, hosted at a cloud provider data center. A public cloud would be open to anyone and everyone. Hydrogenous is a word that does not have relevant meaning in this context.

12. B. The cross-certification model of federated identity requires all participants to review and confirm all the others. SAML is the format most often used for identity assertions in a federated environment. JSON is a communications format for exchanging objects online.

13. B. A copyright protects expressions of ideas, usually creative expression. Music, whether written or recorded, falls into this category. Trademarks are for data that is associated with a brand of a company. Patents are usually for processes or inventions. Trade secrets are business elements kept from public disclosure—music would not usually fit into this category as its value is derived from its distribution in the marketplace.

14. C. In federations where the participating entities are sharing data and resources, all of those entities are usually the service providers. In a third-party certification model, the third party is the identity provider; this is often a CASB. The cloud provider is neither a federated identity provider nor a federated service provider, unless the cloud provider is specifically chosen as the third party providing this function; in this question, option C is more general and requires no assumptions, so it is the correct choice.

15. A. This is the correct process, according to the law. The rest are not proper procedures for complying with the law and are therefore incorrect and inadvisable.

16. B. Copyrights expire after a certain duration and then fall into the public domain, where they can be used by anyone for any purpose. This material certainly exceeds the time of any copyright protection. All other options are invalid.

17. C. Tier 3 should probably suffice for Bob's purposes, providing sufficient redundancy and resiliency. Tier 4 probably offers more than what Bob needs; it will cost considerably more than a Tier 3 implementation and is most likely only necessary for organizations providing health and human safety services (hospitals and trauma centers, for instance). Tiers 1 and 2 are probably not sufficient and might only be considered for non-constant situations, such as archiving and backup.

18. **C.** GLBA mandates requirements for securing personal account information in the financial and insurance industries; Bob's company provides financial services, so he will definitely have to comply with GLBA. If Bob's company is publicly traded, he may have to comply with SOX, but we don't know enough about Bob's company from the question to choose that answer. HIPAA is a requirement only for medical providers and their business associates. PCI is not a law.

19. **B.** Using different vendors for multiple systems of the same type adds not only redundancy but also resiliency; if one product has an inherent manufacturing flaw, the other should not, if it comes from a different producer. The other suggestions are all suitable but do not offer redundancy or resiliency.

20. **D.** Traditionally, it would be optimum if the UPS lasted as long as necessary until the generator is able to resume providing the electrical load that was previously handled by utility power. However, the absolute baseline for battery power is just long enough for all systems to complete their transactions without losing data.

    The other options are incorrect, because they use finite, specific durations; there is no single value that is optimum for all organizations.

21. **B.** It is preferable that your games do not have security flaws in them, but this is not a core aspect of the product you are delivering: you are delivering entertainment, which is the primary goal; security is therefore a nonfunctional requirement.

    If you were creating security products, security would be a functional requirement; games are not security products. A game with security flaws is still a game and fulfills the purpose. Option A is therefore incorrect (although hotly debated among IT security personnel—remember, the game can exist without a security department, but the security department couldn't exist without games).

    Thus far, regulations have not imposed particular security conditions on delivered products by statute. This does not obviate all liability from shipping defective products, of course; the need for due care and due diligence remains. However, this is a much lower threshold than direct statutory guidance, which exists in fields other than software development (to date). Option C is incorrect.

    Outsourcing may or may not be used when performing software security reviews; there is not enough information in the question to determine which method your company uses, so option D is too specific for the vague data provided.

22. **B.** Testing the product in a runtime context is dynamic testing.

    Because this is being done in runtime, it is neither code review nor static testing; options A and C are incorrect.

    Using a small pool of specified individuals is not truly open source, which would involve releasing the game to the public. Option D is incorrect.

23. **C.** The moderator will serve to guide the experience in an objective, dispassionate manner, without influencing the test, as well as to help document the outcomes.

    Having managers in attendance would present a form of unnecessary micromanagement; option A is wrong.

There is no need for a database administrator (DBA) to be involved in the test; option B is wrong.

The security team should use the data gathered from the test, but they don't need to be present for the testing; option D is incorrect.

24. D. It is absolutely essential that the developers are not present during the actual testing as they are likely to influence the test unduly, purposefully or otherwise.

The other parties don't need to participate in the testing process but are not as undesirable as the developers; all the other options are incorrect.

25. B. Having the test participants provide signed nondisclosure agreements is an absolutely essential part of this process; they will be exposed to proprietary material and need to be held accountable for any disclosures they might make.

Managerial oversight is not at all necessary at this level of development and would actually be a form of micromanagement; option A is incorrect.

Health benefits are in no way appropriate for temporary, unpaid testers; option C is only a distractor.

Programmers should be prevented from participating in testing as they have inherent bias and may unduly influence the results; option D is wrong.

26. C. This is not an easy question and requires some concerted thought. The most grave concern to your company is the loss of proprietary information—that is, your games, which are your property and means of profit. Security flaws in your organization could lead to a total loss of your property, which could end your business.

This is one of the very few questions where "health and human safety" is not the correct answer to a security issue; there just isn't much danger involved in either producing or consuming video games (aside from dated, anecdotal reports of seizures resulting from flashing images, which lacked scientific substantiation). Though this will be something you must consider (such as workplace violence issues), it will not be a daily activity. Option A is incorrect.

Security flaws in your products will most likely not be critical or of grave impact; people who hack your game after shipping may be able to include additional functionality or violate some elements of copy protection, but this is not as threatening as pre-release exposure of the material. Option B is incorrect.

Current laws do not dictate much in the way of either content or functionality for software (other than very specific industries, such as health care or financial services); option D is incorrect.

27. C. Software is protected by copyright. All the other options are forms of intellectual property protections but not applicable to software for the most part (trademarked names and characters may be important, but not as important as the copyright).

28. C. This is a very pragmatic and helpful means of gathering inputs that are unpredictable and difficult to simulate and that mimic conditions under which the software will operate.

All the other options are incorrect.

29. C. Fuzz testing is the term used to describe the use of known bad or randomized inputs to determine what unintended results may occur.

Source code review, just like it sounds, is a review of the actual program code; option A is incorrect.

Deep testing is a made-up term; option B is incorrect.

White-box testing is a term used to describe a form of code review; option D is incorrect.

30. C. Digitally signing software code is an excellent method for determining original ownership and has proven effective in major intellectual property rights disputes.

All the other options represent solutions that not only probably lack efficacy but are also often illegal.

31. C. Enforcement of copyright is usually a tortious civil action, as a conflict between private parties.

Only crimes involve arrest, detention, and prosecution; most copyright cases such as this would not be tried as a crime, and the government would not be involved (other than in the form of the judge/court). Options A and D are incorrect.

Public hearings are not used to gain restitution for harmful acts; option B is incorrect.

32. B. A platform as a service (PaaS) environment will likely provide the best option for testing the game; the provider will offer various OS platforms for the game to run on, giving your company the opportunity to reach as many customers (using various platforms) as possible, raising your potential for market penetration.

Although infrastructure as a service (IaaS) is not a terrible option and would give your team additional control of the entire test, it would also require the team to duplicate many different platforms and OSs, requiring a much greater level of effort and additional expertise at what would likely be a much greater cost. Option B is preferable to option A.

A software as a service (SaaS) model will not allow your team to install and run the game; option C is incorrect.

TaaS is a made-up term with no meaning in this context, making option D incorrect.

33. C. To attenuate the risks of inadvertent disclosure inherent in untested software, it is essential to obfuscate any raw production data (such as potential personally identifiable information [PII]) before including it in any test environment.

The other options represent activity that is obviously beneficial but secondary to the importance of masking production data. Think of it this way: even if there is a vulnerability, breach, or malware in the test environment, if raw data is included something of value is lost; if dummy or masked data is the only content included, nothing of value is lost.

34. C. Off-site storage is not intrinsic to the definition of cloud computing; all the other options are.

35. D. Immediate customer support may be an option offered by some cloud providers, but it is not a defining characteristic of the industry. All the other options are.

36. A. In the infrastructure as a service (IaaS) model, the customer is responsible for everything up from the hardware layer.

In platform as a service (PaaS) and software as a service (SaaS), this will be performed by the provider; options B and C are incorrect.

QaaS is an invented term and not meaningful; option D is wrong.

37. D. Vendor lock-in occurs when the customer is dissuaded from leaving a provider, even when that is the best decision for the customer.

These contract terms can be described as favorable only from the provider's perspective; option D is preferable to option A for describing this situation.

There was no description of negotiation included in the question; option B is incorrect.

IaaS is a service model and doesn't really apply to anything in this context; option C is incorrect.

38. B. Ionization detectors usually use a small amount of americium in the detection chamber.

Photoelectric detectors use a light source instead. Option A is incorrect.

Options C and D are incorrect because they are meaningless in this context.

39. D. Because the nature of a life-support effort requires absolute availability, nothing less than a Tier 4 data center will serve your purposes. All the other options are incorrect.

40. B. Bare skin sticks to cold metal.

Most modern systems don't suffer performance degradation at the lower ends of the temperature spectrum; it's the higher temperatures that are of concern for that aspect of the data center. Option B is preferable to option A.

Similarly, high temperature invokes a greater risk of fire, not low temperature, and this environmental aspect is perhaps the factor least impacting risk of fire anyway. Option C is incorrect.

Any regulatory issues stemming from a workplace that is too cold correlates directly with risks to health and human safety, so option B is still preferable to option D.

41. B. This question might be susceptible to overthinking because it is simplistically straightforward: RAID is not a protocol—it's a configuration mechanism.

All the other options are storage protocols that will involve storage controllers.

42. C. While it is important to follow internal policy, industry standards, and regulations when they are applicable, vendor guidance will most often offer the most detailed, specific settings for the particular product in question; the other forms of guidance do not usually specify individual products/versions. This does not mean using the default configuration; the vendor will continue to publish suggestions and recommendations for optimizing performance and security of the product after it goes into distribution in order to meet evolving needs and threats.

43. B. Applying vendor configurations is an excellent method for demonstrating due diligence in IT security efforts. Always remember that proper documentation of the action is also necessary.

Federal law rarely dictates application of vendor guidance, or any other specific security method for individual platforms; option A is incorrect.

Aggressors will almost always be on the offensive and adapt attack methodology faster than our industry creates defenses; even vendor guidance is usually reactive. Option C is incorrect.

Customers rarely have any idea of (or reason to know) configuration settings; option D is incorrect.

44. B. All management functions should take place on a highly secure, isolated network.

The toolset may be available via remote access but is not in any way to be considered public-facing; option A is incorrect.

Resource pooling contradicts direct connections to any particular storage mechanism; option C is incorrect.

Usually, virtualization management will be a responsibility of the provider because it is a crucial element for all customers; option D is incorrect.

45. A. Isolation in the cloud is imperative, largely because of multitenancy (not to support it, as option C implies). In order to do this, the use of technologies like those listed in the question is warranted.

Options B and D have no meaning in this context and are therefore incorrect.

46. A. DNSSEC is basically DNS with the added benefit of certificate validation and the usual functions that certificates offer (the other options). This does not include payload encryption—confidentiality is not an aspect of DNSSEC.

47. C. Default credentials are the bane of security, everywhere. This is definitely the correct answer because it should *not* be part of the baseline build.

All the other options are actual baselining functions.

48. B. Baseline systems need current patches/configuration updates in order to be used to replicate production systems.

All the other options are actual baselining functions.

49. B. Before applying the baseline to the environment, it is important to determine if there are any offices/systems that will require exceptions; not all baselines meet all business needs.

All the other options are actual baselining functions.

50. B. With platform as a service (PaaS), the cloud provider will administer both the hardware and the OS, but you will be in charge of managing the applications and data. There is less likelihood of vendor lock-in with PaaS than software as a service (SaaS), because your data will not be put into a proprietary format (option B is preferable to option C).

With infrastructure as a service (IaaS), your company will still retain a great deal of the administrative responsibility, so PaaS is a better option; option B is preferable to A.

Option D has no applicability in this context and is incorrect.

51. D. Cloud bursting is the industry term usually associated with this type of practice.

All the other options are not terms with any particular meaning in this context.

52. B. While all aspects of cloud computing are necessary to provide a true cloud service, this type of business flexibility is possible because of rapid (close to instant) elasticity, the means to scale your usage up and down as needed.

All the other options are facets of cloud computing but are not as pertinent to the question.

53. D. This is an excellent description of the hybrid model, where the customer owns elements of the infrastructure (the on-premises traditional environment) and the cloud provider owns other elements (the cloud environment used for the temporary additional demand).

All the other options are cloud deployment models but do not suit this particular case.

54. A. A private cloud is the best option for work in highly regulated industries or industries that involve very sensitive assets.

The other options simply are not as preferable as option A for this question.

55. C. A public cloud will be the easiest, least expensive option and probably offer the simplest transition.

The other options are not as preferable as C for this question.

56. B. This is an optimum situation for the use of a community cloud model.

The other options are not as preferable as B for this question.

57. C. The fact that many various customers (including some that may be competitive with, or even hostile to, each other) will be utilizing the cloud environment concurrently means that isolating each is of the utmost importance in the cloud environment.

DDoS is an availability threat, not something to do with confidentiality, so isolation does not serve much purpose in reducing it. Option A is incorrect.

Unencrypted message traffic is not the prevailing, general reason for the need for isolation; it might be one specific, particular aspect of a confidentiality concern, but option C is preferable to B.

Insider threat is not countered by isolation in the same way that isolation protects against threats due to multitenancy; option C is preferable to D.

58. A. Because of European personal data privacy laws, it is extremely important for your company to be sure that the data does not leave the borders of a country approved to handle such data. A private cloud model is the best means for your company to be sure that the data is processed in a data center residing in a particular geophysical location.

The other options simply are not as preferable as A for this question.

59. A. Portability is the term used to describe the ease with which a customer can move from one cloud provider to another; the higher the portability, the less chance for vendor lock-in.

Interoperability describes how systems work together (or don't); because the question did not mention the use of your own company's systems, interoperability does not seem to be a major concern in this case. Option B is incorrect.

Resiliency is how well an environment can withstand duress. While this is of obvious importance to all organizations in the cloud, it is usually seen as a defense against availability concerns, while the question has more to do with portability; option A is still preferable to option C.

Nothing in the question suggests a need for the company to retain some form of governance; option D is incorrect.

60. A. As a cloud customer, the organization is not responsible for making up-front infrastructure purchases, which are capital expenditures.

Cloud customers do, however, make continual operational expenditures for IT resources, in the form of their payments to cloud providers. Option B is incorrect.

Modern business is driven by data as much as any other input, regardless of sector or industry; this does not change whether the organization operates in the cloud or in the traditional IT environment. Option C is incorrect.

The cloud does not obviate the need to satisfy customers. Option D is incorrect.

61. A. These are technical controls, automated systems that perform security functions.

An argument could be made that there is an administrative component to these controls as well: the firewall rules, the DLP data discovery strategy, etc.—these are expressed in the form of a list or set of criteria, which might be viewed as an administrative control. However, the system itself (which is what the question asked) is still a technical control. Option A is preferable to option B.

Because these devices/systems do not deter physical intrusion, but rather logical intrusion, they are not considered physical controls. Option C is incorrect.

"Competing" is not a control type; option D is incorrect.

62. A. The lines themselves are physical, which puts them at Layer 1.

All the other options are simply incorrect.

63. D. Layer 7 is the application's entry point to networking.

All the other options are simply incorrect.

64. A. A virtual private network (VPN) creates a trusted path across an untrusted (often public) network (such as the Internet). It is highly recommended for cloud operations.

Hypertext Markup Language (HTML) is used for displaying web pages; it is not inherently secure. Option B is incorrect.

DEED is an invented term with no meaning in this context. Option C is incorrect.

Domain Name System (DNS) is for resolving IP addresses to URLs; it has no inherent security benefits. Option D is incorrect.

65. C. Tokenization is an approved alternative to encryption for complying with Payment Card Industry (PCI) requirements.

Obfuscation and masking don't really serve the purpose because they obscure data, making it unreadable; storing payment information that is unreadable does not aid in the efficiency of future transactions. Moreover, neither technique meets PCI requirements. Options A and B are incorrect.

Hashing does not serve the purpose because it is a one-way conversion of data; there is no way to retrieve payment information for future transactions once it has been hashed. Option D is incorrect.

66. D. This term has no meaning in this context and is only a distractor.

All the other mechanisms can be (and are) used by DLP solutions to sort data.

67. C. Many security solutions, particularly DLP and similar tools, require a "learning curve" as they become accustomed to new data sets/configurations in order to discriminate between false positives and actual data loss. One week is not enough time to get an accurate determination of the efficacy of these products, and waiting to gather more data over time is a good idea.

The origin of the products probably does not matter in any significant way; options A and B are incorrect.

Hastily migrating out of the current cloud environment (whether to another cloud provider or back on-premises) is reactionary and could prove expensive. Option D is incorrect.

68. D. Senior management is always responsible for determining the risk appetite of any organization, regardless of where and how it operates.

Neither the cloud provider, nor the ISP, nor federal regulators determine the risk appetite of your organization. Options A, B, and C are incorrect.

69. B. Because you will be creating proprietary software, you will probably be most concerned with how it will function across many platforms, in a virtualized environment, and in an environment that you do not own or operate. Interoperability describes how well a system relates to other systems.

Portability is always a concern for cloud customers, as it is an indication of how likely the customer is to be subject to the risk of vendor lock-in. However, because you are using your own proprietary software and not that of another company, this is not a major issue in this case. Option A is incorrect.

Resiliency is how well an environment can withstand duress. Although this is of obvious importance to all organizations, it is usually seen as a defense against availability concerns; the question has more to do with interoperability, and thus option B is still preferable to option C.

Nothing in the question suggests a need for the company to retain some form of governance; option D is incorrect.

70. B. Platform as a service (PaaS) allows a software development team to test their product across multiple OSs and hosting platforms, without the need for the customer to manage each one.

Although infrastructure as a service (IaaS) could offer similar cross-platform benefits, it would require additional effort and expertise on the part of the customer, which would not be nearly as appealing and efficient. Option A is incorrect.

Software as a service (SaaS) does not allow the customer to install software and would be useless for this purpose, making option C incorrect.

LaaS is not a cloud service model and has no meaning in this context. Option D is incorrect.

71. A. Both ISO 31000 and National Institute of Standards and Technology (NIST) 800-37 are risk management frameworks.

Control Objectives for Information and Related Technology (COBIT) is ISACA's framework for managing IT and IT controls, largely from a process and governance perspective. Though it includes elements of risk management, NIST 800-37 is still closer in nature to ISO 31000, so option A is preferable to B.

ITIL (Information Technology Infrastructure Library) is a framework mostly focused on service delivery as opposed to risk management; option C is incorrect.

The General Data Protection Regulation (GDPR) is a European Union law regarding privacy information, not risk management; option D is incorrect.

72. C. The *ENISA Cloud Computing: Benefits, Risks, and Recommendations for Information Security* is the publication.

All the other options are standards bodies but do not have a publication that matches the description in the question as well.

73. D. The Cloud Security Alliance is a volunteer organization that includes members from various industries and sectors and is focused on cloud computing. It relies largely on member participation for developing standards.

All the other options are standards bodies that involve a specific board or other centralized authority for publishing requirements.

74. A. Option A is the definition of the data subject.

All the other options define other privacy-related roles.

75. B. Option B is the definition of the data controller.

All the other options define other privacy-related roles.

76. C. Option C is the definition of the data processor.

All the other options define other privacy-related roles.

77. B. The data controller makes the determination of purpose and scope of privacy-related data sets.

The other options are the names of other privacy-related roles.

78. D. The data custodian is usually tasked with securing and maintaining the privacy data on a regular basis, on behalf and under the guidance of the controller and steward.

The other options are the names of other privacy-related roles.

79. D. The custodian is usually that specific entity in charge of maintaining and securing the privacy-related data on a daily basis, as an element of the data's use.

The compliance officer might be considered a representative of the data controller (your company), or perhaps the data steward, depending on how much actual responsibility and interaction with the data you have on a regular basis. Option A is not as accurate as option D.

The cloud provider (and anyone working for the provider) would be considered the data processor under most privacy regulations; option B is incorrect.

Your company is the data controller, the legal entity ultimately responsible for the data. Option C is incorrect.

80. **B.** The SLA should contain elements of the contract that can be subject to discrete, objective, repeatable, numeric metrics. Jurisdiction is usually dictated by location instead, which should be included in the contract but is probably not useful to include in the SLA.

    All the other options are excellent examples of items that can and should be included in the SLA.

81. **A.** When the cloud customer can ensure that their data will not be ported to a proprietary data format or system, the customer has a better assurance of not being constrained to a given provider; a platform-agnostic data set is more portable and less subject to vendor lock-in.

    Availability may be an aspect of portability; the ease and speed at which the customer can access their own data can influence how readily the data might be moved to another provider. However, this is less influential than the format and structure of the data; option A is preferable to option B.

    Storage space has little to do with vendor lock-in; option C is incorrect.

    A list of OSs the provider offers might be influential for the customer's decision of which provider to select, but it is not typically a constraining factor that would restrict portability. Option D is incorrect.

82. **B.** The contract usually stipulates what kind of financial penalties are imposed when the provider fails to meet the SLAs (for instance, waiver for payment of a given service term). This is a huge motivating element for the provider.

    Regulatory oversight usually affects the customer, not the provider; option A is incorrect.

    The performance details are often included in the SLA but aren't the motivating factor; option C is incorrect.

    In a perfect world, option D would be the correct answer; B is a better answer to this question, however.

83. **C.** The cloud provider is usually allowed to suspend service to the customer if the customer fails to meet the contract requirements (specifically, not paying for the service in accordance with the contract terms). This can be fatal to a customer's operations and is a great motivation to make timely payments.

    Option A is incorrect because the cloud provider would be the entity that would face financial penalties for not fulfilling the SLA.

    Options B and D are incorrect because regulatory oversight and media attention cannot be controlled by the contract between cloud provider and customer.

84. **B.** Audits don't really provide any perceptible effect on user experience.

    All the other options are good reasons for performing audits.

85. **D.** The Cloud Controls Matrix is an excellent tool for determining completeness and possible replication of security controls.

    FIPS 140-2 is a list of cryptographic system products approved for use by U.S. federal customers; option A is incorrect.

The GDPR is a European Union law regarding privacy; ostensibly, an audit could be performed to ensure that an organization is meeting the law's requirements, but the law itself is not a tool for the purpose. Option B is incorrect.

ISO 27001 details the information security management system an organization can adopt; it is not specifically a tool for reviewing cloud security controls. Option C is not correct.

86. D. Federal Risk and Authorization Management Program (FedRAMP) is the U.S. program for federal entities operating in the cloud.

   The International Organization for Standardization (ISO) is an international standards body and does not dictate American government practices. Option A is incorrect.

   National Institute of Standards and Technology (NIST) Special Publication (SP) 800-37 is the Risk Management Framework (RMF) not specifically related to the cloud; option D is preferable to option B.

   The European Union Agency for Network and Information Security (ENISA) is a European Union standards body and does not dictate American government practices. Option C is incorrect.

87. B. A ubiquitous baseline configuration used in a virtualized environment can serve as an artifact for auditors and enhance the audit process.

   The other options are common facets of cloud computing but do not typically serve the purpose of auditing.

88. B. Variables, in general, aren't useful for authentication; authentication requires a match against a template or a known quantity.

   All the other options are typical methods for enhancing authentication.

89. C. This is a nonsense term, with no meaning in this context.

   All the other options are actual common identity federation standards.

90. B. Multifactor authentication doesn't typically utilize associative identification.

   All the other options are typical aspects used in multifactor authentication.

91. D. Because the cloud environment can be accessed from any location (assuming good connectivity), the cloud customer is not required to maintain an expensive operational facility, either for primary or backup purposes.

   All the other options are common aspects of cloud computing, but don't particularly serve BC/DR purposes.

92. A. Rapid elasticity allows the cloud customer to scale cloud operations as necessary, including during contingency operations; this is extremely useful for BC/DR activities.

   All the other options are common aspects of cloud computing but don't particularly serve BC/DR purposes.

93. A. On-demand self-service allows the cloud customer to provision those production resources during a contingency without any delay in ordering or allocating those resources.

   All the other options are common aspects of cloud computing but don't particularly serve BC/DR purposes.

94. B. The data classification process is the organization's formal means of determining value of its assets; this is extremely important to BC/DR efforts in that it can be useful in determining the critical path to be maintained during contingency events.

The SDLC is a system development/acquisition tool; it doesn't particularly assist in BC/DR efforts. Option A is incorrect.

Honeypots are a threat intelligence tool; they don't serve any useful BC/DR purpose. Option C is incorrect.

Identity management is a part of the entitlement process but does not add any value to BC/DR efforts; option D is incorrect.

95. B. DLP solutions typically have the capability to aid in asset valuation and location, both important facets of the BC/DR process.

All the other options are common security tools but don't really serve to enhance BC/DR efforts.

96. A. Because cloud data is typically spread across more than one data center and these data centers can be geographically separated, a single natural disaster event may be less likely to reduce access to the data.

All the other options are common aspects of cloud computing but don't particularly serve BC/DR purposes.

97. C. Egress-monitoring solutions do not typically predict contingency-level events and are not useful for the purpose.

All the other options represent information sources that can aid in predicting BC/DR events.

98. A. A hasty return to normal operations can put operations and personnel at risk if whatever caused the contingency situation has not yet been fully resolved.

All the other options are common aspects of BC/DR preparation and do not typically pose a threat to the organization.

99. D. A full test of the BC/DR plan can result in an actual disaster because it may involve interruption of service; the simulation can become the reality.

All the other options are common aspects of BC/DR preparation and do not typically pose a threat to the organization.

100. A. In containerization, the underlying hardware is not emulated; the container(s) run on the same underlying kernel, sharing the majority of the base OS.

All the other options are aspects of containerization.

101. D. Secure sanitization is not included in all (or even many) SDLC models.

The other options are typical SDLC steps.

102. C. Hardware confirmation is a meaningless term in this respect.

All the other options represent common capabilities of API gateways.

103. D. Cloud customers, with rare exception, will not be allowed to add hardware to the cloud data center.

All the other options are various types of firewalls that a customer could implement in a cloud managed services environment.

104. B. In a typical TLS handshake, the client sends the message (called ClientHello) that initiates the negotiation of the session.

All the other options are incorrect.

105. C. TLS usually relies on PKI certificates authenticated and issued by a trusted third party.

All the other options are incorrect because they are not the *usual* means of establishing trust between the parties in a typical TLS session.

106. A. In TLS, the parties will establish a shared secret, or symmetric key, for the duration of the session.

All the other options are incorrect because they are not the form of cryptography used for the session key in a TLS session.

107. A. In DevOps, the programmers continually work in close conjunction with the production team to ensure that the project will meet their needs.

All the other options are simply incorrect.

108. C. The Agile Manifesto specifically advocates for getting sample systems into the hands of the users as soon as possible in order to ensure that development is meeting customer needs. The Manifesto refutes all other elements of programming that slow down this effort, including documentation, planning, processes, and specific tools.

109. C. Open source software includes programs where customers (or even the public) can view the software's source code.

Freeware and shareware are licensing arrangements and ways of distributing intellectual property. Options A and D are incorrect.

Malware is harmful software designed for attack purposes; option B is incorrect.

110. B. XML works better over the Internet than the binary messaging of the older technologies.

SOAP is not particularly lightweight; in fact, it is kind of cumbersome. Option A is not true.

SOAP is not especially more secure than DCOM or CORBA; option C is incorrect.

SOAP is newer than the other technologies; however, that is not the reason it is preferable in a web context. Option B is still preferable to D.

111. C. REST calls web resources by using uniform resource identifiers (URIs).

Extensible Markup Language (XML) may be used for REST, but it is not a requirement as it is in Simple Object Access Protocol (SOAP). Option A is incorrect.

Security Assertion Markup Language (SAML) is a form of XML used in passing identity assertions; option B is incorrect.

Transport Layer Security (TLS) is a secure virtual private network (VPN) mechanism, not an element of SOAP. Option D is incorrect.

112. A. JSON outputs are common for REST applications.

All the other options are incorrect because they are not the form of output one would expect from REST.

113. B. Sensitive data is often exposed inadvertently because of user error or lack of knowledge about the material. User training can offset a significant portion of this risk by informing users about the value of data assets and the proper use of controls and behaviors.

Physical access control is important, but less for controlling exposure and more for preventing theft. Option B is preferable to A in this context.

Policies are crucial but don't actually offset the risk; they are the underlying structure for creating programs and methods for dealing with the risk. Option B is preferable to C in this case.

Backup power has nothing to do with data exposure, therefore option D is incorrect.

114. B. Administrators will access devices during maintenance mode; blocking admin access would be contrary to the entire point of the activity.

All other options are conditions that are true during maintenance mode.

115. C. Live migration is the term used to describe the movement of functioning virtual instances from one physical host to another and how VMs are moved prior to maintenance on a physical device.

VMs are moved as image snapshots when they are transitioned from production to storage; option A is incorrect.

During live migration, the VM moves in unencrypted form. Option B is incorrect.

Live migration goes over the network; portable media is not necessary. Option D is incorrect.

116. B. IDS/IPS solutions do not elicit user input.

All the other options are mechanisms used by IDS/IPS solutions to detect threats.

117. D. Because the honeypot/honeynet is meant to be observed, production data in any form should not be included.

All the other options are insufficient for the question; D is, by far, the best answer.

118. B. The public does not have a need to know regarding proof of vulnerability scans.

All the other options are legitimate recipients of proof of vulnerability scans.

119. B. Logos and other identifying material are subject to trademark protections.

The other options are also ways to protect intellectual property, but they are not usually associated with logos.

120. C. Intellectual property disputes are usually settled in civil court, as a conflict among private parties.

Because there was no agreement between your company and the competitor in question, there is no contract, so no breach of contract dispute is pertinent. Option A is incorrect.

Although statutes concerning intellectual property protections exist, they are usually in the form of torts (that is, laws that define how civil actions can pursue restitution for private harm). This is not the government prosecuting someone in order to protect the public; criminal proceedings are rare when it comes to enforcing intellectual property rights. Option B is incorrect.

The military does not often get involved in intellectual property disputes and most often uses the civil courts when it does. Option D is incorrect.

121. C. Trademark protection is provided to those who apply for it, to either a state or federal trademark registration body. In the case of conflicting usage (or infringement), courts will take many criteria into account, including which party has first claim on the trademark (that is, who used it the longest), the location(s) where the trademark is used, the possibility for confusion among customers, and so forth. But for a specific location and specific business purpose, the deciding element will probably be which party first registered the trademark in question.

All the other options may be factors the court takes into account when making its decision, but option C is the best answer.

122. D. This is the definition of a SOC 3.

All the other options are SSAE 18 reports but not the correct answer.

123. D. This is the purpose of the SOC 3 report.

All the other options are SSAE 18 reports but not the correct answer.

124. B. Both Australia and New Zealand have privacy laws that conform to EU privacy legislation.

All the other options are examples of countries that do not.

125. A. Japan's privacy law is sufficient to meet EU legislative requirements.

Alaska is not a country—it is a state. Option B is wrong.

Neither Belize nor Madagascar has privacy laws sufficient to meet EU requirements; options C and D are incorrect.

Chapter 8: Practice Exam 2

1. C. A cloud reseller is a firm that contracts with both cloud providers and customers in order to arrange custom services.

The cloud provider(s), in this case, would be those entities selling services to Cloud Services Corp. Option A is incorrect.

The cloud customer, in this case, would be your company. Option B is incorrect.

No aspect of the question describes a cloud database specifically. Option D is incorrect.

2. C. Portability is the aspect of cloud computing that describes the ability to move data and operations away from a given cloud provider (either to another cloud provider or to an on-premise solution).

All the other options are aspects of cloud computing but do not aid in addressing the concerns described in the question.

3. D. While many cloud providers will offer these services (as well as many others), they are not defining characteristics of cloud computing.

All the other options are defining characteristics of cloud computing.

4. B. A platform as a service (PaaS) model will probably best suit your company's needs as it allows the customer (your company) to install software and load data onto a hardware infrastructure owned and operated by the provider.

An infrastructure as a service (IaaS) solution may be viable for this situation, because it allows the same functionality, but it also requires the customer (your company) to install and maintain the OS(s) that run the software. In looking to decrease cost of investment and maintenance, the PaaS model is probably preferable. Option A is not as good as option B, in this case.

A software as a service (SaaS) model does not allow the customer to install software; option C is incorrect.

A hybrid cloud model usually requires the customer to maintain at least part of the hardware infrastructure; in accordance with the description of the situation in this question, option D is not as optimum as option B.

5. A. Platform as a service (PaaS) models are particularly useful for performing software testing because the customer can install and run their own programs across multiple OSs/systems. A hybrid model is used to describe a situation where ownership of the infrastructure is split between the provider and the customer.

A software as a service (SaaS) or infrastructure as a service (IaaS) model would not be optimum for software testing; options B and D are incorrect.

A community cloud model involves the joint ownership of infrastructure among many providers and customers; option C is not correct.

6. D. A software as a service (SaaS) model reduces customer involvement more than the other models; a public cloud deployment likewise reduces customer participation in ownership and maintenance of infrastructure.

Infrastructure as a service (IaaS) and platform as a service (PaaS) models require the customer to participate in some administration of the environment; options A and B are incorrect.

A private cloud entails customer involvement in at least the detailing of governance of the environment; option C is incorrect.

7. C. In a software as a service (SaaS) model, the cloud provider is tasked with acquiring and managing the software licenses; the scale of a cloud provider's operations can allow them to reduce the per-seat cost of software considerably.

The customer is still responsible for some software licensing and maintenance activities (and therefore costs) in infrastructure as a service (IaaS) and platform as a service (PaaS) models; options A and B are incorrect.

A hybrid deployment usually entails the customer maintaining some infrastructure elements, and that usually would also include software licensing requirements. Option D is incorrect.

8. **A.** A public cloud deployment would probably best meet the needs of a company without a robust, trained IT staff. The cloud provider will be responsible for the greatest degree of administration and maintenance compared to the other options.

Options B, C, nor D would not be the optimal choices for a cloud deployment model in this case, because each of those requires personnel with more experience/training. Options B, C, and D are incorrect.

9. **B.** A private cloud arrangement allows the customer to have greater control of the governance and policy within an environment.

All the other options are cloud deployment models that allow the customer less control over the environment as a whole.

10. **B.** A private cloud model can allow the customer to have the greatest assurance of confidentiality compared to the other models.

Options A, C, and D provide less confidentiality than option B and are therefore incorrect.

11. **C.** A community cloud entails all participants to have some degree of ownership and responsibility for the cloud environment; this is the preferred model for cooperative ownership and collaboration among a group with a shared interest/goal.

12. **D.** A hybrid model, where ownership fluctuates between exclusive control of the customer (private) and provider (public) only during times of increased demand, is almost a textbook description of this arrangement and translates very well for cloud-bursting techniques.

13. **B.** A customer using proprietary software in a PaaS environment faces the risk that updates to the underlying OS(s) and/or hardware infrastructure will not be compatible with the customer's software and will affect productivity.

Cloud migration can, however, aid in reducing overhead costs, including energy costs associated with operating a data center, and can enhance BC/DR capability through the provider's increased investment in redundancy and continuity.

14. **B.** The service-level agreement creates financial incentive for the cloud provider to meet the customer's needs on a consistent basis.

Audits and regulators might help this effort, somewhat, by ensuring that the provider adheres to certain mandates and standards, but these are less convincing (and occur after the fact of delivery) than profit motive. Options A and C are incorrect.

Training does not really aid the efforts described in the question; option D is incorrect.

15. **C.** By spreading costs over time, a business can reduce the risk that there will be a lack of money at any given time, impacting operations.

A shift from a capital expenditure scheme to an operational expenditure arrangement does not necessarily mean that overall costs decrease; in fact, costs might very likely increase because the sum of the OpEx installments may total more than the CapEx would have been. Option A is incorrect.

CapEx usually reduces tax exposure because it allows for depreciation of assets, whereas OpEx does not. Option B is not correct.

Whether the business uses CapEx or OpEx financing does not necessarily increase or decrease profit. Option D is incorrect.

16. B. This is a complicated question and requires a significant amount of understanding of control types.

A firewall uses aspects of administrative controls. The firewall policy is a set of rules that dictate the type of traffic and source/destination of that traffic. Option A is incorrect.

Firewalls can be set to change activity in reaction to detected threats, which is a corrective action; option C is incorrect.

Firewall rules can also prevent certain kinds of traffic/access; option D is incorrect.

However, the effect of a deterrent control is the result of its perception by someone who might engage in wrongdoing—unless it is perceived, the control is not really a deterrent. Most firewalls don't function in that manner; they are transparent to both legitimate users and attackers. Option B is therefore correct.

17. A. All of the other options are incorrect. Option D is incorrect because there is no Layer 8 in the Open Systems Interconnection (OSI) model.

18. B. Generic routing encapsulation (GRE) is a tunneling mechanism, specifically designed for the purpose.

Internet Protocol Security (IPSec) may or may not involve tunneling. Option A is incorrect.

Infrastructure as a service (IaaS) may or may not use tunneling for remote access/administration; option C is incorrect.

Extensible Markup Language (XML) is a format for communicating data; option D is incorrect.

19. B. SSH does not offer content filtering. It does offer all the services listed in the other options.

20. B. TLS uses asymmetric encryption to create a symmetric session key.

21. B. ITIL was specifically designed to address service delivery entities (in particular, British telecommunications providers), and how they provide service to their customers.

SABSA is a means of looking at security capabilities from a business perspective; option A is incorrect.

COBIT is designed for all types of business, regardless of their purpose; option C is incorrect.

TOGAF is a means to incorporate security architecture with the overall business architecture; option D is incorrect.

22. D. The TCI does not, specifically, require cost-effectiveness of cloud services.

All the other options are principles detailed in the TCI.

23. B. Tokenization is not typically an aspect of DLP solutions. All the other options are.

24. A. The data discovery facet of DLP solutions can aid an organization in gathering applicable evidence, especially in response to a legal request such as a subpoena (this is often termed e-discovery).

Tools cannot deliver testimony; only people can testify. Option B is incorrect.

DLP solutions do not perform prosecutorial work; that is the function of law enforcement agencies. Option C is incorrect.

While DLP tools can locate intellectual property assets, they do not, strictly speaking, enforce the rights attendant to those assets. Option A is still preferable to D in this case.

25. B. DLP tools can function better if appropriate and accurate classification and labeling is applied throughout the environment and done on a consistent basis.

All the other options are good aspects of a security program but not exactly germane to DLP function.

26. B. Depending on the availability of the archive, it may be possible to use it to recover production data that has been accidentally or inadvertently deleted or destroyed.

Archiving does not really offer any of the other benefits; when data is taken out of the production environment and put into long-term storage, the organization loses the capability to manipulate it and create new assets from it. Options A, C, and D are incorrect.

27. B. Having a suitable backup, away from the main production environment, allows the organization to recover from contingency operations that have interrupted or affected the production environment.

All the other options are not benefits directly associated with data archiving.

28. A. In order to use the archive for recovery (either on a large scale for contingency operations or for granular recovery as a means of data discovery), the data needs to be of a format and type that can be utilized by the organization's systems and environment. Saving data in the wrong format can be equivalent to losing the data.

All the other options are important aspects of a data archiving policy but are not as important as option A (for instance, data that is not encrypted might pose a risk of loss, but data in the wrong format may not be recoverable at all).

29. C. The cloud provider cannot typically require the destruction of the customer's data simply because of its own (provider's) policy. If this is an aspect of the contract between the provider and customer, that is another issue (and listed as another option in this question).

The other options are all sources that may dictate the customer's destruction of data.

30. A. CDNs are often used in conjunction with SaaS services to deliver high-quality data of large sizes (often multimedia).

Databases and data warehousing are typically associated with platform as a service (PaaS), where the provider owns and maintains the infrastructure and data management engine but the customer can install programs and interfaces to manipulate the data. Options B and D are incorrect.

Volume storage is typically associated with infrastructure as a service (IaaS); option C is incorrect.

31. C. The RTO is the measure of time after an interruption at which the company needs to resume critical functions; any service migration must take place within that time.

RTOs vary for every organization; there is no set answer for all organizations. Options A and B might be correct for a given organization but incorrect in the general case because it's impossible to know an organization's RTO without knowing more about the organization.

The RPO is a measure of data that can be lost, not time; option D is incorrect.

32. D. This action defines the archive phase. All the other options are incorrect.

33. A. Data should be labeled and classified as soon as it is created/collected.

All the other options are incorrect.

34. C. Internal theft is not listed in the OWASP Top Ten, probably because the list concerns web application security, not security overall.

All the other options are included in the OWASP Top Ten.

35. B. Backdoors are a particularly prevalent risk in software development because programmers legitimately use backdoors for ease of use and speed of delivery but may mistakenly (or even purposefully) leave the backdoors in the software after development, creating a hidden and significant vulnerability.

All the other options should be concerns of any cloud customer, but they are not of specific or increased concern for this situation.

36. B. Because the cost of creating new instances in the cloud environment is transparent to many users/offices, there is a significant likelihood that users/offices will create many new virtual machine (VM) instances without the knowledge/oversight of management. This can result in a very expensive surprise at the end of the payment period, when the organization receives the bill from the cloud provider.

All the other options are management risks that do not have anything specific to do with the cloud environment and should not affect it/be affected by it.

37. B. The Type I hypervisor is preferable, as it offers less attack surface.

All the other options increase risk and should not be recommended.

38. B. Under current laws, the owner of the PII is legally responsible for data breach notifications, regardless of the circumstances of the breach; in this case, your company is the PII owner.

All the other options are incorrect because those entities are not the owner of the PII.

39. D. If anything, the audit trail for privileged users should be more detailed than that for regular users.

All the other options are recommended techniques for privileged user management.

40. C. Managing the encryption keys on-premises necessitates some elements of a hybrid cloud model; the key management is done on-premises, and the production takes place in the cloud.

A public cloud arrangement would preclude the customer hosting the key management system on its premises; option A is incorrect.

The service model is slightly irrelevant to where the key management system is located; whereas customer-hosted key management is usually associated with an SaaS model, it is not strictly required. Options B and D are incorrect.

41. D. Separation of duties dictates that one person/entity cannot complete an entire transaction alone. In the case of encryption, a single entity should not be able to administer the issuing of keys, encrypt the data, and store the keys, because this could lead to a situation where that entity has the ability to access or take encrypted data.

All the other options are security principles but are not intrinsically applicable to the concept of storing encryption keys away from encrypted data.

42. B. Option A is incorrect because RAID is a storage virtualization technology, used in traditional environments, that combines physical disks components into one or more logical units.

Homomorphic encryption is a theoretical conversion of data into ciphertext that can be analyzed as if it were in its original form. Option C is incorrect.

Option D is incorrect because it uses public and private key pairs to encrypt and decrypt data.

43. C. Option A is incorrect because RAID is a storage virtualization technology, used in traditional environments, that combines physical disks components into one or more logical units.

SSMS involves encrypting a data set, then splitting the data into pieces, splitting the key into pieces, then signing the data pieces and key pieces and distributing them to various cloud storage locations. Option B is incorrect.

Option D is incorrect because it uses public and private key pairs to encrypt and decrypt data.

44. B. This is a description of quantum computing.

Option A is incorrect because it refers to a data transformation.

Option C is a made up term and is therefore incorrect.

Option D is incorrect because it is a data dispersion term.

45. C. Saved virtual instances are simply inert files, and they are very easy to copy and move.

Encryption may be applied to data at rest (even VM snapshots); option A is incorrect.

Insider threats within the cloud data center probably pose just as much risk to the storage nodes as the processing nodes; option B is incorrect.

Option D is incorrect.

46. C. The user interface to the virtualized instance can be handled by a variety of mechanisms, but it is not the function of the management plane.

All the other options are resources provisioned to the virtual machine(s) by the management plane.

47. C. The tabletop testing method is the least intrusive type of BC/DR test. All the other options are BC/DR testing methods that are more intrusive.

48. D. There is no way to know if the backup actually serves the purpose until the organization tests a restoration.

The other options are all backup options but do not actually demonstrate whether the backup is suitable for the business continuity and disaster recovery (BC/DR) requirements.

49. C. The ubiquitous redundancy of systems and capabilities within most cloud data centers not only serves the provider's requirement to meet customer service-level agreements but also enhances the data center's (and the customer's) resistance to disasters and interruptions.

All the other options are characteristics of a cloud data center, but they don't serve much BC/DR purpose; option C is the best choice.

50. C. Returning to normal operations can result in a second disaster if the conditions created by the initial disaster (which created the need to run the BC/DR plan) have not fully been addressed/resolved.

An inadvertent initiation of the plan can result in a disaster, but that would only be one disaster, not two; for instance, if senior management got faulty information during the event anticipation phase and decided to switch to contingency operations, but there was no actual causative event, that would be a single disaster. Options A and D are incorrect.

The act of planning and crafting policy cannot take the form of a disaster. Option B is incorrect.

51. B. The BIA lists the assets of the organization and states their importance, value, and criticality. This can easily be used for BC/DR planning purposes.

The SOC is an audit report; this does not aid in BC/DR planning. Option A is incorrect.

The risk analysis and ALE calculation are used to select reasonable and cost-effective controls suitable for the environment; this does not aid in BC/DR efforts. Options C and D are incorrect.

52. B. Typically, the cost of using the cloud for contingency operations will be much less than creating a physical alternate operating site.

Usually, a cloud solution may also be faster and easier to engineer than a physical solution; options A and D are incorrect.

"Larger," in this context, has no meaning, because the "size" of the cloud is a misnomer; option C is incorrect.

53. B. The Open Web Application Security Project (OWASP) is a volunteer organization that devises standards and solutions for web application development. All the other options are common federation technologies.

54. B. The SOC 2 ,Type 1 audit reviews management's selection of controls for the organization's environment.

The SOC 1 audit reviews the accuracy and correctness of the organization's financial reporting. Option A is incorrect.

The SOC 3 is an attestation of an audit. Option C is incorrect.

There is no SOC 4 report. Option D is incorrect.

55. C. The SLA won't typically include direct mention of the sorts of personnel security measures undertaken by the cloud provider. This may be mentioned, obliquely, in another part of the contract (that is, there may be some language that states that the provider is responsible for ensuring the trustworthiness of its personnel), but it is not a useful SLA element.

All the other options are excellent items to include in an SLA.

56. D. Fire suppression systems are physical control mechanisms commonly found in cloud data centers but are not an element of access control.

All the other options are common physical access control mechanisms in a cloud data center.

57. D. If external vendors need access to the cloud environment, that access should only be granted on an extremely limited and temporary basis.

All the other options are common cloud access types and don't necessarily need to be limited in duration.

58. B. Guest escape is a prevailing threat in a virtualized, multitenant cloud environment and was not commonly found in traditional environments (those environments were typically not virtualized and did not serve more than one customer, the owning organization).

All the other threats are currently faced by cloud customers but also existed in the traditional environment.

59. B. This is the description of a NAS device.

A SAN typically presents storage devices to users as attached/mounted drives. Option A is incorrect.

An HSM is designed for encryption generation and management; option C is incorrect.

A CDN typically replicates multimedia content at multiple, geographically diverse locations to ensure high quality for recipients. Option D is incorrect.

60. C. Because of the multitenant nature of public cloud services, processes and resources that are not properly isolated may create a situation where data could be disclosed to other cloud customers (neighboring tenants). This is a new threat that may result from the migration.

All the other options are existing threats in the company's current environment.

61. A. This is a description of hot aisle containment.

Cold aisle containment is a configuration where the fronts of devices face each other. Option B is incorrect.

Option C is not relevant in this context. Option C is incorrect.

Option D does not describe the data center configuration in the question. Option D is incorrect.

62. A. Unused or poorly managed cabling can impede efficient air flow, increasing HVAC and energy costs and increasing the difficulty of optimizing temperature.

While it is possible that mismanaged cabling could cause slip/trip/fall hazards, this is much less common in modern data centers; option A is preferable in this case.

Cabling does not really have much of an environmental footprint, so discipline applied to cabling won't affect the environment much, one way or the other; option C is incorrect.

Regulators do not usually enforce cable management; option D is incorrect.

63. C. The industry standard is 24 inches. All the other options are incorrect.

64. C. Ideally, raised flooring should be used for no other purpose because any objects in that location would impede airflow. Therefore, options A, B, and D are incorrect because they defeat the purpose of the raised flooring design.

65. B. Cold air is usually put through raised flooring because warm air naturally rises and using the raised flooring to conduct warm air would require an unnecessary and inefficient expenditure of energy.

All the other options are incorrect as they include warmer air.

66. B. Ionization-based smoke detectors use trace amounts of a radionuclide (often americium) to detect the presence of particulate matter in the detection chamber when smoke particles interrupt the constant electric current.

Neither type uses the techniques described in the other options, as they are all incorrect answers.

67. B. Pressure detection is not a common detection technology.

All the other options are common fire detection methods.

68. C. FM-200 is used as a replacement for older Halon systems specifically because it (unlike Halon) does not deplete the ozone layer.

All the other options are true statements about FM-200 used in fire suppression.

69. B. One of the properties that makes it desirable for fire suppression in a data center is that FM-200 does not leave a residue.

All the other options are true statements about FM-200.

70. B. DHCP servers do not normally orchestrate encryption.

All the other options are common functions of DHCP servers.

71. C. This question is challenging because it requires some abstract thought and all answers seem correct at first glance. Intrusion detection systems (IDSs) and intrusion prevention systems (IPSs) do not secure data; they detect attack activity.

Domain Name System Security Extensions (DNSSEC) protects data in transit by reducing the risk of DNS poisoning; Transport Layer Security (TLS) and Internet Protocol Security (IPSec) reduce the risk of eavesdropping and interception of data.

72. D. Administrative access may be limited but not prevented.

All the other options are common steps of OS hardening.

73. B. The baseline configuration can be used as a template of controls applied throughout the environment.

The BIA and financial records may offer an auditor insight into asset valuation/risk but will not provide meaningful data for a control audit. Options A and C are incorrect.

The SOC 3 report is only an attestation by an auditor that an audit has taken place; it does not provide any useful information about security controls.

74. D. During maintenance mode, all maintenance activities should still be logged and tracked.

All the other actions are recommended for a cloud node entering maintenance mode.

75. B. This action is pointless and excessive; the option is a distractor.

All the other options are actions the cloud provider should undertake when conducting scheduled maintenance.

76. B. By definition, the tightly coupled cluster has a maximum capacity, whereas the loosely coupled cluster does not.

The other options do not have a set maximum capacity and are therefore incorrect.

77. C. OpenStack is an open source project for creating cloud environments regardless of hardware brand.

Open Web Application Security Project (OWASP) is an open source web application development project and does not involve the use of any of the tools mentioned in the question. Option A is incorrect.

OAuth is a set of standards for identity federation. Option B is incorrect.

Mozilla is a company that produces and administers open source software such as the Firefox web browser. Option D is incorrect.

78. C. Masking the data (such as replacing the majority of the credit card number with Xs, leaving only the last four digits in view) should suffice for the purpose; it allows the call center personnel to determine which card was used in the sale but does not reveal the card number to the call center.

Encrypting the data in storage but allowing call center personnel to decrypt it creates a vast opportunity for fraud and abuse; option A is incorrect.

Encrypting the data while the call center is trying to make the refund would be counter-productive; the call center personnel would be unable to determine which card gets the refund. Option B is incorrect.

Relying on the customer to provide the correct card number invites inaccuracy and exposes the transaction to fraud; option D is not correct.

79. C. Describe is not a common phase in the SDLC; the software should be described in the Define phase.

All the other options are common phases of the SDLC.

80. D. Business requirements are paramount because they incorporate the elements of all the other options as well as additional inputs.

81. D. A DAM can recognize and block malicious SQL traffic.

A WAF is a Layer 7 firewall that understands hostile HTTP traffic. Option A is incorrect.

An API gateway filters API traffic. Option B is incorrect.

DLP solutions are used for egress monitoring, not incoming SQL commands. Option C is incorrect.

82. B. PaaS is optimum for software testing as it allows the software to run across multiple platforms/OSs.

All the other options are service/deployment models that are not as optimum for software testing as PaaS.

83. C. Sandboxing allows software to be run in an isolated environment, which can aid in error detection.

Software testing should not include raw production data, so there is no purpose for using DLP and DRM solutions; options A and B are incorrect.

The WAF is used to filter web traffic; in the testing environment, there should not be any live traffic going to the software. Option D is incorrect.

84. B. Open source review can detect flaws that a structured testing method might not.

Vulnerability scans will only detect known problems, not programming defects that have not yet been identified; option A is incorrect.

Neither SOC audit nor regulatory review have anything to do with finding software flaws; options C and D are incorrect.

85. D. Programmers have a vested interest in, and a specific perspective of, software they create. They can unduly influence testing outcomes, even unintentionally. It is best to prevent programmers from attending testing of software they helped create.

All the other options are personnel who do not need to be present but will not necessarily cause undue influence of the testing process.

86. B. The Agile method reduces the dependence and importance of documentation in favor of functioning software versions.

All the other options are elements that will most likely be increased by transitioning to an Agile model.

87. C. Agile requires interaction between developers and personnel who will use the software.

All the other options are not essential roles in Agile development.

88. D. Agile development is usually organized in relatively short iterations of effort, between a week and a month in duration.

Dependence on planning is directly contrary to Agile methodology; option A is incorrect.

In Agile, prototyping is favored over testing; option B is incorrect.

Agile relies on cooperative development instead of stovepiped expertise; option C is incorrect.

89. A. Agile development often involves daily meetings (called Scrums).

Agile methodology spurns the use of specific tools and concrete planning; options B and C are incorrect.

Agile also favors customer collaboration and prototyping instead of an elaborate contract mechanism; option D is incorrect.

90. A. SOAP is a web service programming format that requires the use of XML.

REST relies more often on uniform resource identifiers (URIs) than XML; option B is incorrect.

SAML is a protocol for passing identity assertions over the Internet; option C is incorrect.

DLP is a data egress monitoring tool; option D is incorrect.

91. D. STRIDE does not address user security training.

All the other options are aspects addressed by the STRIDE model.

92. D. Every additional security measure might reduce a potential threat but definitely will reduce productivity and quality of service. There is always an overhead cost of security.

93. B. ISO 27034 compliance requires an ANF for every application within the organization.

Under 27034, the organization only needs one ONF, of which every ANF is a subset. Option A is incorrect.

There is no INF. The term is a distractor; option C is incorrect.

SOC 3 reports are for the Statement on Standards for Attestation Engagements (SSAE) standard, not ISO 27034; option D is incorrect.

94. D. Chile does not currently have a federal privacy law that conforms to EU legislation. All the other options are countries that do (Belgium is in the EU).

95. C. South Korea does not currently have a federal privacy law that conforms to EU legislation. All the other options are countries that do.

96. D. Kenya does not currently have a federal privacy law that conforms to EU legislation. All the other options are countries that do (France is in the EU).

97. C. This is an aspect of the current European Union (EU) legislation, known colloquially as "the right to be forgotten"—it is not an aspect of the OECD principles.

All the other options are included in the OECD principles.

98. D. The data subject is the person who is identified by personal data.

All the other options are other privacy-data-related roles.

99. C. The GDPR is the current prevailing EU privacy data legislation. It replaced the Data Directive. Privacy Shield is the program under which entities in non-adhering countries can still be allowed to process the personal data of EU citizens. SOX is an American law.

100. C. The FTC is the local U.S. enforcement arm for most Privacy Shield activity.

All the other options are U.S. government agencies not involved with Privacy Shield.

101. B. Companies that are not in countries that have laws in accordance with the EU privacy regulations can instead opt for creating contract language that voluntarily complies with the laws.

All the other options are incorrect because they do not allow non–European Union companies to process personal data of EU citizens.

102. B. The data controller is legally liable for protecting any privacy data it has. All the other options are other data privacy roles that do not have ultimate legal responsibility.

103. A. Level 1 is the initial level of maturity for a company and its processes; activity may be performed in an ad hoc manner.

All the other options are greater maturity levels of the CMM.

104. A. The ISO 27001 standard reviews an organization's security in terms of an information security management system (ISMS), which involves a holistic view of the entire security program.

ISO 27002 is a standard for applying controls to the ISMS; option B is incorrect.

NIST 800-37 is the Risk Management Framework; option C is incorrect.

SSAE is an audit standard for financial reporting and the controls within an environment; option D is incorrect.

105. D. Because of the sensitive nature of the material covered in the SOC 2, Type 2 report, a cloud provider might not be willing to share it with any entity that does not have a financial stake in the cloud service.

All the other options are entities that are unlikely to receive a SOC 2, Type 2 report from a cloud provider.

106. B. The SOC 1 report reviews the accuracy and completeness of an organization's financial reporting mechanisms.

All the other options are incorrect.

107. C. There are four PCI merchant levels, based on the number of transactions an organization conducts per year.

All the other options are incorrect answers.

108. D. The Common Criteria is a framework for reviewing product security functions, as stated by the vendor.

The UL is a standards and certification entity concerned with product safety; option A is incorrect.

FIPS 140-2 is a standard for certifying cryptographic modules; option B is incorrect.

PCI DSS is a security standard for credit card merchants and processors; option C is incorrect.

109. A. The lowest level of the FIPS 140-2 standard is 1. All the other options are incorrect.

110. C. There are three levels of the CSA STAR program, and 3 is the highest. All the other options are incorrect.

111. B. The CAIQ is the CSA's mechanism for STAR applicants to evaluate their own service.

The SOC reports are part of the Statement on Standards for Attestation Engagements (SSAE) 18 audit standard; option A is incorrect.

The NIST RMF is only mandated for U.S. federal agencies and not part of the CSA purview; option C is incorrect.

The ISMS is one of the ISO standards and not part of the CSA purview; option D is incorrect.

112. C. Cloud carrier is a term describing the intermediary between cloud customer and provider that delivers connectivity; this is typically an ISP.

Options A and B are other typical cloud computing roles; option D is a not a term with any meaning in this context.

113. C. In a centralized broker federation, the broker (typically a third party) acting as the identity provider, creates the SAML identity assertion tokens and delivers them to the relying parties.

All the other options are distractors and not entities that are assigned specific roles in a federation motif.

114. B. The CCM is a tool for determining control coverage for compliance with a variety of standards and regulations.

All the other options are standards or regulations.

115. D. The check involves two kinds of security elements: something you have (the check) and something you are (the biometric control, the signature).

Option A is two elements of the same kind: something you know. This is incorrect.

Option B is two elements of the same kind: something you are. This is incorrect.

Option C is two elements of the same kind: something you have. This is incorrect.

116. D. SLA elements should be objective, numeric values, for repeated activity.

Options B and C are useful elements to be included in the contract, but not specifically the SLA. Options B and C are incorrect.

Option A is too ambiguous; "excellent" is not a discrete value. Option A is incorrect.

117. C. Option A is incorrect because software-defined networking refers to a networking architecture consisting of three layers: application, control, and infrastructure.

Enterprise networking is a general term, not specifically related to the cloud. Option B is incorrect.

Legacy networking or traditional networking is designed for traditional networks that use physical devices and components rather than virtual. Option D is incorrect.

118. D. Quality of service (QoS) refers to the capability of a network to provide better service for certain traffic regardless of network type or topology.

The other options contain uppercase and lowercase letters that may or may not be related to the cloud. Option D is the only option that answers the question correctly. The acronym QoS represents Quality of Service. QoS is used to set priorities for specific types of data to dependably run high-priority applications and traffic.

119. C. Optimized for cloud deployments, the converged networking model combines the underlying storage and IP networks to maximize the benefits of a cloud workload.

120. B. Criminal law is set out in rules and statutes created by a government, prohibiting certain activities as a means of protecting the safety and well-being of its citizens. Violations generally consist of both monetary and/or loss of liberty punishments.

Tort law refers the body of laws that provide remedies to individuals who have been caused harm by unreasonable acts of others. Negligence is the most common type of tort lawsuit. Therefore, option A is incorrect.

Option C is incorrect because civil law pertains to contracts, property, and family law as opposed to crimes like murder and theft that are associated with criminal law.

Contracts are agreements between parties to exchange goods and services; Option D is incorrect.

121. A. Solid-state disks (SSDs) are used in cloud computing today because they operate at high speeds as compared to traditional spinning drives.

Option B is incorrect. SSDs do not necessarily last longer than magnetic drives.

Options C and D are incorrect because SSDs are not noticeably easier or quicker to replace than traditional drives.

122. A. The primary risks associated with virtualization are loss of governance, snapshot and image security, and sprawl.

Options B and C are incorrect. Public awareness and increased costs are not risks associated with virtualization.

Option D is incorrect because the loss of data is not associated with virtualization anymore than the loss of data is associated with non-virtualization.

123. A. The central processing unit (CPU) is the core of any and all systems, handling all the basic I/O instructions as they originate from the software.

The question focuses on the handling of all input/output (I/O) instructions. Only the CPU does that. Options B, C, and D function as a result of the CPU handling all of I/O for the hypervisor, user interface, and supervising application. The CPU is the core of computing systems. Options B, C, and D are incorrect.

124. D. The IETF is an international organization of network designers and architects who work together in establishing standards and protocols for the Internet.

IANA oversees global IP address allocation among other Internet tasks. IANA does not establish standards and protocols for the Internet. Option A is incorrect.

Option B is incorrect because the ISO/IEC develops, maintains and promotes standards in information technology and information communication technology.

Option C is incorrect because NIST is a federal government standards body in the US.

125. D. The Advanced Encryption Standard (AES) is currently used to encrypt and protect U.S. government sensitive and secret data. There are variants, but the most common is 256-bit, which is virtually impossible to break today.

Option A is incorrect because MD5 is a cryptographic hash function used to verify that a file has not been altered.

SSL uses certificates to create a secure connection using encryption. Option B is incorrect.

Blowfish is a symmetric-key block cipher that has been replaced by AES encryption. The U.S. government uses AES and not Blowfish. Option C is incorrect.

Index

I

N

W

X

Online Test Bank

Register to gain one year of FREE access to the online interactive test bank to help you study for your (ISC)² CCSP certification exam—included with your purchase of this book! All of the practice tests in this book are included in the online test bank so you can practice in a timed and graded setting.

Register and Access the Online Test Bank

To register your book and get access to the online test bank, follow these steps:

1. Go to bit.ly/SybexTest.
2. Select your book from the list.
3. Complete the required registration information, including answering the security verification to prove book ownership. You will be emailed a pin code.
4. Follow the directions in the email or go to www.wiley.com/go/sybextestprep.
5. Enter the pin code you received and click the "Activate PIN" button.
6. On the Create an Account or Login page, enter your username and password, and click Login. A "Thank you for activating your PIN!" message will appear. If you don't have an account already, create a new account.
7. Click the "Go to My Account" button to add your new book to the My Products page.

Do you need more? If you have not already read Sybex's (ISC)² CCSP Certified Cloud Security Professional Official Study Guide, 2nd Edition by Ben Malisow (ISBN: 978-1-119-60349-8) and are not seeing passing grades on these practice tests, this book is an excellent resource to master any CCSP topics causing problems. This book maps every official exam objective to the corresponding chapter in the book to help track exam prep objective by objective, challenging review questions in each chapter to prepare for exam day, and online test prep materials with flashcards and additional practice tests.